THE URALS AND WESTERN SIBERIA IN THE BRONZE AND IRON AGES

This book is the first synthesis of the archaeology of the Urals and Western Siberia. It presents a comprehensive overview of the late prehistoric cultures of these regions, which are of key importance for the understanding of long-term changes in Eurasia. At the crossroads of Europe and Asia, the Urals and Western Siberia are characterized by great environmental and cultural diversity, which is reflected in the variety and richness of their archaeological sites. Based on the latest achievements of Russian archaeologists, this study demonstrates the temporal and geographical range of its subjects, starting with a survey of the chronological sequence from the late fourth millennium BC to the early first millennium CE. Recent discoveries made in different regions of the area contribute to an understanding of several important issues, such as development of Eurasian metallurgy, technological and ritual innovations, the emergence and development of pastoral nomadism and its role in Eurasian interactions, and major sociocultural fluctuations of the Bronze and Iron Ages.

Ludmila Koryakova is professor at the Ural State University and Institute of History and Archaeology, Ural Branch of the Russian Academy of Sciences. She has received fellowships from the European Community (INTAS Foundation), the Russian Academy of Science, Centre National de la Recherche Scientifique (CNRS), and the French Ministry of Foreign Affairs, and she is the author of more than eighty publications in Russian, European, and American books and journals.

Andrej Vladimirovich Epimakhov is a Ph.D. Research Fellow at the Institute of History and Archaeology, Russian Academy of Sciences as well as Assistant Professor at Southern Ural State University.

CAMBRIDGE WORLD ARCHAEOLOGY

SERIES EDITOR
NORMAN YOFFEE, *University of Michigan*

EDITORIAL BOARD
SUSAN ALCOK, *Brown University*
TOM DILLEHAY, *Vanderbilt University*
STEPHEN SHENNAN, *University College London*
CARLA SINOPOLI, *University of Michigan*

The *Cambridge World Archaeology* series is addressed to students and professional archaeologists and to academics in related disciplines. Each volume presents a survey of the archaeology of a region of the world, providing an up-to-date account of research and integration of recent findings with new concerns of interpretation. While the focus is on a specific region, broader cultural trends are discussed and the implications of regional findings for cross-cultural interpretations considered. The authors also bring anthropological and historical expertise to bear on archaeological problems and show how both new data and changing intellectual trends in archaeology shade inferences about the past.

BOOKS IN THE SERIES

CAMBRIDGE WORLD ARCHAEOLOGY

THE URALS AND WESTERN SIBERIA IN THE BRONZE AND IRON AGES

LUDMILA KORYAKOVA

Institute of History and Archaeology
of the Ural Branch of the Russian Academy of Sciences
& Ural State University

ANDREJ VLADIMIROVICH EPIMAKHOV

Institute of History and Archaeology
of the Ural Branch of the Russian Academy of Sciences
& Southern Ural State University

CAMBRIDGE
UNIVERSITY PRESS

CAMBRIDGE UNIVERSITY PRESS
Cambridge, New York, Melbourne, Madrid, Cape Town, Singapore, São Paulo

Cambridge University Press
32 Avenue of the Americas, New York, NY 10013-2473, USA

www.cambridge.org
Information on this title: www.cambridge.org/9780521829281

First published 2007

Printed in the United States of America

A catalog record for this publication is available from the British Library.

Library of Congress Cataloging in Publication Data

Koriakova, L. N. (Liudmila Nikolaevna)
The Urals and Western Siberia in the Bronze and Iron ages / Ludmila Koryakova, Andrej
Epimakhov.
  p. cm. – (Cambridge world archaeology)
Includes bibliographical references and index.
ISBN-13: 978-0-521-82928-1 (hardback)
ISBN-10: 0-521-82928-3 (hardback)
  1. Bronze age – Russia (Federation) – Siberia, Western. 2. Iron age – Russia (Federation) –
Siberia, Western. 3. Excavations (Archaeology) – Russia (Federation) – Siberia, Western.
4. Siberia, Western (Russia) – Antiquities. I. Epimakhov, A. V. (Andreĭ Vladimirovich).
II. Title.
GN778.22.R9K668   2006
947'.01 – dc22   2006018216

ISBN   978-0-521-82928-1 hardback

CONTENTS

LIST OF PLATES, FIGURES, AND TABLES

TABLES

FOREWORD

Philip L. Kohl

Wellesley College, Wellesley, Massachusetts, United States

I remember taking an overnight flight from Leningrad (St. Petersburg) to Kyrgyzia (Kyrgyzstan) via Sverdlovsk (Ekaterinburg) in late winter 1986. Just before landing in Sverdlovsk, the stewardess asked me to remove the earphones of a primitive portable cassette player that I had just turned on. Her manner was brusque and peremptory. She demanded to know what I was doing, what I was listening to, and claimed that many passengers believed that I – an obvious, solitary, and clearly suspicious American – must be receiving hidden instructions from someone in the West, perhaps Washington, on this then-novel listening device. I handed her the cassette player and had her listen to the Brahms violin concerto I had been enjoying. . . . Such was Cold War paranoia even as late as the early Gorbachev years in the closed military-industrial center of Sverdlovsk nestled on the Siberian side of the Ural mountains, the same city over which Gary Powers's U2 spy plane had been blown out of the sky in 1960.

In her preface, Ludmila Koryakova refers to the fact that the Urals and western Siberian areas covered in this volume remained a highly restricted military zone until the breakup of the Soviet Union in 1991. Until that time, contacts with the West were practically nonexistent. This isolation affected all fields of knowledge, including archaeology. There was some Western awareness – albeit limited – of Soviet archaeological accomplishments in Central Asia, the Caucasus, and European Russia, but the vast region stretching east of the Urals into western Siberia and northern Kazakhstan was then and has – until the publication of this important study – essentially remained a very large "white spot" on the archaeological map of Western scholars. This volume richly corrects this deficiency. It documents the discoveries of scores of Soviet/Russian archaeologists, ordering and analyzing the Bronze and Iron Age materials from a vast central part of Eurasia. In doing so, it shows us the strengths and distinctiveness of the Russian archaeological tradition.

Whereas Cold War realities clearly inhibited scholarly interaction on both sides of the Iron Curtain, the extent of the information gap varied widely and tended to be sharply asymmetrical: in general, Soviet/Russian archaeologists were far more familiar with the Western archaeological literature, including theoretical developments in Anglo-American archaeology, than Americans or Europeans knew about the accomplishments of their Soviet/Russian counterparts. The authors of this book are well read in Western archaeological theory, but they consciously and correctly, in my opinion, eschew any extended critical discussion of their guiding concepts and proceed with their main task: writing a coherent cultural prehistory of the Urals and Western Siberia during the Bronze and Iron Ages or roughly from the third through first millennia BC. To accomplish their principal goal, they record a sequence of "heuristically useful" archaeological cultures and more generically defined "intercultural communities" (*kulturnaya obshchnost'*), exhibiting greater spatial and temporal stability and "internal horizontal connections" among culturally related peoples. They also focus on shared metallurgical developments and redefine E. N. Chernykh's inductively derived concept of metallurgical provinces (here termed "technocultural networks"). They characterize their general approach as "materialistic . . . presuming causal priority of the material base (in a broad sense) as a primary means of the operation of a society."

With this conceptual and archaeologically appropriate philosophical base, they summarize the evidence. Readers may be overwhelmed by the pageant of archaeological cultures and materials presented, an almost inevitable reaction given the spatial and temporal parameters of their study. This problem clearly reflects the extent of archaeological work undertaken throughout this area and the fact that more investigations almost always document greater cultural diversity, resulting in the definition of even more archaeological cultures. Moreover, the roster of established archaeological cultures also reflects past reality in that it is associated with the mobile types of societies that emerged on the steppes. That is, the bewildering proliferation of archaeological cultures is intrinsic to the nature of steppe archaeology; both "splitters" and "lumpers" of this record can justify their procedures. To some extent, the indistinct differences among many defined archaeological cultures necessarily reflect the dominant herding way of life among steppe peoples, a mobility that fostered intercultural contact and assimilation. There is no correction for this constant merging or mixture of material remains, although it is helpful to be aware of it.

Western readers may be struck by the occasional ethnic, linguistic, and even "racial" attributions of specific archaeological cultures. Koryakova and Epimakhov recognize the problems of such identifications, "their contingent character," and, relatively speaking, attempt them infrequently. They employ them only in "rather clear and well-studied situations," where they can compare such attributions with "well-defined linguistic areas as specialists determine them." Some well-regarded identifications are explicitly accepted even though the evidence they themselves present is sufficiently comprehensive to query them. Thus, E. E. Kuzmina's well-known linguistic attribution of the different variants of the Andronovo cultural tradition, representing essentially "the entire population of the Urals and Kazakhstan of the Late Bronze Age to the eastern Iranians," is regarded as "reliable requiring no additional proof." Later, we read the "support for the Proto-Iranian (or Indo-Iranian) linguistic attribution of the Alakul and Fyodorovo cultures, or related branches of the Andronovo cultural confederation, requires the supposition that the extension of these languages increased and partly overlapped the distribution of the Proto-Ugric languages.... All ... [the] data representing the Andronovo-like cultures in western Siberian forest-steppe and southern forest are evidence for the hypothesis that suggests very active contacts between the Indo-Iranian and Finno-Ugric languages, expressed in numerous mutual borrowings, a part of which relates to the second millennium BC." If read carefully, their discussion reveals some qualification, a degree of uncertainty characterizing even this relatively well-enshrined linguistic identification. The basic problem, of course, is that material remains are nearly always ethnically, linguistically, and "racially" porous, freely adopted by different peoples speaking different languages and exhibiting different physical characteristics.

No "early civilization" arose on the steppes stretching east of the Urals during Bronze Age times. Archaeologists of the ancient Near East or other areas with substantial evidence for cities and large public art and architecture may be puzzled by their descriptions of sites, sometimes less than one hectare in size, as "large" or "monumental." Here a relative, historical perspective is required. The Sintashta/Arkaim planned settlements with their "outstanding characteristics" and "sophisticated system of fortifications" distributed across "The Country of Towns" may appear relatively puny by Near Eastern standards, but they constitute significant, if, still in some respects, enigmatic, discoveries for the archaeology of the Bronze Age steppes. The numerous complex animal sacrifices in burials at Sintashta in particular, as well as the unequivocal evidence of horse harnessing and the use of lighter spoke-wheeled vehicles ("chariots"), and impressive array of metal weapons – all constitute major discoveries. As Koryakova and Epimakhov point out at length, the degree of social complexity evident in these remains, particularly in the relatively uniform and standardized domestic architecture, is difficult to establish.

From its inception, Bronze Age archaeology on the steppes has focused on the excavation of raised kurgans and not concentrated on locating settlements, the cultural deposits of which often are thin and not clearly visible from the surface. This problem is compounded by the fact that dwellings typically consisted of semisubterranean pit houses that were dug into the ground, making them hard to locate. Similarly, many of the Sintashta-Arkaim settlements are not distinctly visible from the ground; most were discovered through the use of aerial photos, confirmed subsequently by helicopter flyovers and on-ground follow-up inspections. Recently, other planned settlements, difficult to discern directly on the ground, have been documented using different remote sensing techniques. Thus, for example, the later transitional Late Bronze to Early Iron

Age planned settlement of Ciça with multiple concentric rings of dwellings extending over c. 8 ha. or nearly three times larger than the largest Sintashta-Arkaim sites were found farther east in the Irtysh-Ob interfluve between Omsk and Novosibirsk in western Siberia. The site was discovered utilizing magnetometer measurements. One can only wonder how many more settlements-habitation and special-purpose sites of various periods will be discovered across the steppes through the use of aerial photography and more sophisticated remote sensing technologies and geophysical explorations. The more general problem evident here and throughout their study concerns the state of current archaeological understanding. How representative is the evidence in hand? Which regions and areas of concern are well investigated and understood and which lack such determinations? The discovery of the Sintashta-Arkaim settlements was unexpected. How many more important surprises still await us?

Perhaps the most basic and important thesis expounded at length in this study (and reflected in its very structure – Parts 1 and 2) is that the Iron Age of central Eurasia qualitatively differed from its Bronze Age. The mobile dominantly cattle herding *pastoralism* practiced during the Bronze Age must be distinguished from the mounted Eurasian *nomadism* that emerged subsequently only during Iron Age times. Koryakova and Epimakhov opt for what they term the "'later' hypothesis" and cite approvingly A. Khazanov's observation that "Eurasian nomadism as an economic and sociocultural phenomenon could not appear earlier because in many respect it depends on the economic and sociopolitical relations with settled statehood societies." These early nomadic societies and ultimately the first steppe empires (and first appearance of "royal" kurgans) came into being in part because they were caught up in larger systems of interregional interaction and exchange, including regular relations with sedentary states to their south (from China to Rome, including the states of southern Central Asia, such as the Parthian and the Kushan states). True Eurasian nomadism, which they believe first emerged farther east on the Mongolian steppe and then diffused west to the area of their concern, required a level of technological control not just over cattle, but also over horses, sheep, and Bactrian camels, each species of which had to adapt or be made to adapt to the climatic extremes of life on the steppes, particularly to forage throughout the long cold winter when the steppe was covered in snow.

Their well-informed account of the ecological, ethnographic, and historical dimensions of nomadism provides an essential overview to this important topic, as well as a detailed introduction to the basic Russian sources. Their discussion on the nature of mounted Eurasian nomadism is most valuable for its characterization of a type of society that dominated the steppes and adjacent regions for millennia almost into modern times. From this perspective, the earlier Bronze Age is seen as a time of experimentation. At a certain point, lighter carts (or "chariots") pulled by horses, supplanted, though never fully replaced, the ponderous, oxen-driven solid wheeled vehicles that had emerged earlier probably in the fourth millennium BC farther to the west. Bactrian camels and wooly sheep also assumed greater and greater importance until they became essential components to the "complete package" of true nomadism. Many questions immediately follow from their presentation. For example, to what extent or how is the advent of iron and the gradual dominant utilization of iron tools and weapons related to the emergence of this new type of nomadism with its full complement of several essential distinct species of animals and technological practices essential to that way of life? How did the gradual shift to the production and exchange of iron implements disrupt or change the nature and extent of interactions among closely related societies across the steppes?

A valuable study raises as many questions as it answers. English readers should be grateful to Ludmila Koryakova and Andrej Epimakhov for making such important and complex archaeological materials available to them. This book undoubtedly will remain the basic reference to the later prehistory of central Eurasia for decades to come. The Cold War barrier that isolated this region from Western consideration has now completely melted away. Among many other welcome advances, our understanding of our shared prehistoric past has considerably grown.

PREFACE

This book would never have been written if our region – the Urals – was still a closed military zone as it was until 1991. Since that time, many Russian archaeologists have been able to discuss our research with foreign colleagues and investigate to what extent our findings represent well-known processes of social change and to what extent our cases are novel and thus especially interesting. Few Western archaeologists have had the chance to examine our work and the prehistoric societies we have studied. Many encyclopedias of archaeology and maps of prehistoric cultures leave northern Eurasia as a blank spot, as if this area was not populated.

Thus, the motive for us to write this book is clear, although the project was daunting. It is difficult to write a book for an audience that has little knowledge of our area, and it is also difficult to write in a second (or third) foreign language.

Once I decided to write this book, I presented lectures to foreign universities, delivered papers at international conferences, and discussed the project with colleagues. In particular, Professor Colin Renfrew urged me (in 1999–2000) to continue with the idea of writing an archaeological synthesis and felt that *Cambridge World Archaeology* would be an ideal place for it. Andrej Epimakhov contributed his work on regions in which he is an expert. We are grateful to Professor Renfrew for his confidence in us and to the editorial board of *CWA* for accepting the book. Two anonymous reviewers have been patient in helping us clarify both substance and style. We hope that readers will be equally patient with the English version of what is undoubtedly a difficult text filled with names of strange territories, artifacts, and cultures.

We managed to write the text while living for periods of time in Russia, France, and England. Thanks to electronic communications, we were always in contact, although we live in different cities in Russia (Ekaterinburg and Chelyabinsk).

Our book is an advanced introduction to the late prehistory of a substantial part of Eurasia – the Urals and Western Siberia, predominantly within the steppe and forest-steppe zones. There is no book in any language that attempts to synthesize information in the Eurasian Bronze and Iron Ages. Naturally, we had to choose among many interesting finds and just as many interpretations and discussions of their significance. Although the book includes our own fieldwork, it surveys extensive literature and archival materials that are not easily accessible, even to Russian archaeologists.

The book was written with the financial help of various bodies, primarily the INTAS Foundation (EU), CNRS (France), Leverhulm Trust (UK), a joint grant of the Ural and Siberian divisions of the Russian Academy of Sciences, and grant 05-01-83104a/U of Russian Foundation for Humanities.

I am deeply grateful to my French colleagues and friends – Marie-Yvane Daire and Luic Langouette – for their generosity and support both in Russia during our joint fieldwork and in France during my stay in Rennes. I thank all the staff of the Laboratoire d'Anthropologie (CNRS) of the University of Rennes 1. I am also most grateful to my other French friends: Francine David, Marie-Celine Ugé, and her parents for their hospitality and constant help.

I finished writing the first draft of this book in Durham, England. It is my pleasant duty to thank Professor Anthony Harding for his help in all phases of my stay in Durham, as well as for his reading of the very raw text. I also thank members of the Department of Archaeology of the University of Durham, and Professor Pavel Dolukhanov from Newcastle upon Tyne, who also read the draft version of the book, and his wife Marianna for her practical support in England. In addition, I thank St. Mary's College in Durham, where I wrote numerous pages of this book. The hospitality of the staff and their lively interest in our work was invaluable.

I cannot express in mere words my gratitude to my very good friend Karlene Jones-Bley, who not only constantly encouraged me but also spent a great deal of her time, and even her health, patiently reading numerous electronic texts and correcting my Russian-English.

I want to thank my Russian colleagues and friends who took a major part of my administrative work and teaching on their shoulders during my absence from Russia. Thank you to Svetlana Sharapova, Sofia Panteleyeva, Natalia Berseneva, Dmitry Razhev, Andrew Kovrigin, Alexander Shorin, Alexei Zykov, and all the other members of the Institute of History and Archaeology and the Department of Archaeology of the Ural State University.

I further thank Gennady Zdanovich who opened the door for me to Bronze Age archaeology and inspired my interest in this subject and Svetlana Zdanovich for her most generous hospitality. Andrej and I appreciate the help, advice, and materials of Iya Batanina, Alexander Tairov, Dmitry Zdanovich, Sergei Kuzminykh, Galina Beltikova, Vladimir Stefanov, Olga Korochkova, Yuri Chemyakin, Viktor Borzunov, Evgeny Chibilev, Emma Usmanova, Nikolai Vinogradov, and Vladimir Kostukov.

I address special words of gratitude to my coauthor – Andrej Epimakhov – for his responsibility, patience, readiness to accept numerous "perestroika" in the text, and his valuable contribution to the first part of the book and to the illustrations.

In conclusion, I want to express my deep gratitude to my family for their constant support and forbearance of my long and frequent absences.

I dedicate this book to the memory of my parents – Anna Maltseva and Nikolai Zmatrakov – whose lives were unfairly difficult and short.

Ludmila Koryakova

INTRODUCTION

The Ural area can be defined in terms of its geographic location as a natural boundary between Europe and Asia. It is characterized by great landscape and environmental diversity: steppe, forest-steppe, forests, and mountains. In late prehistory, these areas were occupied by societies on different social and economic levels (nomadic, half-nomadic, settled pastoralists, specialist metallurgists), and different ethnic attributions (supposedly proto-Iranian and proto-Finno-Ugrian speakers). This area offers an interesting opportunity to examine cultural behavior at an important crossroads, where the influences of the East, the West, the North, and the South meet. This interaction resulted in a great variety of cultural traditions that had either European or Asiatic origins. Therefore, it is quite difficult to separate the prehistory of the Urals and Western Siberia area from that of the rest Eurasia.

This book will focus on the problems of the archaeology of the Bronze and Iron Ages, which are characterized by dramatic changes occurring all over Eurasia in later prehistory.

Historical evidence about the Uralian population is extremely sparse and vague. It goes back to Herodotus, later to the Arabian travellers and merchants. In the tenth century CE, they knew the northern lands called "Ugra," but Russians from the city of Novgorod, who first crossed the Urals in the eleventh century and met the Finno-Ugrian population,[1] undertook the first systematic exploration of this territory. Russians colonized the southern Urals and most of Siberia from the fifteenth century onward. The aboriginal Ob-Ugrians settled in the forest, whereas the Bashkir and Tatar peoples, speaking Turkic languages, occupied mostly the southern Ural and the southern part of western Siberia. They were incorporated into the Russian State, which then consisted of two parts: Moscovia and Siberia. The earliest information concerning environments, resources, peoples, and their culture was collected in the eighteenth century by the first academic expeditions.

Archaeological study of Trans-Urals and Western Siberia, which started before revolution by episodic excavations, became more organized in the

1920 and 1930s. The foundation of Uralian and Western Siberian archaeology is associated with the names of V. N. Chernetsov, K. V. Salnikov, M. P.
Gryaznov, E. M. Bers, M. F. Kosarev, and many others. Since the time of
the first discoveries, the database has greatly increased, especially during the
1970s and 1980s, and local and regional archaeological sequences based on
relative chronologies have been introduced into academic circulation. The
territory between Urals and Ob river basin is huge, and obviously not all of its
regions have been equally studied. There are still a lot of "blank spots" on the
archaeological map of Eurasia.

The aim of this book is to summarize very complex archaeological material
and to give insights into the past of the large area, which is little known to
Western archaeologists and almost completely unknown by a wider audience.
Despite the larger scope of cooperation between Russian and Western specialists, many misunderstandings relating to archaeology and prehistory of that
area can be found in English-language publications. This circumstance forces
us to devote a part of the book to description of archaeological data relating to
the period under review. However, we also will discuss major trends in cultural
and social development of the region.

ENVIRONMENTAL SETTING

In geographic literature, the concept of "Ural" has several meanings. First, it
is accepted that the Ural mountain ridge forms the boundary between Europe
and Asia in the northern part of the Eurasian continent. Second, the river
Ural[2] flows in the southern portion of this ridge. The third meaning, which
at present is known under term of "Great Urals" and which will be used
in our book, sees the Ural in a wider context as the region with common
cultural and economic characteristics. This concept does not conform to the
physical definition of the Ural as a highland. It also does not include the Polar
Ural, which is not populated, nor any part of the Northern Ural. However,
it embraces not only the middle and southern Urals but also the piedmont
lands of the Cis-Urals and Trans-Urals, and a part of the western Siberian
lowland.

Therefore, the area under study comprises the central part of northern
Eurasia, including the Cis-Urals or easterly part of eastern Europe, the Trans-
Urals or the westerly part of Siberia, coinciding with the basin of the river
Irtysh, mainly its western bank. In terms of administrative divisions, this area
covers several provinces (oblast') of the Russian Federation as well as a part of
northern Kazakhstan (Fig. 0.1).

The term "Ural" is of Turkic origin, meaning "a belt." Such a "stone belt"
stretches from the Kara Sea to the Kazakhstan steppe over a distance of over
2,000 km. It consists of several parallel mountain ranges, alternating the large
depressions with river valleys. The Urals's relief is characterized by a strong

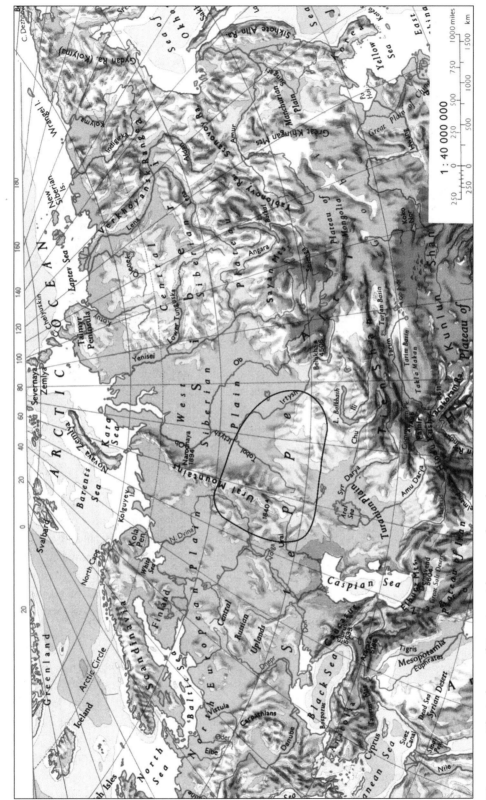

Figure 0.1. Physical map of Eurasia, with area under study.

3

difference between its western and eastern slopes, which form a watershed of the rivers of the Russian Plain from those of western Siberia. Geomorphologically, three basic parts of the Urals are distinguishable: the Northern, the Middle, and the Southern. Traditionally, according to this division, one distinguishes geographical areas: northern, middle, and southern Cis-Urals and northern, middle, and southern Trans-Urals. These parts have differences in their ecological parameters.

The relatively low Ural Mountains are composed of ancient aqueous and igneous rocks. The most elevated mountains are in the north (Narodnaya – 1,894 m), and in the south (Yamantau – 1,640 m). The lowest mountains (600–800 m) are situated in the middle Ural. Within the mountains are widely spread carst caves.

The mountain area of the Urals and also the Trans-Urals are famous for a high concentration of numerous minerals. The ores (iron, copper, gold, etc.), which are chiefly deposited in the eastern slopes, constitute the richest concentrations on earth. Furthermore, a huge variety of semiprecious stones (jasper, crystal, malachite, serpentine, agate, sardonyx, and others) is contained in the Ural metamorphic rocks beneath the surface.

The most significant characteristic of the area under study comprises the alternating landscape-climatic zones, which influence all forms of human adaptation (Fig. 0.2). The climate changes from the cold conditions in the north, where the mean July air temperature is 6–8°C, to the dry steppe in the south, where it is 22°C. The climate is subject to several factors, including the distance from the Atlantic and the closeness to the Arctic, Siberian, and Central Asian high-pressure areas. Nevertheless, the Atlantic air masses influence the Ural climate rather significantly. Because the Urals lie perpendicular to the direction of the predominant westerly winds, the western slopes are considerably more humid than the eastern slopes. This difference is especially noticeable in winter when the forests of the western slopes are bathed in snowdrifts, but the eastern slopes receive much less snowfall. The difference in precipitation is about 100–150 mm. The influx of cold arctic or hot air masses is stronger in the Trans-Urals, where the fluctuation of weather conditions is greater, especially in the transitional seasons.

Although the Ural Mountains are not very high, they can be considered as a west-east ecological factor forming a boundary between the two main climatic regions (Kremenetsky 2003). In addition, their western side, or Cis-Urals, have a more developed river network. The Kama River (the Volga's left tributary) is the largest and most important. In terms of relief, this area relates to the eastern part of the East European Plain with some hills, high bluff interfluves, and large river valleys. Here, the climate is moderately continental, with long cold and snowy winters, warm summers, and well-defined transitional periods – spring and autumn. The precipitation in the plains area reaches 400–500 mm during warm seasons and about 500–600 mm during the entire year. A vast portion

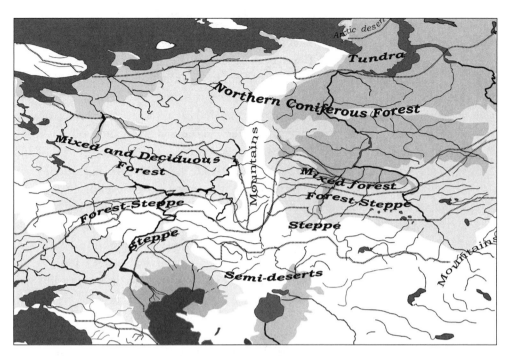

Figure 0.2. Landscape zones of Eurasia.

of this province is occupied by forests: dark coniferous taiga slowly changing first to mixed forest and then to the forest-steppe and then the dry steppe. The river valleys are usually flooded, possessing rich biological resources. In the forest zone, the sod-mid-podzol soils are concentrated, in the left Belaya River bank the podzol-chernozems are spread out. Mixed forests consist of pine, spruce, fir, birch, aspen, oak, rowan, black cherry, and wild apple trees. There is a great deal of frutescent plants, including wineberry and raspberry. The Kama meadows contain many steppe plant species.

The geographic environments of the southern Ural are characterized by arid conditions, which are, however, varied depending on the ecological situation. In the north, there are some high areas and a developed river network, which in the summertime produces rich vegetation in the river valleys. The Ural River, the most southern of the big rivers, flows southward along the eastern slope of the south Ural Mountains, then it sharply turns to the west near the town of Orsk, and it again turns southward and flows into the Caspian Sea (Fig. 0.1). The southern and eastern parts of the southern Urals are represented by dry steppe with poor pastures where there are many salt lakes. The hydrography of this area is influenced by the alternating of wet and dry seasons, each lasting usually about ten years. An important role is played by lakes, which vary in size and origin (elevated, karsts, oxbow). Fresh water lakes are found alongside salty and bitter-salty lakes, which are widely distributed.

The western Siberia area is an almost flat plain with a small northward incline and no abrupt changes in geographic zones, and this is where the largest water systems in Eurasia can be found. The Ob'-Irtysh water basin and a great number of swamps that are predominantly concentrated in the taiga zone. As a consequence, this area possesses the most extensive swamps on the surface of the earth. In the middle Trans-Urals, large areas are occupied by peat bogs and, as a result of higher humidity, unique archaeological objects made from organic materials can be preserved. However, the river network is not very dense. The big transit rivers – the Ob', Irtysh, Ishim, and Tobol – are of the Kazakhstzn type, which is characterized by a high level of spring water (up to 90 percent) and a small water level during other seasons. The rivers flow from steppe to the forest zone, and from early prehistory they have served as the main way of communication between the south and north. Although the navigational season of these rivers ranging from six to three months was a serious obstacle to transportation, pathways formed by the frozen surface of rivers were usually used for overland movement.

The climate is continental. In the warm seasons, warm air comes to the forest-steppe mostly from Kazakhstan and Central Asia and results in droughts and arid conditions. Cold air comes from the Arctic, usually in winter but sometimes in summer, which creates a severe and unstable climate. Additionally, the Ural Mountains retain moisture coming from the Atlantic, and the Altai, Pamir, and Tien-Shan often serve as obstacles to hot air masses.

The general characteristics of the western Siberian climate are the following: rather limited winter snowfall, cold winters, and quick transition to spring, hot summers and constant winds. In the taiga zone, the climate is colder and moister.

Beyond the Ural, the steppe area moves more northward than in eastern Europe (Fig. 0.2). The forest-steppe, situated to the south of the small-leafed forest and represented by multigrass meadows and birch-aspen coppices passes to the steppe, north of which multigrass and feather grass vegetation until recently was predominant. Overall, the landscapes of the Ural-Siberian forest-steppe are characterized by geographic zonality and a mosaic distribution of vegetal assemblages – forests, meadows, swamps, and steppes. Droughts are recurrent here every eight to twelve years. This results in many Trans-Uralian lakes that alternately dry out and then fill with water.[3] The forest zone is inhabited by many species of large animals, including elk, deer, bear, and lynx. The small fur-bearing animals, such as sables, fox, ermine, and squirrels, are also typical in that area.

In the forest-steppe, the fauna is mixed. It is here that both forest and steppe species of animals are found including elk and bear. The Urals and western Siberia represent a variety of landscapes caused by the complex relief, their vast longitudinal extent, and climatic difference between the Cis-Urals and

Trans-Urals. The fauna and flora, naturally, are closely connected to the various landscapes. The differentiating features are clearly manifested in the boundary areas between the basic landscape zones, where there have been some inter-zonal displacements that resulted from climatic fluctuations. These changes are more pronounced for western Siberia, but they are not as visible for the Ural, primarily because of the complex character of its relief. As we have pointed out, in terms of climatic zones, the western Ural is related to the Atlantic-continental region of the temperate zone, but the eastern Ural is included in the continental western Siberian part with its forest and steppe areas. The northern part is almost completely influenced by the Atlantic-Arctic winds (Khotinsky 1977: 22–3). One can say that the climate of the western Urals was changing according to eastern European regularities, whereas the eastern territories demonstrate more "Asiatic scenarios." Moreover, different land-scapes, naturally, do not react synchronically to the temperature and humidity fluctuations.

CLIMATIC CONDITIONS IN THE BRONZE AND IRON AGES

The problem of interrelation between society and environment has always been a focus of attention of various disciplines. This interest was intensified among Russian environmentalists and archaeologists during the past few decades.

Numerous recent publications present historical data on global climate change combined with palynological data, oxygen-isotope analysis, and data concerning lake fluctuations show that there were at least four phases of syn-chronous climatic change in both hemispheres: (1) 560–800 BP – "minor glacial epoch"; (2) 1300–800 BP – climatic optimum of the Early Middle Ages; (3) – 2900–2300 BP – cold of the Iron Age; (4) 6000–7000 BP – last climatic opti-mum (Dergachev et al. 1996: 13). According to Klimanov (2002), in the north-ern hemisphere there were several periods of extreme cold and warm climate. Statistical correlation between twenty-four-hundred-year cycles in C^{14} con-centration and long-lasting climatic changes has recently been revealed (Vasily'ev et al. 1997).

The cycles of global climate were reflected in regional and local fluctuations, forming regional ecological systems. The landscape reacts differently even on synchronic periodic influences. This is expressed in the heterogeneity of mois-ture in different territories (Koryakova & Sergeev 1986; Tairov 2003). Pollen and soil analysis, investigation of Eurasian peat bogs, and new hydrological and geological research undertaken recently in combination with radiocarbon dates did not contradict, in general, these theories, but they detailed more complex climatic dynamics. The scale of regional fluctuation of temperature can differ from one global period to another. In particular, even small global warming (up to 1–1.5°C) is accompanied by greater warming in temperate and high latitudes and smaller temperature changes in northern subtropics. Regional fluctuations also can take place before or after cycles of global climate (Klimenko 1998; 2000; 2003).

The environment of the Volga–Ural–Kazakhstan steppe has been actively studied during recent decades. This research was based mostly on paleosoils under kurgans (Alexandrovsky 2003; Demkin 1997). In the Trans-Urals, a large program of paleoenvironmental research was carried out in the territory of the Arkaim museum-reserve, where a series of pedological analyses comes from (Ivanov & Chernyansky 1996; 2000; Lavrushin & Spiridonova 1999). Substantial information also has been obtained from the middle Urals peat bog sites (Khotinsky 1977; Nemkova 1978) and important evidence has been obtained from the research of lake deposits in the mountain-forest pied-monts of the southern Ural (Duryagin 1999) as well as rich paleogeographic materials received from western Siberia (Ryabogina et al. 2001a; Ryabogina & Orlova 2002; Ryabogina et al. 2001b; Semochkina & Ryabogina 2001). A large series of Holocene sequences also has been received from northern Kazakhstan (Ivanov 1992; Kremenetsky 2003).

Considering all this, we will try to summarize some basic environmental trends, which could have taken place during the period under study.

A society reacts differently to environmental change, depending on its pace (speed) and magnitude. This is most evident in the steppe zone, which, in turn, also has been studied more by archaeologists. Overall, in eastern Europe the fluctuation of moisture did not entail a substantial displacement of the landscape-climatic zones, whereas in western Siberia and Kazakhstan the situation was more complex. Here, the magnitude of fluctuation was greater, and whole zones of landscapes were displaced. As a result, the eastern European population reacted to the environmental change according to an adaptive model, but the Asiatic population chiefly had to follow a migration model.

In terms of geological classification, the Bronze and Iron Ages are related to the middle and later Holocene – its Subboreal and Subatlantic periods, each divided into three subzones. Ivanov (1992) and Ivanov and Chernyansky (2000) summarized all paleogeographic materials of the territory from eastern Europe to Mongolia and correlated them with archaeological periodization (Table 0.1).

The Atlantic period (especially its final stage) is usually considered the time of the climatic optimum of the Holocene, combining the thermal peak with the late Atlantic moistening and when the northern shift of the large leafed for-est reached its maximum (Khotinsky 1977: 81; Nemkova 1978: 43). Although there are some data in favor of the statement that this period was not homo-geneous, one can distinguish several stages of aridization, which has been reflected in the southern Urals pollen spectrums (Lavrushin & Spiridonova 1999: 100). Archaeologically, the Atlantic period is synchronized with the

TABLE O.I. *Climatic fluctuations in the Eurasian steppe (after Ivanov and Chernyansky 1996)*

Time		Periodization					
Thousands years BP	Centuries	Geological	Thermic epochs	Epochs of humidification of Eurasian steppe	Archaeological		
					Epochs	Cultures	
						Eastern Europe	Urals, Northern Kazakhstan
1	2	3	4	5	6	7	8
0	20		Warming	Contamporanity			
1	15	SA³	SA³ Cooling, "minor glacial period"	SA³ Moistening	Middle Ages — Late	Late Nomads	Late Nomads
	10						
			SA² Warming, "minor climatic optimum"	"Early medieval aridization"	Middle Ages — Early		
2	5	SA²		Early Sub-athlantic alternation of micro-pluvilas and micro-arids	Iron Age	Huns	Early Nomads
	0		SA¹ Cooling			Sarmatians — Late	
3	5	SA¹				Sarmatians — Middle	
						Sarmatians — Early	
				Late sub-boreal moistening		Sauromatians	
	10	SB³	SB³ Cooling		Bronze Age — Late	Scythians	
						Cimmerians	Sargary
4	15	SB²	SB² Thermic optimum	Early Sub-boreal aridization	Bronze Age — Middle	Srubnaya	Fyodorovo Alakul
	20					Catacombnaya	Petrovka Sintashta
	25	SB¹	SB¹ Cooling		Bronze Age — Early	Late Yamnaya	Tersek-Botai cultures — Late
5	30					Early Yamnaya	Tersek-Botai cultures — Early
	35	AT³	AT³ Thermic maximum	Late Athlantic Moistening	Eneolithic	Eneolithic cultures	
6	40						Late Neolithic

Eneolithic although in the forest territories the Eneolithic cultures can be seen in parallel with the Yamnaya culture of the Early Bronze Age.

Different scholars studying eastern European and Asiatic areas agree about the characteristics of Subboreal draught and that it was accompanied by significant weather cooling at the beginning of the Bronze Age. To the north of the Caspian Sea, aridity started to increase in the interval between 5200–3700 BP. This process went together with the rise of climatic continentality, and it reached its maximum in the early Subboreal (Early and Middle Bronze Age). This caused the landscape zonation to be displaced at least on one subzone (Demkin & Demkina 1999: 25; Demkin 1997: 158).[4] The second millennium BC is characterized by maximal soil-landscape diversity, and scholars regard this as the time of the beginning of the modern pedological and geographic zonation (Demkin 1997: 152). The continuance of aridity and moisture, if to judge by comparative data from eastern Europe and northern Kazakhstan, was different on either side of the Ural mountains. In the Asiatic part, the warmest period proved to be longer than in the west, and it embraced not only Subboreal-1 and Subboreal-2 but also a part of Subboreal-3; that is to say, it lasted up to the Final Bronze Age. This rise in aridity is diagnosed as gradual (Ivanov & Chernyansky 1996: 152). Some scholars believe the aridity of the second phase of the Bronze Age had catastrophic consequences (Lavrushin & Spiridonova 1999: 100–1).

For the period of the Late Bronze Age of eastern Europe, the humidity is determined as close to modern humidity. It was accompanied by climatic warming, the peak of which coincided with the second and third quarters of the second millennium BC. As mentioned earlier, in northern Kazakhstan aridity continued until the Iron Age and tended to increase. At the second millennium BC, the climatic situation in the Trans-Urals was closer to the climate of eastern Europe. At the beginning of the first millennium BC, it was characterized by a more favorable pattern compared to the western territories, the climate of which evolved to the rising continentality. Consequently, in the mid-second millennium BC, the areas beyond the middle and southern Ural were partly occupied by "insular" forests. The Siberian vegetal complex coexisted together with a prairie one. The end of the second millennium was marked by a general cooling, which resulted in a climatic pattern comparable to the modern pattern. This does not exclude some fluctuation such as a "minor glacial period" of the Subatlantic-3. In the south of eastern Europe, the period of favorable climatic conditions, which provided the flourishing of the Late Bronze societies, in particularly the demographic phenomenon of the Srubnaya culture, ended by the twelfth–eleventh centuries BC (Medvedev 1999a; b). The general cooling reached its peak by the ninth–eighth centuries BC.

The beginning of the Iron Age was characterized by a rise in humidity, which has been recorded for many areas: the northern Black Sea coast, the northern Caucasus, the Trans-Urals, western Siberia, and the area of the Aral Sea (Demkin & Ryskov 1996; Demkin 1997). The degree of this process, however, varied in different areas. It was quite strong in the western Siberian forest zone, which was dominated by north–west cyclones. Moisture backed by cool climate imposed cold and snowy winters and dry summers. The arid zone did not experience such a strong rise in moisture. In the south of eastern Europe at the turn of the second and first millennia BC, the landscapes of the so-called cold steppe had been formed (Medvedev 1999a). A substantial series of palinological data collected from the sites of Trans-Uralian forest-steppe also demonstrated that the transition to the Iron Age was accompanied by climatic change toward the rise of continental climatic conditions (Larin & Matveyeva 1997). Scholars regard the dramatic climatic changes of this period as the ecological stress that affected many areas and the reason for the changes in economic orientation.

The humid phase, however, was replaced by a new cycle of aridity in the mid-first millennium BC, and again it was stronger in the Asiatic part. Many scholars connect this situation with the Sarmatian migration westward to the Volga and northern Pontic areas (see Chapter 6). Hereafter, short time pluvials alternated with dry periods, but their continuity and frequency were less great.

This climate reconstruction demonstrates the changes in the steppe zone and its adjacent areas. In the forest-steppe and, especially, in the forest zone, the changes seemed less pronounced. Here the climatic and landscape variability was not as contrasting as in the south, but it did take place (Matveyeva & Ryabogina 2003). In the forest zone, one cannot see the great displacement of landscape boundaries in a south–north direction. In fact, there is no real frontier between zones; it is more of a statistical nature.[5] The change of general humidity did not entail the transformation of all the forest into the steppe and vice versa. For example, according to observations of wetland specialists, in the taiga of eastern Europe and western Siberia, in conditions of high humidity the forests tended to decrease because of an increase of swampy areas. At the same time, the situation could reverse in the dry periods[6] (Kosarev 1984: 40). No less complex was the situation in the piedmont areas, where the landscapes moved in a latitudinal direction (Duryagin 1999: 55). The disappearance of broad-leafed forests from the eastern slopes of the Ural in the period after Subboreal-2 is witness to such transformations.

Thus, according to environmental research, the climatic and landscape situation in the Holocene changed several times (Table 0.1). It is believed that at least three big climatic fluctuations occurred during the third to the first millennia BC. High humidity took place in the second half of the third millennium BC and at the turn of the second and the first millennia BC. High aridity is thought to have occurred from the middle of the second millennium BC. This is observed particularly in the soil of the southern area. During the period 5000–3800 BP, the soil had mostly meadow characteristics; in the period

3800–2000 BP, it was a meadow-steppe, and finally a dry brown one (Lukashev & Demkin 1989). Since the Neolithic, there has been a considerable differ-ence between the European and Siberian/Kazakhstan sectors of the steppe and forest-steppe belt (Kremenetsky 2003).

The heterogeneity of the Urals region is fully reflected in the history of its climate. Because global changes were diversified in landscape transformations and regional climatic fluctuations, people migrated and adapted their activities to them.

CHRONOLOGY AND PERIODIZATION

The chronological framework of this book – the Bronze and Iron Ages – is determined not only by the authors' preferences and by expertise but also because these two epochs feature a continuity of social and cultural processes although they are separated by crucial changes (Koryakova 1996; 2002). The beginning of the Bronze Age in the steppe and southern forest-steppe is marked by the emergence of food-producing forms of economies. This was based primarily on livestock breeding, which periodically changed its form over a period of almost two thousand years. Nevertheless, despite these changes in form, it always played a leading role up to the eighteenth century. We will try to show that some trends of social development that came to fruition in the Iron Age were rooted in the Bronze Age despite their difference. Nevertheless, working on this book, the authors came upon many expected and unexpected encumbrances.

Chronological Intricacies

Before we pass to the concrete material, we need to turn our attention to the issues concerning a chronological system. The area under study is not only difficult to describe in terms of cultural representation but also in terms of chronology. These difficulties rest on the fact that the human groups of this territory were in contact with those in surrounding territories, as we saw in the previous chapter, and contained sites that had cultural elements of neighboring areas. This has forced scholars to define the chronological position of an area in reference to either the west or east. Meanwhile, there has been no unified chronological system developed for both eastern Europe and western Asia. Archaeologists have been forced to use the existing chronologies based on concrete types of artifacts and complexes and, wherever possible, verify their conclusions. These existing chronologies might, therefore, result in a definite concept of the initial and final dates of various cultural formations – archaeological cultures, groups, variants, and so on.

The literary sources provide rather scarce information about events and processes in the first millennium BC. Moreover, we have no written information at all relating to earlier epochs. Therefore, it is necessary that we rely almost completely on the archaeological evidence. The existing system of chronology applying to the local material is, largely, relative; this chronological system is based almost entirely on methods of a comparative typology of material and cross-cultural analogies combined with stratigraphic observation. For the Bronze Age, the lines of analogy are "attached" to the systems of European, Near Eastern, and Chinese chronology. For the Iron Age, a benchmark role is played by Scythian and Sarmatian chronology, which for its part is tied to East Asia, Greek, and Roman imports and influences. Radiocarbon dating is in the process of being introduced into the practice of regional archaeologies, but as yet it does not form a global chronological net.[7] Additionally, in many cases, especially concerning the Bronze Age, Russian archaeologists face the problems of a contradiction between traditional dates and radiocarbon calibrated dates. The more the calibrated dates come into use, the more one has to lower the date for the cultural formations of the Early Metal Epoch. The radiocarbon dates received for the Iron Age, however, concur with the traditional archaeological chronology, except for the dates of the transitional period. There are also problems with calibration of dates between 800 and 400 BC because of a large "plateau" in the calibration curve (van der Plicht 2004).

Most archaeological sites within the area under examination are of a multilayer composition and often provide good stratigraphic sequences that are indeed of great merit. However, because of the great typological variety of material, especially ceramics, and the use of different field methodologies, it is not always easy to coordinate these sequences from different sites in a satisfactory correlated manner.

In general, there are two absolute chronologies for the Bronze Age: (1) a "long" chronology that is more relevant to the western European (more precisely to the Balkan-Mycenaean) scale, and (2) a "short" chronology that is based on eastern Asiatic (Chinese) analogies. The first one gives earlier dates (longer period) than the second one (shorter period).

We need to note the lack of summarizing publications of radiocarbon dates in Russian archaeology. The rare catalogues of dates issued from some laboratories (Orlova 1995) do not greatly change the general situation. Analytical selections of absolute dates relating to the Circumpontic metallurgical province and a summarizing review relating to the Late Bronze Age have recently been published (Chernykh 2002). These dates, however, are not greatly significant for the area under study; additionally, against this general background, the number of eastern European absolute dates is rather limited. There are only a small number of radiocarbon dates recorded for the most eastern part of eastern Europe (Kuznetsov 1996b). In 2002, the first series of radiocarbon dates for the Eneolithic and Early Bronze Age of the Cis-Urals was obtained. For the time being, it is published only in a summarized form (Chernykh & Orlovskaya 2004; Morgunova et al. 2003; Morgunova & Turetski 2002). These sites fall into the period between the second half of the fourth and third quarters of the third millennia cal BC (Table 0.2). Moreover, judging by funeral ritual and inventory this group does not look homogeneous.

Nevertheless, as a result of this work, the chronological framework of the Circumpontic province (see Chapter 1) was well marked (3300–1900 cal BC), and it has become possible to distinguish the earlier (Early Bronze Age) and later (Middle Bronze Age) phases in its development. However, some dates within the period 2800–2500 cal BC have turned out superimposed, and the probable border between the earlier and later phases has been attributed to 2700–2600 cal BC.[8]

A similar situation has been noticed for the transitional period between the Middle and Late Bronze Age, and when one attempts to divide the Late Bronze Age into phases, we see that the sectors of superimposed dates covered 250–300 years (2300–1600 cal BC, 1900–1250 cal BC, and 1500–900 cal BC). The critical line of the Early Iron Age was marked better around 900 BC (Chernykh et al. 2002b: 21). It is, however, worthwhile to recall that for the enormous territory of the Eurasian metallurgical province only 237 radiocarbon dates from all those collected by Chernykh's team are available for use. Recently, a series of forty dates relating to chronologically different sites of Trans-Uralian Bronze Age have been recorded in the Oxford laboratory (Table 0.3). These dates are the basis of Table 0.4.

One way or another, the disagreement between the two dating systems for the Bronze Age remains. We must wait for serial analyses that will fill in the chronological and geographical "blank spots" that, in turn, will help to create the standard cultural and chronological scales for some regions with their further correlation.

The chronologies of the transitional periods are particularly uncertain. This statement can be fully applied to the transitional period from the Bronze to the Iron Age, although the introduction of iron technology into Eurasia is more or less clear (see Chapter 5). Nevertheless, there are a number of cultures with general parameters that correspond to the Iron Age, but they were based on the production and use of bronze. "Transitional" sites are, in many cases, poor with regard to datable material, or they do not provide any organic remains for radiocarbon analysis. Consequently, one of the constantly debated problems in Russian archaeology is, in a narrow context, that of the origins of the Scythian culture and, in a wider context, that of nomadic cultures. The discovery of the Arzhan kurgan in Tuva was of great importance for this issue and by now a representative series of radiocarbon dates displaying its early age have been obtained (Zaitseva et al. 1997a; Zaitseva et al. 1997b). However, some scholars (Chlenova 1997) still insist on its later date, based on a number of cross-cultural parallels. Meanwhile, the calibrated radiocarbon determinations for Arzhan, Tagisken (Aral Sea area), and some other sites of Inner Asia has demonstrated the older dates for the beginning of eastern nomadic cultures (Hall 1997).

TABLE O.2. *Radiocarbon dates of the Yamnaya sites of the Cis-Urals (after Morgunova et al. 2003)*

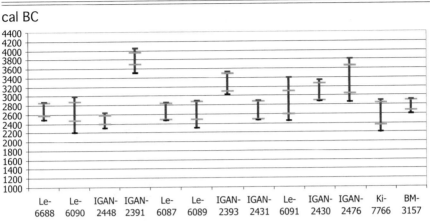

Series of radiocarbon dates also were obtained for key Scythian sites of the northern shore of the Black Sea (Zaitseva et al. 1997a). They correlate with archaeological dates and allow us to coordinate them with sites from southern Siberia.

In general, the chronology of the Iron Age is better established than that for the Bronze Age (Table 0.5). There are several chronologies based on detailed typologies of grave goods, primarily of arrowheads, coming from Eurasian kurgans (Khazanov 1971; Medvedskaya 1980; Milukova 1964; Moshkova 1974; Skripkin 1990; Smirnov 1961). The last few decades have been marked by discoveries of several spectacular unrobbed nomadic graves in various parts of the

TABLE O.3. *Radiocarbon dates of the Bronze Age sites of the Trans-Urals and western Siberia: Samples: 1 – Seima-Turbino; 2–15 – Sintashta; 18–20 – Petrovka; 21–23 – Petrovka-Alakul; 16–17 – Early Srubnaya; 28–30 – Alakul; 24–27 – Fyodorovo, Fyodorovo-Alakul; 31–37 – Final Bronze Age (for details, see Chapter 2)*

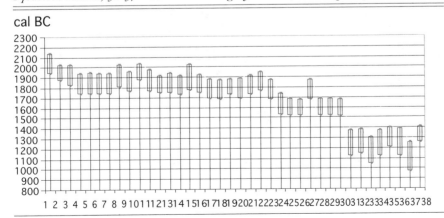

TABLE O.4. *Chronology of the Bronze Age*

Periods	Dates (BC)	Cis-Urals				Trans-Urals			Western Siberia	Northern Kasakhstan
		Volga	Steppe	Forest-steppe	Forest	Steppe	Forest-steppe	Forest		
Early	3200	Yamnaya	Yamnaya	Early Bronze Age cultures	Eneolithic cultures Garinskaya groups	Tersek	Surtandy	Early Bronze Age cultures		Botai
	3100					—	—			—
	3000	Catacombnaya				?				—
	2900					—				—
Middle	2800	Poltavka				—			Cultures of the combed-holed ceramic	—
	2700					Yamnaya Poltavka?				—
	2600	—					?			—
	2500	—				—	—			?
	2400	—	?			?				—
	2300	?		Abashevo	Balanovo	?		Tashkovo	Krotovo	—
	2200									—
	2100									Krotovo-Elunino
Late	2000	Potapovka Pokrovsk	Sintashta Petrovka Alakul Srubnaya Fyodorovo			Sintashta Petrovka Alakul Fyodorovo			Tashkovo	
	1900	—	—			—				
	1800	Srubnaya		Srubnaya Alakul			Petrovka Alakul Fyodorovo	Cherkaskul		Petrovka Alakul Fyodorovo
	1700	—				Sargary				
	1600	—				—			Alakul	
	1500		Sargary			—				
Final	1400	Nur-type	—	Mezhovka	Kurmantau Erzovka groups Mezhovka		Cherkaskul Mezhovka	Mezhovka	Andronovo-Like Cultural Horizon	Sargary Dandybai Dongal
	1300	—	—	—			—	—		
	1200	—			—			Berezki		—
	1100								Irmen	—
	1000								—	—
	900									

16

TABLE 0.5. *Chronology of the Iron Age*

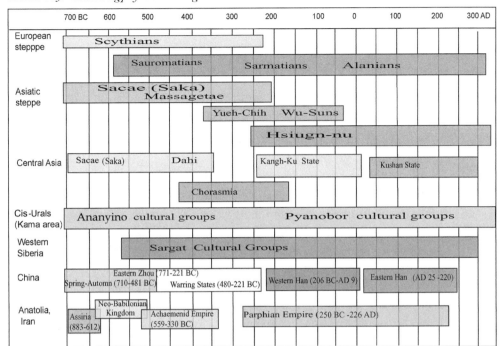

Eurasian steppe and forest-steppe. They contained exclusively rich imported materials that could help precisely mark their chronological positions and date the grave complexes. Nevertheless, here we are waylaid by a different danger deriving from written sources that mention certain nomadic tribes that inhabited the Eurasian steppes. The attempts to find their archaeological expressions have led scholars to endless debates in which the questions of chronology are a major part.

Periodizations: Remarks about Terminology and Structure

Cultural and social development is a multidimensional process, and the determination of its temporal parameters plays a very important role in the formulation of questions we want to answer and explanations we want pertaining to this process.

The division of "age" or "epoch" into early, middle, and late periods is commonly accepted in archaeology, though not always used. The concept of "period" can have two meanings: (1) as a time span, during which a process occurs, and (2) a stage of a certain development. At the same time, if the concept of "stage" or "phase" is relating to a stadial structure of periodization, then one "period" is a marker of its temporal structure (Evdokimov 2000). In Russian literature, the term "stage," in its strict sense, is not widely used, as it is applied mainly to the global process such as metallurgy or livestock development. Instead, the term "phase" or "etape" can easily be found in pages of many publications.

The archaeology of the early epochs also uses the term "chronological horizon." This term is not typical of Iron Age archaeology, although Yablonsky (2000) has recently suggested that it should replace the concept of "Scythian and Siberian Unity," which is really not relevant but common, with the term "Scythian chronological horizon." According to Klein (2000: 489), the difference between period and chronological horizon is that the dating of a period is extensional within some interval of time, whereas the dating of horizon is discrete and not precise.

For modeling and synchronization of global processes that occurred in Eurasia in the Bronze Age, the concept of metallurgical provinces based on the grouping of technologically and morphologically similar objects played a great role (Chernykh 1978). Thanks to this concept, the basic chronological horizons have been determined as well as some regional scales coordinated. Accepting and using Chernykh's concept in its content, we should make some comments pertaining to its terminology. The term "province" is usually used in two basic meanings: (1) as a part of a large taxonomic system as, for example, a climatic or landscape system in geography; or (2) as a contraposition to a certain center. In fact, the provinces determined by Chernykh are of a single-level formation in terms of their territorial disposition, and they can, indeed, serve as the centers rather than provinces. Furthermore, their English loan-translation does not reflect their meaning. Therefore, we think that it would be better to use the term "technocultural network" than province.

Following tradition, we divide the Bronze Age into the Early, Middle, Late, and Final periods (Table 0.4). This allows us to see the similarity of the cultural processes in different landscape zones of the Cis-Urals and Trans-Urals and to find their common and individual features. The absolute dates are sometimes discordant with the traditional concept, but, in this case, we prefer to rely on the recent series of radiocarbon dates (Chernykh et al. 2000a). The dates of synchronous cultural occurrences also have been corrected. For the Bronze Age chronology of eastern Europe, we used the scheme suggested by Trifonov (1996a; 1996b, 2001).

In addition to these periodizations, in Russian archaeology there exist some other systems, taking different criteria for its definition, especially with regard to the Iron Age.

As the nomads played a very significant role in Eurasian prehistory, Russian archaeologists have distinguished two basic periods (or epochs) in the Iron Age: Scythian (from the seventh to the third century BC) and Hunnic-Sarmatian (second century BC to fifth century CE). Gryaznov (1983) brought to light the so-called Arzhan-Chernogorovo phase of Scythian and Siberian cultures (ninth to seventh century BC). It also has been suggested that the Early Iron Age be called "the epoch of ancient nomads" as opposed to "the epoch of the late or medieval nomads."

We will rely on a general periodization comprising the concepts of "age," "period," and "phase." The local periodizations will be used in a limited scale.

Hence, the temporal sequence we shall be dealing with extends through the period of the late third, second, and first millennia BC. Because of the clearly manifested landscape-climatic zonality (Fig. 0.2), the regional chronological and cultural sequences do not coincide in detail. We can note, however, that most cultural similarities are to be observed within the corresponding geographic zones, where more or less stable historical and cultural associations had been evolving. Such associations of cultures can be united by concrete cultural and chronological horizons that are more characteristic for the Bronze Age than for the Iron Age, which can be described in terms of cultural worlds.

Chronologically, the time under study consists of several basic periods the boundaries between which are to some extent conventional:

The Early Bronze Age (3300–2600 cal BC); the Middle Bronze Age (2500–1800 cal BC); the Late Bronze Age (1800–1500 cal BC); the Final Bronze period (1400–800 cal BC); the Early Stage of the Iron Age (800–300 cal BC); the Middle or True Stage of the Iron Age (200 cal BC–300 AD), and the Late Iron Age (400–600 AD).[9] This scale is deemed reasonable for the southern part of the region (steppe-forest-steppe). A part of the northern (boreal zone) includes different periods conditioned by a slower technological evolution. The Bronze Age in these northern areas actually lasted up to the fourth century BC.

GENERAL DEFINITIONS

Philosophically, the book is mainly based on a materialistic approach presuming causal priority of the material base (in a broad sense), as a primary means of the operation of a society. The environment is considered rather important among many interplaying factors stimulating social development. Among the latter, technology plays a significant role. Sociopolitical and ideological factors are regarded as powerful factors as well.

The elements of approaches characteristic of the current state of Russian archaeology (Koryakova 2003) will be used in relevant cases. Dealing with such a vast area and extensive chronological period, we have to depart from the cultural-historical approach, which is still of great significance in Russian archaeology. This approach allows us to account for the variation within the large amount of chronological and geographical evidence in the archaeological record. An interesting remark, supporting this statement, was made by Gosden: "Although out of favour with elements of archaeology more oriented towards theory, the interest in local distinctiveness and sequence found in culture history may well marry together with recent interests in the links

between material culture and ethnicity and so-called 'contextual archaeology'"
(1999: 476).

We believe that archaeological culture, as a heuristic archaeological device
(Veit 1994) and a marker of similarity and patterning given by archaeological
material, has a good reason to exist.

We do not attempt to identify ethnic groups as ethnic identifications of
any "archaeological cultures," although we assume that ethnic heterogeneity
existed in the past. In earlier prehistoric periods, a degree of ethnic heterogeneity was rather small; it became higher as the population increased. This
ethnic temporal and spatial uncertainty and alterability causes so-called cultural
"flowability" ("fluidity"), which is characterized by diffusive cultural boundaries (Arutunov 1989: 44–5). Archaeologically, it is expressed in morphological and ornamental (in particular) continuity when the sites, collections, and
assemblages differ by one or two traits, forming continuous sequences, in which
the least similar complexes are situated at the periphery of these sequences.

In general, given the possibility of certain correlation between archaeological
and ethnographic groups, we are aware of the contingent character of this
relationship. Therefore, we shall not go into details of ethnic attributions, unless
it concerns rather clear and well-studied situations, as, for instance, regarding
cultural continuity through many centuries in the forest areas. Dealing with
archaeological occurrences of a large distribution, we can compare them with
some well-defined linguistic areas, as specialists determine them. For the Iron
Age, the probability of archaeological, linguistic, and ethnic correspondence is
presumably higher than in the Bronze Age.

Although we deny the strict correlations between certain archaeological and
particular social entities, we believe that archaeological patterns, give insights to
the cumulative image of spatially expressed human experience (human culture),
which was realized at certain times in certain territories and related to certain
groups of people.

At the same time, we would like to clarify the semantic context of the
term "archaeological culture." When using such expressions as, for instance,
people of the "Yamnaya culture," or "Yamnaya people," we have in mind the
cumulative image of people who have left the sites, united by us with the name
of Yamnaya.

The concept of "archaeological culture" has obvious limitations. A study of
historically known people testifies to the great complexity, variety, and hierarchy of social and cultural formations. Despite its limited nature, archaeological
information indicates that such a variety existed in the past. But its reduction to
nothing but the concept of "archaeological culture" hinders our understanding
of the totality of cultural processes, leading archaeologists into blind alleys of
terminological disputes and overestimations of local developments. To avoid
this localism, one can use some other concepts of archaeological (cultural)
taxonomy.

Some areas maintain spatial stability through centuries, irrespective of cultural groups who inhabit it. Analogous ecological conditions have an effect on the formation of similar cultural stereotypes, reflected in economic activity, everyday life, and belief.[10] These create a common cultural background, in which internal horizontal connections between peoples, irrespective to their age, play very important roles. The concept of cultural intercommunity (*obshchnost'*) is used to denote this phenomenon. It is determined by a considerable number of interconditioned manifestations of human activity (culture) which are characterized by the similarity of basic material and nonmaterial cultural stereotypes within certain areas and in certain periods. Taxonomically close but not identical to the latter is the concept of "family of cultures," which we introduce in order to emphasise possible genealogical relations within certain areas. It is determined as the diachronic and genealogically organized group of cultures, which being interconnected by relations of common origin and succession, reflect stable diachronic development of core-traditions within certain periods.

We also use the term "cultural world." This is understood as a conglomerate of economic, social, ethnic, political, and other determinants (Shchukin 1994). "World" is characterized by specific style or some structural unity of a certain cultural model that resulted from social development in conditions of historical closeness.

As we stated earlier, the specifics of the area under study are determined by its intermediate position both in its geographic and cultural aspects. This means that local societies were predestined to various interactions, which are not always expected to be symmetrical. Another very important factor is that the period we are dealing with – the second and first millennia BC – is in an area characterized by growing technoeconomic complexity and growing influence from statehood societies, especially in the Iron Age with its first World Empires.

PART ONE

THE BRONZE AGE: THE RISE OF ECONOMIC AND CULTURAL COMPLEXITY

CHAPTER I

THE DEVELOPMENT OF BRONZE METALLURGY

From the very beginning, Russian archaeologists studied both historical and technological aspects of ancient metallurgy. However, until recently, many Russian archaeologists regarded this categorizing of artifacts as a means of synchronization and used it primarily for cross-cultural comparisons. At present, such a narrow use of the metal material has nearly been discarded as a result of the advances of analytical studies of the technology of metal production and the work of specialists such as Yessen (Yessen & Degenom-Kovalevski 1935), Chernikov (1949, 1935), Bochkarev (1995a, 1995b), Sunchugashev (1969, 1979), Ryndina (1998), and Chernykh (1966, 1970, 1992).

Ryndina has summed up the basic approaches that relate to the problems of the beginning of the Bronze Age. She considers the cultures in which metal ornaments and thrust and cutting tools appeared only sporadically as Eneolithic. The cultures with a large number of objects made of artificial alloys can be classified firmly as Bronze Age cultures (Ryndina & Degtyareva 2002: 18).

Chernykh (1989) regards metals as a major determinative factor that resulted in great changes, apart from metallurgy, in other areas of human culture and entailed enormous consequences. He describes it in terms of the theory of metallurgical focuses and provinces, which corresponded to one or another archaeological culture. He combined the types of copper-based alloys with morphological types of metal artifacts and plotted the quantitative relationships between the different compositions that were characteristic for particular cultures.

Such observations have formed the basis for the identification of the metallurgical or metalworking centers.[1] These centers often were directly correlated with particular archaeological cultures, or their variants, and were seen as the distinctive productive elements in such cultures. Subsequent research has revealed more complicated links between archaeological cultures and centers of metal production.

According to Chernykh, a metallurgical province, a "technocultural network" in our terminology, is a unified productive system with similar traditions of metallurgical development. Such a network could emerge from the active trading relations between those societies that possessed mineral resources and those that did not (Chernykh 1992). Metal consumers received from producers not only raw material, which stimulated the new centers of metalworking, but also technical ideas necessary for their development (Ryndina & Degtyareva 2002: 41). It was in the area of circulation of such knowledge that the metallurgical centers were set. The term *center* is understood as a region where similar metal and metal artifacts were produced professionally by a distinct group of skilled craftsmen. The evidence for various types of production rests on and is largely determined by four indices: (1) the type and category of artifacts presented; (2) the technological means of production; (3) the particular chemically and metallurgically defined groups of copper and bronze used; and (4) the structure or social organization of production (Chernykh 1992).

In all centers, metalwork exists as a special craft maintained by professional groups. Within a village, it can be a community craftsman, transmitting his skills and knowledge to his descendants; this is an individual-familial form of craft organization. Clan organization represents another form, which presumes an existence of clan groups of metallurgists. They engage in mass production that is predestined for long-distance exchange (Ryndina 1998; Ryndina & Degtyareva 2002). All data provided by history, archaeology, and ethnography testifies that metallurgical production was, from the beginning, rather specialized. Therefore, in all cases, the social status of metallurgist was especially high. Bochkarev (1995b: 116) regards metallurgy as a very important subculture.

In order to make particular subjects relating to the area under study clearer in our future reasoning, we must review briefly at the general evolution of Eurasian metallurgy.

THE STAGES OF METALLURGICAL DEVELOPMENT IN EURASIA

According to Chernykh (1989), the early metallurgy in Northern Eurasia passed through three main stages.

Pure copper objects that were found in several cultures of the fifth–fourth millennia BC characterize the first stage. Geographically this stage corresponded to the Balkan-Carpathian metallurgical network (5000–3800/3700 cal BC), which originated under influences from Anatolia. Conversely, after it spread to southeast Europe in the fifth–fourth millennia BC, it developed rapidly and was accompanied by significant social and cultural changes. Societies appeared here that were both producers and consumers. This development had the effect of an explosion followed by transformation. The end of the first stage was marked by a visible desolation of the Eneolithic cultures of the Balkans and Carpathian areas and rejection of many technological achievements. This occurrence led to a deep collapse, the reason for which remains mysterious (Chernykh 1989; Chernykh at al. 2000).

The transition to the Bronze Age lasted several hundreds years (3700–3300 cal BC). A new system of metallurgical production replaced the old one. Its territorial expansion grew greatly, and its influence spread even wider (to about 4–5 million km²). This was the second stage of the development of Eurasian metallurgy; the centers were formed with the Circumpontic metallurgical network,[2] which existed from about 3300 until 1900 cal BC (Chernykh et al. 2002b; Chernykh et al. 2004). All centers of this system produced objects of similar form and technology. At this stage, which was associated with the Early and Middle Bronze Age (the third and very beginning of the second millennia BC), local metallurgical production had emerged in many areas, including the Caucasus, where the centers mainly produced arsenical bronze and pure copper.

The Circumpontic network embraced the metallurgical and metalworking centers of the Caucasus, Balkans and Carpathians, northern Coast of Black Sea, and Asia Minor (Fig. 1.1-A). The metal objects penetrated to the north and were introduced into the steppe cultures of northern Pontic area. These cultures played a very important role in the northward and eastward transmission of metallurgy and, within it, an advanced economy. The typological and functional variability of bronze tools became much more advanced.[3] The innovations are characterized by the casting technology, especially in the manufacture of socketed axes in closed molds that replaced the open two-pieced molds (Ryndina & Degtyareva 2002).

The third stage, corresponding to the Late and Final Bronze Age (beginning of the second millennium BC–beginning of the first millennium BC), was characterized by the further geographic spread of metallurgy over northern Eurasia.[4] The three most influential zones were the Balkano-Carpathian, Caucasian, and Uralian. The new metallurgical networks that were formed were the European, Caucasian, Eurasian, and Central-Asiatic networks. Population movement and the transformation of various cultures accompanied this process. It is very important to note that in all these areas, the new tin and poly-composed bronzes came into wide use, and the number of mined ore deposits was greatly increased.

The main features of the Middle and Late Bronze Age of northern Eurasia were the extraordinary northeastward expansion of metallurgy and metalworking, the large introduction of tin bronzes, the beginning of the newly developed technology of metalworking, and the typological standardization of finished objects. These were inherent to the Eurasian network, which covered a huge area from the Altai Mountains to the Dnepr River, including the steppe and forest landscapes (Chernykh 1989: 267). In the Eurasian network, many new metallurgical and metalworking centers came into being, based on the ore deposits of the Urals, Kazakhstan, Tien-Shan, and the Altai mountains (Fig. 1.1-A). Tin was extracted in central Kazakhstan and the Altai and transported to the western metallurgical centers. The following types of bronze artifacts were in common use throughout Eurasia: tanged knives with flat notch and waist, curved sickles, socketed poleaxes, socketed gouges, and hammered and cast spearheads with various grooved ornaments (Chernykh 1992: 213).

The technoeconomic and cultural networks of every chronological period are characterized by the emergence and dissemination of new technological innovations, which directly or indirectly stimulated cultural changes. The Urals played its own part in this process.

THE URALS' BRONZE METALLURGY

The Beginning

In recent decades, research has considerably advanced our knowledge of metallurgy in the Urals. This advancement, which has been made with both field discoveries and analytical and experimental work, are summarized in several recent works (Chernykh 1992, 1997b, 2002; Chernykh et al. 1999; Grigory'ev 2000b; Grigory'ev & Rusanov 1995). These works have contributed greatly to our knowledge of the Urals' metallurgy.

One can confidently affirm that throughout the entire Bronze Age and into the beginning of the Iron Age, the Urals was one of the major metallurgical centres in north-central Eurasia. In this section, we will give a general overview of the Urals metallurgy, focusing primarily on its technological aspects. In later chapters, we will consider its economic, cultural, and social aspects.

The Ural Mountains contain numerous deposits of mineral resources including metal ores. As a geological and metallurgical region, the Urals are divided into western and eastern areas. The western area mostly contains very rich copper sandstone; the eastern area has mainly oxidized sulphide ores, in which copper carbonates (malachite and azurite) prevail. Because the Urals' mineral resources have been intensively exploited in historic times, it is difficult to find, at present, traces of prehistoric mining. Nevertheless, in the eighteenth century, the members of the first Russian academic expeditions to Siberia and travelers informed about the local mines (*chudskiye kopi*) reported seeing evidence of prehistoric mining; this also was confirmed by Russian classical geologists (Zaikov et al. 2002: 417). Russian archaeologists Chernykh (1970), Kuzmina (1962), and Yessen (1946, 1948) later explored some of the mines (Elenovka, Ush-Katta in the Orenburg district, Gumeshki near Ekaterinburg, Tash-Kazgan in the Trans-Urals – Fig. 1.1-B) and, most recently, a team of Russian geologists and mineralogists systematically investigated the ancient copper mines of the Southern Urals (Plate 1.1, Fig. 1.3).[5] This latter group also discovered some mines that had not been known previously to archaeologists (Zaikov et al. 2002). Grigory'ev (2000a) has studied the mining and metal production of the Sintashta culture. Systematic research was undertaken by Chernykh's team in the Kargaly complex, which preserved the remains of mining and metallurgical activity of both the prehistoric and historic periods.

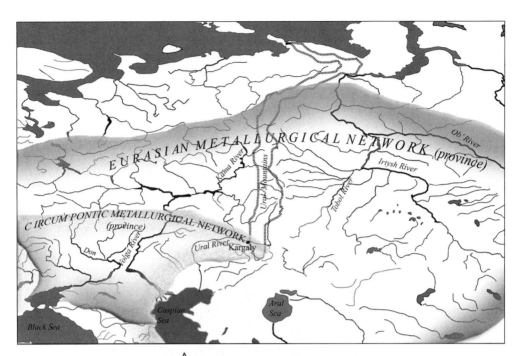

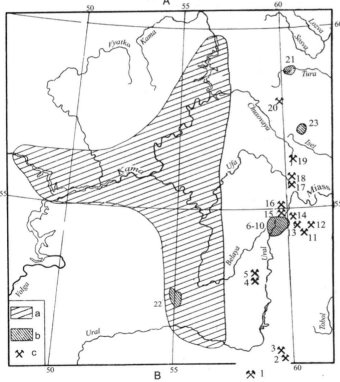

Figure 1.1. Schematic map of Circumpontic and Eurasian technocultural networks **(A)** and map of distribution of Ural copper deposits **(B)**: (a) area of copper sandstone ores, (b) groups of mines; (c) copper deposit; (1) Dzhengana, (2) Ush-Katta, (3) Elenovka, (4) Kamyshly-Uzyak, (5) Bakr-Uzyak, (6–10) Kiryabinskoye, Urgun, Voznesenskoye, Polyakovskoye, Naralli, (11) Polyanovskoye, (12) Kichiginskoye, (13) Tash-Kazgan, (14) Nikolskoye, (15) Mednaya Gora, (16) Berezovaya Gora, (17) Soimonovskoye, (18) Sugurskoye, (19) Gumeshki, (20) Mednorudyanskoye, (21) Verkhoturinsky mines, (22) Kargaly mines, (23) Blagodatnyi mines (after Chernykh 1970).

Plate 1.1. The Kamensky mine in the South Urals.

We are convinced that internal and intercultural relations were greatly influenced by the level of development of metallurgy, which, in turn, was greatly influenced not only by mineral resources but also by social factors. Meanwhile, we are not inclined to regard all socially significant events in the life of the Urals' population of the Bronze and, a fortiori, the Iron Age under one "metallurgical" point of view. There is no doubt that metallurgy played a very important role in the general social advancement. However, as a rule, at the very beginning of metallurgical development, the Eurasian pastoral and hunting-fishing societies were not directly dependent on the use of metal tools. The

Plate 1.2. Aerial photo of the Kargaly mining area (after Chernykh 1997).

composition of the early metal inventory, especially of the Early and Middle Bronze Age, shows more evidence of its military and ritual character than of its utilitarian function. The appearance and sporadic use of metal tools per se did not yet entail a change in the economic base and social relations, as has been well demonstrated in the Ural sites of the preceding Eneolithic period.

The metal objects of the Eneolithic are represented by a rather modest quantity of copper artifacts of the simplest forms, and no traces of production have been discovered. However, we must confess that this period is not well studied; the number of investigated sites is quite limited, compared with the Bronze and Iron Age. On the whole, the role of metal tools in the life of the population following the hunting and fishing economic way of life was minimal, and, correspondingly, metal production did not hold an essential place.

Metallurgy was really established at the beginning of the Bronze Age first in the Cis-Urals steppe zone together with the appearance of the Yamnaya culture (see Chapter 2). Although the Yamnaya sites are exclusively represented by kurgan burials, there exists a whole series of data that testify to the development of local metallurgy in the southern Cis-Urals. The countless copper sandstone deposits here started to be exploited earlier than those of the Trans-Urals. Archaeological sites of the Cis-Urals yielded the remains of metal production: the fragments of smelting and casting forms, drops of metal, copper tanged knives, and awls. However, there are no remains of either furnaces or slag relating to this period.

The most impressive discovery relating to ancient metallurgy of the eastern part of Europe is associated with the Kargaly mining and metallurgical complex that marked the eastern border of the Circumpontic network (Fig. 1.1-B) (Chernykh 1997a, 1997b; Chernykh et al. 2002b; Chernykh & Easteo 2002).

This copper-ore mining and metallurgical center is located in the northern zone of the Eurasian steppe in Orenburg oblast within a typical multigrass and mat-grass landscape. The ore deposits cover an area of 50 × 10 km (Plate 1.2). Rich copper mineral deposits are found at the side of the Ural River basin, especially its right tributaries. The richest deposits are concentrated along the Kargalka, a small steppe river. The Kargaly deposits are related to a type of copper sandstone and shale and are included in a southern copper-bearing zone. The mining sites are marked by endless surface traces of ancient and historical mining: vertical shafts and horizontal day-drifts, pits, cavities, and waste heaps. As Chernykh noted, the great number of shafts were of an underground character, which cannot be completely described. About twenty settlements and four kurgan cemeteries are recorded within the Kargaly complex (Chernykh 1997b, 2002).

The excavations of the Kargaly mining area have yielded data that gives evidence for the beginning of its exploitation and is radiocarbon dated to 3000 cal BC (Chernykh 2002: 135–7).

Unique materials discovered in the burial grounds of the Orenburg district give evidence for the high level of Cis-Uralian metallurgy: socketed chisels, axe-hammers, two-back hammers, massive spearheads, and adze-planes made from copper and iron (Morgunova 2002; Morgunova & Kravtsov 1994). Pieces of sandstone ore and the earliest objects made from pure copper have been found in some graves of the Yamnaya culture (the late fourth–third millennia BC). They were manufactured according to western patterns, but the raw material was mainly local (Fig. 2.4). Analyses show that the copper for manufacturing the objects discovered in the Orenburg burials was extracted from the Kargaly copper sandstone deposits. Additionally, some of these burials yielded pieces of Kargaly ore.

The early metallurgy of the Urals had thus been developed under influence from the Caucasus. However, the production of the Caucasus center, which supplied almost all of eastern Europe in the late third millennium BC, was made from arsenical bronze. Arsenical bronzes were very rare at that time in the Urals, where pure copper was dominant. Despite its peripheral location, the Kargaly center used almost all of the advanced technologies and produced the same set of objects as the western centers. The difference was the complete absence of tin alloys. Deposits of tin minerals were not available in the Urals. The interesting point is that almost all of the metal produced had only a westward distribution. The objects smelted from Kargaly ores are frequent in the kurgans of Volga-Ural area, but they never are found beyond the Urals.

Moreover, the materials from the forest zone of eastern Europe between the Urals and Scandinavia demonstrate that some primitive metal production that did not have a direct relationship with Circumpontic types existed here. There are now about 184 radiocarbon dates from metal-producing sites of this area indicating the period between 3500 and 1900 BC (Chernykh et al. 2002b: 17).

As mentioned earlier, in the Early Bronze Age, the productive economy – pastoral stockbreeding and metallurgy – had emerged in the steppe zone. Regional economic specialization and new types of social relations and connections also were formed during this period. Mining and metallurgy demanded professional knowledge, which, in an archaic culture, was of a mysterious and sacral character (Baiburin 1981). This created a separation of professional groups from other members of society who organized the productive process, and distribution of production. All this changed internal social relations and relations between different societies. Direction and length of trade-exchange contacts in the third millennium BC in eastern Europe were determined by the movement of metal from different mining sources (Ryndina & Dektyareva 2002: 115).

Further Developments

The further development of Urals metallurgy was associated with the latest phase of the Middle Bronze Age and the early phase of the Late Bronze Age. It was stimulated by the disintegration of the Circumpontic metallurgical system and the formation of the Eurasian technocultural network, which covered an area of about 7–8 millions km^2 (Chernykh et al. 2002b; Chernykh et al. 2004). In the Urals, this period was marked by the appearance of two brilliant cultural formations embodied in the Sintashta and Abashevo sites (Fig. 2.5–A). For the moment, we will not address this correlation. We will simply note that these two occurrences were mutually connected and functioned in parallel on both sides of the Ural range.

The remains of major metallurgical and metalworking activity have been recorded at many settlement sites in the western and eastern Urals region. A number of the structures investigated at the settlements of Beregovskoye, Balanbash, and Urnyak in the Belaya basin in the southwest Urals region, contained smelting vessels, crucibles, slag, and the remains of waste from casting tools and ornaments (Salnikov 1954: 54–60, 1967). Two major centers are associated with the Abashevo cultural area. The first one was located in the Don River basin, in an area that lacked ore but was still a metalworking area. It used scrap metal imported from the Urals. The second, the Balanbash center, in the southern Cis-Urals, was metallurgical, and it produced copper for a

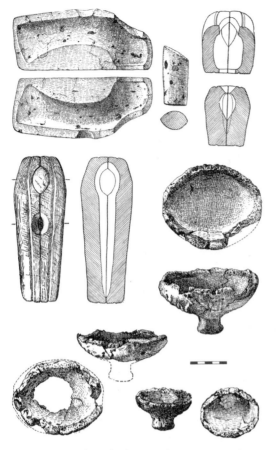

Figure 1.2. The Abashevo culture: casting forms and melting pots from grave 1 of the Pepkino kurgan (after Khalikov, Lebedinskaya, and Gerasimova 1966).

large territory (Fig. 2.1-B). There are numerous copper-bearing sandstone outcrops in the Belaya basin and elsewhere, which first provided an ore base for the southern Urals centers. Some villages of the Abashevo metallurgists have been discovered in the forest-mountain zone 300 km to the east of the general Balanbash territory (Borzunov & Bel'tikova 1999).

Originally, the Balanbash metallurgists produced objects made from pure copper. The smelting of ores was accomplished in settlements where the remains of slag, smelting pots, and finished objects have been encountered. However, the remains of smelting furnaces have not been found, but they could have been of the simplest construction from which only burned spots would have remained (Grigory'ev 2000b: 513).

Metalworkers were able to cast objects in one- or two-sided casting molds, usually made from clay or stone (Fig. 1.2). The shaft-hole axe is the most distinctive metal type from the Abashevo sites. The shaft hole is elliptical in section. Knives often have a waisted tang, which tapered toward the hilt end. Flat adzes had relatively wide heels in relation to the blade edge. The Abashevo people did not know how to cast socketed spearheads and made them by forging them from a single sheet of copper. Such spearheads and also some types of small sickles or single-edged curved knives occur on sites in the far western Urals region.

A substantial part of the Abashevo metal inventory was made from arsenical copper, which was connected by Chernykh (1970; 1992) to the copper-arsenic Tash-Kazgan deposits situated on the upper reaches of the Ui River in the southern Trans-Urals (Fig. 1.1-B; Fig. 1.3). According to Chernykh, this copper-arsenic ore was transported westward over the low-lying Ural range (a distance of about 250–300 km through the mountains). The variation of arsenic concentration in the Abashevo artifacts is rather high (1–7 percent). Grigory'ev (2000b: 503), who analyzed a series of metal slag, states that the Tach-Kazgan ore could be smelted on-site or in the Cis-Urals settlements, and

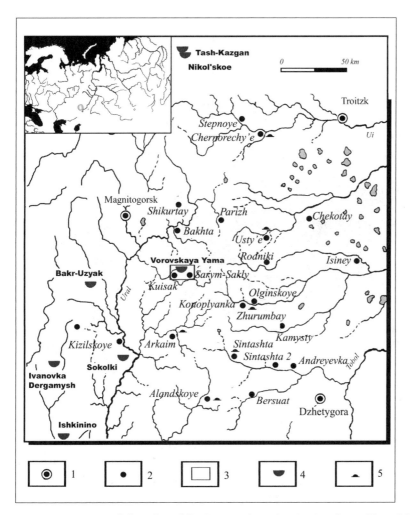

Figure 1.3. Map of the of Middle Bronze Age sites in Southern Trans-Urals and ancient copper mine locations: (1) modern settlements; (2) fortified settlements; (3) areas of geoarchaeological research; (4) surveyed ancient copper mines (after Zaikov, Yuminov, Bushmakin, Zaikova, Tairov, & Zdanovich 2002).

that the metal was transported further to the Abashevo and Sintashta areas. He further states that the metal of the Tash–Kazgan origin is not arsenical copper but arsenical bronze. However, the European materials show that the extraction and smelting of arsenical minerals in the Bronze Age is highly unlikely, and that the presence of arsenic in copper objects reflects the use of secondary copper ores containing arsenates, which can easily be reduced to form copper-arsenic alloys (Harding 2000: 202). We can, therefore, see that the character of the technology of copper-arsenic bronzes is far from completely understood.

It is commonly accepted that Tash–Kazgan copper gradually decreased. Nevertheless, tools made from it have been found at Abashevo sites as well as at other cultural sites on the Don. Nearly the entire inventory of metal objects

Plate 1.3. The remains of the Sintashta furnace from the Usty'e settlement (photo by N. B. Vingradov.)

from the Abashevo sites is made of arsenical copper. There are, however, some copper-silver objects; specialists connect these with the Nikolskoye copper-silver deposit. The Nikolskoye ores produced billon, which consisted of silver and copper. Silver occurs widely in Abashevo sites of the eastern and western Urals and the Volga regions. Tin bronzes were completely unknown in the Abashevo area (Chernykh 1992: 202).

Abashevo metallurgy had a great deal in common with the metal production of the Sintashta culture, yet the latter is much better represented archaeologically and its mineralogical base is well known (Fig. 1.3). The prehistoric mines in the Southern Urals in the area of the Sintashta sites are usually open pits 20–80 m in diameter and up to 12 m deep. The ores are represented by various types of copper minerals: (1) nickeliferous ores in serpentenites; (2) zinciferous deposits in volcanic rocks; (3) streaky-impregnated ores containing garnet and tourmaline; and (4) sulphide-quartz and carbonate veins. Some of the mines are surrounded by waste rock dumps (Dergamysh and Vorovskaya Yama) and traces of the processing of minerals (Elenovka Mine) have been found. They were exploited in the Late Bronze Age as well (Zaikov et al. 2002: 430).

The remains of processed minerals, mining and ore-processing tools, slags, ruins of furnaces, and finished objects are encountered in almost all Sintashta settlements. Traces of metallurgical activity were registered in almost every house. The basic parameters of smelting technology were inferred from a series of analytical and experimental works carried out by specialists in the museum-reserve at Arkaim (Grigory'ev & Rusanov 1995). The smelting took place in the rounded multifunctional cupola ovens that measured 0.7–1 m in diameter and were, in a majority of cases, attached to wells that were also in the houses (Plate 1.3; Fig. 1.4).[6] Reproduction of the process has demonstrated that such construction provided additional afflux because of the difference between the temperature in an oven and a well. The ore was crushed into small pieces, mixed with flux and placed into a warmed oven. Wood charcoal was used as a combustible that facilitated a reductive-oxidative regime with a small loss of copper. The temperature could reach

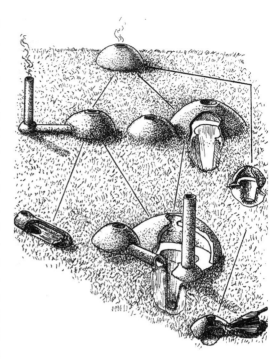

Figure 1.4. Scheme of evolution of metallurgical furnaces during the Middle Bronze Age (after Grigory'ev 2000b).

1200–1300°C. One smelting could provide an ingot of 50–130 g. The Sintashta metallurgists were responsible for the invention of the horizontal chimney,[7] which archaeologically has been traced by a narrow groove. A two-part bellows for constant blowing was also part of the metallurgists' equipment (Grigory'ev 2000b; Grigory'ev & Rusanov 1995). The Sintashta metallurgists produced mostly pure copper, arsenical copper, and arseniferrous bronze.[8] For example, 48 percent of the metal objects that came from the Sintashta settlement were made from arseniferrous bronze, 34 percent from arsenical copper, and the remainder was from pure copper. Specialists can only assume that either arsenic-bearing ores were used, or that copper in some way was alloyed with arsenic-containing minerals (Zaikov et al. 2002: 431). The majority of metal from the Arkaim settlement is of pure copper. Among the Sintashta metal artefacts there also are some silver copper alloys and gold objects that were manufactured from locally extracted gold. Typologically, the Sintashta metal objects are, in some respects, similar to the Abashevo objects, which are to some extent similar to the Seima-Turbino objects. These are represented by two-edged knives, elegant shaft-hole axes, socketed spearheads, adzes, sickles, chisels, harpoons, awls, and hooks (Fig. 1.5). Ornaments include temple pendants wrapped with golden foil, rings, and bracelets.

In the Abashevo and Sintashta centers, metallurgy was based on local mineral deposits. The whole cycle of work, from smelting to final treatment, is well

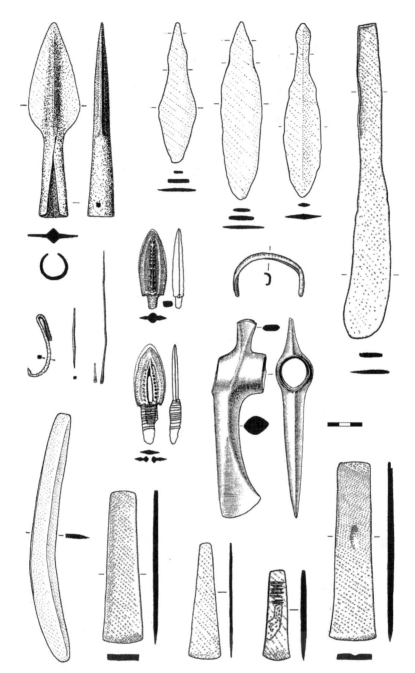

Figure 1.5. Metal artifacts from the Sintashta cemeteries (after Gening, Zdanovich, & Gening 1992).

represented in the settlement materials. Typological characteristics of artefacts allow us to conclude that, on the one hand, the Abashevo and Sintashta met-alwork continued the basic patterns of the Circumpontic tradition, but, on the other hand, they reflect the formative stage of the Eurasian technocultural system.

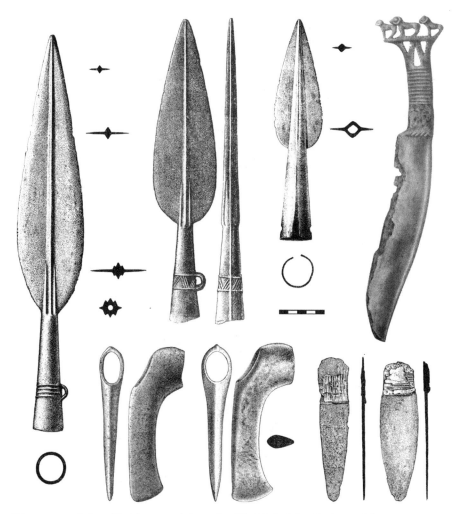

Figure 1.6. Seima-Turbino metal from the Cis-Urals (after Bader 1964).

This event coincided with an impulse that came from the east. In Russian archaeology, this impulse is known as the Seima-Turbino transcultural phenomenon, the concept of which was substantially developed by Chernykh and Kuzminykh (1989). It is represented by several hundred metal objects and molds coming from five major burial grounds located on both sides of the Urals (Seima, Turbino, Reshnoye, Rostovka, and Satyga). Many metal objects were found in different areas within the vast territory of Eurasia, from Mongolia to Finland and the Carpathian Mountains. These are splendid weapons: celts-axes (axes with closed sockets), spearheads, daggers with impressive sculptures on the handles, and knives (Fig. 1.6). The new technology principally used closed thin-sided molds and shafts were employed for casting. The shaft-cast socket is the most remarkable innovation in the bronze production. The metallurgists knew how to produce high-quality tin-bronze, which had not previously been possible. According to Chernykh and Kuzminykh (1989), such technology emerged in the Sayan and Altai area and originally was based on its rich mineral resources. It was quite unexpected because the local culture looked to be rather primitive. The Seima-Turbino technology had broken the monopoly of the Caucasus metalworking traditions, which had at their disposal rich copper sources but were poor in tin.

Specialists distinguish two groups of objects from the Seima-Turbino sites based on the chemical composition of their metals. The first group includes objects that are encountered in all regions of distribution of Seima-Turbino sites; these are made from copper-tin and copper-tin-arsenic alloys. The second group contains alloys based on combinations of copper, arsenic, silver, and so on, without tin. The latter are exclusively characteristic for eastern Europe, and connected to the Urals mineral deposits. There are no substantial tin deposits in the Urals. Thus, the finds of copper-tin alloys here can be interpreted as evidence of imported of bronze, or tin, or ready objects from the east. There are many tin mines in eastern Kazakhstan, where they stretch in a large zone along the Upper Irtysh River up to Xingjian (Chernikov 1960: 119).

The number and quality of copper-tin bronzes in Siberia exceeds those in eastern Europe by many times. In addition, the majority of molds are concentrated in Siberia. All finds of Seima-Turbino objects are encountered in the forest and forest-steppes of Eurasia as well. This indicates an area of northwestward movement of objects or technologies, which cannot be transmitted without people, through the west Siberian taiga and Ural Mountains to the forested plains of eastern Europe – the so-called Great Tin Road (Chernykh & Kuzminykh 1989: 174, 275).

Technologically, the Seima-Turbino phenomenon gave a strong impetus to the development of metallurgy in northern Eurasia. It was responsible for the introduction of bronze technology into the forest zone. If the initial metalworking came to the east European forest zone from the south, then more advanced types of bronze objects came here from the distant area of western Siberia (Fodor 1975).

The Apex of Uralian Metallurgy: Expansion and Perfection

The next stage in the development of Eurasian metallurgy is characterized by a decrease of long-distance migratory activity and a general cultural unification and stabilization. This resulted from the Abashevo and Sintashta heritage, combined with an eastern Seima-Turbino impulse, which was responsible for the introduction of thin-walled casting and the use of tin alloys. Consequently, in the steppe and forest-steppe, where the bulk of metal artifacts and traces of production were found, two zones have been configured: the European and Asiatic.[9] Bochkarev (1991, 1995a) states that for the Late Bronze Age the Urals metal-mining center was comparable with the highly developed centers of the Carpathian metal industry, whose production dominated the Balkan and Carpathian regions.

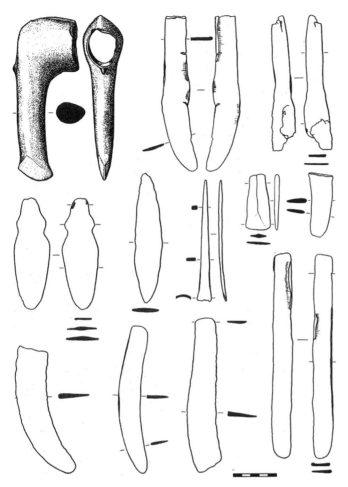

Figure 1.7. Metal objects of the Petrovka culture (the Kulevchi settlement).

According to the latest reports, it is commonly believed that the tradition of the Sintashta technology was continued and developed by Petrovka metallurgy. The Petrovka sites (see Chapter 2) have the reputation of "metal-giving" sites, which yield numerous copper slags, ingots, metal drops, tuyeres, smelting pots (crucibles), molds, and finished objects. Some of these finished objects, such as double-edged and single-edged knives, sickles, and adzes, were manufactured from sheet metal, a technique that goes back to the Circumpontic prototypes (Fig. 1.7). The sheet technique is also characteristic of female decorations. Thin blades were used for grooved bracelets (with hollow bows), spiral pendants in one and half turns, oval clothing decorations, and so on (Chernykh 1992: 213).

In the Late Bronze Age, new copper resources in the Altai, Kazakhstan, and in the north of Middle Asia began to be exploited. This gave rise to new metallurgical centers and technological innovations and achievements. For example, bigger ovens with deeper floors, which were rather rare during the Sintashta period, became usual in the Petrovka settlements (Grigory'ev

2000b). Although tin bronzes accounted for only 15–20 percent of all metal items from Petrovka sites, new closed molds and some special types of heat-treatment had been invented (Ryndina & Degtyareva 2002: 187).

From the second quarter of the second millennium BC, the Urals population started to mine widely the Trans-Uralian mineral deposits and to use oxidized copper ore. As has been stated, several independent centers of metallurgy were formed in Kazakhstan (the Andronovo area) and the Altai. Together with other centers in eastern Europe, they composed the Eurasian metallurgical network mentioned earlier.

Some new kinds of weapons and tools appeared, including tanged and sock-eted arrowheads, battleaxes with a cross rib around a socket, single- and double-edged knives, and daggers with distinctive handles, sickles, razors, adzes, and chisels (Fig. 1.8). The number of ornaments also greatly increased. These included earrings of various shapes; pendants for braids; forged hollow ear-rings; figure-eight-shaped, cross-shaped, and ring-shaped pendants; and sewn-on plaques with astral symbols. Bracelets with spiral ends also appeared.

The Andronovo metal was predominantly made of tin alloys, the produc-tion of which was based on the rich central Kazakhstan copper oxide-bearing minerals and eastern Kazakhstan and Altai deposits of cassiterite. Hundreds of mines are known in the territory between the southern Urals, Kazakhstan, and Rudny Altai (Fig. 3.5). Gold deposits were worked at Stepnaya in north-ern Kazakhstan and in the Kuzylsu Valley in the Altai as well in the Urals (Zaikov et al. 2002). Metallurgical centers of the Andronovo area are rightly considered the most productive in Eurasia. The weight of smelted copper from Kenkazgan ores alone is estimated at approximately 30,000–50,000 metric tons (Alexeyev & Kuznetsova 1983: 211) and from Dzhezkazgan about 1,000,000 metric tons (Chernykh 1992: 212). The Ksyzkazgan mine in central Kazakhstan produced around 800,000 cu m of copper ore. The bulk of extracted cassi-terite from the mines of eastern Kazakhstan is estimated to be about 130 metric tons (Matushchenko 1999a: 120). The Andronovo metallurgists worked with copper oxide ores, which were close to the surface, followed the ore-bearing channels, and used axes and hammers to extract the ore. The hard and solid ores were first heated by fire, then cooled with water, and then carried out in leather baskets.

In the Late Bronze Age, mining and metal production had recommenced at Kargaly. The so-called living-producing complex relating to this period (Srubnaya culture) was investigated at the Gornyi settlement (1650–1330 cal BC). It consisted of five parts: (1) living house; (2) the smelting yard, where there was a great amount of ore debris, copper slag, waste, and ash; (3) the ore yard, where minerals were assorted and prepared for smelting; (4) "sacral shaft"; and (5) a pit for waste. The layer with remains of small underground house-pits measuring 3–5 m^2 underlined the main complex (1550–1450 cal BC). House-pits are dated to 1700–1600 cal BC. Archaeologists have recorded traces of destruction of the "living-producing complex," which was burned in a fire in approximately mid-1500 cal BC. There also is some indication of invasion: a tin-bronze arrowhead, different from those of local production, was stuck in a roof. After this catastrophe, the local people built new houses, which were much simpler, and their remains are less traceable. After the decline of the Srubnaya culture, the complex did not function for several centuries until the 1800s CE (Chernykh 1997b, 2002).

The Kargaly production moved to the west. At the same time, the Kargaly center functioned in concurrence with new metallurgical centers, which began work in the east. Metallurgical production of the Andronovo area was based on the richest raw materials: Kazakhstan copper and tin deposits and almost inexhaustible wood resources. Compared with the preceding periods, the landscape and cultural boundaries

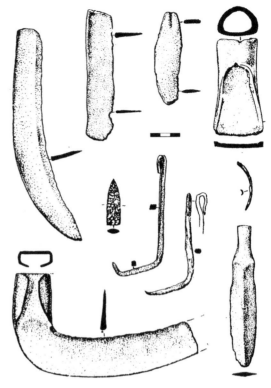

Figure 1.8. Metal objects from the Andronovo (Alakul) site Uk-3 (after Koryakova, Stefanov, & Stefanova 1993).

did not get in the way of "expansion" of eastern metal.

The Urals metal spread to the west up to the Dnepr River and replaced Caucasian bronze in some regions of the western steppe zone. Metal hoards, containing bronze tools, which are interpreted by scholars (Morozov 1981) as objects predestined for exchange, appeared. The metal was diffused not only in the form of ready-made objects but also in the form of ingots. The Urals population was engaged in a system of long-distance connections acting in the vast area between the Altai Mountains and the Black Sea – within the Eurasian technocultural network.

During the second millennium BC, the common forms of metal tools were widespread throughout temperate Eurasia. The evidence, mentioned earlier, of specialized metal production causes scholars to think that it existed in the form of a community craft, which primarily supplied the needs of the local territory, but a part of the production went into the exchange network. In Bochkarev's (1995: 20) opinion, the craftsmen-metallurgists possessed a special status in society as well as the specialists supplying the needs of the elite. This is evidenced by special burials of metallurgists throughout of Eurasia[10] and an admirable quality of metal goods, primarily weapons of high quality (Solovyev

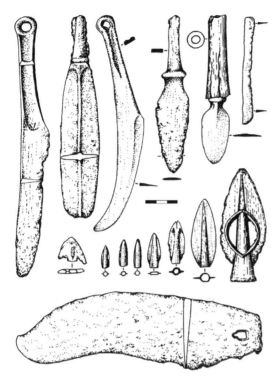

Figure 1.9. Metal objects of the Final Bronze Age from Kazakhstan (after Varfolomeyev 2003).

2003). Burials of metallurgists appeared in the third millennium BC within the Yamnaya (Pershino burial; see Chapter 2) and Catacombnaya cultures.

In the period of the Final Bronze Age, the Eurasian metallurgical area was extended northward where the new centers of metalworking started to function. Nevertheless, by the turn of the Bronze and Iron Age, a general productive decrease of many centers was already noticeable, especially on the European side of the Urals. This is evidence of some crisis of the system, which, perhaps, could no longer properly maintain long-distance connections. There is the appearance of hoards. Most widespread were double-edged tanged and socketed arrowheads of the pre-Scythian type. The ridged-axes come into use, as well as entirely cast daggers and spearheads with perforated blades (Fig. 1.9). The crisis could have been generated by a shortage of mineral supplies, in particular, the outcrop copper ores. However, it is most probable that the industrial decline was only part of a general process that preceded a drastic alteration of the entire lifestyle.

CHAPTER 2

THE ACHIEVEMENTS AND COLLISIONS OF THE EARLY AND MIDDLE BRONZE AGE

In this chapter, we will emphasize the emergence and development of a productive economy in north-central Eurasia. The Early and Middle Bronze Age is represented by several cultural core traditions, reflecting the eastward spread of western complexes connected with the Yamnaya, Catacombnaya, Abashevo, and Early Srubnaya cultures.

The dynamics of interaction between populations of different landscape zones can be seen even at the beginning of the Bronze Age. The primary impulses emanated from the southern regions, where their inhabitants received and mastered new forms of economy and technology earlier than in the north. The steppe population played the role of transmitter of new ideas, which become a source of cultural transformation for those in the northern territories. The main distinction between the southern and northern cultural zones is that in the steppe area development was not continuous, and an important role was played by migrations. This was in opposition to the northern zone, which was defined by a gradual evolution without any fundamental replacement of population.

However, the role of the forest-steppe and south taiga peoples was not passive. First, southern innovations filtered into traditional cultures that rejected some of these innovations but retained others. Second, the history of the Abashevo and Seima-Turbino groups comprise evidence for the advantages arising out of long-distance migrations, even into a different landscape zone.

This chapter will illuminate the asymmetry in the cultural and economic development between the steppe, forest-steppe, and forest zones, which was characteristic for the beginning of the Bronze Age.

THE YAMNAYA CULTURE IN THE CIS-URALS

The Yamnaya culture, which was first distinguished by Gorodtsov (1916), is sufficiently known to Western readers thanks to the work of Childe (1927, 1929) and Gimbutas (1965, 1997), who drew the image of militant Kurgan people who destroyed the Eneolithic Balkan cultures. Since that time, its archaeological outline and content as well as their interpretation has changed dramatically. There is, however, no doubt that the Yamnaya culture was of key significance for many fundamental problems of Eurasian prehistory, including the origins of the Indo-European peoples, pastoral economy, diffusion of metallurgy, and wheeled transport.

Actually, the Yamnaya culture, which in Russian literature is called a "cultural and historical intercommunity," consists of several regional subcultures, differing in some details in its archaeological material. It originated in the Eneolithic, continued into the Early Bronze Age, and was the first huge cultural entity that covered an enormous territory, stretching from the north shores of the Black Sea to the Trans-Urals – between the Don River – the Volga, and the Urals (Merpert 1974). Within this vast area that was occupied by people sharing common canons of material culture and funeral rituals, more than a dozen local variants can be traced. This culture is chiefly known by its huge number of kurgan burials and small number of settlements. The first kurgans appeared in the Eurasian steppe during the Eneolithic. The deceased were usually buried in a deep rectangular pit on their back or side in a crouched position (rarely extended), with ochre sprinkled over them, and a rather poor set of grave goods.

The great majority of Yamnaya sites are known in the western part of this area due to years of excavation; those of the eastern part were represented originally by a very small number of kurgans and considered a distance periphery, only very recently have they begun to be studied systematically (Fig. 2.1).

Archaeological Characteristics

The sites of the Bronze Age in the steppe zone of the Urals are represented by barrows (kurgans), discovered by archaeologists during the last two decades and related to the Yamnaya culture. In fact, the real discovery of the southern Urals variant of the Yamnaya culture took place in the 1980s. For the most part, the investigated burials are concentrated in the southern Cis-Urals (Bogdanov 1998, 2000c, 2004; Bogdanov et al. 1992; Bytkovski & Tkachev 1997; Morgunova 2002; Morgunova & Turetski 2003; Mosin 1996). On the eastern slopes of the Ural range in the basins of the Ural and Tobol rivers, there are only isolated ceramics finds (Mosin 1996) and single burials (Salnikov 1962) of the Yamnaya culture. The total number of investigated kurgans of this cultural group is close to 120, and 112 of them relate to the later phase (Bogdanov 1998; Tkachev 2000). The Yamnaya cemeteries in the southern Urals are situated within the steppe landscape and contain usually only a few of mounds, or just single kurgans, the dimensions of which vary rather significant: from 10 m up to 64 m in diameter and up to 6 m high (Merpert 1974).

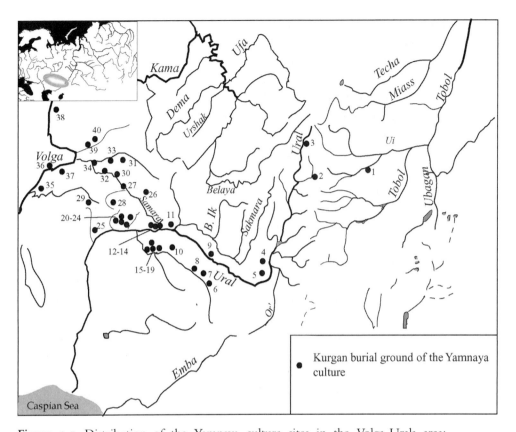

Figure 2.1. Distribution of the Yamnaya culture sites in the Volga-Urals area: (1) Burly-II; (2) Aleksandrovskii IV; (3) Malo-Kizilskii-II; (4) Ishkinovka-I, II; (5) Novotroitsk-I; (6) Zhaman-Kargala-I; (7) Vostochno-Kuraily-I; (8) Tanabergen-II; (9) Buranchi-I; (10) Uvak; (11) Nizhnaya Pavlovka-V; (12) Pyatiletka; (13) Krasnokholm II; (14) Kardailovo-I; (15) Bliznetsy; (16) Linevskie kurgany; (17) Izobilnoye-I; (18) Izobilnoye- II; (19) Tamar-Utkul-VII, VIII; (20) Shumayevo kurgany; (21) Gerasimovka-i, II; (22) Boldyrevo-I, IV; (23) Trudovoye-II; (24) Baryshnikov; (25) Kamennoye; (26) Grachevka; (27) Medvedka; (28) Efimovka; (29) Tambovka-I; (30) Gvardeitsy-II; (31) Bereznyaki-I; (32) Utevka-I, III, V, VI; (33) Kutluk-I, III; (34) Spiridonovka-II; (35) Ekaterinovka; (36) Kashpir-II, III; (37) Perepolovenka; (38) Suskan; (39) Lopatino-II, III; (40) Nizhnaya Orlyanka-I.

The site localization is quite standard, and it does not depend on a cemetery composition, but it is correlated with the close proximity of a small river or ravine. All sites are situated on the first fluvial terrace, and they usually consist of kurgans of different sizes. It is believed that the cemetery originated from the erection of the biggest kurgan (Bogdanov 1999: 9). Quite specific characteristics of this area can be marked by the almost complete absence of multiburial kurgans; only four kurgans contained two burials under one mound. In the remaining cases, a mound was erected for only one burial occupying the deep central pit (Fig. 2.2-A). It must be stressed that in all reliable cases, the above grave constructions, including the very big ones, were created shortly after the funerals. There is another clear pattern: big kurgans (more than 2 m high) primarily contained mature males (very rarely female); the kurgans of more than 5 m high contained only males. Two-thirds of the total number of mounds are small kurgans (under 1.2 m high), which contained a more variable composition of deceased, but male burials were dominant here as well. Single kurgans are identical in architecture and grave goods to the kurgans in cemeteries, but they did not contain human remains.

The burial pits are rectangular in form with vertical walls, supplemented sometimes by steps running along the upper part of the pit. Very often, we can find a wooden roof in a pit. Dromoses are recorded in a very few graves (Izobilnoye 1, kurgan 3 – Fig. 2.2-B).

The dominant burials, containing males and females of twenty to fifty years old,[1] were in a contracted position either on the back or on right side, and the hands were near the knees. Such a position is an ethnographic feature of the Cis-Urals variant of the Yamnaya culture, whereas in other areas, these are considered quite late characteristics. In several cases, the archaeologists recorded traces of fibrous ropes with which the arms or legs of deceased had been bound (Grachevo, kurgan 2). The orientation of the skeletons is rather stable: to the west-north-west. At the same time, some nonstandard positions are also noted (Bogdanov 2000a).

Bogdanov (1999: 12; 2004: 147–54) divides all Yamnaya burials into the following ritual groups.

1. In some burials the deceased was in a contracted position on its back and the head oriented to east-north-east. Ochre traces were noted around the skull and feet. These burials were executed in simple pits and are regarded as the earliest in the Cis-Urals area.

2. The most numerous group of burials are those that contain skeletons in a crouched position placed on the right side and oriented east-north-east. Ochre was also used (Fig. 2.2-A).

3. Two burials contained the remains of people placed on bent knees, propped against the wall and oriented to the north.

4. The fourth group is composed of nonstandard (extraordinary) burials, including collective graves and those with dismembered and partial skeletons (Fig. 2.3-A).

Double burials were discovered in only eight cases. In four of these burials, we can clearly see which is the main burial and which is the companion burial. Among the latter, two partial skeletons were found (Fig. 2.3-B) (Bogdanov 1990). Two severed skulls lavishly covered with ochre and accompanied by rich grave goods were buried in the big kurgan at Gerasimovka (Bogdanov 2000a). Cenotaphs are known in this series as well (Morgunova 1992: 22).

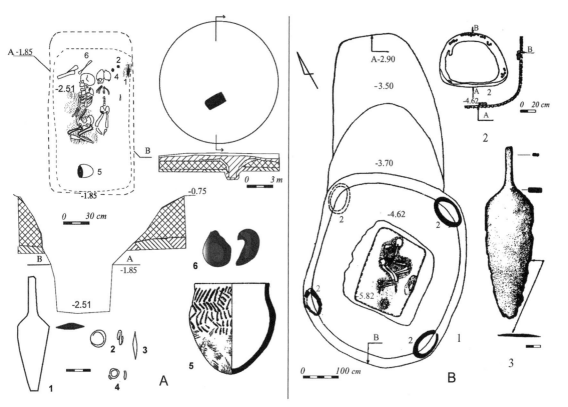

Figure 2.2. Yamnaya culture. **A:** Tamar-Utkul-VIII burial ground. Kurgan 5, grave 1: (1–4) copper; (5) clay; (6) shell (after Morgunova and Kravtsov 1994); **B:** Izobilnoye burial ground, kurgan 3, grave 1: (1) a view in plan; (2) shape of the clay wheel; (3) a copper knife-dagger (after Morguniva 2002).

The funeral ritual of the Yamnaya tradition is also characterized by the wide use of various bedding material (for example, poplar bark and grass) on which the deceased lay, and sprinkles of ochre, chalk, or charcoal that covered the skeleton or its parts (face, hands, feet) and the bottom of the pit.

Compared with western areas, the burials of this culture produced more grave goods. The set of grave goods includes some (but not a great number) of round-bottomed bowls, pots of a small dimension with hemispheric bodies either profiled or were without a clear neck. Pots are decorated with a comb stamp. One one-side casting mold made of clay was recovered in this area.

As we wrote in the previous chapter, metal objects are manufactured from pure copper, which is chemically identical to copper found in the Kargaly mine. An interesting burial of a twelve- to thirteen-and-a-half-year-old teenager accompanied by a kit of metallurgical instruments was excavated within the Pershino kurgan 1 located in the Kargaly area (Bogdanov 2001; Chernykh & Easteo 2002; Chernykh et al. 2000b). This can be interpreted in the light of idea that the profession of metallurgist was an inherited one.

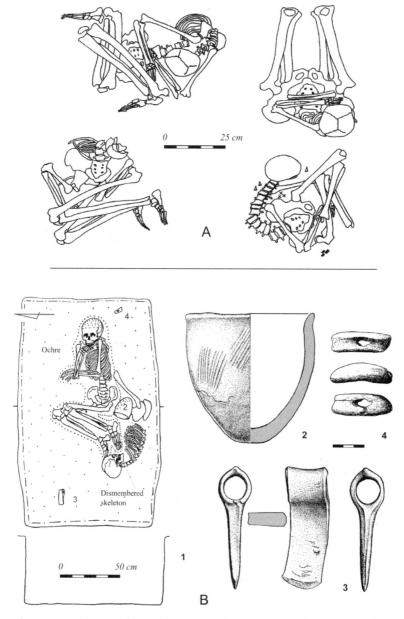

Figure 2.3. A – Partial burials from the Tamar-Utkul-VII, kurgan 4 (after Bogdanov 1998); **B** – Tamar-Utkul burial ground VIII, kurgan 4, grave 1: (1) view in plan; (2) clay pot; (3) copper axe; (4) bone object (after Bogdanov 1990).

Metal tools include four-sided awls with and without stops, knives with leaf-shaped or triangle blades and straight handles, socketed axes with rounded edges, adzes, hammers, and bimetallic devices for which meteoritic iron was used along with copper. The only reliable objects that can be defined as a weapon is a leaf shaped spearheads with a forged socket found in the

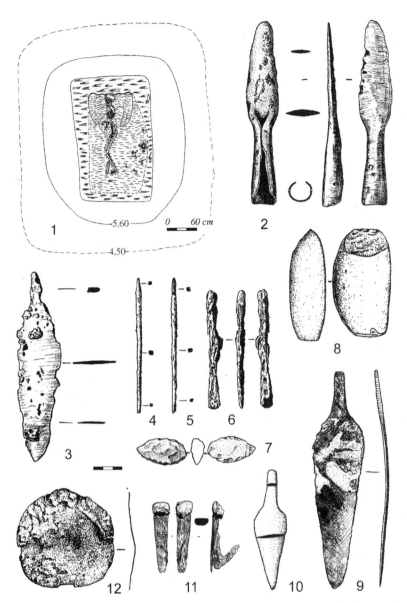

Figure 2.4. Yamnaya culture. Materials from Bolshoi Boldyrevsky kurgans: (1) burial 1; (2) copper spear; (3) copper knife; (4, 5) copper awls; (6) iron chisel; (7) stone scraper; (8) stone pestle; (9) copper dagger from kurgan 2; (10) copper knife from kurgan 10; (11) bimetallic object from kurgan 1; (12) iron disk from kurgan 1 (after Morgunova 2000).

Tamar-Utkul-VII cemetery and Bolshoi Boldyrevsky kurgan (Fig. 2.4) (Morgunova 2000; Morgunova & Kravtsov 1994).

Rare ornaments are basically represented by small tubes made from blades, round pendants with puanson decoration, and spiral earrings. Among the bone objects, "horned pins" should be mentioned. Stone pestles and grinders are numerous. In several cases, seashells and river shells, ore, and pieces of iron have been found in burials. Animal bones are not numerous. Traces of wagons, which are not very frequent within the main territory of the Yamnaya culture, are well recorded in the Cis-Urals area (Fig. 2.2-B). They are represented by wheel imitations, which were cleaned up in the grave of the kurgan 3 (Izobilnoye cemetery). These were located at the steps and in the corners of the grave. A part of a wooden wheel was found in the Gerasimovka–1 cemetery (Morgunova 1992: 23), and remains of wagons with four solid wheels were discovered in the Shumayevo burial ground. The latter was very well preserved, with clear traces of use. Their radiocarbon date is 2900–2600 cal BC (Morgunova et al. 2003, Turetski 2004).

The Uralian Yamnaya culture has some specifics against the background of western variants: individual kurgans with single central tomb are dominate; more variables in kurgan size and funeral ritual (a rather large group of non-standard burials); numerous pieces of evidence of metallurgy, including iron and bimetallic objects, carpentry, and four-wheeled wagons.

Chronological Variants and Their Cultural Attributions

The internal chronology of Yamnaya antiquities is based on the material of Eastern Europe, and mainly from the Volga area. In 1974, Merpert suggested the theory of the evolution of the funeral ritual of the Yamnaya culture. He analyzed several parameters of the funeral rite, in particular, orientation and position of skeletons, and some groups of grave goods. The ritual groups of burials that he distinguished had chronological meaning as well. According to his classification, the Cis-Urals variant cannot be considered an early variant. Taking this into account, Merpert (1977: 72) excluded it from the areas of culture formation. The same observation has been used as an argument in favour of the hypothesis covering the "archaic" and "conservative" character of the Cis-Urals Yamnaya sites, as compared with the western ones. Scholars also interpret some elements of Catacombnaya cultural influence noted in local sites as evidence of their late age (Malov & Filipchenko 1995; Tkachev 2000: 45–6).

The system of absolute chronology for the Cis-Urals region is at its early stage (Table 0.2). According to C-14 dates for the Volga area, the time period of the Yamnaya culture in that area falls between 3500 cal BC and 2200 cal BC, and if some cemeteries of the Poltavka culture (latest version of the Yamnaya tradition) are added, then this period can be extended down to the turn of the third and second millennia BC (Kuznetsov 1996b). These C-14 dates can be used as a *terminus ante quem* for the Cis-Urals area, so much so that between these two areas there is a great deal of common archaeological material (Tkachev & Gutsalov 2000).

As we have noted, the Cis-Urals area is not the homeland of the Yamnaya culture, and its appearance here is the result of its eastward expansion. Unlike the Volga area, where there are Eneolithic sites such as Khvalynsk and Syezheye that have some genetic links with the Yamnaya culture, the Cis-Urals region so far has produced only a small number of similar complexes, and these have only been discovered recently (Bogdanov 2001; Tkachev & Gutsalov 2000).

The "peak" of the kurgan tradition's second ritual group coincides with the second half of the Early Bronze Age and three-quarters of all burials relate to this period.

Some archaeologists believe that the Yamnaya culture and the Afanasyevo culture in Siberia are genetically connected (Danilenko 1974; Posrednikov 1992). But this idea is as yet not well grounded, because within the huge expanse between the Ural River, southern Siberia, the Altai, and Tuva areas only a few isolated sites of this time period have been discovered (Evdokimov & Loman 1989).

In fact, the Cis-Urals area can be regarded as the eastern periphery of the Yamnaya cultural zone. It has, however, some specifics of funeral ritual and material culture, and it may have had its own center of metallurgical production situated at the eastern margin of the Circumpontic metallurgical network. This is confirmed by the chemical composition of Cis-Urals metal, relatively numerous finds of massive copper objects, and the evident skill of local people to work with meteoritic iron (Morgunova & Kravtsov 1994).

Morgunova (2002) reviewing the Volga-Urals Yamnaya culture describes it in terms of three phases: early, classical, and late. The early phase is represented by some settlements, small kurgans (20–25 m in diameter), and Repin-type pottery.[2] The archaeological expression of the funeral ritual is close to the common early canons typified here by the Gerasimovka-II cemetery, which relates to the beginning of the Early Bronze Age. The classical (or developed) phase, which is archaeologically much better represented than the previous one, is notable for the "unification of the funeral ritual, round bottomed pottery, the disappearance of settlements, and the prevalence of wheeled transport" (Morgunova 2002: 258). Kurgans differed in size, ritual details, burial arrangements, human sacrifices, and the composition of grave goods. The elite burials are easily distinguishable from ordinary ones by labor investment and metal goods. Some scholars regard the late or conclusive stage, which continued into the Middle Bronze Age, as the Poltavka variant, which is contemporaneous with and connected rather closely to the Catacombnaya culture. It continued traditions of the previous phase with the appearance of flat-bottomed pottery, enormous kurgans such as Boldyrevo (D = 64 m) and Izobilnoye (D = 40 m) with rather sophisticated grave chamber constructions and sets of grave goods containing wheels and bimetallic (copper-iron) craft tools. The biggest kurgan in the Boldyrevo-I cemetery contained the grave of an adult male on his right side in a crouched position (Fig. 2.4). The body was covered with a matt made from plant fibres and decorated with a bird wing shaped appliqué made from white bark; the head was crowned with white bark as well. The deceased was accompanied by unusually rich offerings (Morgunova 2002). Such rituals might have expressed the elements of a new ideology reflected in the kurgan tradition, the crouched body position (adoration), and the lavish sprinkling of ochre, which could have been associated with some sacrifice to the gods.

Some archaeologists believe that it is possible to include the Poltavka sites within the Catacombnaya culture (Telegin 1985). This period is characterized by the rise of connections between the Volga-Urals area population with that of the Northern Caucasus. The form of this interaction is still not clear, but a migration of some groups from these areas looks quite probable, stimulating the cultural transformation in the Volga-Urals area (Kuznetsov 1996c).

Were the Folk from the Yamnaya Kurgans Socially Organized Pastoral Nomads?

One of the debated problems connected with the Yamnaya culture is the nature of its economy and society. The Eneolithic and Early Bronze Age data allowed Merpert (1974) to put forward the theory that nomadic pastoralism, with a sheep-breeding focus, originated in the third millennium BC, which in turn allowed the population of the Yamnaya cultural groups to assimilate a vast portion of Eurasia. According to Shilov (1975: 80–5), who studied this problem in the Lower Volga area, some groups of the Yamnaya people could practice the nomadic way of stock-breeding, with limited distances of transmigration. These were perhaps the first attempts of adaptation to open landscapes.

No one doubts the Yamnaya-culture economy was based on pastoral forms of livestock breeding, yet some scholars insist on its nomadic character (Morgunova 2000, 2002). They argue that all barrows are connected with the steppe landscapes, and the steppe environments were not conducive to agriculture at that time; consequently, there are neither long-term settlements, nor implements of agricultural labor. However, in the south, in the area closer to the Caspian Sea, there are some long-term settlements yielding Yamnaya pottery. Some scholars interpret them as winter habitations and use this fact to reconstruct the form of seasonal longitudinal transmigrations (north-south movement in fall-winter time and south-north movement in spring-summer time) of a nomadic character (Bogdanov 2000c: 12).

By contrast, it is commonly accepted that the Yamnaya flocks did not go far beyond the river valleys. From the viewpoint of classical nomadism theory, this form of seasonal transmigration can be regarded as no more than a mobile pastoralism form or, at best, a seminomadic one. Paleozoological material coming from the burials includes bones of cattle and sheep. It is quite well known that it is not possible to develop a nomadic mode of life and economy without horses in a herd, but horse bones are extremely rare in the kurgans. It is possible, however, to say that the absence of horse bones in the mortuary complexes can be explained by ideological reasons. To do justice to this, however, one needs to refer to Anthony's theory, according to which a horse was ridden in the period of the Botai culture (3500–3000 cal BC) in Kazakhstan area. Then a horse was spread to eastern Europe (Anthony & Brown 2003: 66), that could influence the Yamnaya culture as well. However, Benecke and von den Driesch (2003: 81), who state that during the Neolithic, Eneolithic, and Early Bronze periods, horses were widely used as a source of food and raw material, contest this point of view. According to their analysis, morphological changes are only visible on the horse bones of the Middle and Late Bronze Ages that is after 2500 cal BC.

Another argument in favor of nomadism of the Yamnaya population is the existence of ox-drawn wheeled transport, which was used as a means of transportation and habitation (Turetsky 2004). However, the number of Yamnaya-culture graves with remains of vehicle is still small against the total number of graves (Ivanova 2001), and this type of transport is too heavy to execute long-distance migrations.

Meanwhile, a larger group of specialists shares the idea that classical steppe nomadism appeared in the first millennium BC. They rightly ask, "Were prehistoric mobile pastoralists real nomads?" After detailed analysis of the Eneolithic sites of the Black Sea Steppe, Rassamakin came to the conclusion that "Neither the Usatovo nor the Yamnaya culture became nomadic, and there is no evidence that the subsequent cultures did either" (Rassamakin 1999: 156).

Classical nomadism as an economic and cultural phenomenon (see Chapter 6) was not possible in the Eneolithic for another reason. Specialized nomads cannot exist without a connection with a settled population, and this is very doubtful in the Yamnaya case, especially for the Cis-Urals area. The similarity with the Scythian burials (big labor consuming kurgans with human sacrifices), which sometimes were used by adherents of the Eneolithic pastoral nomadism hypothesis, is very superficial, because the rest of society is not represented archaeologically, and, consequently, we cannot speak about the entire social-funeral structure.

The assessment of the social organization of the Yamnaya culture can only be based on the material of the funeral ritual and on its heterogeneity evaluation. Despite the lack of direct evidence, we cannot, however, regard the Yamnaya society as egalitarian. Quite clear features of early social complexity characterize Yamnaya society. The difference in labor investment in different kurgans and burials is evident. To distinguish the concrete social groups is not easy because of the small series of burials distributed over the lengthy time period of about five hundred years. Meanwhile, some scholars state that the funeral ritual of the Cis-Uralian region was evolving toward the rise of complexity (Morgunova 2002: 236; Morgunova & Kravtsov 1994: 71). Reconstruction of demographic parameters of society is also rather difficult. One can say that the structure of the population of investigated burials does not correspond to a "normal" one. There are no small children, among whom the mortality is usually very high; furthermore, even the group of teenagers is quite limited. The dominant group is represented by adult male burials (Yablonsky & Khokhlov 1994: 118–41).

There is no doubt that to be buried in a kurgan was some sort of privilege (or rule) for a special societal group. This, consequently, also can be considered evidence of status differentiation within any concrete social group.

The big barrows appeared in the valley of the Volga River and to the west of the Urals in the second half of the third millennium BC. In the Southern Urals these barrows make up 30 percent of the ninety barrows of the Yamnaya and Early Poltavka cultures. Morgunova distinguished four groups of barrows on the basis of mound size and burial chamber construction. She stressed the high status of the individuals buried under the large mounds that contained carpentry and metalworking tools made of copper. This is interpreted as a reflection of a situation in which craft specialization became socially significant. It is worthwhile to refer to Bochkarev (1978: 52), who concluded that burials of specialized metallurgists are immanent to these cultures, where craftsmen were integrated into society, and the funeral ritual displayed the professional position of the deceased.

Some graves contained objects designed for religious and ritual activities (dismembered parts of the body, horned pins, powdered ochre, and pieces of iron ore). The largest barrows (40 to 50 (or more) m in diameter) are dated from the first quarter of the second millennium BC. That is to say, chronologically speaking, they appeared later than the small and medium-size barrows, and they indicated the conclusive establishment of a hierarchy.

Axes, spears, bows and arrows, daggers, and wagons (Morgunova 1992) represent warrior attributes. Following on from this analysis, we can note that social divisions within the Yamnaya culture were of a highly ritualized nature. Bogdanov (2000b) has suggested an interesting hypothesis. He thinks that the crouched body, irrespective of what side on which it was placed (or turned, as the result of tissue decomposition) expressed the idea that the deceased was regarded as a human sacrifice to the gods. In this connection, the "accompanied goods" should be regarded not as his personal property but as a part of the sacrifice on behalf of the group. In several burials, the deceased were in a kneeling position.

The distinctive social positions depended ideologically on ritualized kinds of activity. Probably, E. Kuzmina (1981: 34) is right to point out that in the Yamnaya culture we can see more social and ideological ranking than ranking based on property.

Yamnaya culture is traditionally connected to the problem of Indo-European origins. As a whole, nobody denies its affiliation to the Indo-European world, yet some researchers interpret it as an Indo-Iranian one (Kuzmina 1974). Mallory (1989; 1998: 187), sharing this hypothesis in general, is more careful saying that the Yamnaya culture could reflect a Greco-Armenian-Indo-Iranian continuum (late Indo-European). Carpelan and Parpola (2001:130–1) relate the late Yamnaya variant (Poltavka tradition) to the Proto-Aryan language. Hence, the discrepancy lies in the point that concerns the speed of the process of language differentiation in the framework of an Indo-European continuum.

Thus, the third millennium and the very beginning of the second millennium BC was of great importance for cultural and social history. Culturally it was the continuation of traditions derived from the Yamnaya contexts. In Bochkarev's (1995b) opinion, it was the Volga-Urals area where the process of the cultural genesis was extremely active; therefore, this area had a major influence on the preconditions of the formation of later cultures.

THE ABASHEVO CULTURE

The Abashevo cultural area extended through the forest-steppe region of eastern Europe; its sites have also became known far to the east into the Tobol basin. The main groups of sites or cultures within this intercommunity have been identified in the Don basin and the right bank of the Volga, in the Middle and Upper Volga, and in the Urals (Pryakhin 1976: 164–6) (Fig. 2.5). It is currently believed that this culture was formed in the very early second millennium BC in the middle Don area in the northern periphery of the late Yamnaya culture and between the Catacombnaya, Fatyanovskaya, and Sredne-Dneprovskaya cultures (Pryakhin & Khalikov 1987). The Abashevo culture inherited some elements of the Corded Ware cultures and was strongly influenced by mixed Yamnaya-Catacombnaya groups (Kuzmina 2001).

In the Urals area, the sites of the Abashevo culture occupy mostly the western slopes of the Ural Mountains, partly into the Trans-Urals. They usually take up the forest-steppe landscapes, but some sites have been encountered in the forested Volga-Vetluga interfluves and mountain areas (Borzunov & Bel'tikova 1999; Goldina 1999; Petrin et al. 1993; Pryakhin & Khalikov 1987). A kindred population inhabited the Middle Volga area and the Don and Volga interfluves. The Urals variant of the Abashevo culture, known also as the Balanbash, is a part of the larger massive cultural group. However, it differs sharply from classical Abashevo.

The long history of the study[3] of the Abashevo culture has caused a broad range of interpretations, to which various sites have been inscribed. Yet, some years ago, all Uralian metallurgy was attached to this culture. Initially, after its first discovery, the Sintashta fortified settlement also was regarded as an Abashevo site. Such a conclusion was made as a result of the chronological priority of the Abashevo tradition of metalwork and the resemblance of some pottery types.

Researchers have investigated the specifics of the Volga and Ural regional groups quite well. According to Kuzmina (1992: 74), the Volga-Uralian group directly follows the earlier groups without any chronological break. However, we should remember that the earlier materials are represented exclusively by burials and occasional finds. The metal richness of the Volga Abashevo sites

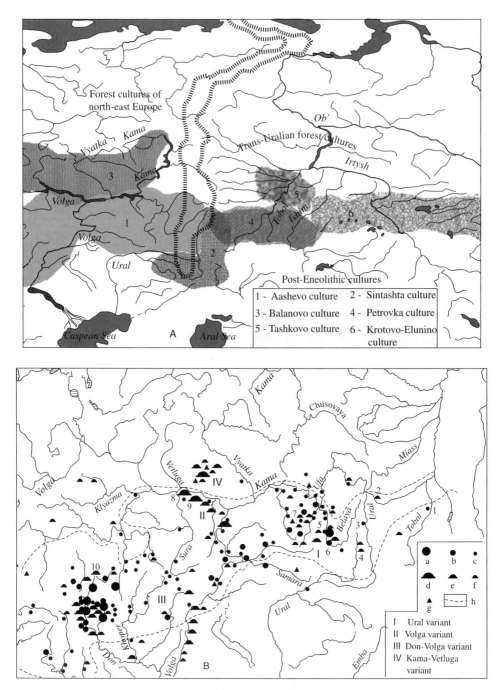

Figure 2.5. A: Schematic map of the Middle Bronze Age cultures (steppe and forest-steppe zone) and **B:** map of distribution of sites of the Abashevo culture: (a) six to ten settlements; (b) two to five settlements; (c) one settlement; (d) six to ten burial grounds; (e) two to five burial grounds; (f) one burial ground; (g) flat burial ground; (h) limit of forest-steppe; (1) Alexeyevskoye; (2) Stepnoye-1; (3) Malo-Kizilskoye; (4) Almukhametovo; (5) Balanbash; (6) Beregovskoye-1, 2; (7) Davlekanovo; (8) Pepkino, Vilovatovo; 9) Abashevo; (10) Staro-Yuryevo (after O. Bader, D. Krainov, and M. Kosarev, eds. 1987).

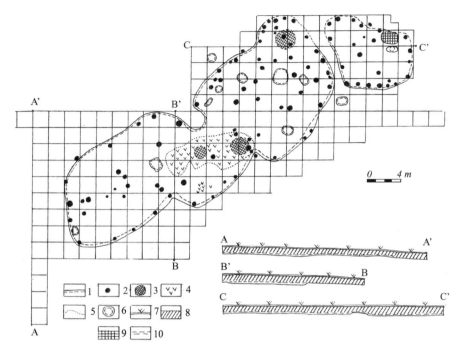

Figure 2.6. The Abashevo settlement of Beregovskoye I: (1) house limits; (2) posthole; (3) fireplace; (4) ash accumulation; (5) the limits of ash accumulation; (6) storage pit; (7) topsoil; (8) humus; (9) recent pit; (10) clay soil (after Gorbunov 1986).

is usually overstated, and there is no direct evidence of metallurgy. Another hypothesis synchronizes the Volga Abashevo culture with the Sintashta tradition (Besedin 1995; Epimakhov 1993). It is based on the identity of metal objects, bone (antler) "spades," and disklike cheek-pieces, found in the sites of both cultures.

The latest chronological boundary of the Urals Abashevo sites is more definite than that of the early boundary. It is limited by the end of the Late Bronze Age, and this is confirmed by stratigraphy: deposits containing pottery of the Srubnaya culture always overlap those of Abashevo. At the same time, scholars have noticed some elements of continuity in their pottery design. This has allowed some archaeologists to consider a longer period of the Abashevo tradition (Pryakhin & Khalikov 1987). There are also some Abashevo elements in the funeral ritual of the later Alakul culture of the Trans-Urals. Unfortunately, because of the indefinite character of its general chronology, there is still no internal periodization of the Abashevo culture.

The Cis-Urals Abashevo culture is represented by two kinds of sites: settlements and burial grounds. Despite the quite large number of these settlements (more than fifty), it is very hard to find well stratified sites among them. Only about ten settlements have vigorous monocultural archaeological deposits and contain distinguishable house remains (Balanbash, Beregovskoye-1 (Fig. 2.6),

Malo-Kizilskoye, Urnyak, and Tubyak). The other sites are usually multi-layered.

In general, the Urals Abashevo settlements are located on the promontories of the first river terraces or in the high valleys. In two cases, one can speak about the presence of simple fortifications. The occupied area of the biggest settlements does not exceed more than several thousand m². As a rule, one to three houses are visible within the settlement, but their number might be more because some of them could have had aboveground constructions with underground depressions. In most cases, Abashevo ceramics, which have characteristic designs, are only distinguished from settlement collections typologically.

The living architecture of the Cis-Urals Abashevo settlements is represented by limited material (Gorbunov 1986). Investigated dwellings differed in size (from 6 × 6.5 to 13 × 14 m), but they are quite close in construction, and only organic materials were used. The supporting and framing posts were dug into a slightly deepened foundation pit. Some storage pits and fireplaces are recognized on the floors. It is possible to suppose that the difference in size and interior design was conditioned on functional factors; these factors are partly supported by the concentration of evidence of metalworking activity in small rooms.

Abashevo collections contain mainly fragmented pottery and animal bones. Four basic types of Abashevo pottery are distinguished: (1) jugs, (2) bowls, (3) cans, and (4) miniature vessels with sharply formed shoulders. The diagnostic feature of Abashevo ceramics is the special form of the rim, supplemented by an internal rib (Fig. 2.7-B).

All pottery is decorated, except single cans (straight-walled pots). Small comb stamping and drawing are dominate among the technical devices. Various geometrical motifs, straight lines, and holes characterize ornament (Mochalov 1997). O. Kuzmina (1992: 106–7) supposed that this ornament might imitate some motifs of clothing decoration.

As mentioned earlier, the Abashevo settlement material contains instruments of metallurgy and metalworking (pestles, "anvils," abrasives, and crucibles), waste (slag and drops of metal), and ores. In the Balanbash settlement, bone disk-shaped cheek-pieces have been found. Rosette appliqués used on ornaments and clothing headdresses are considered a specific indicator of the Abashevo culture (Fig. 2.7-A). Small rings, pendants, pennanular bracelets, and large torques are also typical of the Abashevo tradition (Chernykh 1992: 202–3).

The series of Abashevo metal comes from occasional finds – hoards, the majority of which territorially gravitates to copper deposits in the Urals and Trans-Urals (Fig. 2.8). No hoards are known on the Volga right bank. However, some hoards have been discovered beyond the Abashevo area in the forest zone, and these may trace the direction of distribution of Abashevo metal.

Figure 2.7. Female ornaments and pottery from the Abashevo sites in the Kama area.

The evidence coming from burial grounds is more numerous and various than from settlements. The Urals Abashevo cemeteries usually include a small number of kurgans – around ten on average. The maximum number, twenty-six kurgans, was investigated in the Staro-Yabalaklinsk burial ground

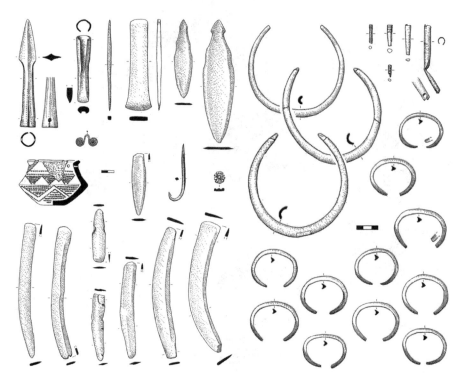

Figure 2.8. Metal artifacts and pot from the Verkhne-Kizilski hoard of the Abashevo culture.

(Gorbunov & Morozov 1991). Cemeteries occupy the river terraces, and there are some elements of regular row planning in the positioning of barrows, which usually are not high (80 percent of them are not higher than 0.5 m, the remaining are no more than 1 m) (Gorbunov 1986). Mounds are mainly round in form, but there are some barrows of oval shape, which result from to the additional graves added into the original kurgan. About 55 percent of the mounds are made of earth, but one can find some added elements – such as circular ditches, stone and wooden fences – which in some cases were erected around a central grave pit (Fig. 2.9-I).

Funerary chambers are rectangular in form and have different dimensions that are connected to the age and number of individuals buried in one grave. One can see that the funeral chamber was destined only for the deceased and his belongings. The average depth of graves does not exceed 1 m. Aside from the simple pits without any additions, there are a number with wood and stone inner constructions such as walling and roofing. The presence of stone is an ethnographic feature of the Cis-Urals Abashevo sites (Fig. 2.9-II).

All investigated barrows contained individual inhumations. Collective burials are very rare both in the Cis-Urals and in the Middle Volga areas. Khalikov excavated an interesting collective burial in 1961 in the Pepkino kurgan (Volga area, Fig. 2.5-B) (Khalikov et al. 1966). Twenty-eight young men were buried

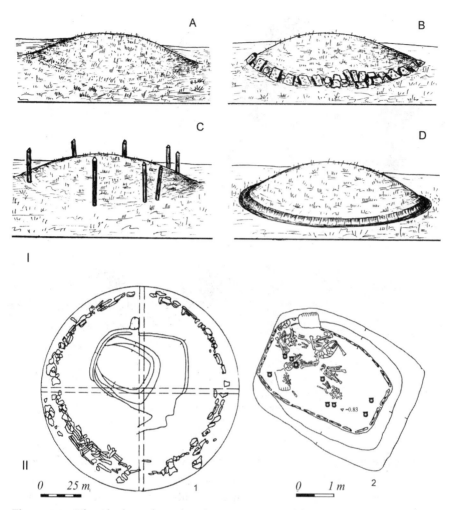

Figure 2.9. The Abashevo funeral tradition: I – types of the Urals Abashevo kurgans; II – The Baishevo IV kurgan: (1) view in plan, (2) grave in plan (after Gorbunov 1986).

in a pit over 11 m long (Fig. 2.10). Traces of injuries – broken bones and skulls pierced with metal axes and stone arrowheads of the Balanovo type (see later) – were detected on the bones of a large number of these skeletons. The bodies of some of the skeletons had been dismembered. Among those buried in this grave was a bronzesmith, who was distinguished by his powerful build. A two-part mold for a shaft-hole axe, a crucible for smelting copper and other smithing artifacts were found with him (Fig. 1.2).

Evidence of cremation has not been recorded, although traces of fire use are quite numerous: remains of fire, ash and charcoals in the pit, on the roof, and in the floor. In some cases, burials were arranged on the ancient soil level.

The position and orientation of the deceased are not well determined. However, the presence of some valuable goods in graves does not allow for the accepted traditional explanation that disturbed burials were the result of

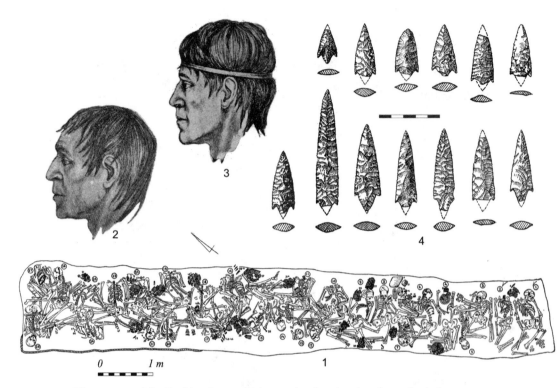

Figure 2.10. The Pepkino kurgan: (1) grave in plan; (2, 3) anthropological reconstructions of two of the deceased; (4) set of stone arrowheads (after Khalikov, Lebedinskaya and Gerasimova 1966).

robbery. It is possible that these people practiced some partial burials or other complicated rituals. The position of the deceased has been traced in the Volga area materials where they were placed at the entrance with raised knees; this is different from other synchronic Middle Bronze cultures. This and the sporadic use of ochre can be regarded as reminiscent of the archaic Yamnaya tradition.

Animal sacrifices played a limited role in the funeral ritual: cow and sheep bones were discovered in the pit filling. Grave goods are represented by pots, some bone and metal objects, including chisels, knives-daggers, sickle-like tools, awls, and hooks. Stone and bone arrowheads represent either weaponry or hunting. Bone objects conditionally called "spades" are well known in the Abashevo area. The most characteristic part of the grave goods complex is related to the numerous ornaments: bracelets, rings, hollow ribbed tubes, rosette-like, and semi-circular plaques.

The analysis of material yielded by settlements and funerary sites has allowed scholars to model some subsistence patterns of the Abashevo population. A number of animal bones, mostly from settlements, attest to livestock breeding. These bones are mainly from cattle (68–78 percent), then sheep and pigs (Table 2.1). The Abashevo culture contrasts with other cultures of the Middle

TABLE 2.1. *Animals from the Abashevo Cis-Urals settlements (after Gorbunov 1986)*

| | Settlements | | | | | | | |
| | Balanbash | | Urnyak | | Beregovkoye-1 | | Beregovskoye-2 | |
Species	MNI	Percent	MNI	Percent	MNI	Percent	MNI	Percent
Bos taurus	214	61	544	77,8	78	62,9	53	71,5
Ovis aries and Capra hircus	46	22	44	9,9	14	11,3	8	10,8
Equus caballus	6	2,8	7	1,6	15	12	12	16
Sus scrofa domestica (pig)	32	14,2	41	9,1	17	15,7	1	1,4
Dog	–	–	–	–	–	–	–	–
Wild animals	–	–	2	1,6				

and Late Bronze Age by the limited presence of horse bones in settlements and their absence in funeral sites. There are also horse harness details, which, as a rule, were found in settlements. Such a correlation of animals represented in the earlier-mentioned proportions testifies to a rather stable mode of life and the necessity to store up forage for the winter period.

Scholars traditionally interpret the presence of pig bones as evidence of agriculture, because pigs can be fed agricultural products, but they also can be fed acorns. It is interesting to note that pig bones were discovered only in the Cis-Urals area, where oak forests are available. This can be evidence of a natural forage basis for pig breeding, and the question of agriculture can only be settled after special analysis.

One also should be careful in the sociological interpretation of the Abashevo materials because of lacuna of related information. In some cases, scholars distinguish an elite necropolis referring to a disproportion in the demographic structure: the predominance of adult males (Gorbunov 1992). Taking the limited number of fully investigated burial grounds into account, one should accept such a conclusion as hypothetical. However, it is worthwhile to agree with statements about the posthumous selection of individuals who deserved to be buried in kurgans. Unfortunately, the settlements do not provide even any indirect evidence of an elite existence.

Some burial grounds containing the remains of ritual performed for the people of a distinctive position have been excavated in kurgans along the Don River within the traditional Abashevo area, particularly the Filatovka and Vlasovo cemeteries (Sinuk & Kozmirchuk 1995). These are characterized by the composition of elements connected with the Late Catacombnaya culture, the Mnogovalikovaya (Multibanded) ceramic cultures, and the Sintashta, Abashevo, and Alakul cultures. From the social point of view, the burials displayed distinctive elements of a system of prestige goods – expressive warrior attributes. These burials were originally interpreted in terms of a return migration of eastern Abashevo groups. Currently, however, they are attributed to the Potapovka version of the Sintashta tradition or as a component of the Novokumaksky horizon and providing evidence of a westward movement from the Volga-Ural area. Newcomers possessed a powerful social and political organization as well as chariots. In the Don area, they met people of the Catacombnaya culture and those of the Abashevo culture. Otroshchenko (2000) states that the westward impact of the Sintashta and then Petrovka groups was rather strong, and it could have changed the classical Abashevo appearance. Finally, it also could have inspired the process directed to the formation of the early Srubnaya culture in its Pokrovsk (east) and Berezhnovka (west) variants.

Despite the rather modest material expression of the Abashevo culture, its influence can be traced in many Eurasian cultures of the Middle Bronze Age. The mechanism of this influence is something of a mystery. We should perhaps consider the mentality of the bearers of the Abashevo cultural tradition as rather cosmopolitan toward the outside when we remember that the Seima-Turbino populations, having come to the Urals, had established distinctive contacts with the Abashevo groups (Chernykh et al. 2004). By contrasrt, the earlier-mentioned Pepkino kurgan is clear evidence of serious conflict that came about between the Abashevo and forest Balanovo groups.

Paradoxically, despite the tremendous amount of material confirming the Abashevo culture, the image of its society is still hardly visible and mysterious. However, in the late stages, it occupied maximal territory comparable only with the territorial expansion of the Catacomnaya culture.

THE SINTASHTA CULTURE

The Sintashta materials have been the subject of intense and often heated debates. This cannot be explained exclusively by their relatively recent discovery and extreme originality, because the fact is their significance goes far beyond regional importance. The Sintashta traditions played a very important role in the formation of the Srubnaya and Andronovo cultural families of the Late Bronze Age. The Sintashta antiquities and especially the Arkaim fortified settlement became known during a rather difficult period of Russian history and through the force of many political and ideological reasons, they were in the focus of actual life of Russian society.

The discovery and investigation of the eponymous site of Sintashta (Plate 2.1) came about in the 1970s (Gening et al. 1992), but the awareness of its value only occurred later. Initially, the Sintashta site was not distinguished from the numerous Andronovo sites that had been known in abundance in the southern part of the Chelyabinsk district in the late 1960s. These sites were then regarded within the Salnikov's concept of stadial evolution and its application to the Andronovo culture. The specific character of the sites, which later would

Plate 2.1. Aerial photo of the Sintashta archaeological complex (Arkaim Reserve Museum).

be referred to as the Sintashta culture, was first emphasized by Smirnov who excavated the Novyi Kumak cemetery in the South Cis-Urals. In his book with Kuzmina (Smirnov & Kuzmina 1977), this material was used for distinguishing the so-called Novokumakski cultural and chronological horizon indicating the Middle Bronze Age in the Eurasian steppe. Only after subsequent large-scale excavations at the Sintashta settlement and cemeteries as well as at the Arkaim settlement, which illuminated the extraordinary characteristics of these sites, did scholars begin to change their views regarding many questions relating to the archaeology of the Bronze Age.[4]

Thanks to the wide use of aerial photography and site recognition, the area of site distribution, their number, size, and settlement pattern are now well established. In the Trans-Urals steppe, these systems of closed fortifications are only connected to the final period of the Middle Bronze Age.

The settlements and cemeteries of the Sintashta type are concentrated in the northern steppe of the southern Trans-Urals (Fig. 1.3). Characteristic of this area is the high deposition of copper ores and the nearby large forest massifs (Zaikov 1995). As a rule, Trans-Uralian settlements are accompanied by cemeteries. These compactly located sites were united under the conditional name of "Country of Towns," assigned by their principal investigator, G. Zdanovich (1989, 1995, 1997b; Zdanovich & Batanina 2002; Zdanovich & Zdanovich 2002). Some archaeologists accepted this term as a sort of metaphor; others commented on it rather vociferously.

All settlements are situated on the tributaries of the Tobol and Ural rivers. Only one site (Chekatay) is located on a lake bank. Conversely, the burial grounds are known in wider areas, including Kazakhstan (Kaliyeva et al. 1992; Logvin 2002), Cis-Urals (Tkachev 1995, 1998; Khalyapin 2001), and the Volga area (Vasily'ev et al. 1994). However, settlements have not yet been found in these regions.

Twenty-two fortified settlements have been discovered during the past three decades. Most of them contained from one to four building horizons (Yaminov & Savely'ev 1999; Zdanovich & Batanina 2002). Out of the twenty-two settlements, seven have been excavated to varying degrees. The best studied are Sintashta, Arkaim, and Ustye.[5] Twelve cemeteries are known in the Trans-Urals, but this number cannot be regarded as final because cemeteries have not been discovered for several settlements. Conversely, a few cemeteries have no visible connection to settlements. In the Trans-Urals, five cemeteries have been excavated (they comprised two hundred burials), in the Cis-Urals eight cemeteries (one hundred burials), in northern Kazakhstan, one cemetery (twenty-eight burials), and in the Volga area two cemeteries (thirty-three burials). In the Cis-Urals, the Sintashta burials and kurgans are included in multistage cemeteries, and very often their number is limited, as was observed in the Novyi Kumak burial ground (Smirnov & Kuzmina 1977).

Overall, the database of the Sintashta culture is rather rich, but the full extent of its potential has not yet been realized. At the risk of tedium, we, however, must dedicate some pages to the detailed description of the archaeological material because of its outstanding character and extremely interesting meaning.

Archaeological Materials

SETTLEMENTS

The settlements are usually located at a distance of 40 to 70 km from each other, in the central parts of the large river valleys, near a stream or ravine and river mouth (Plate 2.2). They occupy spacious flat, dry ground of the first fluvial terrace, yet the naturally fortified grounds were rarely used. The proximity to a water source and natural boundaries forming some sort of island during the time of the spring floods was very important for the placement of the settlement (Zdanovich 1999; Zdanovich & Batanina 2002). A water barrier usually separated the necropolis from the settlement, which is situated to the north of the necropolis.

The architecture of the Sintashta settlements, for which a closed system of fortifications is characteristic, is quite well described. Their sophisticated character and complexity in comparison with other sites of Eurasian steppe zone are very impressive and intriguing. One can trace three basic layouts. The first two layouts are represented by oval- or round-shaped plans with radially grouped houses and entrances turned to the center: Alandskoye (Plate 2.2-A), Bersuat, Kizilskoye, Sintashta, Arkaim (Plate 2.3), Sarym-Sakly, Kuisak, and Isenei. The

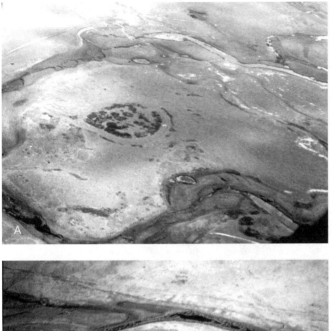

Plate 2.2. Settlements of the Sintashta culture. **A:** The Alandskoye settlement. **B:** The Andreyevskoye settlement (Arkaim Reserve Museum).

second is based on the linear principle. The houses are inserted into a rectangular plan of fortification: later layers of Ustye, Chekatai, Andreyevskoye (Plate 2.2-B), and Chernorechy'e-III. Some scholars interpret rectangular fortresses as of a Petrovka type; stratigraphically, these are later than the circular sites of the Sintashta type. According to Zdanovich and Batanina (2002), the oval layout is the earliest form of such a fortress type. In some settlements, the traces of reconstructions are recorded both archaeologically and by aerial photography.

The diagnostic feature of the Sintashta settlements is the closed fortification that consisted of ramparts and ditches, surrounded by a fence or wall. This feature is based upon either the round or rectangular plan, or a combination of the two. Fortified grounds enclose from 6000 to 35,000 m². The fortresses are provided with counterforces, towers, and other constructions protecting entrances and the access to water. Four entrances have been discovered in

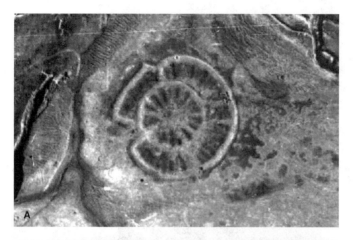

Plate 2.3. Arkaim settlement. **A:** Aerial photo of the 1950s. **B:** Excavated and partly reconstructed house: modern view (Arkaim Reserve Museum).

the Arkaim outer wall (Fig. 2.11; Plate 2.3-A). Two of the entrances have been excavated. Only the left gate of the main entrance, which exited to the west, led directly to the circular street, the other entrances were narrow labyrinths arranged inside the walls (Zdanovich 1995, 1997b). The ditches were 2–4 m wide, about 1.5 m deep, and had some pits dug out in the ditch bottom for removing the surplus water. Excavations have demonstrated that the ditches contained deposits of ruined walls: its upper part consisting of burnt soil with charcoal inclusions was underlying the remains of the wall foundation that consisted of natural clay. The wood and earth building technique was in common use. First, the turf bricks formed two parallel walls, which served as an encasement that was filled in by natural native rock taken from the ditch, and then the wooden frames were placed on this foundation. The frames were filled with loam soil, which has a cementlike quality after it dries.[6] As a result, the wall could reach 5–6 m in height. The use of stone is recorded in two fortresses: Olginskoye[7] and Alandskoye (Plate 2.4), where stone was used on the outside plastered defensive wall.

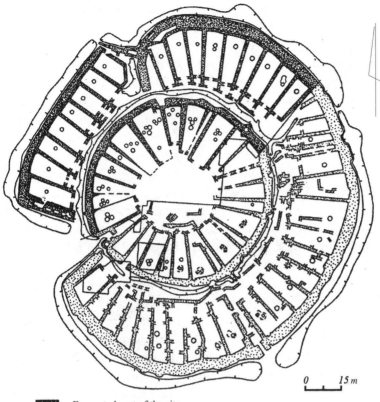

- ▨ – Excavated part of the site
- ▨ – Walls
- [O₀] – Wells, ovens

Figure 2.11. Arkaim fortified settlement (after Zdanovich 1997).

Plate 2.4. The Alandskoye settlement: ditch section (excavation of D. Zdanovich).

The internal space of the settlements is almost entirely occupied by edifices, organized into sectional blocks. Some settlements consisted of one circle of houses (Sarym-Sakly); the others comprised two concentric circles of house structures. In particular, Arkaim has two protective circles, two circles of standard dwellings, separated by a street and a central square. The external wall, built from a special soil, placed into timber frames, covered by bricks made of local soil, was 160 m in diameter and 4 m thick (Zdanovich 1989). Sixty-seven houses were joined by a common internal wall (Fig. 2.11). They were situated in a radial direction and were entered at the circular internal street.

As a rule, the center of the settlement was free of any buildings. The number of houses, which are usually rectangular or trapezoidal, correlates with the size of a settlement. The house sizes are very similar, usually between 100 and 250 m² (Fig. 2.12). The houses are usually found on foundations dug 20–30 cm into the natural rock, postholes, wall ruins, and some other features relating to the interior are also found. The construction principles are standard; a frame-pillar construction was used exclusively. It consisted of several longitudinal rows of posts that supported a roof and served as a basis for lighter partitions within the houses (Plate 2.3-B). Building material consisted mostly of soil and wood. The long longitudinal walls were adjacent to the next house. A short transversal wall served, at the same time, as a section of a defensive line. The archaeologists noticed that the structure of the ground at the defensive wall foundation and corresponding to different houses was also different. This allowed the excavators to think that the people who built each house were responsible for building that part of the defensive wall that adjoined their house (Zdanovich, verbal communication). Therefore, the additional character of the construction of groups of houses allows us to see the "residential blocks." Such a manner of settlement organization offered to its residents the advantage of a modest expenditure in construction and heat savings during the winter.

All houses had a standard floor plan: an economic area, living area, and a small antechamber or porch fronting to the center of the settlement. Zdanovich (1997, 1997b) points out that along with entrances facing the center there were corner exits leading to a house roof or to the top of the defensive wall. On both sides of the entrance, there were sections where the oven chimney was arranged (Gening et al. 1992). This chimney served for heating the house. In fact, the heating system of such a big house was rather economic and efficient: on three sides, it was isolated from the cold by adjacent houses and the defensive wall, and the fireplace in front of the entrance created some sort of heat air lock. Every house contains one or several wells next to which the remains of a cupola-shaped furnace with traces of metallurgy are recorded (Fig. 1.4). It has been experimentally established that the spatial proximity of well and oven is conditioned by specifics of the metallurgical process: such a connection allowed increasing natural air traction. The well walls were whickered; at their

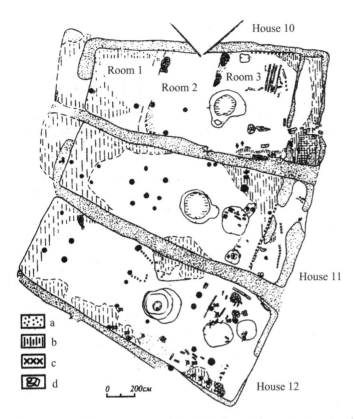

Figure 2.12. Houses 10–11 of the Sintashta settlement: view in plan: (a) yellow clay; (b) dark loam; (c) charcoal, burnt wood; (d) clay bricks (after Gening, Zdanovich, & Gening 1992).

bottom (on the aquiferous level), the remains of vertical wood posts standing on the well perimeter were found. Some pottery sherds and animal bones also have been found in the well infillings. The floor around the wells was more foot worn than other parts of these dwellings. The living space occupied an area of 35–65 m², which might accommodate not more than twenty to thirty people (Epimakhov 1996; Grigory'ev 2000a). In the Alandskoye site, the remains of water conduits (clay and wooden tubes) were discovered, but the limited scale of the excavation does not allow us to speak about it in more detail.

The excavated sites yielded mostly ordinary material: animal bones, pottery fragments, spindle whorls, instruments for leather working, and so on. Yet a large number of finds connected to metal production and metalworking (pestles, abrasives, nozzles, slag, metal drops) is also typical for the Sintashta sites. These traces usually are evenly distributed on the surface of a dwelling.

The settlement pottery of the Sintashta culture is rather variable although it is easily recognizable in the collections. Big can-shaped and smoothly profiled

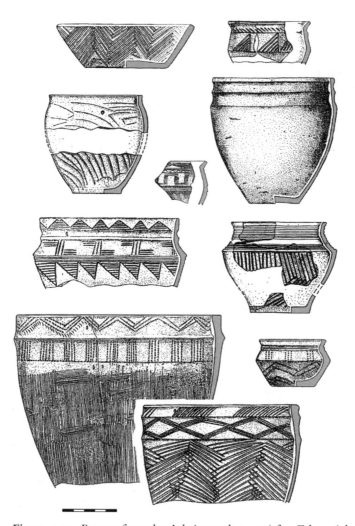

Figure 2.13. Pottery from the Arkaim settlement (after Zdanovich 1997b).

vessels, decorated on the upper part by two-three sticked bolsters, represent the diagnostic settlement pottery type (Fig. 2.13). Large and very large vessels (from 16 to 50 liters) constitute about 20 percent of the Arkaim collection. The pots are also very specific with sharply designed shoulders and an inner rib at the neck. This type is widely found amongst funeral pots as well. There are also less "outstanding" but widely used types; these are pots with vertical necks, ornamented on the shoulder with chevrons and can-shaped vessels that have a smooth profile. The closest parallels to one group of the Sintashta pottery can be found in the Abashevo collections. Some pots, however, have stylistic similarities to the Potapovka, Petrovka, Pokrovka, and Mnogovalikovaya pottery.

Technologically, one can see some variability in clay composition, but the method of pottery making appears to be about the same. Practically all vessels were made on a solid mold, sometimes with the use of an upside-down pot

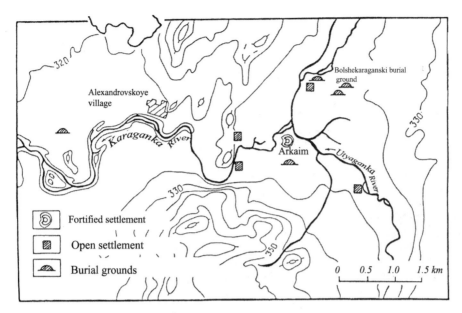

Figure 2.14. Location of sites in the valley of the Karaganka and Utyaganka rivers, Arkaim valley (after Zdanovich 2002).

covered by a piece of cloth. Most of the pots have characteristic cloth imprints on their internal surface.

The metal inventory coming from the settlements is represented by sheet-based instruments demonstrating the decline of traditions of the Circumpontic metallurgical complex and the forming of Eurasian metallurgical prototypes. Compared to the large number of finds connected to metal production, the number of stone molds is not large. Special objects or markers of social status are almost completely absent in the settlement collections. Therefore, the settlement finds cannot be used to reveal socially determined areas nor specialized buildings and blocks. However, we should reiterate that no settlement has yet been completely excavated.

CÉMETERIES

The Sintashta cemeteries occupy the flat portion of the first and second river terraces. The number of funeral complexes within one cemetery can vary from five pits to several dozen. Burial grounds, as a rule, are related to the settlement fortress forming the model "one settlement – one cemetery" (Fig. 2.14). The only difference between burial grounds is the degree of their compactness. The Sintashta Big Kurgan is interpreted by its researchers (Gening et al. 1992) as a common sanctuary or temple. However, we should point out that this attribution is so far arguable, particularly when we remember there are no analogous structures in other territories. In addition, the pottery complex from that site does not allow us to make unambiguous definitions, because it included fragments of typologically different pots.[8]

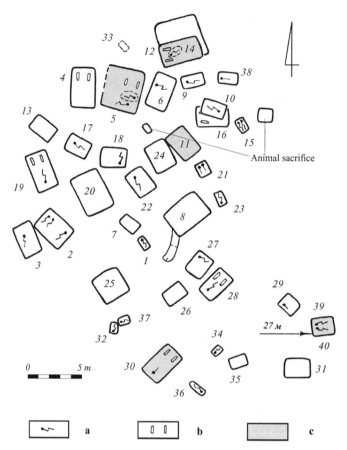

Figure 2.15. Plan of the Sintashta burial ground: (a) skeleton position; (b) traces of chariot; (c) finds of cheek-pieces (after Gening, Zdanovich, & Gening 1992).

At present, funerary sites are visibly represented by kurgans. The only exclusion is the Sintashta burial ground in which the complexes of SM and SII did not have any visible above ground constructions (Fig. 2.15). Nevertheless, they were organized according to a common pattern and every grave was supplied with an individual construction, which does not allow them to be considered as a separate type. According to some scholars, however (Grigory'ev 2000a; Zdanovich 1997b), the Sintashta burial ground did not have a common mound, and every grave was marked by a special construction that took the form of a small mount before being destroyed. Above-grave constructions were made of wood and soil; there are no reliable examples of the use of stone, except these of the Cis-Urals area. Sacrificial deposits consisting of parts of animals and pots were placed into the grave and the surface under the barrow, which constituted the major elements of the funeral area.

The ways of organizing the space under the kurgan – number, composition, orientation, and locality of graves with regard to the central grave – are varied. About 85 percent of multigrave barrows have a quite clear planning structure.

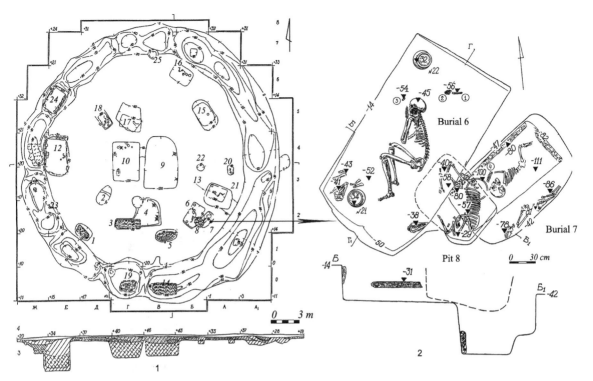

Figure 2.16. Bolshekaraganski burial ground: (1) general plan and kurgan profile; (2) burials 6 and 7, and pit 8: general plan and profile (1 – knife and remains of scabbard; 2 – crystal; 3 – astragali) (after Zdanovich 2002).

The funeral area was limited by a circular ditch (sometimes in composition with a small bank, with entrances or causeways (Bolshekaraganski kurgan 25 – Fig. 2.16) (Zdanovich 2002a). The biggest (3–4 m in length) or double graves usually had the central location. In the Sintashta period, they were oriented along the N-S line; later in the Petrovka period, this orientation would be replaced by a W-E direction. Other structures were situated around central complexes with different degrees of regularity. Therefore, within some barrows a clear contrast can be recognized between the "center" – more significant – and the "periphery" – of lower status, but undoubtedly connected with the central grave (Epimakhov 1995). A special place within this structure was given to animal sacrifices.

Stratigraphic observations confirm the multistage character of the mortuary complex formation. One could see that some burials were secondary to the primary complex. Alongside such an established pattern, there were some digressions. For example, there are the barrows with a single central grave, but there are also instances with three graves, among which the central one was not distinguishable. The earlier-mentioned multistage process of barrow formation can explain this.

TABLE 2.2. *Composition of the "sacrificed herd" of Bolshekaragansky kurgan 25 (after Zdanovich and Gaiduchenko 2002)*

Species, group	MNI	Percent
Horse	22	19,3
Cattle	29	25,4
Sheep	48	44,2
Goat	11	9,7
Swine (wild boar)	2	1,7
Dog	1	0,9
Korsak	1	0,9
Duck	1	0,9
Total number	115	100

The pit graves differ in size and complexity. They are more or less similar in form – rectangular with a stable ratio between length and width (3:2). All grave constructions were of wood and earth; stone is very rare. The mortuary chamber was furnished with a wooden frame covered by one, two, or even three ceilings made of logs and straw. The space between the wooden frame and pit walls was filled with earth. Vertical pillars supported the roof. Sometimes the excavators managed to record the remains of bedding on the floor of the funeral chamber: this bedding could be wood, grass, or animal skin (Zdanovich 1997b).

The big graves yielded individuals of various sex and age compositions; all ages are represented. However, 5 percent of graves contained couples: a man and woman lying in a position facing each other. Some of the larger graves contained up to eight individuals (Plate 2.5). Nevertheless, 52 percent of the burials were single individuals, mostly children.

About half of all burials show traces of intrusion. In several cases – as is documented by stratigraphy and field observation – the time between burial and intrusion was rather short (this is covered by the term "ritual robbing"). The deceased were placed on an organic bedding on the left (rarely on the right) side in a contracted position with hands near the face. In their orientation, the northern, western, and northwest directions are predominant. This is especially characteristic for female burials.

One the most outstanding characteristics of the Sintashta funeral ritual are the abundance and variability of animal sacrifices, chiefly domestic animals: horse, cattle, sheep, and dog, including other canines (wolf, fox). Detailed archaeozoological and taphonomic research undertaken by D. Zdanovich and Gaiduchenko (2002: 208–9) at Bolshekaragansky cemetery near Arkaim demonstrated a very complex and meaningful structure of the use of animals in the funeral ritual. The authors write: "Female individuals of four main species of sacrificed animals makeup 80 percent of the "sacrificed herd." Only stallions represented the mature horses – they make up 10 percent of "the herd." The remaining 10 percent were young animals under one year old." Most likely, the sex of young animals was not that significant in choosing them for sacrifice. The females of all species, as well as perhaps stallions, were at the age of active reproduction. No ritual selection of sheep and goat existed. One hundred fifteen animals were sacrificed for about twenty-four people buried in one kurgan of the Bolshekaragansky cemetery (Table 2.2; Fig. 2.16).

The variability is also expressed in the numerous combinations of different animal body parts and where they were located. Whole skeletons obviously

Plate 2.5. Kamennyi Ambar burial ground, kurgan 2, grave 12.

cannot be interpreted as funeral food; this is especially true in relation to horse depositions in combination with chariot traces or with finds of cheek-pieces. These are found only in the Sintashta cemetery.

There is some regularity: a horse usually accompanied a man; children and young woman were usually given small horned animals, which, being numerous, occupied, the lowest position in the hierarchy of species of sacrificed animals. The horse was on the top of this hierarchy (Zdanovich & Gaiduchenko 2002). D. Zdanovich distinguished the following forms of representation of animals in sacrificial complexes: "whole" animal, "partial" animal, and "part" of animal. The latter – an artificially organized group of bones, consisting of complete skull and legs – is dominant (Zdanovich 2005:13).

Grave goods are numerous. The most frequent is pottery, varying in size, in decoration, and, to a lesser extent, in technology. Pottery collections coming from cemeteries are characterized by richer ornamentation and the presence of some types that were not common in settlements. Above all, this is related to small sharply ribbed vessels – "lamps" resembling typical pots of the Abashevo culture.

Metal goods fall into the following categories: weaponry – spearheads, axes (Plate 2.6–1), knife-daggers, arrowheads, darts; implements – knives, sickles, needles, awls, gouges; and ornaments – pendants for braids, beads, spiral pendants in one and half circles. Many objects are made from bone and horn. Above all, the disklike (shield) cheek-pieces should be noted.[9] The bone complex also includes arrowheads, small "spades" (Plate 2.6–2), knife handles, and spindle whorls. The set of stone articles consists of numerous arrowheads of two types: tanged and with a truncated base, pestles, "anvils," and abrasive stones. There are no luxury goods.

In some cases, there are combinations of the remains of two-wheeled chariots, with 10–12 spoke-wheels and an imitation of pair-horse harnessing

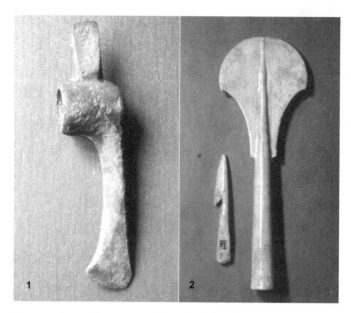

Plate 2.6. 1 – Bronze axe from the Sintashta cemetery. 2 – Bone arrowhead and "spade" from the Sintashta cemetery.

(Fig. 2.17). As a rule, the wheel traces are recorded in the form of two parallel oval-elongated depressions with a lens-like section. They are usually situated 130–160 cm from each other. This distance can be regarded as the gauge of a chariot. We would not insist that the ritual required placing the whole chariot into the grave[10] (yet, undoubtedly, such examples are well known), but, rather, similar gauge size supplies evidence in favor of this hypothesis. These "wheel fosses" are also correlated with post holes, which were usually located in or near the center of a grave bottom. Such "charioteer's graves" (14 percent) usually contained adult males accompanied by numerous weapons. Most of these are collective graves, and they can be located either in the center or on the periphery (Epimachov & Korjakova 2004).

Sex and age of the diseased was a condition of the composition of the goods included in the grave. Weaponry except for knife-daggers (which may have been considered a tool rather than a weapon) was an accessory of male burials. Ornaments, awls, and needles are considered female attributes. This differentiation appears to have been made for diseased at about five years old. The objects interpreted as the markers of social status and social power – maces, spearheads, chariots – are encountered both in central and in peripheral graves.

Hence, the Sintashta funeral ritual is distinguished by its high variability when compared with the background of other Ural Bronze Age cultures. However, it is not easy to interpret these data.

Statistic diachronic analysis shows that the funeral ritual was evolving on the way to the gradual elimination of its most expensive parts: normal metal

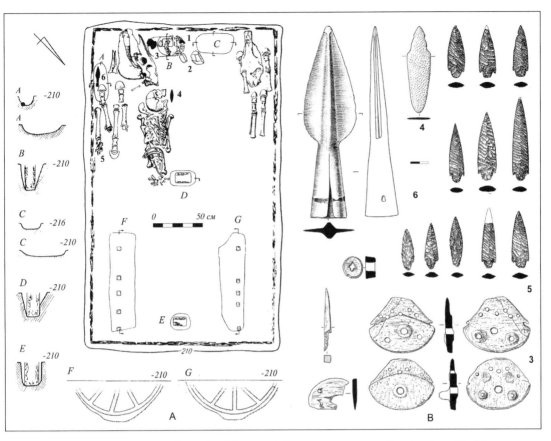

Figure 2.17. Krivoye Ozero burial ground, kurgan 9, grave 1, view in plan: (1)–(3) pots; (4) stone and bone arrowheads; (5, 6) antler cheek-pieces; (7) bronze arrowheads; (8) bronze knife-dagger; (9) abrasive (after Vinogradov 2003).

objects were being replaced by miniature imitations, whole vessels tended to be replaced by incomplete or repaired items, whole sacrificed animals were being replaced by the parts according to the principle "pars pro toto." At the same time, it was more common for whole animals to be immolated in the eastern part of the area of the Sintashta ritual expansion (Zdanovich & Gaiduchenko 2002).

Available data allow us to think that such elimination also was expressed in the decrease of the portion of nonstandard variants of funeral rituals. This tendency was realized in the Petrovka culture, the "daughter-branch" of the Sintashta culture.

THE PETROVKA CULTURE

This cultural formation was first recognized thirty years ago and is well grounded on the materials of northern Kazakhstan where a number of settlements and burial grounds have been investigated (Zdanovich 1973). The stratigraphy of some sites clearly demonstrated the early position of the Petrovka deposits over those of Alakul (Zdanovich 1988, 165). Currently, the territory of the culture has been extended to cover the Trans-Uralian steppe and forest-steppe (Potyemkina 1985; Vinogradov 1995a), central Kazakhstan (Tkachev 2002),[11] and the Middle Tobol area (Matveyev 1998) as well. Tkachev (1998) also includes into this culture some sites of the southern Cis-Urals. Despite the fact that the culture occupies quite a large territory (Fig. 2.18), no local spatial or chronological variations have been distinguished. Only some specifics of central Kazakhstan (Nurtai type) have been preliminary determined.

About a dozen settlements, occupying up to 3.5 hectares,[12] with rectangular fortifications are currently well described. They are located in similar topographic conditions taking up flat river or (rarely) lake terraces. A few sites are situated on promontories near vast meadows. Access to a water source and the presence of lowland were the important factors of village location.

In several cases, Petrovka fortified settlements were implanted over the Sintashta settlements.[13] The ground within the defensive line is densely built up. Blocks of several houses having a common roof, separated by streets or walls, are recorded there. Unlike the Sintashta sites, the Petrovka settlements have a linear street layout. Fortifications vary greatly. For example, in the Kulevchy site the fortification was practically symbolic being represented only by a simple enclosure. A full-scale defensive system, as at the Usty'e settlement, consists of a wood and earthen wall with a ditch (Vinogradov 1995a: 17).

The above-ground and mainly rectangular houses at the Petrovka settlements were of a frame-pillar construction and were adjacent to the defensive wall as at the Sintashta sites. They are usually of a standard size within a settlement but vary in general between 80 and 160 m². [14] The corridor-shaped and ramplike entrances were in the corner of the house and fronted on the street that separates two blocks. The interiors were likely to be divided into partitions. The floors of the northern Kazakhstan houses preserved the traces of clay daub; those of the Urals provided traces of wooden planking. Child burials are found underneath house floors. A well and an oven furnished each house. The number of wells, which are usually situated along one long wall within a house module, can vary, but it is likely that only one functioned at a time. We think that the interior was laid out before the walls were erected. As mentioned earlier, the ovens of the Petrovka houses are numerous and often used in the metallurgical process. Ovens are well marked by stone foundations. The Petrovka pottery is also found in the open villages of the Late Bronze Age (Nelin 2000). This is especially true for the central Kazakhstan region.

Hence, on the one hand, the Petrovka settlement architecture has much in common with that of the Sintashta culture, but, on the other hand, it demonstrates the clearly visible tendency to a decline in sophistication. The linear layout of settlements looks like the intermediate stage in their development toward the open villages of the Late Bronze Age with their freestanding houses.

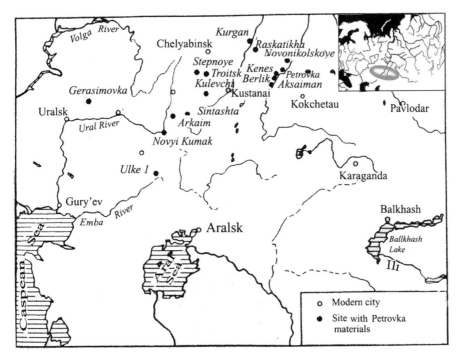

Figure 2.18. Distribution of the sites with Petrovka materials.

The settlements of the Petrovka culture produce abundant collections of fragmented pottery, animal bones, and metal objects among which tools are dominant (Fig. 1.7). The majority of metal objects are manufactured from pure copper, secondarily by tin bronze, and there are a few tin–arsenic alloys.[15] Although the second group of alloys is typical of the Late Bronze Age, tin bronze was not in wide use at the beginning. The ore deposits located between the Mugodzhary Mountains and central Kazakhstan could have served as a resource basis for the Petrovka metallurgy (Degtyareva et al. 2001: 34–5). As mentioned earlier, the chemical composition of the Petrovka metal is essentially different from that of the Abashevo and Sintashta cultures and closely akin to the Alakul metal.

The Petrovka-culture mortuary sites have been well studied, especially in the Urals. The first Petrovka burials were investigated by the early 1960s (Matveyeva 1962; Stokolos 1962), but the situation became clearer after excavation of outstanding cemeteries such as Alabuga and Raskatikha (Potyemkina 1985), Krivoye Ozero and Kulevchy-VI (Vinogradov 1984; 2000), Stepnoye-7, and Troitsk (Kostukov & Epimakhov 1999). Only the Krivoye Ozero cemetery displays a definite connection with a settlement: this is Chernorechy'e-III with its closed rectangular layout.[16] The Kulevchy-VI cemetery is related to the Kulevchy-III village, where the elements of fortification are, however, rather vague.

The cemeteries of the Petrovka culture occupy the first river terraces. It is hardly possible to estimate credibly the full size of the actual necropolis.

However, it is clear that together with large cemeteries comprising dozens of kurgans there were smaller ones with three–five mounds. A number of the Petrovka burials have been discovered in multiperiod cemeteries.

The kurgans are relatively small: 0.5–0.7 m in height and 20–25 m in diameter. Very often, they are hardly traceable in the surface, and only large-scale and all-over excavations allow archaeologists to determine the cemetery structure as has been demonstrated at the Troitsk-7 site. We can, however, state that above-grave constructions were built of wood and earth; stone was used only sporadically as rectangular fences.

The Petrovka kurgans usually contain many burials, although there are exceptions to this rule. Two variants of spatial structure are inherent to them: (1) based on a central-periphery principle and (2) linear. The former is a continuation of the Sintashta tradition, the origin of the latter is not clear. If in the Sintashta culture, we saw a parallelism in the layout scheme of the settlement and funeral sites, then in Petrovka we do not. Transformation of the settlement planography has entailed the changes in the funeral practice. Sometimes a kurgan could be delimited by a small circular ditch – very rarely by a stone fence, but very often without any archaeologically visible demarcation. Some of the later burials were arranged on the periphery including the ditch; others were inserted in the mound without any relation to the center.

The deceased represent all sex and age gradations, but those interred in the Petrovka cemeteries almost never reached the age of fifty. The grave size also depended on the burial character (collective or individual). Statistically, the grave pits are shallower than those of the Sintashta culture. The people were buried in a contracted position on the left side and oriented either to the west or to the east. In paired burials, the deceased laid facing each other.

As a rule, the center of a kurgan was marked by a large and deep tomb containing the remains of one, two, or several adult persons. All of these burials have been robbed. However, the large graves have preserved not only rather rich inventories but also some construction details. The tombs were furnished with wooden constructions: roofing, frames, and wall covering, which were fixed by vertical pillars. In the Troitsk-7 cemetery, traces of evidence that the grave was partitioned into three sections and made of wooden boards was found.[17]

Like the Sintashta cemeteries, the Petrovka kurgans produced abundant animal sacrifices, essential parts of which were outside the burial chamber either on the paleo-surface or in special pits, which seem to bear no relation to actual burials. Wild animals were not used for sacrifice.

In Kazakhstan, the horse-paired burials are well known imitating a paired-horse harness that was usually arranged to the west of the grave. The Urals' animal sacrifices are highly complex; horses were given to men, sheep accompanied the children. Here, the "charioteer complex" is also well documented archaeologically by the traces of wheels[18] on the grave floors,

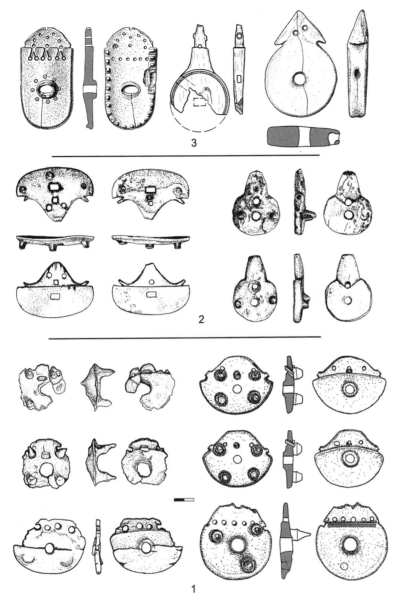

Figure 2.19. Bronze Age cheek-pieces: (1) Sintashta type; (2) Petrovka type; (3) Alakul type.

cheek-pieces, and horse remains. At the same time, the shield-horn cheek-pieces were being transformed through a reduction of number and size of the thorns, and general simplification (Fig. 2.19).

Male burials produce objects of weaponry: spearheads, battle-axes, bone and stone arrowheads, stone maces; the female graves produce ornaments: grooved bracelets, double twisted pendants, oval- and crosslike pendants, and metal and paste beads. In addition all graves yielded an abundance of pottery.

Flat-bottomed pots with profiled or straight walls and a series of mixed forms characterized by talc and chamotte temper represent the Petrovka ceramics (Fig. 2.20). In certain respects, this pottery resembles the Abashevo and early Srubnaya ceramics, although it is more decorated (about 40 percent of the pots were completely covered with incised decoration), with zigzags, wavy lines, and hatched triangles. Vessels with a sharply carinated body are common. Pots were manufactured on a model for which the old pots were covered by cloth. They differed from the Sintashta pots by the absence of an internal "rib" in the transition from neck to shoulder and the external roll under the rim. A relatively limited number of elements composed the zonal ornamental scheme: diagonal shaded isosceles triangles, horizontal zigzags, and horizontal lines, made with the tracing of a flat comb stamp. One can easily see that the Petrovka pottery complex has its stable traditions, which contrast with Sintashta pottery-making with its great variability.

WHAT WAS BEHIND THE SINTASHTA AND PETROVKA ANTIQUITIES?

It would not be a mistake to say that the above-described archaeological materials with their outstanding characteristics have often bewildered scholars and have been hotly discussed.

The first questions asked after having gained an acquaintance with the sites of the Sintashta and Petrovka cultural formations concern the basic material and social structures, and the ideology of people whose experience is imprinted in their sites. The second group of queries is connected with the interpretation of the cultural situation at the very beginning of the second millennium BC. This was very much dependent on the role of the Sintashta culture and its relationship with the Petrovka culture. In addition, of course, many scholars are interested in their ethnic interpretation. However, we will touch on the last point only to a very small extent because we do not consider ourselves experts in this domain. Some aspects of interpretation will be highlighted in other chapters jn this book.

Economic Sphere

Pastoral livestock breeding was the basis of the of the Sintashta economy. That statement is not in any doubt: all sites without exception yield a great number of animal bones. The economy of the Petrovka communities has much in common with Sintashta but with a few differences.

Archeozoologists (Gaiduchenko 1993; Kosintsev & Varov 1995) regard the probable herd composition of the Middle Bronze period as evidence of its limited mobility. The bones of big horned cattle are quite dominant (46–60 percent) in the osteological collections coming from Sintashta settlements.

Figure 2.20. Petrovka type pottery from burial grounds.

The archaeozoological collections of the Petrovka sites demonstrate some rise in the proportion of sheep bones and a shortage of cow bones, although the latter were still dominant – 45–50 percent (Kosintsev 2000).

The problems arise when we try to imagine how a stockbreeding economy functioned and was organized; what were its forms. There is no direct evidence concerning a special selective activity that could be connected with intensive economic development: the breeding technology is not visible through the tool complex.

This picture is different if we depart from the idea of a specialized character of the Sintashta and Petrovka economy and focus on metallurgical production with cattle serving as the means of payment for metal. Theoretically, one can suppose that cattle obtained from the outside as a result of such exchange

TABLE 2.3. *Distribution of bones of domestic animals from the sites of the Sintashta and Petrovka cultures (southern Urals and northern Kazakhstan, percent) (after Kosintsev 2000)*

Species				Sites			
	Arkaim	Sintashta	Mirny IV	Petrovka-II	Kulevchi-III	Novoni-Kolskoye-I	Ushkatta
Bos Taurus	60,4	46,2	67,5	46,6	49,8	56.0	43,4
Ovis aries and Capra hircus	24,2	8,1	26,2	27,6	39,2	26,3	41,3
Equus caballus	15,4	5,7	6,3	25,8	11	17,7	15,3
Number of bones	6782	829	1425	2715	5108	3404	843

might skew the picture of animal age distribution because of a decrease of young individuals. However, this question has not been investigated so far. It is also not easy to assess the exchange role.

By contrast, some selective activity can be exemplified by a variety of different morphological types of animals discovered in the Bolshekaraganski cemetery: runty and semi-thick-legged (8.3 percent), runty and semi-thin-legged (25 percent), middle and semi-thick legged (8.3 percent), middle, and semi-thin-legged (41.67 percent) that corresponded to their economic utility (Gaiduchenko 2002c).

There is no doubt that the number of animals was limited by the ecological capacity of a given territory; an excessive number of animals would have quickly led to pasture degradation. Taking 20–30 km as the average distance between fortresses into consideration, it is possible to outline the "territorial districts" as 1300–2800 km². So far, there are no strong models for pastoral husbandry accounting for the ecological capacity of pasture. Therefore, we must refer to the material of later pastoralists, who worked out an optimal variant of pasture use. According to Zhelezchkov's (1983) estimation, ideally the territory of 500000 km² could feed two million sheep or 150,000 horses or 120,000 cows.

Archeozoological collections yielded from excavations of the Sintashta sites demonstrate the following quantitative proportion of animal bones: big-horned livestock – up to 60 percent, small-horned livestock – 30 percent, horse – up to 15 percent (see Table 2.3) (Gaiduchenko 2002b; Kosintsev 2000). Gaiduchenko (2002b) thinks that the portion of the latter was higher, and in most of the excavated settlements (except Bersuat) the horse was in second place after cattle.

However, we can conditionally rely on these data as a departure point to estimate the probable number of animals that might have subsisted on a "terri-torial district" of 2000 km². Therefore, the probable number of animals would be twenty-four hundred sheep, three hundred cows, and sixty horses. Because of the limited mobility of the population, the use of the whole territory is unlikely. As is known from ethnography, a pastoralist needs about one hundred hectares of territory for his subsistence. Therefore, the Sintashta district could nourish about two thousand people in conditions of a nomadic economy, but, for the Bronze Age, this figure should have been lower because of a much less mobile form of livestock breeding. According to Gaiduchenko's calculation (2002a: 412), the Sintashta pastures were located not further than a few dozen kilometres from the settlements.

The cattle of the Sintashta and Petrovka cultures were mainly hornless. Gaiduchenko (1995, 2002c: 412) relates the origin of these cattle with the regions of more ancient breeding, from the south. Horse breeding was aimed at the development and use of the horse's working qualities: speed and energy. It was used only partly as meat. The preliminary isotopic analysis demonstrates that horse meat or milk was not of great importance in the diets of these people (from the Bolshekaraganski cemetery), although cattle and sheep meat and milk were significant dietary staples (Privat 2002). Sheep and the small number of goats provided wool (Gaiduchenko 2002c; Kosintsev 2000).

The natural biological resources of the area in question supplemented the needs of the local population: the remains of almost all wild animals and fish were found in the sites. The same relates to the floral remains, which represents the whole spectrum of vegetation of this landscape, except oak and plum, which supposedly were imported (Gaiduchenko 2002b).

The latest finds of millet grains[19] and traces of a cultivated field (supposedly) at Arkaim[20] and Alandskoye allow some scholars (Zdanovich 1995) to argue the idea that the Sintashta population also was engaged in agricultural activity. Gaiduchenko (2002b), who studied the plant remains and content of vessels, thinks that cereal played a significant role in the nutrition of the inhabitants of the Sintashta settlements. Still, the conditions and specifics of the zonal taphonomic process in the Eurasian steppe negatively influences grain preservation. However, taking into account the severe climatic conditions of this area, one cannot expect to find that this kind of economy would be greatly developed. This thesis is partly supported by the absence of large storage facilities. Until cultivation is proved by a large series of analysis, it will always be under some doubt. We can, however say, at least generally, that the inhabitants of some Sintashta settlements were acquainted with elements of cultivation.

Metallurgy and metalworking are highly technical fields, depending on necessary qualifications and group or individual specialization as well as on the availability of natural resources. At the same time, specialists pay attention to the technical level of metal processing, which was still relatively low; many necessary skills were still developing and thus are reflected in the large proportion of waste articles in the collections (Degtyareva et al. 2001).

Some particular case studies illuminate the changes in economic development, which occurred at the beginning of the second millennium BC. A case in point is the study of textile imprints on pottery. Chernai analyzed a series from pots of the Eneolithic and Bronze Age that came from the southern Urals and northern Kazakhstan. According to his observation, the development of nonwoven textiles, which were characteristic for the local Eneolithic cultures, stopped and did not reach the advanced level seen in eastern Europe. These felt textiles were replaced by semiwoven textiles, which were not known in this area earlier. These changes paralleled changes in ceramic technology: the pot's body was formed on a model with the use of textiles, and then the potter attached a shoulder and neck. Chernai (1985: 109) says that so rapid a change in technology could only happen as a result of a rise in the productive economy and technological innovations brought from the outside. This method of pottery modeling was in use later in the Alakul and Srubnaya cultural traditions. Usachuk (2002) also deduced an interesting conclusion from his detailed investigation of the technology of shield cheek-piece manufacturing. He is sure that specialized artisans made all these articles. In addition, there is no doubt that chariot making was a specialized craft.

There were some other economic fields including pottery making, leather processing, weaving, and so on, which were likely to have been carried out at the domestic level.

Summing up, we can expect that this economy could provide not only subsistence but also a surplus, based on the a great number of sacrificed animals lavishly represented by bones found in burial grounds. Where and how could this surplus be spent? Who was responsible for its distribution? These questions are closely related to the question of the nature of Sintashta-Petrovka society. Did that society have an elite element? Livestock breeding as a major branch did not require strong centralization and constant control from the elite side. Control over the mineral resources and long distance exchange seems more likely to need an elite group. At a certain stage, these functions could be performed by special group of "managers-warriors." Settlement setting also required an organizational activity, but archaeological material does not provide us with unambiguous information.

Social Contrasts

In Sintashta society, there was a sophisticated system of fortifications at the settlements that was organized into regular blocks of houses. These astonishing sites had clear regular planning; all details had been thoroughly thought out. This planning would not have been possible without some organizing power and societal knowledge adequate to follow that power. Many interpretations have been suggested in relation to the Arkaim site – military fort, proto-city, proto-town, and ceremonial and religious center. The latter hypothesis appears reasonable if we bear in mind that the set of artifacts found in the site

was not typical for intensive everyday use. It is not easier to accept the interpretation put forward by those researchers who regard sites such as Arkaim
as administrative and ceremonial centers, where people (about one to two
thousand), apart from some craftsmen and aristocracy, gathered periodically to
perform rituals (Berezkin 1995). It is difficult to imagine how such a number
of people could live all at once within such a close and limited space over
a long period of time. However, it is also possible that so far we simply do
not have appropriate historical or ethnographic models for this interpretation.
In any case, it appears that some of the fortresses were one-layer settlements
(Arkaim) and others (Kuisak), have traces of reconstruction and were reset-
tled two or more times. In Zdanovich and Batanina's opinion (2002: 137),
the defence function of the fortifications was of primary significance. However, we still do not know who the enemies were. Some scholars (Medvedev
2002a; Pyankov 2002) also support a mythological meaning for the settlements. In particular, they pointed out the similarity between Arkaim and cult
complexes such as Dashly 3, Kuldug-tepe in Afghanistan and temple-fortress
Koy-Krylagan-Kala in Chorasmia, on the one hand, and between them and
the Avestan town *Var* that was built by *Yima*[21] in order to save people, on the
other.

Nevertheless, a proto-type for circular fortified settlements, containing central squares and houses siding on a wall, is known in the Early Bronze Age in
Anatolia, the Aegean, and South-Eastern Europe (Korfmann 1983; Merpert
1995a, 1995b; Yakar 1985). According to Kuzmina (1994), similar fortresses of
a circular layout dating from the second quarter of the second millennium BC
have been discovered in other regions (e.g., the Crimea and the Don Valley)
and could stem from the idea of a military camp, which existed in the steppes
for a long time.

It is interesting to take Korfmann's interpretation of Demircihuyuk in
Anatolia, which demonstrates a striking similarity with Arkaim:

> The construction of row houses at Demircihuyuk offered the residents the
> advantage of modest expenditure in construction and additional insulation
> in the winter. Such collective architectural planning had its disadvantages.
> Its disadvantages lay in the fact that, should any one house need repair, the
> roofs of all would be affected; this also was true, for example, in the event
> of fire. Cooperative effort at Demircihuyuk is apparent not only in the
> domestic architecture but also to an even greater degree in the conception
> of the embanked fortification wall. The existence of an architectural tra-
> dition that is, of an established building pattern, postulates the affluence as
> well. This architectural system implied that both material and labor stood
> in reserve for anyone who for any reason was unable to contribute his share
> toward the renovation of his dwelling. Overall, as well as the the impor-
> tance of wealth, communal solidarity must have been valued (Korfmann
> 1983).[22]

There is no doubt that continuity of this architectural tradition, which lasted for at least two hundred years, is evidence for a stable and strong social organization.

However, it is not easy to recognize any differences between the fortified settlements in size or complexity. Differences in form are explained by chronology (Zdanovich & Batanina 1995), but the idea of chronology does not seem to us seriously grounded because the great majority of settlements have not yet been studied. For the time being, there is also not enough evidence about the "agricultural neighborhood" – some groups of open settlements as satellites of the fortresses. According to preliminary observation, they did exist, but we must be cautious until excavations produce results and these results are analyzed. There is no doubt that the basic part of economic activity (pasturing and mining) – not to mention hunting, fishing, and gathering – occurred outside the fortification. It is probable that ceramic fragments found in various parts of the Arkaim Valley document this activity as well.

The analysis of mortuary remains produces further controversial ideas. On the one hand, funeral sites of the Sintashta cultural continuum show that burial practices were associated with a new system of prestige and its symbolic expression had been established. This system was based on communal ritual, but with visible symbolism relating to some individuals as well. Animal sacrifices (mostly cattle and horses) became an essential part of this rite and most of them were connected with a specific person or persons. Researchers distinguish three kinds of animal sacrifices: those that were represented by whole animals, those that were for the owner's destination, and those connected with communal rituals. The first were placed under the funeral chamber's roof, the second were usually next to the grave (in a special pit), and the third were concentrated in special places within the funeral area (Gening et al. 1992; Sinuk & Kozmirchuk 1995; Zdanovich & Gaiduchenko 2002). The burials differ by the number and kinds of sacrificed animals. Some people were accompanied by one or two animals or their parts; others were buried with a number of animals (Gening et al. 1992). Indexes of a biomass of sacrificed animals and consumed amount of meat calculated by Gaiduchenko and Zdanovich (2000) correlates with the age, sex, and social position of the buried persons. D. Zdanovich (2005:15) notices thatchild burials were accompanied by about 25 times less animal matter than adult male burials, possibly because a child's buriel would attract fewer mourners thus less meat was consumed. Female burials were given a smaller amount of animals compared with males. The biggest sacrifices connected with some distinguished persons included up to twelve animals (Stepnoye 7–4, Sintashta and Khripunovo cemeteries). The funeral of such persons could attract hundreds of people. Another relevant fact is that male burials containing weaponry objects, chariots, and harness elements indicate a military makeup. We also can refer to such objects as stone maces and bone "spades" (Plate 2.6–2), which were definitely of prestige character.

At first glance, the burial grounds that have been studied look homogeneous in terms of wealth differentiation. No cemeteries can be determined as a separate necropolis of the high social stratum. Burials are undoubtedly characterized by some variation in the number and composition of grave goods, but this variation is not striking. We cannot see clear property stratification, although most scholars believe in the existence of an elite (Bochkarev 1995a; Vasily'ev et al. 1992). Attempts to confirm this statement (Epimakhov 2002b; Zdanovich 1997a) have resulted in the conclusion that: (1) an elite was not materialized during "a lifetime" (there are no traces of its existence in the settlements, and the traces are not numerous in the ritual); and (2) Sintashta funeral rituals represent, first of all, sex and age gradations, and less visibly social positions.

Despite this, the rather stable presence of charioteer graves in the communal cemeteries testifies to the fact that the people, who definitely had a different status, shared the same living conditions with other members of society. Interesting results relating to the male and female social roles were obtained from the excavation and anthropological examination of the Bestamak cemetery in western Kazakhstan. Logvin (2002) writes, that the uniform standard of internment in single male and female burials suggests that men and women of the Bestamak community had much in common in public status. At the same time, an analysis of grave good composition allowed him to distinguish the social group, which is represented by burials of men owning the axe-adzes, indicating higher status than other members of the community (Fig. 2.21).

As stated earlier, a relatively high level of metallurgy and metalworking is well documented. Pieces of slag, ore, drops of metal, and metalworking tools are found in some burials (Epimakhov 1996).

Meanwhile, simple demographic calculations (Epimakhov 2002a) demonstrate that only a third of the dead were honored with the privilege of being buried under kurgans. It is important to note that all age-sex groups were found and the level of mortality is near normal.[23] Therefore, the rest of society was buried in a different way.

Because not all the deceased members of this society are accessible to archaeological investigation, a reconstructed societal structure based on funeral sites can only be incomplete and skewed. However, all conclusions about the level of Sintashta society must rely on the results of mortuary sites.

At the same time, the Sintashta burials that produce an abundance of sacrificed animals and grave goods, are distinctive compared with other steppe and forest-steppe Bronze Age sites. Although the number of luxury goods is limited, scholars interpret some goods (maces, battle-axes, spearheads, chariots) as markers of power. Such objects found at the sites of the European Neolithic and later Iron Age are considered signs of social power and features of a chiefdom level (Bradley 1991; Kristiansen 1991).

A simple conclusion can be drawn from this situation: the elite part of society can be distinguished only if we regard some categories of goods, amount and sophistication of animal sacrifice, and the central locality of graves as markers of social status. D. Zdanovich (1997), who has analyzed the funeral ritual of Sintashta society, states that although the society "knew" the institute of elite, elites were not dramatically distinguished from others, at least from the evidence of the kurgan burials. We think that the Sintashta elite's main function was administrative and organizational, including and perhaps, first of all, ceremonial activity, which seems to have been of great significance in Sintashta society.

It is difficult to determine the number and proportion of societal strata in Sintashta society. Yet, we can state that ranking, as a characteristic of complexity, is visible especially in regard to the specialization of economic activity. One also can suppose that part of the population could have had easier access to material resources, as it has been described in some theoretical works (Carneiro 1981; Kristiansen 1991; Tainter 1988), but again archaeological representation of such social characteristics is not univocal.

The specific attributes of the Sintashta archaeological complex can be characterized by the following: (1) systemic character of site localizations; (2) highly organized settlements with elaborated fortifications and sectional architectural planning; (3) complex burial sites with a high concentration of the remains of sophisticated ritual practice comprised of several variations in the association between human bodies and animals; and (4) the significant presence of metal objects, weaponry, wheeled transport of rather advanced construction for that time, and an eclectic set of ceramics.

Social complexity is usually connected to specialized production, the monumental character and variation of architecture, settlement hierarchy, increase in the size of the society, and the stratification of funeral ritual. The Sintashta society was much more complex than aboriginal post-Eneolithic society based on nonproductive economies.[24] Although the settlement sizes do not correspond to the Near Eastern proto–urban standards, they are comparable with some towns of the Asia Minor, some of which, like the Troy II, were not more than 2 ha (Masson 1989). Although at present level of our knowledge it is unlikely possible to measurably assess the level of the Sintashta society, one cannot deny that such a concentration of population within rather compact territory (60000 km²) is outstanding against the usual steppe landscape occupancy.

Some social groups existed that were partly or fully involved in different fields of economic production, including crafts and the management of settlement planning and construction, as well as the organization of religious ceremonies. It is worth mentioning that an emphasis on ritual activity points to a close connection among leadership, hierarchy, and religion (Wason & Baldia 2000: 224).

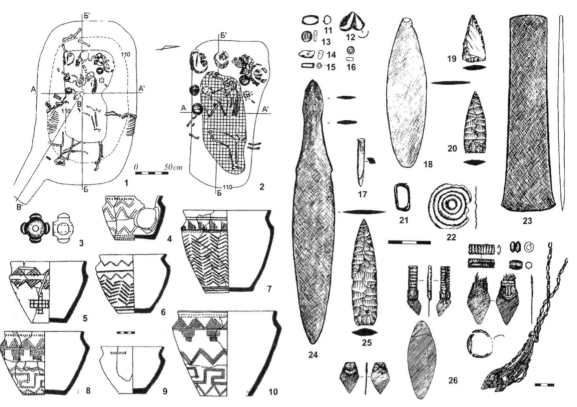

Figure 2.21. The Bestamak burial ground: double burial from pit 5 with pottery and mace-head: (1) burial of three horses; (2) male-female burial; (3) stone mace-head; (4–10) pots; (11–26) grave goods from male-female burial; (11, 13–16) necklace ornaments; (12) pendant; (13) bronze nail; (18) knife; (19, 20, 25) flint arrowheads; (21) bracelet; (22) flat plaque; (23) axe-adze; (24) bronze knife; (26) plait covering (after Logvin 2002).

It appears that the Petrovka society was slightly different from that of Sintashta. At least this seems evident for the Urals area. The size of settlements and, consequently, their demographic capacities, are somewhat comparable. There are differences in the scale of structural complexity between the various rectangular settlements, that is to say, we deal with gradual cultural simplification. It is hardly possible to rank the population using only materials from the settlement. The burial grounds, however, show the process of societal changes.

One can see that the new order determines the formation of the funeral site. Pottery prototypes were also well established. During the Sintashta time, only a portion of the dead were buried under "kurgan" mounds; during the Petrovka periods, the situation was different. The individual graves of children arranged in the kurgan's periphery become more numerous. The number of grave goods accompanying the children becomes fewer. The same tendency, although not in such an expressive manner, is seen in adult burials. In other words, during the Petrovka period, the labor investment in the funeral practice definitely decreases.

The Petrovka series of burials do produce some prestige goods, especially, weapons (which are, however, less numerous). Nevertheless, it seems that some sort of "individualization" takes place: the number of individual adult graves rises and grave goods are more specifically attached to the individual. One can suppose that a kin component (not only by blood but also by marriage) of social relations comes to play a more significant role in the Petrovka societies.

The probable ethnic attribution of the Sintashta sites has been the center of scholarly interest practically from the first publications (Gening 1977; Smirnov & Kuzmina 1977). Gening and Kuzmina thoroughly explored the Indo-Iranian hypothesis. The list of arguments can be added when comparing the hierarchy of sacrificed animals used in Sintashta funeral rituals with an analogous list reconstructed from written sources such as the *Rig Veda* and *Avesta* (Zdanovich 2005). The Sintashta funeral rituals of offering exactly correspond to the Indo-Iranian hierarchy of ritual significance of three basic animals – horse, bull, and sheep. The dog (wolf) burials do not contradict this attribution. The location of this kind of animal between the grave bottom (underworld) and daily surface (living world) does not look accidental. The mediating functions of a dog between the worlds of the living and dead are well known (Kerberos, four-eyed dog of the *Avesta*). Jones-Bley (2002), who examined the Indo-European burial ritual as it is presented in the *Rig Veda* and *Avesta*, compared it with archaeological materials and concluded, "The Sintashta burials include all the elements that go into the main body of Indo-European burial and also includes what has been regarded as an aberration, that of excarnation" (Jones-Bley 2002: 78).

The Origin and Ultimate Fate of the Sintashta Cultural Core-Tradition

We think that the historical fate of the Sintashta population is closely connected to its genesis. In general, the following model can represent, in some sense, the origin of Sintashta society.

At the end of the Middle Bronze Age, a destructive shift ushered in the transformation of the Circumpontic metallurgical network that had functioned with large-scale connections between the southern and northern cultural areas. This destruction concerned not only the Catacombnaya cultural formation, whose heritage is somewhat reflected in Sintashta sites, but also the entire eastern European steppe-forest-steppe. Some scholars explain the displacement of the bearers of the Catacombnaya tradition from the northern Caucasus to the Pontic steppes by migrational processes which swept over the Circum-Pontic and Aegean area at the turn of the third and second millennia BC (Chernykh 1989: 24; Zdanovich 2005: 17).

Destruction does not mean that all cultural prototypes were abolished, if the point is not to annihilate the bearers of tradition. In extreme situations, the system of social priorities is changed, and some prototypes, which were on the periphery of social consciousness, are generated or are culturally selected. It is worthwhile to refer to the climatic factor as well. Specialists state that in the early second millennium BC, the area of the Sintashta culture experienced maximum aridity, spread of saline soils and deforesterization (Lavrushin & Spiridonova 1999; Zdanovich & Zdanovich 2002). This factor could push the mechanism of migration and produce radical change in social and economic strategies.

Despite the different origins of its initial components, the Sintashta culture that formed in the South Trans-Urals, introduced new traditions of settlement, funeral architecture, and the rapid development of metallurgy. We can suppose a synchronic appearance of Mnogovalikovaya Ceramic, Abashevo, and Sintashta cultures resulting from the destruction of the old cultures of the Middle Bronze Age. The spasmodic character of metallurgical development, building construction, and woodworking is well represented. The remains of chariots, the production of which could have taken place locally, are evidence of this.

All of these cultural occurrences are connected with the southern part of the Circumpontic and adjacent areas, namely, the Caucasus and Balkans. The very characteristic attribute of the Sintashta and Petrovka cultural tradition – sophisticated system of animal offering and sacrifice – has no parallels in local cultures, but its closest forms (indeed, not identical) can be found also in the Catacombnaya culture sites (Gei 1999; Sinuk 1996; Zdanovich 2005).

The genesis of the Petrovka core-tradition is clearly connected with that of Sintashta. No one doubts this. The questions under discussion are about the degree of the contribution of aboriginal groups of central and northern Kazakhstan in the formation of regional variants as well as the chronological relationship between them and the partial synchronization of the Kazakhstan sites with those of Sintashta.

The Petrovka culture is also closely connected with the Alakul culture (see Chapter 3). Here, however, there is some disagreement between scholars. Most scholars share the hypothesis suggested by G. Zdanovich (1973) and developed by Vinogradov (1982) about the Petrovka origin of the Alakul tradition. However, some archaeologists do not rule out their separation and prefer to put an equal sign between the terms "Petrovka" and "Early Alakul" (Vinogradov 1983). An alternative position is held by Potyemkina (1995), who thinks that the Alakul culture was primarily based on the Eneolithic groups of the Trans-Uralian forest-steppe, yet the Petrovka elements played a secondary role. Grigory'ev (2000a) claims that the Alakul prototypes originated with the Cis-Urals Sintashta variant.

Hence, we should confess that there is no common opinion about the taxonomic level of all the antiquities described earlier or about the interpretation of some sites. It can be explained by the series of real similarities between Petrovka and Alakul materials, on one side, and by the fact that many sites are of a mixed character. Additionally, the images of both cultures were formed, above all, on the burial materials and, especially, on the pottery.[25] The investigation of settlements always complicates an analysis that is reflected sometimes in such a concept as the "Sintashta-Petrovka" culture.

Nevertheless, we are convinced that the Petrovka and Sintashta sites are distinctive. Their synchronic character is proved for the Urals. In central and northern Kazakhstan, Sintashta sites are not known, and, thus, the Petrovka materials do in fact indicate the beginning of the real Bronze Age in this area.[26]

As we stated earlier, the chronological position of the Petrovka culture is well established by aerial photography analysis and the stratigraphy of some settlements and cemeteries. The excavation of the Usty'e settlement (Vinogradov 1995a) confirms these observations. Kurgan 10 of the Krivoye Ozero cemetery produced the same stratigraphy demonstrating the later position of the Petrovka complex in relation to the Sintashta complex. Tkachev (1998), who studied the Cis-Urals materials, came to a similar conclusion.

When investigating the correlation between the Petrovka and Alakul cultures, we have less expressive evidence. As Matveyev (1998) states about the cemeteries of the Middle Tobol area, the Petrovka features gradually played out during the early stages of the Alakul culture. The stratigraphy of the Troitsk-7 cemetery confirms this statement (Kostukov & Epimakhov 1999).

Summing up, the many elements of the Sintashta cultural complex have no local roots in the southern Trans-Urals; their parallels lead us to the west and southwest. However, these elements have got a systemic character here, in the Uralian land.

THE CULTURAL FORMATIONS IN THE FOREST ZONE

The interrelations of societies possessing a more advanced economy (livestock-breeding and metallurgy) with post-Neolithic and Eneolithic local groups constituted an essential part of the cultural process occurring in the forest zone in the Early and Middle Bronze Age. These contacts covered the entire zone of leafed forest and southern taiga of eastern Europe and western Siberia. Yet, because the cultural processes in the forest zone are usually much slower and less expressive then in the south, it is hard to find unambiguous results in the gradually developing local cultures.

Cis-Urals Subarea

While the cultures of the southern part of central Eurasia were rapidly transformed, those of the north continued in the traditional patterns until the more radical changes paralleled by the emergence of the Yamnaya complexes on the steppe and Abashevo in the forest-steppe occurred. We will briefly describe them just to show contrasts, which divided the southern and northern areas (Fig. 2.5-A).

In the major part of the forest zone, the Eneolithic period lasted until the beginning of the second millennium BC. The cultures evolved slowly, although in a general sense this process was associated with great economic changes. The southern areas were under the influence of productive economies, the elements of which were introduced into the traditional hunting and fishing mode of life. The first bronze objects that appeared in the early second millennium BC marked the beginning of the Bronze Age.

Archaeologists reveal two cultural and archaeological subareas in the forest zone of north-central Eurasia that were situated on both sides of the Ural Mountains − Volga-Uralian and Trans-Uralian-Kazakhstan − in which several regional variants are revealed (Shorin 1999). All of these were united by traditions of combed geometric patterns in pottery decoration.

The hypothesis that this area was inhabited by proto-Finno-Ugrian speakers is commonly accepted: the Volga-Ural subarea is connected with the beginning of Finno-Permian linguistic group; the Trans-Uralian subarea is attributed to the proto-Ugrian and Samoyed speaker populations. These statements derive from the general theory of the origin of the Uralian peoples, largely based on linguistics, linguistic-paleontological approach,[27] archaeology, and ethnography (Fodor 1975; Goldina 1999; Hajdu 1985; Napolskikh 1997; Shorin 1999). We have no reason to disbelieve these.

According to this theory, the disintegration of the Uralian proto-language occurred from the sixth to the late fifth millennia BC, proto-Finno-Ugric was divided into two main branches (proto-Finno-Permic and proto-Ugric) within the period of second half of the third millennium BC, and the proto-Ugric spread out into the northern and southern branches by the end of the second millennium BC.

Archaeological materials show that in the forest zone, subsistence was based on the effective hunting of big hoofed animals (reindeer, elk, antelope, wild pig, bear, and beaver), gathering,[28] and productive fishing (sturgeon, grayling, pike, chub, idus, tench, etc.). The remains of special sophisticated instruments (hooks, harpoons, and nets) and an abundant quantity of fish bones and skin bear witness to this. These people built rather large wooden houses that were connected to each other and with farmyards by roofed passages (Goldina 1999). Rectangular houses were arranged in rows along the riverbanks.

Metal objects were obtained from the Caucasus center through the Balanovo and Abashevo groups during the early second millennium BC. Later, as the analysis demonstrates, metal objects were made from local sandy copper stones. The metal from the Kama area reflects the formation of the earliest, but still primitive, local metallurgy in the forest Cis-Urals area (Chernykh 1970; Kuzminykh

1977). As a result of the high level of hunting and fishing, which assured a stable food supply, and gradual rise of productive economy, demographic parameters of local societies were augmented. Archaeologists record the settlement concentrations (open villages) usually at the confluence of the rivers. However, these villages could not house more than a few hundred people; these small communities were based on kinship relations as it was illustrated by ancient words denoting "kin" and "kinship" in the Finno-Ugric vocabulary (Hajdu 1985: 186).

Significant events occurred in the forest zone of eastern Europe in the Early Bronze Age. These events were provoked by the eastward diffusion of cattle breeders and farmers, such as the Corded Ware and other similar cultures. The early sites of these latter were similar to each other in pottery design, stone tools, and funeral ritual allowing them to unite into cultural and historical formations, which occupied the vast territory from the eastern Baltic and southwest Finland to the Middle Volga and Kama areas.

Russian scholars consider the diffusion of the eastern European Corded Ware cultures as a long process of segmentation and settling in the new territories that may have been caused by ecological factors (Bader et al. 1987). Characteristic features of all eastern European Corded Ware cultures show flat and kurgan burials containing crouched skeletons, accompanied mostly by globular short-necked vessels and stone battle-axes.

We will only briefly dwell on the northeast province of the Balanovo culture as the most eastern culture of the Corded Ware massive occupying the Kama-Vyatka-Vetluga interfluves (Fig. 2.5–1). It was discovered in the nineteenth century and first was considered as a variant of the Fatyanovo culture. Hundreds of sites – villages, cemeteries, and numerous stone axes found by chance, represent the Balanovo culture. The sites are usually situated on the high hills of the riverbanks. The villages consisted of several above-ground houses (16–28 m^2) built from wooden logs with saddle roofs, and joined by passages (Fig. 2.22–2, 5).

The cemeteries are both of the flat and kurgan type, containing both individual and collective graves. Men were buried on the right side, women on the left side, both in contracted position (Fig. 2.23). The dead were wrapped in animal skins or birch bark and placed into wooden constructions. The funeral chambers were arranged in the ground in rectangular pits. The bones of domestic pigs and sheep as well as copper ornaments and tools have been found in Balanovo graves together with the human skeletons (Fig. 2.24). The set of grave goods depended on sex, age, and social position: copper axes only accompanied only persons of a high social position; stone axe-hammers (Fig. 2.22–4) were given to men and teenagers, flint axes to everyone, including children and women, except the chiefs. Many amulets are found in the graves as well.

Recent investigations demonstrate that the Balanovo archaeological layers are basically connected with or overlapping the late Volosovo and Garinskaya

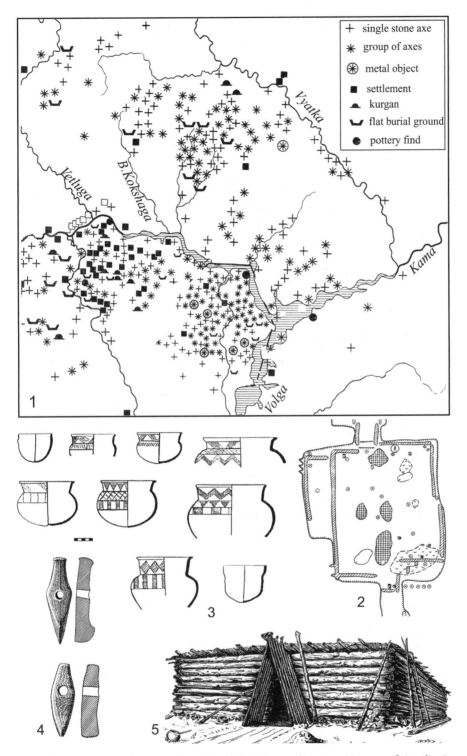

Figure 2.22. The Balanovo culture in the Kama-Vyatka area: (1) map of site distribution; (2) house from the Galkina Gora settlement; (3) Balanovo pottery; (4) stone battle axes; (5) artistic reconstruction of the house from Vasilsurskoye settlement.

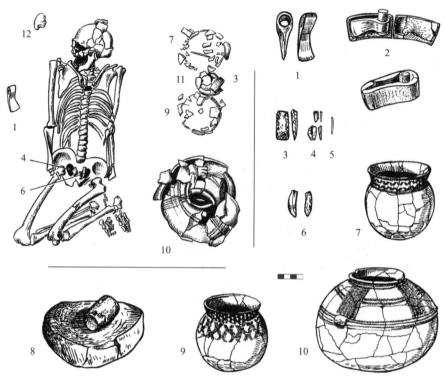

Figure 2.23. Churakchinskii kurgan, burial 2: (1) copper axe; (2) melting forms; (3) flint axe; (4) stone flake; (5) awl; (6) bear tooth; (7, 9–11) pots; (8) grinding stone and pestle; (12) stone (after Bader & Khalikov 1987).

layers (Eneolithic cultures). According to Solovyev's analysis (1994), the earliest Balanovo presence was noticed in the high hills of the right bank of the Volga and the Vyatka-Vetluga area, whereas the Eneolithic sites occupied forested lowlands. The Balanovo pottery, which sharply differs from Eneolithic ceramics, constitutes about 17–36 percent in the settlements. That is to say, in the second quarter of the second millennium BC, the people with the Balanovo core-tradition occupied some former Eneolithic sites. The newcomers[29] partly coexisted with the late Volosovo population (mixed Balanovo-Volosovo sites)[30] and partly displaced them (collections with Balanovo pottery domination). They brought with them a more advanced economic and cultural tradition than that of their neighbors. They bred domestic animals: at the beginning of the second millennium BC, primarily pigs and sheep, but closer to the mid-second millennium BC cattle and horses that corresponded more to local ecological conditions. The newcomers used draught cattle and two-wheeled wagons (Goldina 1999). The Balanovo people exploited the local copper sandstone deposits and pioneered the swidden method of farming (Krasnov 1971).

In the Late Bronze Age, the cultures of the Prikamsky subarea (Prikazan-skaya, Erzovskaya, Lugovskaya, Kurmantau, Buiskaya) continued the traditions

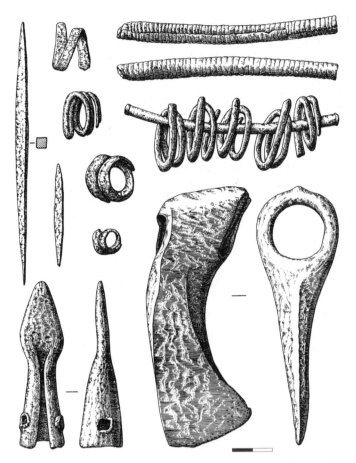

Figure 2.24. Copper objects from the Balanovo burial ground (after Goldina 1999).

of the preceding period, first of all, in pottery and house designs, reflecting some cultural continuity. Scholars interpret the latter as the same stage of development as the proto-Permian language (Goldina 1999: 164–5). Subsistence was based on stable animal husbandry supplemented by hunting and fishing. They bred cattle, horses, and, to a much smaller extent pigs and sheep. Some stone, bone, and bronze tools have been interpreted by scholars as evidence of cultivation. Further evidence comes from millet grains found in the Lugovskoye-I settlement (Zbruyeva 1960). However, it is unlikely that cultivation was essential. Despite the continuing influence issued from the Andronovo-Cherkaskul side, the local groups of the Cis-Urals forest zone kept their identity and passed their traditions on to their descendants as they entered the Iron Age.

The Forest-Steppe and Southern Taiga of Western Siberia

The archaeological study of the Trans-Urals and western Siberia started before the Russian revolution with episodic excavations and gained an organized form in the 1920–30s. The foundation of western Siberian archaeology is associated with names of V. N. Chernetsov, K. V. Salnikov, M. P. Gryaznov, E. M. Bers, M. F. Kosarev, and others. Since the first discoveries and determinations were made, the database has greatly increased, and local and regional archaeological sequences based on relative chronologies have been introduced into academic circles. The territory between the Urals and Ob' river basin is huge, and obviously not all areas have been studied equally.

The Trans-Urals-Kazakhstan subarea with cultures producing pottery with combed geometric patterns covers the territory of several geographic zones: from the tundra to the steppe of central and eastern Kazakhstan. This occurrence is unique only for the Eneolithic period (Shorin 1999). Since the Bronze Age, the cultural division was strictly correlated with this or that ecological zone. However, we should stress that "south–north" cultural connections are evident in all later epochs within this subarea.

In the forest zone of the Urals and western Siberia, the settlements are situated partly on promontories and on riverbanks away from the water. (For the Urals, this was the time of the climatic optimum of the Holocene and transition to the Subboreal.) The population of this area developed an economy composed of hunting and fishing of various forms. Archaeological sites of the Ob' basin clearly demonstrate the leading role of fishing (Kosarev 1984; Matushchenko 1999a). The diagnostic marker of all Eneolithic cultures is pottery decoration. The decoration is rather complex with varying geometric ornament that has a predominantly horizontal design that covers round and pointy-based straight walled vessels.

The stone inventory is more homogeneous. Characteristic for all cultures is the full domination of the flake technique of the lithic industry. The tool set is more or less standard and includes knives, scrapers, arrowheads, spearheads, and drillers, made from Uralian jasper. Copper, as a new material, appeared in the third millennium BC, but its use was extremely rare. Some sporadic copper items come from peat-bog sites, which are common in the Urals. The bog sites also provide rich collections of wooden objects: paddles, floats, cuirasses, net spreaders, fishing tools, scoops, birch bark boxes, and so on.

An important point concerning the cultural situation in the Tobol-Irtysh basin is its intermediate position between the forest and steppe. The periodic drift of steppe elements into this area was a serious factor in its development.

The Pre-Andronovo Horizon in the Western Siberian Forest-Steppe

The first bronze artifacts appeared in southwestern Siberia at the end of the third millennium BC. Since that time (the Middle Bronze Age of the general chronology), practically all of the forest-steppe and southern forests, from the Trans-Urals to the Yenisei River, were occupied by several cultures and groups: Tashkovo (Middle Tobol), Loginovo (Middle Ishim), Odino, Krotovo, and Elunino[31] (the Middle Irtysh, Upper Ob', and Altai areas) as well as the

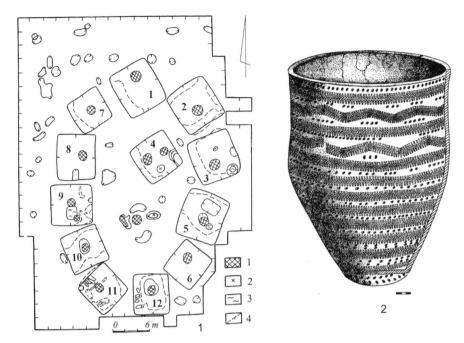

Figure 2.25. The Tashkovo culture: 1. The settlement of Tashkovo; 2. Plan of excavation: (1) calcinations; (2) charcoal; (3) clay; (4) the border of the dark-grey layer with remains of charcoal (after Kovaleva and Ryzhkova 2002); 2. Big pot from the village YUAO-XIII (after Kovaleva, Ryzhkova, & Shamanayev 2000).

Samus' culture (Tom-Chulym rivers) (Molodin & Glushkov 1989) (Fig. 2.5). They constituted the so-called pre-Andronvo cultural horizon, which is generally dated from the first quarter of the second millennium BC and display clear evidence of the diversified economy contributed by the productive and non-productive branches (Korochkova et al. 1991; Matushchenko 1999a; Molodin 2001).

The chronology of these antiquities is mainly based on the evolution of the pottery morphology and decoration in which the alternating holed and combed motifs that cover the entire pot's surface and reach back to the earlier epoch were dominant. Among them, the Tashkovo and Krotovo cultures are more significant. The latter is thought to continue into the Late Bronze Age (Gening & Stefanov 1993; Molodin 1985). In general, one can say that these cultures seem rather distinctive and are only slightly touched by steppe influence. Yet they definitely contributed to the later cultural formations in western Siberia. The Tashkovo culture is represented by villages with a circular or semicircular layout of ten to twelve houses situated on the banks of small rivers or lakes and yielding a great number of richly decorated flat-bottomed ceramic vessels (Fig. 2.25). At least three of these villages have been excavated completely (Kovaleva 1997; Kovaleva et al. 2000). Open dispersed settlements with one- or two-chamber houses of the semisubterranean type and flat burial grounds constitute the Krotovo culture.

The funeral sites are known only from the eastern regions of the "pre-Andronovo" horizon (Middle Irtysh and Upper Ob'). These are flat burial grounds situated on elevated riverbanks or terraces (Abramovo XI, Sopka-2, Rostovka, Elunino). The graves formed several parallel rows and contained the remains of inhumations and cremations. Some extraordinary details have been recorded: sprinkled ochre, burials of separated skulls or skeletons without skulls, collective multilayered burials, and secondary fractured burials (Matushchenko 1994). Some graves are rather rich with metal objects, among which are those of the Seima-Turbino type (Rostovka – Fig. 2.26, Elunino, Sopka-2).

Sites of the Seima-Turbino Type

We have already written about the Seima-Turbino metallurgy in previous chapters. We will discuss its cultural aspect in the following section.

In 1912, two sites, Seima burial ground on the Oka River and Borodino hoard in Moldavia, were discovered. They produced a number of splendid metal objects. Later, in 1924–1927, near Perm city (Cis-Urals), the Turbino cemetery yielding similar material was excavated. Since that time, the problem of cultural, chronological and technological attribution of these antiquities has been known under the name of Seima-Turbino phenomenon, which is still one of the most mysterious riddles in Russian archaeology.[32] The third big burial ground, Rostovka, which produced numerous metal objects of the Seima-Turbino type, was excavated in western Siberia in the 1970s. It consisted of thirty-eight flat burials with inhumations (in supine or contracted position) and cremations executed "outside." A pit "crematorium" was discovered there as well. The cemetery has yielded a rich collection of grave goods, among which there are many metal objects paralleling the Seima-Turbino materials of the Volga-Kama area. The pottery is close to that of the Krotovo-Elunino pottery (Matushchenko & Sinitsina 1988). During the last decades, several settlements with such pottery have been discovered in the Omsk area (Matushchenko 1999b).

A substantial collection of material of the Seima-Turbino type comes from the Reshnoye burial ground on the Oka River (Volga tributary) and Satyga burial ground on the Konda River (northwestern Siberia), which were investigated in the 1970s. Separate burials have been recently discovered in the Kama area (Cis-Urals).

The cemeteries and separate burials contained splendid and easily recognizable bronze weapons and tools: spearheads with closed sockets (Fig. 1.6), celts, and knives-daggers (Chernykh 1992), but few graves have yielded any human remains. Moreover, they do not abound with pottery. The pottery, in its turn, usually does not produce any characteristic appearance nor does it

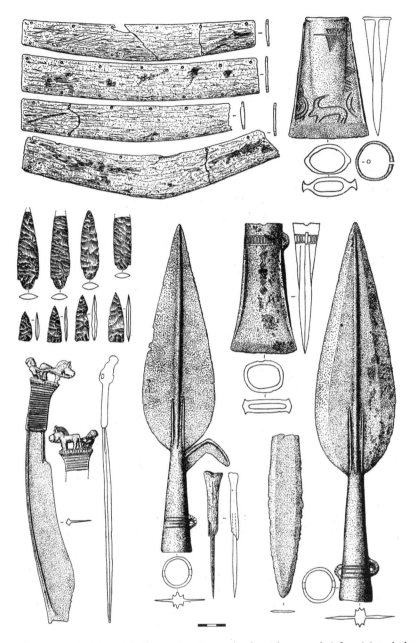

Figure 2.26. Materials from the Rostovka burial ground (after Matushchenko & Sinitsina 1988).

exhibit local traits. There are no settlements that could be associated with the cemeteries. These sites have been the focus of academic discussions since they were first discovered. Specialists have debated the origin of the Seima-Turbino phenomenon, its cultural attribution, and chronology. The dates suggested by different scholars vary between 1700 and 800 BC.

The most popular theory of the Seima-Turbino phenomenon was put forward by Chernykh and Kuzminykh (1989). According to them, two main components appear to be responsible for the emergence of this phenomenon. The first, and probably the dominant, component could be connected with the metallurgists and horse breeders who inhabited the Altai Mountains, steppe, and forest-steppe (descendants of the Afanasyevo and Okunyevo populations which were familiar with tin-bronze production); the second component could be related to the hunters and fishermen of the taiga around the Yenisei River and Lake Baikal. This area is known to be rich in nephrite from which some objects found in the Seima-Turbino cemeteries were made. These people were highly advanced metallurgists and possessed the secrets of advanced technology of tin bronze production in closed thin-walled casting forms. They also knew how to cast objects in the lost wax method. The Seima-Turbino man-to-man weapons were most effective in northern Eurasia in the mid second millennium BC. As the experimental works and micro-wear analyses showed, some long spears (up to 44 cm) with short shafts could be used as daggers (Solovyev 2003: 28). The weaponry set included richly decorated socketed axes, two-edged daggers, socketed spears, and curved knives. The Seima-Turbino warrior also had a lamellar body armor made from long horn blades (Fig. 2.26).

According to Chernykh and Kuzminykh (1989), the possession of advanced weaponry and the ability to use sleds with draught horses as shown in one of the bronze figurines on the knife top (Fig. 2.26), allowed Seima-Turbino craftsmen groups to move northwestward and to cross huge distances within a relatively short period. They left their cemeteries along their routes. These cemeteries are discretely situated in the forest-steppe and forest zone between the Altai and Cis-Urals.

In the light of new discoveries in the Altai area, it seems that Kirushin (1992, 2002) is right in his hypothesis that the Seima-Turbino metallurgy emerged in the Altai foothills in the eighteenth and seventeenth centuries BC within the Elunino context, and the Elunino people moved northward under the pressure of incoming Andronovo colonists. This occurred not later than the eighteenth century BC (Kirushin 1992).

However, to our mind, it is difficult to imagine, that they moved through the wild and dense Siberian forests. Most probably they used the water ways – the Ob' and Irtysh rivers. This hypothis is supported by the fact that the northern sites with Seima-Turbino metal (Satyga and Kaninaskaya cave) are usually found in the swampy-taiga zone of the lower Ob' basin.

We should refer also to E. Kuzmina's model (2004: 57) of Seima-Turbino phenomenon. Kuzima states, that a substantial part of Seima-Turbino metallurgy originated in eastern Kazakhstan, on the basis of the Fyodorovo and Krotovo-Elunino cultural components.

Nowadays, it is becoming clearer that Seima-Turbino bronzes were produced in several metallurgical centers situated in eastern Kazakhstan and the Altai that possessed an advanced form of technology from that period (Kuzmina 2004; Parzinger 2000). These centers originally supplied most of western Siberia with metal, whereas the southern Urals and eastern Europe were oriented to other centers, as we saw earlier. We can suppose that at least in the beginning, the Seima-Turbino metallurgy might be a clan-based craft. Some of clan groups under the leadership of elite warriors moved north and westwards following the flow of metal goods. Along the way, some groups of craftsmen-traders could have formed some sort of colonies to which the earliermentioned cemeteries could correspond. The colonists, especially in distant areas from their homeland, could use the local pottery and live in local-style houses; thus they are not identified by these attributes.

Kuzmina (2004: 52), supposes "that prestigious Turbino weapons were the property of the military elite, in that case, only famous warriors, not craftsmen, could bring them to the Borodino (in the west) and China (in the east)."

After the Seima-Turbino groups reached the Urals, three additional paths are archaeologically traceable. The first passed the southern Urals through the Abashevo territory and stopped in the Middle Kama area where it is represented by the Turbino and, Zaosinovo-4 cemeteries (Goldina 1999). Evidently, the migrants had contact with the Abashevo people from which they adopted their metallurgical skills using the local copper and silver sources. Therefore, in the Turbino burial ground there were also objects of the Abashevo forms.

A second group passed along the northern periphery of the Andronovo territory and stopped in the Lower Kama and Middle Volga (the Sokolovsky cemetery and a handful of occasional finds of Seima-Turbino objects). The third group crossed into middle and northern parts the Urals and reached the Pechora basin, also leaving cemeteries in north-west Siberia.

Technologically, the Seima-Turbino groups appear superior to the aboriginal populations not only in metallurgy but also in their stone industry. Their stone arrowheads and knives were much better manufactured and have close parallels in Siberian cultures (Fig. 2.26). There are two zones, western (European) and eastern (Siberian), within the area of the Seima-Turbino bronze distribution. In the Siberian zone, tin bronzes are dominant whereas in the west there are a great number of arsenic and copper-arsenical bronzes. The object repertoire is also different (Chernykh & Kuzminykh 1987). About 41.4 percent of all tools are made of tin bronze. The Seima-Turbino metal is also associated with objects made from nephrite, deposits of which are available in the Lake Baikal area. The Great Nephrite Road of the Bronze Age is said to have linked southern Siberia and Europe.

Despite its attractiveness, the model described earlier has some uncertain points. The first is the time of origin of the Seima-Turbino metallurgy. Until we have a substantial series of radiocarbon dates (which in many cases are not possible because of the absence of bones in the burials), this problem will remain open. As mentioned earlier, according to the latest data, which are, unfortunately, not numerous, this time should be moved toward the very beginning of the second millennium BC. Second, it is not clear what factors, except the availability of rich raw material resources, conditioned the formation of such an innovative bronze industry. Third, it is not clear whether there was a directional migration of metallurgists or a network of warrior-traders distributing high-quality weapons and other metal objects and objects made of precious stone in the forest-steppe and forest. It seems that both these occurrences might have taken place, but their social context is rather mysterious. It is important to understand the reason for such a long-distance movement or trade. We can more definitely explain why this movement did not pass through the steppe area, because the steppe people were their own metal suppliers and consumers. In this case, we have to conclude that in Eurasia, in the beginning of the second millennium BC, two competing technological systems could exist.

In any case, we cannot deny that the Seima-Turbino phenomenon, despite its unclear nature, played a significant role in the life of Eurasian populations during the second millennium BC.

In conclusion, we must stress that, during the Early and Middle Bronze Age, the life of the Urals and western Siberia populations was far from quiet. It was a time of innovations, new technological discoveries, assimilation of new territories, and formation of communication networks. It also was a time of sharp regional and interregional contrasts in the economic, ideological, and social spheres. It was an interesting time, which we will address again in the final chapter of this book.

CHAPTER 3

STABILIZATION, COLONIZATION, AND EXPANSION IN THE LATE BRONZE AGE

In the Late Bronze Age, the steppe, the forest-steppe, and the Ural region became an arena of interaction between the two biggest cultural formations – Srubnaya and Andronovo. These cultural systems, occupying the Eurasian steppe and forest-steppe are represented by a great number of sites: settlements of different sizes consisting of many dwellings and burial grounds manifesting a great diversity of mortuary practices. The most characteristic trait of these groups is the pottery, represented by several types and differing in decoration and form.

THE URALIAN VARIANT OF THE SRUBNAYA FAMILY OF CULTURES

The Srubnaya culture was first distinguished by Gorodstov (1916) on statistically processed materials of the Donets area. The culture was named for the burials that were found inside wooden structures placed into the funeral chamber. Only later did it become apparent that such structures in fact occurred rarely: about 2 percent of the total number of burials. As with other cultures that were widely dispersed, the name of the burials became the name of the cultural and historical intercommunity (Merpert 1985).

Several basic features are characteristic of this culture: the vast territory that it covers; an abundant number of sites, some already studied and others continually being discovered; and the striking uniformity of its material. However, the total number of Srubnaya sites is not even calculated. Thousands of settlements, concentrated mainly in the forest-steppe region, and hundreds of kurgan burials with thousands of excavated burials have been recorded up.

In fact, the Srubnaya culture occupies the same area that had previously been occupied by the Abashevo culture. The main difference is that the Srubnaya sites and Srubnaya materials are distributed both further east (up to the

Trans-Urals and even Middle Asia) and further west than Abashevo sites (Fig. 3.1). All researchers agree that there are a large number of early Srubnaya settlements and burials in eastern Ukraine, but some scholars extend the area of the earliest Srubnaya sites as far as western Ukraine. In regions where Abashevo and early Srubnaya sites are encountered together, the latter occupies a slightly later chronological position as it has been established in multiphase settlements in the Don basin (Shilovskoye, Mosolovskoye) and in the western Urals region (Beregovskoye, Tubyak, and Staro-Yabalaklinski). The Srubnaya culture can by no means be thought of as homogeneous because of its huge territorial expansion and long-lasting existence. We have designated it as a family of cultures, in consideration of its geographic and chronological variations. However, unlike Andronovo, the difference between the Srubnaya variants is not as clearly delineated.

Some elements of the Srubnaya culture also have been discovered in the Low Amu-Dary'a (Chorasmia), where they are mixed with the Alakul elements representing the Tazabagy'ab culture (Itina 1961, 1963, 1977). According to Otroshchenko (2003), the Srubnaya cultural family is composed by two large chronoterritorail units. The group of Pokrovskaya cultures (seventeenth–fifteenth centuries BC) is the earliest indication of the Srubnaya culture, and can be seen in the Volga-Ural area. The Berezhnovsko-Mayevskaya group is the later Srubnaya manifestation occupied the Dnepr-Donets steppe.

It is not our objective to review all the Srubnaya cultures; we will dwell only on the Urals variant.

Archaeological Characteristics

Srubnaya sites are situated in the Urals within the forest-steppe landscape and represent the eastern periphery of the active cultural zone. The northern periphery of this local variant is related to the left side of the Kama River; the northeast boundary passes along the left bank of the Belaya River. The southern and eastern limits are quite vague, at least at the level of present-day knowledge. It is clear, however, that active cultural contacts with Alakul and Fyodorovo populations occurred within this area. The study of the dynamics of these interactions are, to some extent, limited by the weakness of the Srubnaya and Andronovo internal chronologies and – this is very important – these chronologies are not mutually well coordinated.

Some scholars distinguish the Trans-Uralian variant of the Srubnaya culture (between the Ural River and Ural mountains), others interpret these as traces of Srubnaya influence. Meanwhile, the series of sites with early Srubnaya materials, which are usually in combination with others, are located in the Trans-Urals, particularly in the area of the Sintashta culture where they relate to the latest layers. Attempts have been made to distinguish several stages in

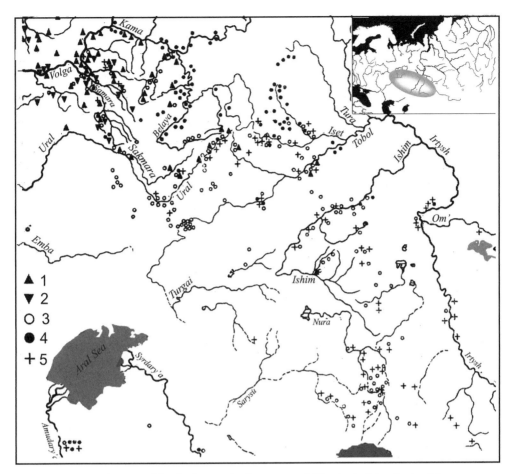

Figure 3.1. Distribution of the Srubnaya, Andronovo, and Cherkaskul sites in the Cis-Urals and Trans-Urals: (1) Srubnaya, (2) Late Srubnaya, (3) Srubno-Alakul, (4) Alakul, (5) Cherkaskul-Fyodorovo (after Grigory'ev 2000a).

the history of the Cis-Ural variant of the Srubnaya culture, but the differences are traced only in the burial material and partly in the pottery.

Settlements, burial grounds, hoards, and menhirs represent the sites of the Srubnaya culture in the Urals.

Settlements are quite numerous: there are more than eight hundred within the territory between the Trans-Volga and Belaya river basin (Obydennov & Obydennova 1992, 40),[1] and about 8 percent of these have been excavated. However, large-scale (500–3,000 m²) excavations have been carried out at only six settlements. Almost all of these settlements contained material from Abashevo, Mezhovka, and other cultures. Srubnaya settlements vary in size, but large settlements (occupying more than 10,000 m²) are not numerous. Some settlements are indicated only by the presence of some pottery sherds.

The difference in size and saturation of archaeological layers has allowed scholars to establish a hypothesis about the existence of economic and cultural centers within the area under question, two of which have been studied in detail. These are: (1) Beregovskoye, where, in a limited territory, fifteen sites were discovered, and (2) the Tubyak micro-regions (Gorbunov 1992: 81–3). According to Gorbunov, these centers comprised large settlements with traces of metallurgical production and some smaller settlements and necropolis.

The settlements usually occupy either the terraces of small rivers or the remains of terraces. The exception to this rule is represented by the settlement of specialized metallurgists in the Kargaly micro-region (Chernykh 1997b; 2002). Some archaeologists believe that there also were settlements for the specialization of leather processing and bone carving (Morozov 1981).

Despite the long history of study of the Srubnaya culture, only about twenty-five dwellings have been completely excavated, but no general statement can be made regarding their placement. In individual cases, traces of ditches have been reported.

Judging by the difference in size (from 15 to 200 m^2), rectangular and square houses differed not only in construction but also in function. Houses were built from wood and earth but some house basements were faced with stone. These houses were fairly substantial. They were semisubterranean constructions, with basements 0.5–1.2 m, vertical pillar frames. These houses required numerous man-hours to build; in this case, basements were deeper – 0.5–1.2 m. Other houses were built above ground but with a similar pillar frame construction (Morozov 1982). The houses usually had only one entrance. Open fireplaces, storage pits, and wells are found within the houses (Fig. 3.2).

As we have already seen, one of the most impressive sites of the Srubnaya culture is the Kargaly mining and metallurgical complex, the study of which has continued since the end of the 1980s. Within the huge territory occupied by mining pits relating to the period from the Early Bronze Age to the eighteenth century BC, about twenty Srubnaya settlements have been discovered. One of them (near the former farm of Gorny) was systematically investigated over a period of several seasons. Hundreds of finds connected with metallurgy and metal working were found including slag, pestles, molds, smelting waste, and completed objects. Metal from the Kargaly center penetrated over to the Don area, which clearly indicates the large scale of production. The Uralian metallurgists exchanged mineral ores for cattle and horses, the bones of which have been found in abundance at the Kargaly site. The osteological collection comprises more than a million domestic animal bones, 80 percent of which were cattle, and represents approximately twenty thousand cows (Antipina & Morales 2003).

In general, the material culture of the Srubnaya settlements is represented mainly by collections of fragmented pottery and implements reflecting various kinds of economic activity. Practically all bronze tools – knives, sickles, awls,

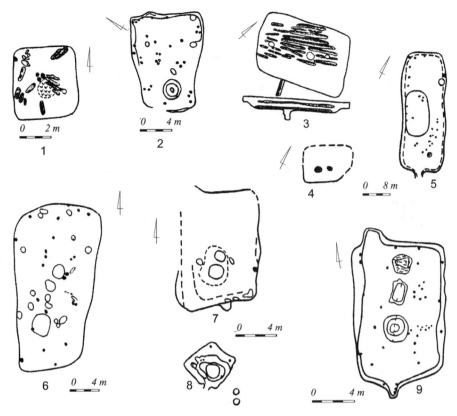

Figure 3.2. Srubnaya culture. Dwellings. (1) Suskanskoe-II; (2) Suskanskoe Levobe-rezhnoe; (3) Suskanskoe Pravoberezhnoe; (4–5, 7–9) Beregovskoe-I; (6) Kushtiryak-skoe (after Obydennov and Obydennova 1992).

fishhooks – belong to the category of the blade technology. Stone was used for making pestles, abrasives, and rarely for arrowheads, but these had straight bases.

Among the bone tools, shank-shaped or disk-shaped cheek-pieces take a special place. They are regarded as important for absolute and relative dating, as well as for social reconstruction.

Compared with settlements, there are many more Srubnaya cemeteries in the territory between the Volga and Belaya rivers; more than three hundred kurgans containing about eleven hundred burials have been excavated. The proportion of burials between the early and later chronological groups is about 1:6 (Obydennov & Obydennova 1992). Several hundred burials are known in the Trans-Urals as well (Grigory'ev 2000a; Salnikov 1967).

Burial grounds are situated in the same topographical conditions as settle-ments. In addition to kurgans, a number of flat burials have been discovered as well. The cemeteries usually consist of three to eight kurgans. The only exception is the Staro-Yabalaklinski cemetery, where more than one hundred complexes have been excavated (Gorbunov & Morozov 1991). Kurgans differ in size: diameters vary between 8–10 and 30 m (Fig. 3.3). In southern areas, kurgans are bigger than in the north. About 80 percent of the mounds were round in shape, but in several cases kurgans had an oval form. The mounds are all made of earth. Sometimes they are surrounded by small circular ditches or clay moats, and demonstrate traces of special acts connected with special preparation of the burial ground by means of its burning (Bogdanov & Khalyapin 2000: 45). The mounds also contain the remains of fire, animal bones, and pottery fragments. Stone arrangements are found sporadically in the Trans-Urals area.

The later chronological group of sites demonstrates a tradition of placing pots outside the burial in the southeast part of the kurgan; this occurs in 8 percent of all burials. Complete animal skeletons are infrequent.

Usually in the first stage, each kurgan would contain from one to five burials. In the second stage, some kurgans with twenty to twenty-five burials are known. They are situated either around the central grave or in a row. The latter principle is recorded for cemeteries in which kurgans form a chain. Pit graves are of a rectangular shape but not deep (about 0.4–0.5 m). There are three groups: small (from 0.2 to 1.0 m²), medium (from 1.0 to 2.3 m²), and large (3–3.5 m²) pits. The most frequently found graves are of the medium size (Obydennov & Obydennova 1992: 80–1). Only big pit graves are furnished with elaborate elements. These elements include wooden constructions such as roofs and posts, and steps (as a rule, on one sidewall). Wooden frames placed on the pit floor are very rare. The majority of the deceased were interred according to the inhumation ritual. However, there are a fair number of secondary burials and burials with dismembered skeletons. The dead were usually placed in a contracted position on the left side with hands located in front of the face, and the head oriented to the north or northeast. Other positions, on the right side or on the back, are very rare, as is the use of ochre, chalk, or charcoal in the ritual.

Burials are predominantly individual. There are some paired or collective graves in which the deceased were in the standard positions. Only one burial has been found in which the dead were placed face to face. In some cases, when a child accompanied a woman, the child was placed behind her back. Although we admit that some of the deceased might be dismembered, as Merpert (1954: 142–6) supposed, it is well known how difficult it is to trace such a ritual in the field. Therefore, we are inclined to be more careful in suggesting the existence of body dismemberment in Srubnaya society. Nevertheless, when dismemberment is suggested, all such skeletons belong to adult age categories.

Grave goods are not very rich and very often are represented only by pottery (74 percent). Metal tools and ornaments are more rare. About one-third of children's burials and every fifth adult burial are without any goods. Statistical analysis shows that the tradition of putting pots and hands near the face was dominant. Animal bones as the remains of funeral food are found exclusively in adult burials. Children were given only pots.

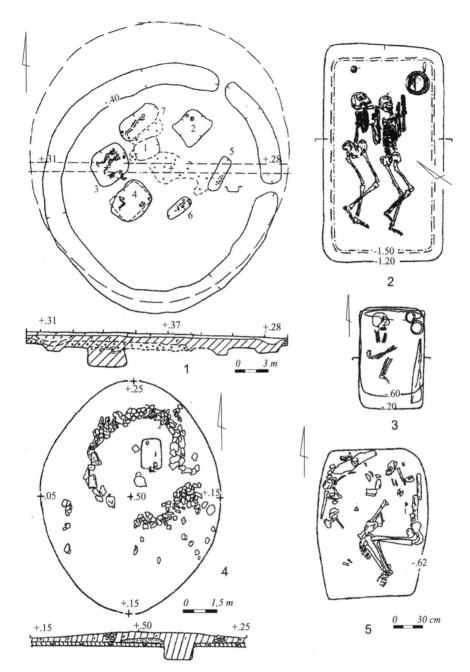

Figure 3.3. Burial grounds of the Srubnaya culture: (1) Bolshekaragansky kurgan 20, view in plan and profile; (2) grave 3; (3) Ilyaska kurgan 10, grave 1; (4) Ilyaska kurgan 1, view in plan and profile; (5) Ilyaska kurgan 1, central grave (after Lubchansky and Ivanova 1996; Botalov et al. 1996).

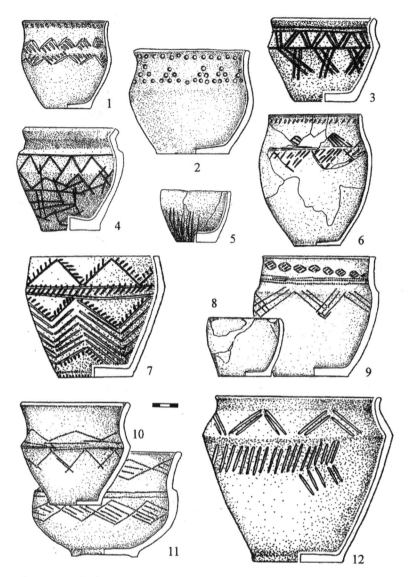

Figure 3.4. Srubnaya type pottery: (1, 2, 6, 8–11) Ilyaska burial ground; (3, 5–7, 15) Bolshekaragansky burial ground (after Grigory'ev 2000a).

Pottery is the most common find in Srubnaya sites (Fig. 3.4). All vessels are made by hand from a clay mixed with chamotte, sand, and crushed shell. Among the pots we can distinguish are straight-walled pots and dishes (tureen bowls). A specific feature of Srubnaya ceramics is the particular manner in which the potter smoothed over the pot's surface with a comb stamp, tufts of grass, or with wooden chips, that left traces in the form of so-called scratches.

About one-third of the pottery was not decorated. The remaining vessels were ornamented only on the upper part. The most popular motifs are zigzags,

Plate 3.1. Menhir of Akhunovo (photo by E. Chibilev).

triangles, notches (69 percent), rhombuses, and herringbone patterns made with comb and plain stamps, or by carving and pressing. The pots with ribbed shoulders are diagnostic for the early group. The technique of shaping the vessel on a solid mold was used. This, however, was not typical for the Srubnaya cultural tradition. This is close to the Petrovka tradition, and forces scholars to think that the latter took part in the Srubnaya cultural genesis. The pots decorated with hole tubes also belong to the early stage. These patterns went out of use in the later stages when the decoration become poorer and the number of its motifs become minimal.

Metal objects are represented by tools: bronze knife-daggers, awls, fishing hooks, and ornaments including bronze bracelets, beads, and elongated pendants; the ornaments are sometimes covered with golden foil. There are numerous glass and bone beads, sometimes designed in a complex plait decoration, perforated animal fangs, and shells. From this list, only elongated pendants can be attributed as ethnographic elements of the Srubnaya culture. The remaining objects have their greatest analogues not just in the Urals but also in the Volga area, Kazakhstan, and Siberia.

Megalithic constructions have been discovered during the last five to six years in the southern Trans-Urals. Their systematic study is in the early stages; therefore, we will only briefly mention them. They were discovered in the area of Srubnaya-Alakul contact, and the first excavations did not reveal undoubted evidence of their cultural attribution, except some ceramic sherds of the Late Bronze Age that have some Srubnaya-Alakul characteristics.

Uralian megaliths are represented by solitary menhirs, rows, and groups of menhirs made from flattened and more or less massive erected stones (Plate 3.1). Many of these were destroyed or damaged in earlier times and are therefore only slightly visible on the surface.

They are usually situated near settlements or cemeteries and inserted into the axis "village – megalith – cemetery," to be a part of the organized landscape. Each element of this composition occupies its own topographic position: the settlement in the first terrace; menhir on the hill slope, and the burial ground on the most elevated point (Polyakova 2002).

Another category of Srubnaya site is the hoard, thirteen of which have been discovered in the Cis-Urals (Obydennov 1996). As a rule, they are connected to the territory of settlements or kurgans and found in the basins of small rivers. The hoards are composed of simple (Andronovo type) and hooked (Srubnaya type) sickles (eighty-one items) (Plate 3.2), lop-headed axes (nine items), ingot, molds, and stone pestles. Their affiliation to the Srubnaya culture is determined typologically; in two cases, they are confirmed by accompanying ceramics.

Summing up, one can say that the source base for the Srubnaya culture is quite large. Srubnaya sites are the most numerous Bronze Age sites in the Cis-Urals. We should, however, confess that no modern systematic work has been done to analyze and synthesise the data coming from the area under question.

Economic and Social Aspects

By and large, the Srubnaya sites – both settlements and burials – look modest, similar, and even poor in terms of material culture. For a long time, its standard and monotonous character had served as an argument to interpret the Srubnaya society in terms of an egalitarian structure.

Among the new ideas concerning interpretation of the available materials, we should point to those concerning economic and cultural centers put forward by Gorbunov (1992) and the discovery of the settlements in Kargaly that specialized in metallurgy (Chernykh 1997a). Special areas for metal production also were noted at Beregovskoye, Tubyak, and the Tavlykayevskoye settlements. However, they are not comparable in their scale of production with the Kargaly center.

Nevertheless, the Srubnaya subsistence economy was mainly based on live-stock breeding (Chernykh et al. 1997). This is evidenced by site location and the composition of osteological collections coming from settlements. Ninety-three percent of all animal bones that have been discovered are represented by domestic species: cow, sheep, horse, and pig (Kosintsev & Varov 1995). The pig was slightly more important in the forest-steppe (Otroshchenko 2003: 326). There are some dog bone finds. The difference in composition of archeozoo-logical collections reflects the environmental conditions of a concrete region.

Traditional interpretation presupposes quite a significant role for plant culti-vation, but we do not have direct evidence in favor of this hypothesis. Scholars have used as evidence some stone tools and sickles that could have been used in cultivating practices, but no paleobotanical analysis has been carried out for the Cis-Urals area. Nevertheless, samples have been taken from thirty-four sites located in the area between the Urals and Ukraine (Pashkevich 2000).

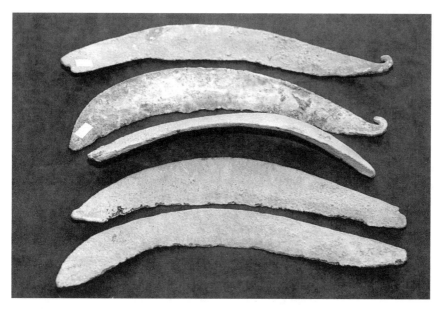

Plate 3.2. Bronze sickles from the hoard on the Lebyazhy'e settlement (photo by E. Chibilev).

Their analysis has demonstrated that traces of cultivation appeared in eastern Europe not earlier than the middle phase of the Late Bronze Age – notably in the Srubnaya time period. It is also noted that agricultural remains (cereal grains) were found in the Bereznovka-Mayevski variant of this culture occupying the steppe area of Ukraine and south Kalmykiya. The Pokrovsk variant of the Srubnaya culture – in the forest-steppe of eastern Europe, including the Cis-Urals area – did not know cereal agriculture. Its inhabitants were livestock breeders and metallurgists.

Considering this data, we can conclude that the role of cultivation in this region was limited. It is possible that intensive gathering was much more significant, and it supplemented the traditional milk-meat diet.

It seems rather probable that the division of labor and connections between societies corresponding to different cultural groups within the Srubnaya area played a significant role.

The funeral practices described here are characterized by a high level of uniformity. Therefore, they cannot serve as a strong basis for the reconstruction of social structure. But it is the uniformity of religious practice within this large area that presumes a high probability of ethnic homogeneity of the Srubnaya societies. This unification in ritual and in pottery decoration increases toward the late period. Obviously, the existence of sex and age groupings is without doubt in Srubnaya society.

The settlement size assessment allows scholars to suppose that they could host approximately two hundred to two hundred fifty individuals, which corresponds to a large community. Such a collective has a de facto look of egalitarianism, but we should not exclude the possibility of strict ideological restrictions to wealth manifestation.

The egalitarian interpretation of Srubnaya society has recently been criticized. An attempt was made to distinguish the group of elite burials in the Volga area (Malov 2002). Analysis of the distribution of scepters and maces allowed scholars to work out a variant of an internal elite hierarchy that was inherent to the Pokrovsk variant of the Volga-Urals Srubnaya culture (Dryomov 2002; Tsimidanov 1997). Otroshchenko (2003: 326) consider the burials where the bones of domestic animals are found as belonging to this elite (this constitutes from 2 to 15 percent of Srubnaya burials).

However, it is difficult to extrapolate this interpretation to the Cis-Urals area, where no social markers have been found in the burials. At the same time, Gorbunov (1996: 16–17) supposed that this unification existed as a result of a "special despotic regime of power," which secured the mass recruiting of the male population to mining work and "educated" people in the spirit of undoubted passivity.

The complex and large-scale mining system in Kargaly required a great labor investment, as well as ore and metal transportation, which is supposed to have been done by men. Indirect evidence of such a situation is reflected in the huge amount of animal bones, mostly of cattle (Antipina & Morales 2003: 327), which gives insight into the amount of meat eaten. Another argument in favor of this hypothesis derives from the small male representation in the burials of the Poksrovsk variant (Otroshchenko 2003: 322).

However, it is hard to believe that such a hypothesis will attract many supporters because of its weak argument, although it is interesting from a theoretical point of view. The unification of life can issue from the existence of a unified ideology among an ethnically similar population. In general, the organization of metallurgical production did not require mass participation by the entire population. It was the destiny either of separate clans or their separate members.

It is traditionally believed that the Srubnaya culture originated in the Volga-Ural area where the greatest number of early sites is concentrated. The process of its formation was contributed to by Poltavka (late Yamnaya variant), Abashevo, and late Catacombnaya groups (Agapov et al. 1983). However, it is currently believed that the main basis of the Pokrovsk group is connected with the Potapovka superstratum (Vasily'ev et al. 1994). From the beginning, the early Srubanya population groups (Pokrovsk variant) were in close contact with the Alakul population groups. Therefore, Otroshchenko (2003: 319) emphasized the role of military and technological impulse deriving from the South Urals center of cultural genesis, namely, with the Sintashta influence.

Paradoxically, the "eternal" problem of linguistic interpretation of the Srubnaya population is not currently debated in the literature. All scholars relate it to the Iranian linguistic group, relying on a connection between the

Srubnaya culture and the Scythians.[2] This is true for the Volga area, which was the core territory of the Srubnaya culture and where the transition to the Final Bronze and Iron Ages is traced quite well.

In the Cis-Urals, the Srubnaya sites are succeeded by Mezhovka sites, which scholars interpret as belonging to the Finno-Ugrian linguistic group. To coordinate these two points of view is hardly possible, because it is difficult to determine archaeologically the linguistic affiliation of a population, whose culture is represented on a very defective scale. It is more important to stress that in similar economic conditions and mutual interests in interaction, linguistic differences could play a secondary role.

THE ANDRONOVO FAMILY OF CULTURES

The Andronovo cultural zone covers an enormous portion of western Asia. Its western flank constitutes a contact zone with the Srubnaya culture in the Volga-Ural interfluvial and extending eastward to the Minusinsk depression (Fig. 3.5). Sites are found as far south as the foothills of the Koppetdag, the Pamir, and Tien-Shan mountains, whereas the northern boundary is unclear when it reaches the taiga zone. Moreover, there is a chain of Andronovo-type cultures in the forest-steppe zone of western Siberia. This cultural formation is more concerned with the area under study then the Srubnaya culture; therefore, we will devote more time to it.

It is not an exaggeration to say that no one culture in Russian archaeology has so many controversial interpretations and paradoxes as does the Andronovo culture. First is its name. It comes from the small village of Andronovo on the Yenisei River (southern Siberia) that is in the very eastern periphery of the culture. In 1914, near this village, several burial grounds containing skeletons in crouched position and pottery with very rich decoration were discovered.

In the 1920s, Teploukhov (1927) began to study the Andronovo antiquities. He classified the materials known at that time and created the first cultural and chronological sequence of the Bronze Age of southern Siberia. That sequence consisted of the following cultures: Afanacyevo, Andronovo, Karasuk, Kurgannay'a, and Tashtyk. He dated the Andronovo culture to the second millennium BC. Therefore, from the beginning, this term was related to sites of the Minusinsk lowland, but, gradually, it was applied to the territory from southern Siberia up to the southern Urals. Gryaznov (1927) refined its general chronology (fourteenth–eleventh centuries BC) and defined some western and eastern characteristics of the Andronovo culture.

In the 1940s and 1950s, Salnikov excavated the cemeteries near the Fyodorovka village and the Alakul Lake in the southern Urals. The sites differed in ritual and ceramics. Having analyzed the available material, he revealed the Fyodorovo (eastern) and the Alakul (western) stages of the evolution of the

Andronovo culture. The former (fifteenth–twelfth centuries BC) was represented by burials with cremations and richly decorated pots with comb ornament and rounded shoulder; the later (eleventh–ninth centuries BC) was characterized by burials with inhumations and pots with sharp shoulders decorated
with triangles, and executed with a flat stamp. The latest stage (eighth–seventh
centuries BC), the Zamarayevo stage, was singled out as well (Salnikov 1951).
Later, after several stratigraphic observations particularly made in the southern
Urals, Salnikov (1967) corrected his periodization and changed the dates of
the stages: Fyodorovo (eighteenth–sixteenth centuries BC), Alakul (fifteenth–
twelfth centuries BC), and Zamarayevo (twelfth–eighth centuries BC).

Other scholars, especially those concerned with the chronological framework and the interpretation of stages, criticized many points of this scheme.
In particular, Fedorova-Davydova (1964, 1973) argued that the earlier date of

Figure 3.5. Distribution of sites within the Andronovo area: (1) Nurbakovo;
(2) Novo-Burino; (3) Bol'shaya Karabolka; (4) Tomilovo; (5) Tuktubaevo; (6) Bishkil';
(7) Chernyaki; (8) Sosnovka-I, III; (9) Sineglazovo; (10) Smolino-I, II; (11) Isakovo-
I, V; (12) Sukhomesovo; (13) Churilov-II; (14) Fyodorovka; (15) Alakul; (16) Sub-
botino; (17) Baklanskoe; (18) Berezovski; (19) Chernorechy'e; (20) Stepnoye-I;
(21) Kinzerski; (22) Urazaevski; (23) Troitsk; (24) Bashnya Tamerlana; (25) Kulevchi-
III, VI, Nikolayevka-II; (26) Mirny-III; (27) Tsarev Kurgan; (28) Kamyshnoye;
(29) Raskatikha; (30) Verkhnaya Alabuga; (31) Evgen'evka; (32) Alekseyevka; (33) Pere-
leski; (34) Spasskoye-I; (35) Orsk; (36) Nikel'; (37) Aktubinsk, poligon; (38) Aktubinsk,
ptitsefabrika; (39) Pyatimary; (40) Emba; (41) Putilovskaya Zaimka; (42) Priplod-
nyi Log; (43) Urefty; (44) Naurzum; (45) Kenes; (46) Petrovka; (47) Semipalatnoye; (48) Burluk-I; (49) Alypkash; (50) Efimovka; (51) Kalachevski; (52) Kenotkel';
(53) Kokchetav; (54) Chaglinka; (55) Kokshkarbai I; (56) Biyrek-Kol'; (57) Obaly; (58)
Borovoe; (59) Nurmambet; (60) Balykly; (61) Zhilandy; (62) Algabas; (63) Botakara;
(64) Kosagal; (65) Sangru II; (66) Zhamantas; (67) Buguly I; (68) Taddy; (69) Baibala;
(70) Egiz-Koitas; (71) Akshatau; (72) Kanattas; (73) Bes-Oba; (74) Dzhamantas;
(75) Satan; (76) Taldy; (77) Tas-Bulak; (78) Krashnaya Krucha; (79). Bat'kin Payek;
(80) Akmola; (81) Lebyazh'e; (82) Malyi Koitas; (83) Zevakino; (84) Predgornoye;
(85) Oblaketka; (86) Karadzhal; (87) Sarykol'; (88) Academic Radlov's excavation;
(89) Nizhnyaya Suetka; (90) Novo-Aleksandrovka; (91) Elovka-II; (92) Yurt Akba-
lyk; (93) Vakhrushevo; (94) Ordynskoye; (95) Barnaul; (96) Blizhniye Elbany-XII;
(97) Blizhniye Elbany-XIV; (98) Khomutinka; (99) Shipunova; (100) Volchikha;
(101) Zmeyevka; (102) Ur; (103) Kytmanovo; (104) Ikonnikova; (105) Prigorodnoye
khozyaistvo; (106) Bol'shepichugina; (107) Andronovo; (108) Orak; (109) Yzhur;
(110) Solenoozernaya; (111) Pristan'-I; (112) Sukhoe Ozero; (113) Yarki -I; (114)
Yarki-II; (115) Ust'-Erba; (116) Kamenka-III; (117) Kamenka-I; (118) Lanin Log; (119)
Lebyazh'e-I; (120) Tepsei; (121) Podkuninski Ulus; (122) Berlik; (123) Aksaiman; (124)
Ulubai; (125) Kuropatkino-II; (126) Pavlovka; (127) Chistolebyazhski; (128) Ak-Tobe-
I, II; (129) Ashi-Ozek; (130) Maitan; (131) Nurtai; (132) Tashik; (133) Shapat; (134) Ak-
Tobe; (135) Sovkhoz Kirova u Karagandy; (136) Efimovka; (137) Betkuduk; (138) Dzhar-
tas; (139) Belokamenka; (140) Ermak; (141) Abramovo-4; (142) Polturino; (143)
Krivoye Ozero; (144) Berezovski; (145) Shibayevo I; (146) Alandskoye; (147) Ust'e;
(148) Ikpen'-I; (149) Satan; (150) Nurtai; (151) Lisakovka; (152) Solntse-Talika.

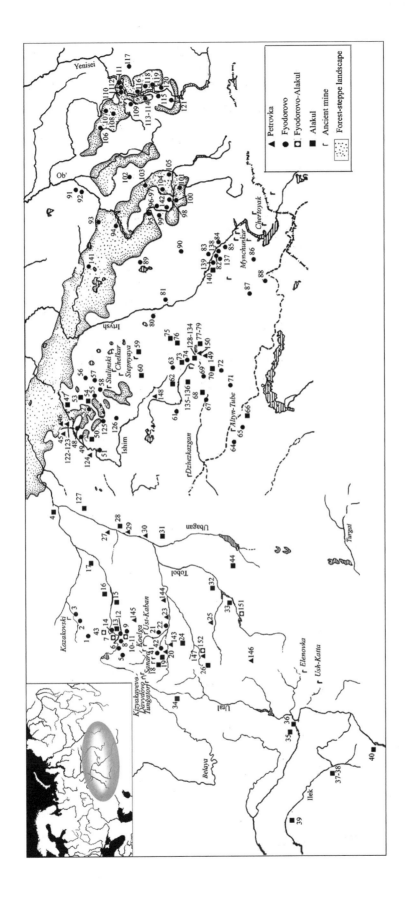

Legend:
▲ Petrovka
● Fyodorovo
▣ Fyodorovo–Alakul
■ Alakul
Γ Ancient mine
⸬ Forest-steppe landscape

Yenisei
Ob'
Irtysh
Chertovyak
Mynchunkur
Stalinski
Chelkar
Stepnyaya
Altyn-Tube
Dzhezkazgan
Ishim
Ubagan
Turgai
Tobol
Kazakovski
Koelga
Ust-Kaban
Samara
Kizyakuyevo
Davydovo
Tungatovo
Elenovka
Ush-Katta
Belaya
Ural
Ilek

the Alakul sites and, consequently, its independent position with respect of the Fyodorovo ones. It was suggested that these formations be considered as separate cultures within the Andronovo cultural and historical intercommunity.[3] However, in the 1960s and early 1970s, the stage model of the Andronovo culture dominated Russian archaeology. Its influence was so strong that it did not allow scholars to see the essentially different lines of evolution represented by the Alakul and Fyodorovo materials. That model had some regional variations and a number of mixed forms. Obviously, the problems of origin and ethnic attribution of the above cultural formations were and still are hotly debated. By the mid-1980s, Andronovo studies seemed be in a cleft stick. The impulse was given by new discoveries, which, if they did not resolve all the problems, then at least opened the way to new areas of research.

In the past twenty years, some new cultures relating to the Andronovo area have been discovered, and the names "Petrovka" and "Sintashta" have been placed on them. As we saw in the previous chapter, the first occupied chiefly the eastern area (Tobol–Ishim interfluves); the second, the southern Urals (Zdanovich 1988). They had several characteristics in common, but the earlier excavated Sintashta settlement, which had not been understood in the beginning, because it differed from classical Andronovo and contained certain Abashevo features, now began to be understood. In 1976, Smirnov and E. Kuzmina revealed "the Novokumaksky stage," which was interpreted as the early stage of the Andronovo culture and dated to the fourteenth century BC.

Hence, the Andronovo cultural formation, which takes up a vast area of the steppe and forest-steppe of western Asia, is considered to be of great importance. In the course of its study, an enormous amount of concrete material has been amassed. This resulted in the appearance of different and partly controversial systems of periodization and structuralization of this cultural formation. Today, the main cultures composing the Andronovo family are represented by the Petrovka, Alakul, Fyodorovo, and Sargary-Alexeyevka, but the main disagreement between scholars lays in the interpretation of the interrelationship between the Alakul and Fyodorovo complexes, and in a definition of intermediate types. This is reflected in different models of their correlation.

1. The unilinear model was suggested by Zdanovich (1988) and Avanesova (1979; 1991). It supposes the linear genetic evolution from the Eneolithic to the Iron Age, but unlike the scheme of Salnikov, it places the Alakul culture before the Fyodorovo culture.

2. A parallel model or model of partial coexistence is supported by E. Kuzmina (1994), Potyemkina (1985), Kosarev (1981), Evdokimov (2000), Tkachev (2002), and Grigory'ev (2000a). According to this model, the Alakul and Fyodorovo cultures coexisted in a certain period but have different origins and different lines of evolution.

3. Matveyev (1998) has suggested a phylogenetic model. He unites all cultures of the second millennium BC in the Trans-Urals and western Siberia into

the concept of the "Andronovo family of cultures" defined as a diachronic aggregate of congenial cultures. Matveyev summarized the basic discriminating marks of the Andronovo cultures. These include the following types:

- productive economy;
- dominance of livestock breeding (chiefly cattle, small cattle, and horse, but not pig);
- primarily stable permanent settlements and houses, represented basically by frame-pillar semisubterranean constructions;
- the presence of ash accumulations in the settlement area;
- the burying of the dead in purposely created constructions, above ground, part of which was made from mud or turf bricks or stone;
- the use of wood, stone, or their combinations for the funeral chamber arrangement;
- biritualism: the coexistence of inhumation and cremation, and sometimes secondary burials of the nonarticulated bones;
- a special role of fire and dogs in the funeral ceremonies;
- earthenware richly decorated with geometric designs: zigzags, meanders, triangles, and so on;
- stone tools used in metallurgical production;
- bone dice.

According to Matveyev, all cultures of the Andronovo family can be traced back to the Sintashta and Petrovka subcultures of the Novokumaksky association, which were transformed into the Alakul culture. The development of the latter has produced a number of descendent cultures: Fyodorovo and Cherkaskul (earlier generations), Mezhovka, Alexeyevka-Sargary, Irmen, and Karasuk (later generations).

The main idea of this model seems rational and, despite the apparent peculiarity, this model stresses the same basic links between cultures within the Andronovo area as that which have been noticed by other scholars.

The Alakul Culture

The Alakul culture is traditionally regarded as one of the basic composite components of the Andronovo family. The concept of the Alakul culture has changed several times and today there is no common opinion even about the possibility of considering it as a cultural unity. In particular, until the late 1970s (Zdanovich 1973), the Alakul culture comprised the Petrovka sites that were (and still are) regarded as a variant of the early Alakul tradition. We do not deny the Petrovka-Alakul succession, but we think that the confusion in terminology is on the way to the correct understanding of the cultural process. Therefore, we distinguish the concepts of the Petrovka and the Alakul occurrences.

ARCHAEOLOGICAL CHARACTERISTICS

The Alakul sites are found across a huge territory within the steppe and forest-steppe zones of the Trans-Urals, northern, western, and central Kazakhstan (Fig. 3.5).[4] The eastern boundary is marked by the Ermak 4 cemetery in western Siberia (Khabarova 1993). The western limits are more vague because the Late Bronze Age sites of the Ural river basin are characterized by a combination of cultural traits of the Alakul and Srubnaya groups. In the Trans-Urals and steppe Cis-Urals, the Alakul component prevailed, and in the forest-steppe Cis-Urals, Srubnaya stereotypes were dominant. The bearers of the Alakul tradition assimilated all the Trans-Uralian forest-steppe included in its northern area; mortuary materials document this. In the south, the Alakul territory was limited by the steppe zone.

The Alakul antiquities are represented by settlements and cemeteries[5] (Fig. 3.6). Among them, the sites of the steppe and forest Trans-Urals (excluding its northern periphery) and Kazakhstan are the best studied; although now, just as ten years ago (Zdanovich 1988), no one settlement has been excavated completely. Usually one or two houses are excavated, and therefore we do not have enough material to characterize in detail a settlement as an architectural complex.

The settlements are located on the first river terraces or in the low lake banks, usually very close to a large valley, and only very rarely can one find traces of the Alakul presence on high ground. The general settlement surface does not exceed 10,000 m²; the biggest settlements are located in the eastern territory. Potyemkina (1985: 76–103) certifies an increase in the of size of settlements up to 35,000 m² in the late stage of the Alakul culture. She also discovered the remains of a primitive defensive construction in the Trans-Urals settlement of Kamyshnoye-II, which is in the periphery of the Alakul territory.

The planning structure of settlements is predominantly linear; the houses are organized into one row or, rarely, into two rows running along the river bank (Stefanov 1996; Stokolos 1972). A settlement was formed gradually by means of adding a new house to a row. The structures in every local group differed in technological detail. The wide use of stone in the building process is typical for the steppe area of the Cis-Urals or for central Kazakhstan that lacks forests. Such a tradition is not known in the Trans-Urals and northern Kazakhstan.[6] This, however, cannot be explained only by utilitarian reasons because stone is available in abundance in the foothills of the Urals.

The Alakul houses are rectangular, measuring 140–270 m² in surface, dug into the ground 0.5–0.7 m (Fig. 3.7-A, B).[7] The entrances were designed as entryways in a corner or in atransversal wall. The numerous postholes (up to three hundred) on a floor give evidence to the postframe construction of a building. The quantity of posts correlates with house size and construction. In some cases, several rows of postholes are traced along the long axis of the house.

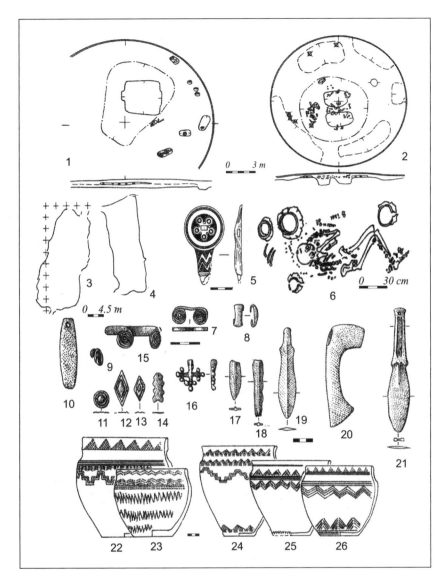

Figure 3.6. Complex of the Alakul material culture: (1) Semipalatnoye burial ground, kurgan 2; (2) Alypkash burial ground, kurgan 32; (3) Kulevchi-III settlement, house 7; (4) Petrovka-II settlement, house 1; (5, 25) Novonikolskoye burial ground, kurgan 5, grave 2; (6, 15, 22–23) Alypkash cemetery, kurgan 32, grave 4; (17, 18) Semipalatnoye cemetery, kurgan 5, grave 5; (19, 20, 24) Tsarev Kurgan, grave 7; (21) Novonikolskoye-I settlement; (26) Alakul cemetery, kurgan 18, grave 8 (5 – bone; 7–21 – bronze; 22–26 – clay) (after Zdanovich 1988).

The roofs are thought to be two slopes (including an asymmetrical variant) and a pyramidal type (Zdanovich 1988). The internal house space was divided into partitions.

Wells, storage pits, and fireplaces, the number of which can reach five to seven in a single house, are typical elements of Alakul interiors. Among the fireplaces, a group of metallurgical furnaces consisting of one or several parts can be distinguished. The fireplaces were built with the use of stone and specially baked small clay bricks. It is interesting that the bricks were not numerous enough to plaster a fireplace, and they were sometimes decorated. Thus, their function is not clear. A substantial number of the fireplaces were very simple, and they were recorded only on tempered spots on the floor.

Settlements produce the typical set of finds. These include animal bones, a great deal of fragmentary pottery, stone tools for metalworking, bone tools for leather processing, spindles, awls, and needles (Fig. 3.7). Metal tools are represented by knife-daggers, sickles, socketed chisels, gouges, hook, and so on (Fig. 1.9). Weaponry finds are rarer. Bronze, stone, and bone arrowheads were found as well as maces. Horse equipment, flat cheek-pieces without thorns, were only encountered in individual cases.

Pottery, which serves as a cultural marker for many Bronze Age cultures is quite peculiar, and this allowed Salnikov (1952), who excavated the Alakul cemetery in the Urals in the 1950s, to single out the western variant of the Andronovo culture. All vessels have flat bottoms and a striking profile; they have a ledge between the neck and shoulder, and their surface is carefully treated (Fig. 3.8). More than half of all pots are decorated by flat or comb stamps, including a toothed comb, incised techniques, drawing, and pressing. Decoration usually covers the neck and the shoulder but rarely the lower part of the body. The most popular motifs include isosceles and rectangular hatched triangles, zigzags, and rhombus. Such a feature as an undecorated band on the low part of the neck has for a long time been considered typical of the Alakul decorative style. However, it is now argued that it is not obligatory on settlement ceramics (Stefanov 1996: 46). We should not forget that the Alakul pottery image has been formed on the basis of funeral material, which is quite substantial and has rather explainable specifics. Settlement collections usually produce bigger pots, a smaller number of vessels that are decorated, and the pot motifs are simpler.

The Alakul funeral sites are represented by a series of sporadic child burials within settlements and by kurgan cemeteries. The former are usually quite poor, and grave goods are limited basically to pottery. It is possible that the child burials were associated with building sacrifices. It does not, however, mean that people were killed before or in the course of house building. Perhaps in this case we can see some survival of an archaic form of ritual that had existed earlier, as it was recorded among Slavs and other European peoples (Baiburin 1983: 80–3). In the Alakul ritual, there was not "visible" demarcation between the "world of dead" and "world of living," as has been observed for Sintashta practice.

Cemeteries are situated in the same topographical areas as settlements. The Alakul burial grounds are quite numerous, and the biggest ones comprise

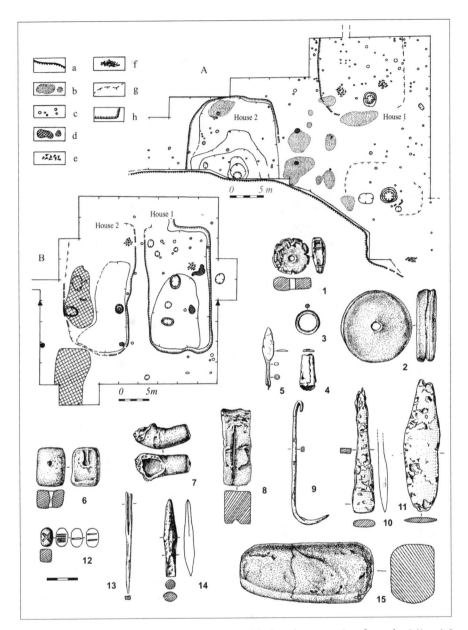

Figure 3.7. Houses and materials from the Alakul settlements: **A** – from the Mirnyi-I settlement; **B** – from the Mirnyi-III settlement: (a) steep bank, (b) ashpit, (c) posthole, (c–d) stone fireside, (e) accumulation of animal bones, (h) unclear contour, (g) border trench; (1, 2, 6, 8) stone; (3–5, 9–11) bronze; (3, 12–14) bone; (7) clay (1–8, 12, 14 - Mirnyi-II; 9–11,13 – Mirnyi-II) (after Stefanov 1996).

dozens of kurgans (Matveyev 1998; Potyemkina 1985; Salnikov 1952; Stokolos 1962; 1972). Although the term "kurgan" is not fully correct with regard to Alakul cemeteries, especially in the case of multigrave funeral sites that usually have one or two big graves in the center and many others, primarily children's

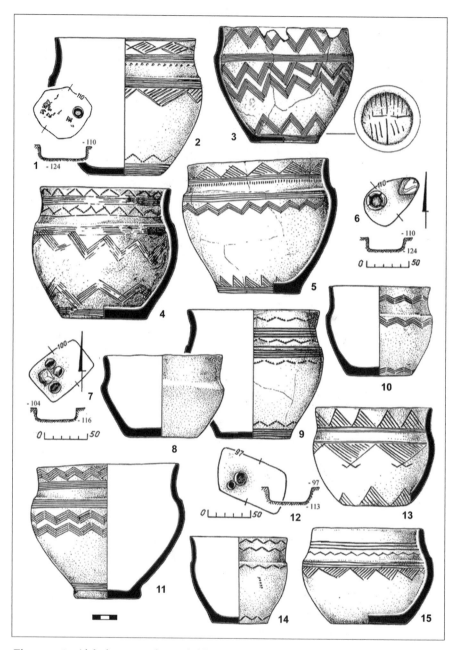

Figure 3.8. Alakul pottery from children graves of the Urefty burial ground, kurgan 2: (1, 2) grave 6; (3) grave 7; (4) grave 8; (5, 6) grave 9; (7–10) grave 10; (11, 12) grave 12; (13–15) pots from the pits near grave 12 (after Stefanov & Korochkova 2006).

graves, located around the center (Fig. 3.9). Such complexes frequently have circular ditches. The main portion of the above-grave construction was dedicated to the central graves, yet the other burials necessitated the addition of more earth. As a result, what the archaeologist sees as the whole assemblage

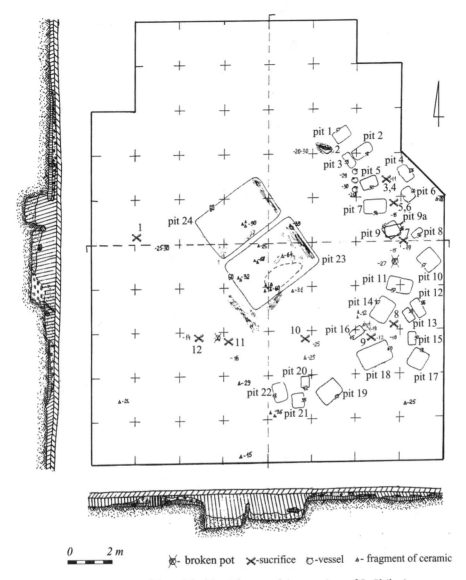

0   2 m

☒- broken pot   ✕-sucrifice   �-vessel   ▲- fragment of ceramic

Figure 3.9. Kurgan 20 of the Alakul burial ground (excavation of S. Shilov).

was built in several stages. Such kurgans can contain up to forty to fifty burials. The above-grave construction size depends on the quantity of burials, but in general, kurgans rarely exceed more than 20 m in diameter and 1 m in height. Moreover, there are also single-grave kurgans. The correlation between these two types is not clear.

The variation of the peripheral grave orientation can be explained by the system of their location. In the other cases, latitudinal orientations prevail especially in the Cis-Urals (Sorokin 1962) and in some cemeteries of central Kazakhstan. All grave pits are rectangular, and their size is completely determined by the age of the deceased although none is deep. The internal grave constructions are quite simple. In the forest-steppe, the tradition of using wood for the grave walls, plastering, and roofing is recorded. Stone was used more for fencing, roofing, and cyst construction in the steppe zone from the Cis-Urals up to central Kazakhstan. In the late stage, when archaeologists certify the rise of the Fyodorovo influence, we can see the appearance of stone constructions in the Trans-Urals as well (Vinogradov et al. 1996).

The Alakul funeral ritual is characterized by the absolute domination of inhumation. Sporadic cremation existed when the deceased was burned somewhere outside the area, and, then, the remains and ashes were placed into a grave. However, this ritual is encountered in complexes having some features of the Fyodorovo culture. All central graves, excluding the rarest cases, were robbed. Yet, it is possible to recognize the basic traits of the initial situation. The majority of graves contained single individuals placed in a contracted position on the left side with hands in front of the face (Fig. 3.10). There is a series of paired (male and female) burials in which the dead were placed face to face (man – on the left side, woman – on the right side). There are also graves with three individuals: man, woman, and child. In their orientation, the latitudinal directions are predominant.

Compared with the preceding period, sacrifices are represented by separate animal bones and their compositions. A complete animal body was replaced by its head and extremities. At the same time, the composition of selected animals remained similar to that of the Petrovka culture: the first place is occupied by cattle, then sheep, then horse. Similarly, an animal sacrifice was performed in special pits or at the edge of the grave pit. Usually, sacrifices are connected to large burials. It is interesting to notice the series of complete or partial dog sacrifices, which are more characteristic of the Trans-Urals (Matveyev 1998).

Fire played quite a significant role in the Alakul rituals; however, to connect its occurrences and specific burials is not possible. Generally, fire use is reflected in sporadic cremations,[8] fire traces on ancient surfaces under kurgans, and burned wooden interior constructions of big graves that supposedly belonged to adult women. Sometimes ochre was used as a substitute for fire.

Our ideas about grave goods are probably not adequate to the real situation because the central graves were robbed. Nevertheless, the Alakul burials usually yield quite a large number of artifacts.

Pottery is the most frequently found artifact but ornaments are also numerous: beads, amulets made from animal canines, gutter-shaped bracelets of two types (with spiral-like ends and with open ends), rings, crosslike and spectacle-like pendants, flat plaques, forged hollow earrings, and other items. The complex female hair decorations include pendants for braids (nakosniki) should especially be noted (Fig. 3.11). These are not only ethnographic markers of the Alakul culture (Evdokimov & Usmanova 1990) but also indicated social status and age status of the buried female. It is very interesting to note that the ethnographic costume of the Kazakh women has similar hair decorations.

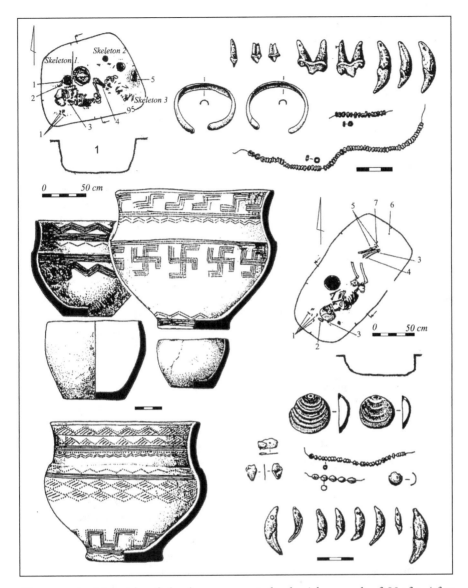

Figure 3.10. Materials of the kurgan 21 at the burial ground of Urefty (after Korochkova and Stefanov 2004).

Traditionally, scholars are interested in horse bridle objects, the number of which sharply decreases in the Late Bronze Age. The shieldlike cheek-pieces, some of which are found in settlements, were changed: the thorns disappeared, some items decorated with complex ornaments, and therefore they look more like ritual, not functional, objects (Fig. 2.19–3). One can state that there was a decline in chariotry, which is indirectly confirmed by a decrease of a horse sacrifice.

Very often the burials, especially those of children, produced only some pots. Ceramic collections are well represented by complete forms that allow us to create a more informative classification of pottery. In the series of proper Alakul ware coming from cemeteries, we have the same three basic forms as in settlements: can, can-pot, and pot. In the early stage, some portion of pottery with sharply designed shoulders and collars formed rims is preserved, but it is combined with typical Alakul vessels with ledge-designed shoulders. In ornamentation, the flat stamp still prevails.

Later, the collarlike rim disappears, ledge-designed forms replace sharply designed shoulders, and gradually the comb stamp comes into use. Ornamental motifs are supplemented by meanders, oblique triangles, and others. The decoration patterns tend to develop toward a greater role of the geometric in composition with wide use of the comb stamp. The pots gradually take on a smoother profile.

COMPLICATION OF INTERNAL CHRONOLOGY AND
THE ORIGIN OF THE ALAKUL CULTURE

Chronologically, the Alakul culture is related to the Late Bronze Age, and it is contemporaneous with the Srubnaya culture. In terms of the paleometallurgical periodization, the Alakul antiquities are connected to the Eurasian metallurgical network (according to Chernykh), of its first and partly second phases. The latter is dated differently, depending on the system used: traditional or radiocarbon. Radiocarbon dating considerably lowers the initial date – down to 1700 cal BC. The earlier date: turn of the third and second millennia BC – is defended by Matveyev (1998: 370–71), who excavated and dated, by C14, two necropolis situated in the north periphery of the Alakul territory. However, this hypothesis is not shared by many scholars, because the acceptance of such a variant of the chronology synchronizes the Alakul sites not only with the Petrovka sites (Matveyev states) but also with the Sintashta culture.

Until recently, the internal periodization of the Alakul culture has been weakly grounded; therefore the interpretation of concrete sites depended on the assessment of the Fyodorovo culture component in the pottery collections. The point is that supporters of the hypothesis that state the genesis of the Fyodorovo culture is based on Alakul made this reasoning. The general direction of ceramic evolution, which still serves for the reference, was established many years ago, but the evolutionary character of the changes makes all the variants of the internal periodization vulnerable.

Usually, scholars speak about early, middle, and late groups of material, relying on their ideas about the preceding and succeeding cultural formations. For example, according to Zdanovich (1988), the Alakul culture is genetically connected with the Petrovka culture. Potyemkina (1985) states that Petrovka originates in the southern Trans-Urals and northern Kazakhstan. She bases this on the basis of the Early Bronze Age local cultures intensive contacts with other formations such as the Sintashta, Abashevo, and Poltavka that entailed the formation of the Petrovka culture, which in turn is regarded as the early

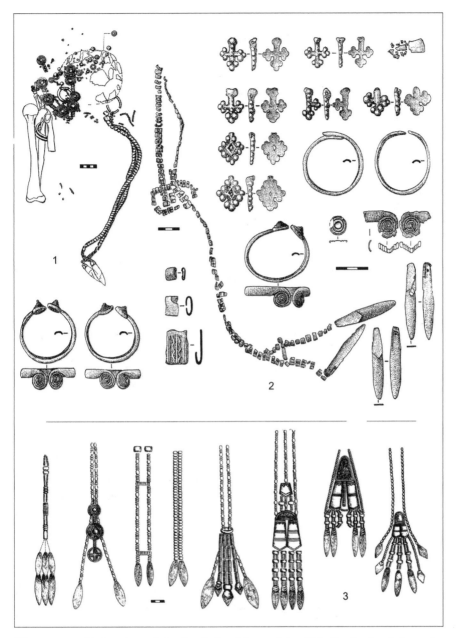

Figure 3.11. Decoration of the female headdress of the Alakul style: (1–2) from the Kulevchi burial ground; (3) reconstructions of the Alakul female hair decorations (after Usmanova and Logvin 1998).

stage of the Alakul culture. In every case, the internal periodization is based on the pottery and the evolution of its decoration, supplemented by stratigraphic observation.

Hence, the chronological issue of the Alakul culture concerns the problems of its origin. Nevertheless, it has hardly been discussed until recently, because its being the successor of the Petrovka culture had not been doubted. Matveyev thinks the genesis of the Alakul tradition was a multicomponent with the Sintashta culture taking dominance. It is true that the Petrovka sites investigated in northern Kazakhstan do not contain the whole range of Alakul characteristics. However, to think about a direct connection between the Sintashta and Alakul traditions means to simplify the real situation. The Petrovka sites of the Trans-Urals display some specific elements, a part of which would be seen later in the Alakul materials. As to the later position of the Petrovka culture compared to the Sintashta culture, this sequence is proved by a solid stratigraphic basis as well by other factors that we have indicated earlier.

By contrast, Grigory'ev (2000a) returned to the idea suggested earlier by Fedorova-Davydova (1964). He states that the Alakul culture originated in the southern Cis-Urals. According to Grigory'ev, the Alakul culture derives from a combination of the late Abashevo and Sintashta cultures, and in the sixteenth century BC, it turned outward into the Trans-Urals as a result of an eastward migration of its population. This hypothesis appears to be rather sophisticated, but is not well grounded.

The fate of the Alakul population is not clear but this is partly reasoned by the indefinite chronological correlations between the Alakul and Fyodorovo sites. Despite the multivoiced character of these internal interpretations of the origin of the Alakul culture, it is commonly accepted that it is related to the Sintashta-Petrovka line of evolution.

The Fyodorovo Culture

The Fyodorovo culture was revealed more than sixty years ago (Salnikov 1940), but it is still heavily debated. In particular, its position and role within the Andronovo area is interpreted differently. In turn, this results in different interpretations of the Andronovo cultural formation itself. According to one extreme hypothesis, the Fyodorovo culture should not be included in the Andronovo family. Nevertheless, Siberian archaeologists often identify the Andronovo culture by appealing to the Fyodorovo antiquities that were first discovered in the Minusinsk depression in the early 1920s.

The spread zone of the Fyodorovo sites is indeed vast. These sites are found in the area between the Urals and southern Siberia. Some separate features of the Fyodorovo burials and pottery are encountered in the area to the west of the Urals up to Ukraine. It is, of course, hard to expect a completely uniform culture over such a huge territory; meanwhile, scholars characterize the Fyodorovo sites in terms of a common culture. Geographically, the Fyodorovo sites are more connected to the forest-steppe landscapes. This is particularly notable in the Trans-Urals, where all large cemeteries are concentrated in two areas: around Chelyabinsk and around the Uvel'ka and Ui rivers. The latter marks the frontier between the northern steppe and forest-steppe (Fig. 3.5).

Beyond the Trans-Urals, the distribution of the Fyodorovo sites is not sufficiently clear. They do not form a continuous territory to be registered in
northern, central, and eastern Kazakhstan, and their "traces" are quite visible
up to the Tin Shan and Xingjian (Mei 2000; Mei & Shell 1999). In a more
or less "pure" form and out of the Alakul territory, they are recorded in east-
Middle Asia, eastern Kazakhstan, Altai, and the Minusinsk lowland (Kuzmina
1994). In central Kazakhstan, there are quite a number of sites with a mixed
appearance.

The relative chronological position of the Fyodorovo antiquities in the
Trans-Urals, northern, and central Kazakhstan within the Late Bronze Age is
undoubted. It is based on an elaborate typology of artifacts and by good stratigraphic observations. However, on the level of absolute dating, some scholars
come to different conclusions concerning the relationship between Fyodorovo
and Alakul sites. This has resulted in two cultural formations, either of which
are placed into a synchronic and parallel context or into their genetic connection with the late position being given to Fyodorovo.[9] We believe that the
materials of the Trans-Urals and western Siberian show evidence more in favor
of the second hypothesis without sharing the idea of a strong genetic link.

The Fyodorovo culture is almost exclusively represented by burial grounds,
which serve as cultural markers together with pottery that has a quite peculiar design. The situation with settlements is even more difficult. Some separate fragments of Fyodorovo pottery are not infrequently in found in settlements, but its percentage is, as a rule, rather limited. The number of authentic
Fyodorovo habitats is extremely small, and they are just single houses. In some
cases in multihouse settlements the structures, with so-called Bishkul ceramics,
which are considered by some scholars as a settlement variant of the Fyodorovo
type, are revealed. Taking this indefinite character of the Fyodorovo settlements
into account, it is reasonable to begin the characteristics of the culture of the
area under study with its funeral sites.

ARCHAEOLOGICAL MATERIALS
The Trans-Uralian Fyodorovo kurgan cemeteries are characterized by their
occupation of the flat banks of water reservoirs (Plate 3.3-A). Such topographical placement is in contrast with that of the preceding time periods when
populations preferred the mostly flat terraces. The number of mounds within
a cemetery varies from several dozen to hundreds, and the largest cemeteries
are concentrated in the area between Ui and Uvel'ka rivers. A spatial structure
can be traced in several cases when the number of kurgans is large enough
to form chains. In some burial grounds, the Fyodorovo structures are distinguished in the periphery of the Alakul structures occupying outlying position
(Korochkova 1993; Korochkova & Stefanov 2004). In western Siberia (Middle
Irtysh), flat cemeteries are dominant, but in the Upper Ob', the Fyodorovo
cemeteries are composed of both flat and kurgan burials.

Plate 3.3. Kurgans of the Fyodorovo culture type. **A** – Excavation of the Fyodorovo burial ground. **B** – A kurgan with stone fence and burials in stone boxes.

The Fyodorovo kurgans are smaller than the Alakul mounds, but they have better expressed relief. In some cemeteries, there are oval-shaped barrows, which is the result of subsequently adding new burials (Salnikov 1967). The most characteristic marker of the Fyodorovo funeral complex is the custom of building circular or rectangular fences around the cemetery (Fig. 3.12). Such fences are made of stone by cyst or masonry lying or they are covered by an earthen mound along the outer contour (Plate 3.3-B). The number of rectangular fences increases when moving from the west to east. The fences built from vertically erected stone slabs are numerous in the eastern regions of the territory of the Fyodorovo tradition, where, there are even mounds made exclusively from stone. At the same time in the Trans-Urals, one can sometimes discover mounds without any stone.

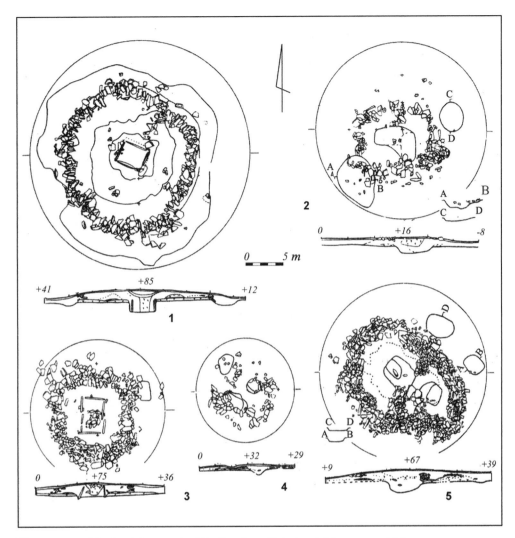

Figure 3.12. The burial ground of Putilovskaya Zaimka: (1) kurgan 7; (2) kurgan 3; (3) kurgan 2; (4) kurgan 8; (5) kurgan 6 (after Zdanovich 1988).

As a rule, the Fyodorovo kurgans contain one rectangular grave pit. However, these graves differ dramatically in their arrangement even within one and the same cemetery. In the Trans-Urals the following variables are recorded: (1) wooden frames on the pit bottom, (2) stone walls, (3) stone boxes, and (4) simple pits. All of these were combined with wood or stone roofs. Outside the Urals area, one can find the stone boxes covered by stone slabs. The diagnostic feature of the Fyodorovo ritual, especially in the Trans-Urals area, is the dominant role of cremation executed out. This tradition slowly decreases toward the east. There are also some other expressions of fire use: burned pit walls, piles of charcoal in the mound, and evidence of burning on the roof of the tomb. Inhumation is characteristic for the Kazakhstan and southern Siberia areas.

The graves usually have an east–west orientation. The linear model of the spatial organization of the mortuary ground is predominant (Fig. 3.13). According to this model, a barrow was enlarged by means of a new mound being attached to the earlier one. It is believed that multigrave barrows (up to five pits) are related to the later stage of the Fyodorovo tradition (Kuzmina 1994). The flat cemeteries of western Siberia contained numerous burials organized in parallel rows. The majority of burials comprised the remains of single individuals although in the eastern regions some double burials, in particular, those of a woman and child are known.

Overall, to judge the demographic characteristics of the deceased is quite difficult because of the almost total predominance of cremation. At the same time, we can discern the fact that the deceased were burnt together with sacrificed animals or their parts. Beyond the Urals, in the case of inhumation, the deceased were in a left-side crouched position with hands near the face.

In addition to the grave construction, the Urals Fyodorovo burials are characterized by quite a minimal series of ritual variables and a rather limited set of grave goods that distinguishes them from those of previous and later cultures. Animal bones were not as abundant as in Alakul burials: several ribs, horse scapula, horse or sheep head, and extremities. In a few cases, dog burials have been recorded. The variability of funeral rituals is much higher in the western Siberian regions of the Fyodorovo culture.

Grave goods include bronze ornaments such as trumpet earrings, palmate shaped pendants, bracelets with conical spirals at the ends, and round shields.[10] Some knife-daggers with slightly outlined head and nervure are also found. However, the most frequent item is pottery. The typical pots are well made, thin-sided, and with a smooth profile (Fig. 3.13–6, 7). They are regarded as the diagnostic feature of the Fyodorovo cultural complex. The technology of their construction differed from that of the Alakul culture: making of the Fyodorovo pot started from the body, whereas the Alakul vessels were manufactured on a model. Surfaces were carefully treated, sometimes they were polished and the bottom was designed as a pedestal (poddon). Proportions were strongly maintained – the mouth diameter is usually equal to the height of the pot. Most impressive is the Fyodorovo decorative system, consisting of three zones, each of which was designed according to a strict canon.

Small comb stamps decorated the pots; ornament is represented by complex geometric motifs based on an oblique grid (swastikas, meanders, triangles). A part of the decoration was represented by rows of small holes or cannelures (grooves). Triangles with oblique strokes can be found mostly on the neck; meanders were plotted to the body (Korochkova & Stefanov 2004: 91). One should notice that the described ceramics are most expressive but not very numerous in the Fyodorovo burials, including those in the Urals.

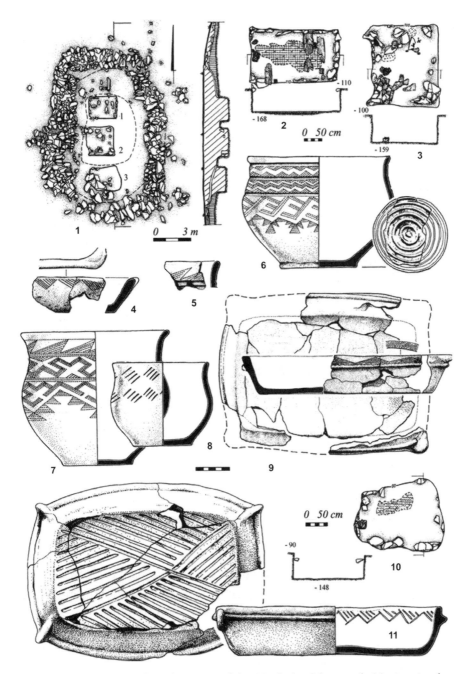

Figure 3.13. Materials from kurgan 6 of the Urefty burial ground: (1) view in plan and profile; (2, 4–6, 9) grave 1; (3, 7, 8) grave 2; (10, 11) grave 3 (after Stefanov & Korochkova 2006).

Among the most common exclusions from this rule are the pots decorated with rows of horizontal lines made with a flat stamp. The pottery of the Urals also includes rectangular and oval dishes, which are usually not included in the ceramic inventory of other regions of the Andronovo area (Fig. 3.13–9, 11).

The cemeteries also comprise some structures, which cannot be considered the real funeral complexes. They had the external form of a kurgan, but they did not contain any graves. Large piles of burnt human and animal bone as well as ceramic vessels have been discovered under these mounds. It is quite probable that these served as the cremation places.

Numerous authentic Fyodorovo settlements have not been discovered in the peripheral zone – either in the northern forest-steppe or in central Kazakhstan. In the Urals, there is only one settlement, Kamennaya Rechka, which is situated on the Ui-river. In all other cases, the Fyodorovo component is revealed either typologically or stratigraphically in multilayered settlements.

The known settlements are situated on the first river terraces, near the large river valleys. They can comprise from four to five to several dozen houses, situated according to a linear pattern. Their inhabited space varies between 30 and 300 m². The two basic types of construction encountered in the settlements are light framework dwellings and big semi-subterranean, multiroomed buildings (Malutina 1990; Matveyev 1998). The houses usually have storage pits, niches, wells, and hearths. Big buildings combined the functions of living house and place for young livestock. The heterogeneity of the Fyodorovo architectural tradition can be explained by the fact that the studied Fyodorovo settlements are located in very different parts of the cultural area. For example, in central Kazakhstan the architecture of daylight surface dwellings displays an influence coming from Central Asia. The connection with Central Asia is evidenced also by the pottery of the Namazga VI period, found among the Fyodorovo pottery assemblages (Malutina 1991). The semisubterranean houses are obviously of local origin.

Material collections from settlements are, to some extent, richer than those from burials. They contain, aside from pottery, numerous other artifacts. Metal objects are represented by socketed arrowheads, chisels, awls, hooked sickles, knife-daggers, etc. The bone inventory includes instruments for wool and leather processing, as well as many bone arrowheads. The metal work is documented by clay casting molds, abrasives, pestles, and slag, which are more typical for the sites of central Kazakhstan.

THE PROBLEM OF THE ORIGIN OF THE FYODOROVO CORE-TRADITION

The most difficult question concerns the origin of the Fyodorovo cultural core-tradition. All opinions on this point fall into two basic hypothetical versions: the "forest" and the "steppe" hypothesis. The former regards the Fyodorovo sites as a result of the evolution of the Trans-Uralian forest cultures expanding their influence into vast territories (Salnikov 1967). This version also presupposes the

Ugrian attribution of the Fyodorovo culture. The second hypothesis, which is shared by many archaeologists, arises from the assumption of its southern origin and, consequently, in its Iranian affiliation.

We should stress that neither version has indisputable arguments. On the one hand, the area that is traditionally regarded by adherents of the "northern" birthplace of the Fyodorovo tradition was assimilated by people with the Alakul tradition rather early on (Matveyev 1998), and consequently, the Fyodorovo culture could not have originated there because of its later chronological position.

On the other hand, the version that takes central Kazakhstan as the place of origin is also chronologically ambiguous. At the present time, there are no closed archaeological complexes containing pure Fyodorovo and pure Alakul forms of ceramics. The areas of both cultures only partly overlap. This, together with other factors such as an inability to reveal dependable late Alakul sites, force us to think about their asynchronic character. Stratigraphic observation made on the Atasu settlement in central Kazakhstan supports the idea of the later position of Fyodorovo pottery in relation to that of Alakul pottery. (Kadyrbayev & Kurmankulov 1992; Kuznetsova & Kurmankulov 1993). This does not contradict the fact that the Final Bronze Age assemblages contain more Fyodorovo elements than those of Alakul.

These variants of the Fyodorovo genesis obviously do not deplete numerous nuances of interpretations that can be found in Russian publications. In particular, Grigory'ev (2000a; 2002) believes that the Fyodorovo tradition has a trans-Caucasian and Near Eastern origin (territory of Iranian Azerbaidgan). According to him, some small proto-Fyodorovo groups participated in the frontal northeast migration of the Sintashta population.

Korochkova (1993) thinks that the Fyodorovo funeral tradition was not determined by cultural factors but was the reflection of a social process, according to which the Fyodorovo graves belonged to some group of people having special social status. Such an approach helps to understand the lack of 'pure' Fyodorovo settlements against the background of an enormous number of typical Fyodorovo barrows.

In any case, the Alakal and Fyodorovo funeral traditions are rather different, that obstructs the seeking for the straight genetic connection between them.

It is currently believed that the Fyodorovo population contributed to the Valikovaya (banded) pottery cultural horizon (Final Bronze Age – see Chapter 4). However, in the time of the Final Bronze Age, cremation practically disappears from the funeral ritual. The Fyodorovo heritage is recorded not only in the Trans-Urals, but also in the forest-steppe Volga area, where the Suskan type, which combines some western and eastern traditions, has been revealed (Kolev 1991). This area was of an intermediate character between the Fyodorovo territory and the area of the Late and Final Bronze Age of Ukraine where some Fyodorovo elements, including numerous and typical

Fyodorovo pots, have surely been traced (Berezanskaya & Gershkovich 1983). Researchers interpret these elements as evidence of a gradual penetration of the Fyodorovo groups into the west (Gershkovich 1998). This also can be explained by active contacts between eastern and western regions of northern Eurasia.

Economic and Social Dimensions of the Andronovo Cultures

As we stated in the Introduction to this book, environmental conditions of the Late Bronze Age in the Eurasian steppe were favorable to extensive livestock breeding. Yet, the local specifics in plant-formation, precipitation, and wind activity can recoil upon diverse ecosystems, which in turn influenced herd composition.

Particular ecosystems are dominated by particular plant species, which have different biological and fodder productivity. For example, the plants-xerophytes such as mat-grasses have rather large root systems (up to 1 m deep). Their biological productivity is about 3,000 kg per 1 ha, whereas the fodder productivity is 300–700 kg/ha in springtime; 200–500 kg/ha in summer; 100–300 kg/ha in fall; and about 150 kg/ha in winter. In every ecosystem, the vegetal biomass prevails over the mass of phytophagous animals, which in turn dominate the predatory birds. Therefore, the animal biomass is "more expansive" (more energy-consuming) than the former, but in the climatic conditions of the Eurasian steppe agriculture that, in principle, is easier to realize, it required greater physical effort with little outcome (Evdokimov 2000).

In order to survive, the pastoralists maintained a rational balance between the number of animals and the state of a pasture. According to the statistical data of the nineteenth century collected by Kosarev, one Kazakh family consisting of four to six persons should have had twenty-four head of animals (in comparison to a horse).[11] The pastoralist family with limited plant cultivating should have eighteen head, a semisettled family fifteen units, and a farming family could have only twelve head of animals. Kosarev (1991: 38) believes that one can statistically determine the minimal norm for the Bronze Age family: twelve animal head. He states that for more or less stable herd reproduction a slaughter should not be more than one-quarter of the total animal stock; one conventional Andronovo family of five persons could have eaten during a year no more than three head of horses, which corresponds to 3.6 cows or 18 sheep. He calculates that such a family having twelve animals required on average about 1 km² of pasture.

On the subject of the economy of the Alakul population, it did not greatly change from the preceding period. As in the previous period, livestock breeding was the basis of population subsistence. The stable settlements are witness to the pastoral character of Alakul livestock breeding. The animal bones collected from the settlements with Fyodorovo ceramics allow us to a imagine major branch of the economy. It also was based on livestock breeding, the form of which, however, is not clear. Cattle were predominant in herds (60 percent), followed by sheep (22 percent), and horse (15 percent). The horses were three breeds: (1) runty, with withers of 128–136 cm; (2) middle – 136–152 cm in withers, and (3) high, grace horses with 152–160 cm in withers. Great and small cattle were of an eastern European breed (Kuzmina 1996b: 89). In the northern zone, fishing and hunting, basically elk, played quite a notable role. Traces of metalworking were recorded in some settlements (Zakh 1995).

There is no direct evidence for plant cultivation although its existence is suggested because some artifacts interpreted as agricultural tools (hoes and grinding stones). Potyemkina (1985: 320–1), however, doubts this, coming to the conclusion that low labor productivity and crop capacity do not allow us to consider the role of cultivation as essential in the Alakul area. We are inclined to share this opinion.

Archaeological material clearly gives evidence about other economic activities: weaving, leather processing, wood processing, and so on. No one doubts the existence of metallurgy, but its concrete forms are not clear yet. For the time being, in the Alakul area no one has distinguished such specialized metallurgical settlements analogous to Srubnaya sites such as Gorny I in the southern Cis-Urals or the Mosolovo settlement in the Don area. However, many of the Alakul habitats produce traces of metalworking or copper production, not to mention the great quantity of metal coming from the sites (Fig. 3.14).

It seems that the Trans-Ural mines continued to function, and their production was actively supplemented by Kazakhstan and Cis-Ural (Elenovsko-Ushkatta deposits) metal. The appearance and wide use of tin bronzes testifies to connections with eastern Kazakhstan where the largest deposits of cassiterite were available.

Generally, referring to the image of the Alakul archaeological representation, we can say that the Alakul society can be characterized in terms of a kinship social organization. Sex and age structures are clearly diagnosed by funeral rituals, but it is difficult to say anything about other societal gradations (professional or religious). However, it seems that the contraposition of central and peripheral burials was a reflection of social structure stressing different social statuses of buried persons. Cremation burials do not differ from inhumation burial in terms of basic characteristics. Potyemkina (1985) has noted a correlation between the ages of the dead and the types of sacrificed animals: bones of horses have been found more often accompanying adults in central graves, those of cattle were in the burials of adults and juveniles, and the bones of sheep and goats were associated more frequently with infants.

It is clearly visible that the labor investment in funeral rituals became smaller although all of basic elements of rituality and set of offerings were preserved (retained). Symbols of power and prestige (maces, spearheads, axes, and chariotery complexes) maintain a similar tendency. Conclusions drawn from the

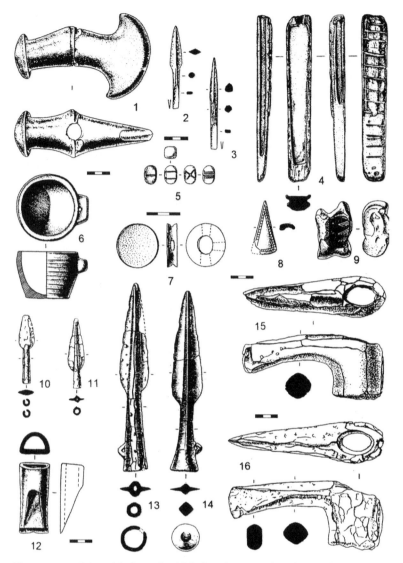

Figure 3.14. Materials from the Alakul settlement of Korkino (after Chemyakin 2000).

analysis of funeral rituals correspond well to those of settlement studies. Judging from the settlement size, one can say that they accommodated not more than several hundred people.

The size of a necropolis surely allows us to suppose that they served as lineage cemeteries. Unfortunately, the state of anthropological collections is not good because of soil conditions and the extensive robbery of adult burials. Because of this, it is not possible to verify the hypothesis that inhumation was characteristic for all buried people, although this looks to be the case. Some identified female cremations in the Alakul cemeteries can testify to the marriage connections with the Fyodorovo groups.

The question of the organization of Fyodorovo society is also not easy to address. Before we turn to that discussion, we will briefly dwell on its demographic parameters. One completely excavated settlement, Cheryomukhovyi kust, allows us to assess the number of its inhabitants. According to Zakh, its excavator (1995: 73), this settlement might have accommodated about 110 to 120 individuals at once. This statement points to a lineage-based organization. Such a small society contrasts with the quite big cemetery. Yet, if we suppose that the cemetery was used for a long period, then this contradiction does not look so sharp.

We do not have direct evidence about the degree of social ranking within this population group although a certain, amount of diversity in the above ground and in-grave arrangements can bear witness its connection with social diversity. We can also compare the labor investment of every burial. As a criterion for distinguishing the socially significant grave, one can take a set of rare artifacts, such as a "knife-dagger" and a javelin. At the same time, it is also possible to expect that the rareness of metal in graves can be explained by the easy accessibility to robbers. This is particularly true in the Kazakhstan area, where graves do not have solid above ground constructions.

We can conclude that the economy in the Andronovo and Srubnaya zones was based on animal husbandry supplemented with some agriculture, hunting, fishing, and domestic crafts. Andronovo stockbreeding is close to that of eastern Europe with respect to herd composition and animal characteristics. It developed from settled pastoralism that gave rise to mobile pastoralism by the end of the second millennium BC.

Plate 3.4. Polished stone ax from the Mirnyi-2 burial ground. According to petrographic analysis undertaken in the Ural Geological Academy, this ax is made from volcanic tuff of basalt composition. Such rocks are encountered in trappean formation of Russian platform and in southwest Byelorussia.

Metallurgy was quite advanced and concentrated in several centers whose products were distributed throughout temperate Eurasia. If, however, we consider the grave goods with which the deceased were furnished, we do not find great wealth differences, and the number of imported objects was limited. We should note, however, that the Andronovo society knew and appreciated gold although it was not in wide circulation. Additionally, the Alakul and mixed Srubnaya-Alakul cemeteries of southern Urals produced a series of splendid polished stone axes (Fig. 3.14–1; Plate 3.4) closely reminiscent of axes from Troy and the Borodino hoard.

In a general sense, one can see that the level of social stability was higher in the Srubnaya and Andronovo periods; there are neither fortresses nor sophisticated constructions. A prestige grave-good system is not clearly displayed. Funerary rituals do not provide evidence of unquestionable social stratification although the diversity of funerary rituals and a series of valuable objects can also correspond to a diversity of social categories. None of the available facts contradicts the hypothesis of population growth and a relatively stable economy including various craft production. The extent of the Andronovo cultural network increased greatly, and there were exchange networks linking most of central Eurasia through common metallurgical traditions. The population of the Urals used many inventions that came about in the first half of the second millennium BC, especially military developments such as war chariots, which were predominant during the period 2000–1500 cal BC in the Eurasian steppes. This period can be considered as a time of stabilization and colonization that however did not exclude military conflicts between communities.

Linguistic attribution of the Alakul and Fyodorovo cultures is argued in full by E. Kuzmina (1994). On the basis of complex analysis of the Andronovo culture, supplemented by linguistic, paleoanthropological, and ethnographic data relating to the culture of the Indo-Iranian peoples, she related the entire population of the Urals and Kazakhstan of the Late Bronze Age to the eastern Iranians.[12]

We agree with her argument and believe it to be rather reliable, requiring no additional proof. In this connection, it is interesting to mention the problem of time and place of contact between the Indo-Iranian and Finno-Ugrian groups, which are well established linguistically and toponimically.

In the material of the Alakul culture, some traces of the northern cultural complex are found as well. In particular, the presence of the Cherkaskul culture (see Chapter 3) is most visible. Its pottery is found even in Kazakhstan. It is quite probable that since the time of the "classical" Alakul the vector of interrelationships between steppe and forest groups had changed.

NORTHWARD EXPANSION

In the second quarter of the second millennium BC, the Alakul groups and, slightly later, Fyodorovo communities struck out into the forest-steppe, toward the northern taiga. This movement is evidenced by numerous settlement sites with diagnostic decorated wares. The aboriginal population accepted pastoralism and began to use more tin-bronze. The model of their interaction may be defined as "Stock breeders, hunters and fishers" or "Stock breeders, metallurgists and hunters." The consequence was a redistribution of people and a cultural transformation within the vast area to the east of the Urals.

The character and time of the shift of steppe population into the forest zone was different in different regions of this area. However, researchers are of the same mind to date this process by the early Late Bronze Age. For example, in the Trans-Urals northern forest-steppe, both the Alakul and Fyodorovo materials are represented quite well (Korochkova et al. 1991; Koryakova et al. 1991; Matveyev 1998; Stefanov & Korochkova 2000; Zakh 1995). Therefore, the forest-steppe regions of western Siberia were strongly impacted by the steppe groups, from direct colonization and assimilation of the local populations. In its turn, in the forest zone the syncretic cultures, which are known in the literature under the name of "Andronoid" or "Andronovo-like," came into being. After the first wave of the Andronovo colonization, which seems to have been stronger from the side of the Fyodorovo groups, than others, and mixture with the local population, some internal transformations took place. On the one hand, one can see an astonishing similarity in the material culture within the forest-steppe, but, on the other, some differences are also clearly visible.

The Andronovo-Like Cultural Horizon

The Andronovo-like cultural horizon is composed of several subcultures, among which the most important are: Cherkaskul (Middle and southern Trans-Urals); Pakhomovo – Middle Irtysh and Tobol), Suzgun (taiga area of the Middle Irtysh), and Elovka (forest area of the Ob'-Irtysh river basin) (Fig. 3.1; 4.1). All these subcultures and some other smaller groups are characterized by similar ceramics – flat-bottomed pots with high or middle shoulders, short necks, and compact decoration consisting of alternating geometric motives in which the forest "images" and "Andronovo spirit" are easily recognizable. Yet the concrete combinations of the ceramic forms and designs determine the specifics of each subculture. Moreover, they have some similarity with synchronous formations of pre-, Trans-Urals, and eastern regions of western Siberia. The introduction of the Andronovo-type geometric design into the local pottery has reduced the area of the local hole and combed ornamental scheme, which, however, still covered the major part of the taiga and Polar area (Potyemkina et al. 1995).

The sites of the Cherkaskul group are mainly concentrated in the southern forest and northern forest-steppe of the Ural mountains (Fig. 3.1). Some elements of this cultural complex are known far beyond the core-area – even in the steppe zone (Evdokimov 1983). Therefore, the Cherkaskul sites are sometimes considered as belonging to the Andronovo family as a later version of Fyodorovo tradition (Matveyev 1998).

Cherkaskul pottery has much in common with that of Fyodorovo pottery: it is characterized by the frequent use of carpet design in ornamentation, which is, however, denser and more sophisticated than that of the Fyodorovo tradition. The flat-bottomed pots have a smooth and pleasing profile (Fig. 3.15-A). The local clays that have a lavish admixture of talcum were used for pottery manufacture. Although the Cherkaskul ceramics are widely spread over the Trans-Urals, it is difficult to find any site with a "pure" Cherkaskul layer because most of the local sites are multisettled. For the same reason and also because of specifics of local soil, the residential architecture of this culture is modestly represented in the archaeological record. In the mountain-forested areas, the basements of houses were not deep, with shallow rectangular pits. They served as the grounds for building of small (about 22–50 m²) frame-pillar wooden constructions with internal hearths (Fig. 3.15-B). The houses had the corridor-like entrances. However, in the southern locations, in the forest-steppe and steppe environments, the houses were larger (100–200 m²) and with deeper basements. Some more or less "homogeneous" settlements produced a great deal of evidence for a stable and settled life – tools for hunting, fishing, as well as bones of predominantly domestic animals, bone dice, and the remains of developed metallurgy (Fig. 3.16). The remains of deep wells and ash accumulations are features of the Cherkaskul settlement layers.

The Cherkaskul core-tradition demonstrates an interesting funeral practice. Here, two major rituals: cremation and inhumation, are known. The first was characteristic for the southern area, the second one for northern and western regions. Funeral constructions vary greatly as well. In the south, these are represented by small kurgans with stone fences and mounds, covering individual burials with traces of cremation, which was executed outside the burial ground. Some cemeteries, as for instance, Bolshekazakbayevo kurgan 19 (Fig. 3.17) give the vivid example of ritual contamination. Four deep grave pits suitable for burying adult persons contained only the remains of cremations, which were spread out on the pit bottom. From one to four pots were placed to the pit corners.

Inhumations usually were in shallow pits in contracted left-sided position and accompanied by rather modest grave goods. After its formation in about the fourteenth century BC, the Cherkaskul population moved to other regions. They successfully joined with neighboring groups living within the Andronovo and Andronovo-like zones.

The Pakhomovo groups (twelfth–eleventh centuries BC), constituting the southern part of the Andronovo-like massive, are located in the northern forest-steppe and forest of the Tobol-Irtysh basin and were represented basically by settlements and, to a smaller extent, by burial grounds. The pottery of this group has much in common with that of Fyodorovo pottery in morphology, decoration and manner of surface treatment. Nevertheless, the Pakhomovo collections always contain pots covered by monotonous ornaments of the forest style in which very various holes and figured stamps were very popular (Korochkova et al. 1991).

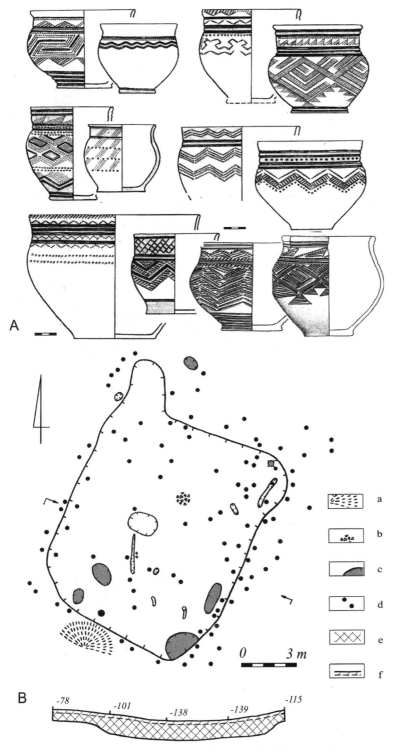

Figure 3.15. Cherkaskul type pottery **(A)** and **(B)** Cherkaskul house-structure from the Shukubai-II village: (a) rock; (b) fireplace; (c) bone accumulation; (d) post-hole; (c) gray clay; (f) top soil (after Evdokimov 1985).

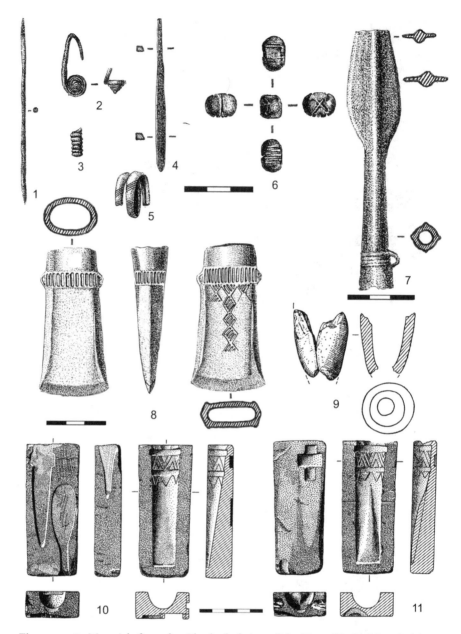

Figure 3.16. Materials from the Cherkaskul sites of the Trans-Urals: (1) awl; (2) earring; (3) bead; (4) knife; (5) finger ring; (6) dice; (7) spearhead; (8) socketed axe; (9) twyer; (10–11) stone molds from the settlement of Lipovaya Kury'a (after Shorin, unpublished manuscript, drawing by Timoshek and Khlobystin 1976).

The settlements are not very large: 4,500 m² on average; the excavated houses are varied but not numerous (Pletneva 1994). They are above ground or semisubterranean (rarely), about 100 m² in size, rectangular, wooden built with vertical pillars supporting a pyramidal roof. The houses were furnished with

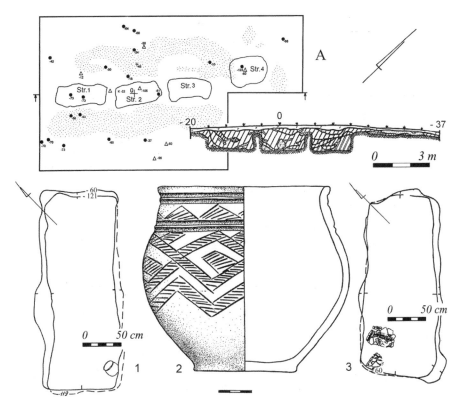

Figure 3.17. Burials and pottery of Bolshekazakbayevo kurgan 19: **(A)** site – plan; (1) grave 1; (2) pot, (3) grave 2.

open hearths, and storage pits. The fixed hearths were arranged with various details, including wooden frames, clay plastering or bricks. Households also included some small wooden constructions of economic use. Water pits and ash accumulations, recorded in the Pakhomovo villages, together with hearth constructions are clearly paralleled with the Andronovo house building.

The inventory of the Pakhomovo archaeological sites comprises not only pottery which, of course, is dominant, but also large quantity of tools relating to hunting and fishing, the traces of metallurgical activity (crucibles, smelting molds), and metal objects themselves (awls, needles, ornaments). The composition of archeozoological collections and hunting tools testify to the significant role of meat hunting and fishing, supplemented by cattle and horse breeding (Korochkova et al. 1991).

There are only a few modest burials and thirteen fractioned human skeletons discovered in the ash accumulation at the Novo-Shadrino settlement (Middle Tobol) relating to the Pakhomovo culture (Korochkova 1999).[13] Together with fractioned individual and collective burials of the other Andronovo-like cultures (see later), these burials shed light on some aspects of the funeral rituality of the Late Bronze Age forest societies.

Suzgun groups (twelfth–ninth centuries BC) occupy the area to the north of the Pakhonovo territory and partly overlap the latter in the northern Ishim and Irtysh forest-steppe (Polevodov 2003). Some sites are situated on the high promontories of the Irtysh river valley; the others on the low fluvial terraces. Terrain relief, size, and the economy conditioned the settlement layout.

Elevated sites such as the Suzgun II and Chudskaya Gora are interpreted in terms of sanctuaries (Potyemkina 1995). The settlement layout is recorded only for the Chudskaya Gora, yet one should be very careful in its extrapolation to the other regions of the Suzgun area because of the specific character of this site (Fig. 3.18). Ten long rectangular houses (8–12 × 3.5 m) with corridor-like entrances have been excavated in the Chudskaya Gora site. Twenty-five to thirty houses were situated inside a wooden walled enclosure, along the ground perimeter, and were very close to each other. The house remains consisted of vertical pillars forming perpendicular rows. They probably were conjoined above into the rigid frame supporting a flat roof. The authors of the site publication see here elements of Andronovo architecture (Potyemkina et al. 1995).

The site has produced a great number of various artifacts, especially ceramics (eleven hundred pots), which were deposited in the assemblages inside the houses or dispersed between them, as well as the animal bones, among which there were dog skeletons, separated dog skulls, and fish-scales. Part of the bones had been burnt and this is reflected in the ash and carbonized bone accumulations. Many whole pots were found upside-down. This is how the authors of site publication interpret such a situation:

> The amplitude of pottery and the system of its deposition in composition together with other factors can be interpreted as evidence of mass ritual actions that were connected with sacrificing and common eating of obla-tional food. These actions were executed in the promontory part of the site. Over quite a long period, settlement inhabitants and people from the neighbourhoods periodically visited the sanctuary. (Potyemkina et al. 1995: 36–7)

Hence, the main conclusion drawn from detailed analysis of the Chud-skaya Gora site is that it served as the ritual and administrative center where some people responsible for maintaining the customary observance might have lived.

Only several solitary inhumations found occasionally within the cemeteries of different periods, and recently discovered collective burials containing the remains of various ritual actions represent the mortuary practice of the Suzgun culture. All of these were executed on the ancient soil; the dead were chiefly in extended supine positions. The burial grounds at Ust-Kiterma-V and two settlement burials Ust-Kiterma IV discovered between the Ishim and Irtysh

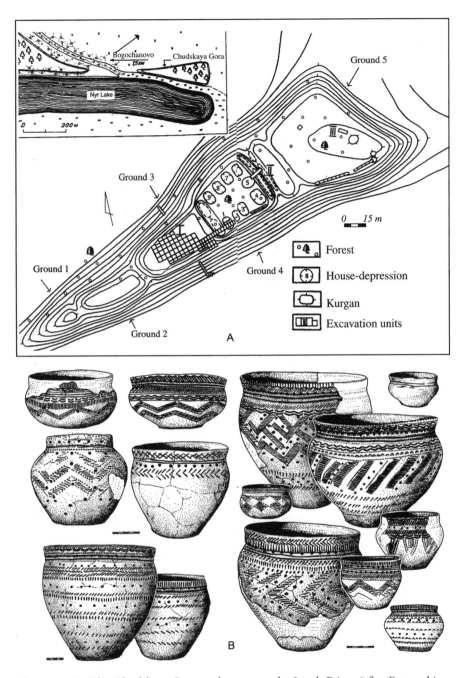

Figure 3.18. The Chudskaya Gora settlement on the Irtysh River (after Potyemkina, Korochkova, and Stefanov 1995).

rivers are very interesting. The first was located under a small mound and contained thirty-seven partly cremated or burned skeletons, the second one individual inhumation, and ten partly burned skeletons. These graves were built after the settlement had ceased functioning (Polevodov & Trufanov 1997).

Two types of burials represent the Suzgun mortuary practice: (1) small kurgan burials with round and oval shaped mounds, under which from one to four graves can be found; and (2) the collective burials with dozens of individuals, which had been subjected to some cleaning procedures. There are both inhumations and partial cremations. Some elements of the Suzgun funeral ritual go back to the pre-Andronovo time period, the others are paralleled in the Andronovo-like cultures of the Late Bronze Age (Polevodov 2003).

As previously stated, pottery is the most abundant category of artifact in the sites of the Suzgun culture (Fig. 3.18). The collections consist of flat and round bottomed pots with well pronounced profiles and decorated with geometric motifs (hatched bands, triangles, rhombuses, etc.) (Kosarev 1981).

In the Suzgun inventory, which include clay spindle whorls, plummets, bone-picks, and arrowheads, there is a series of objects relating to the bronze metalworking. This fact is rather distinctive if we remember that this area is rather poor of any copper resources. Metal is most abundantly represented in the collection of the Chudskaya Gora site, which allows us to think that metalworking may has been a part of ritual actions.

The economic profile of the Suzgun populations reconstructed on the analysis of archeozoological and artifact collections was of diversified character. Among the domestic animals cattle was dominant, and horse occupied second position. Hunting and especially fishing constituted an essential part of subsistence economy, but their correlation varied. Researchers pay attention to the fact that the latest sites of the Andronovo-like cultures produce the greater proportion of the horse bones and smaller number of sheep bones (Kosintsev 1989).

All the Andronovo-like cultures are close to each other not only geographically and chronologically but also economically and socially. All of them are oriented to a diversified economy consisting of producing and non-producing branches, the proportions of which must have been varied according to concrete conditions and external influence. The strongest stimulation came from the south – from the Andronovo cultural area; its forms varied from the direct shift and assimilation of some aboriginal groups up to the introduction of selected elements. The local traditions, however, have turned out to be stable and the Andronovo component has been transformed in different degrees but preserved some nuances, colors, and elements, which allow us to recognize it. The question is, what kind of mechanism conducted such stimulation. How far to the north did the Andronovo groups penetrate? As research shows, the Andronovo groups (first – the Alakul, then the Fyodorovo communities) did go to the south forest, mainly concentrating in the forest-steppe areas. Their traditions, in a rather transformed form, were brought to the forest by the decedents of the first waves of Andronovo colonization. One should remember that by the time of the formation of the Andronovo-like cultures, around the thirteenth century BC, the Andronovo cultures themselves no longer existed in the steppe area.

Against the background of the brilliant classical Andronovo formations, the Andronovo-like cultures display a clear decrease in the number of metal objects. This can be explained by several factors: first, the absence of own sources of ores and ligature, and second, a metal had not entered into the main economic activity of the forest societies. Bone, horn, and other tools, the manufacture of which was not as labor-intensive as the metal objects, and which were nearly as effective, remained in use for a long time. During this period, the latitudinal connections between different groups in western Siberia were strong.

The demographic parameters of the Andronovo-like communities were rather modest. They were limited by the capacity of the forest ecological niches. Hunting and fishing, and, obviously, gathering were of greater significance here than in the south. In addition, this, in its turn, naturally required more space. The population density of the forest-steppe and especially the forest was relatively low. Communities were concentrated in clusters chiefly along the rivers, which served also as the paths of migration and communication. The material culture does not demonstrate any serious markers of complex social hierarchies. An absence of funeral sites in the vast area adds to our difficulties to understand the social context of the Andronovo-like cultures. The available burials display more ritual diversity connected with the spiritual sphere of these cultures than the social one. Ritual and ceremonial activity played a very important part in the social and economic organization of local communities.

At the end of the Bronze Age, marked by changes in the life of western Siberian population, the Andronovo-like types had been transformed. In the steppe, eastern variants of the cultural horizon of the Valikovaya pottery tradition came into being. Because of cooling and the overmoistening of the humid zone, the cultures with Cross-Stamped ceramic of the taiga forest origin appeared along the northern border of the forest-steppe (see later).

The support for the Proto-Iranian (or Indo-Iranian) linguistic attribution of the Alakul and Fyodorovo cultures, or related branches of the Andronovo cultural confederation, requires the supposition that the extension of these languages increased and partly overlapped the distribution of the Proto-Ugric languages, the area of which is traditionally determined within the western Siberian forest and forest-steppe. Despite southern influence, the Andronovo-like cultures preserved some substantial elements of the local aboriginal cultures of the Eneolithic and Early Bronze Age (in pottery, house types, and funeral rituals). The solution of this problem is far from final. Yet, it is interesting to note that some "classical" Andronovo ornamental motifs such as "meanders," which were adopted from the south, are well represented in the forest zone, where they is preserved in very late historical cultures of the Ob-Ugrians: Khanty and Mansi peoples. Specialists also pay attention to the similarity between Indo-Iranian and Finno-Ugrian mythology. The two gods of the Indo-Aryans: Varuna and Mitra, are paralleled with Finno-Ugric deities Numi-Torum and Mir-Susne-Hum (E. Kuzmina 1994, 2001; Steblin-Kamenskij 1995). All of this, representing the Andronovo-like cultures in the western Siberian forest-steppe and southern forest, are evidence for the hypothesis that suggests very active contacts between the Indo-Iranian and Finno-Ugric languages, expressed in numerous mutual borrowings, a part of which can be traced to the second millennium BC (Carpelan & Parpola 2001; Napolskikh 1997).

CHAPTER 4

ON THE EVE OF A NEW EPOCH:
FINAL BRONZE AGE

Around the fourteenth/thirteenth centuries BC, the societies of the Andronovo-Srubnaya area were gradually transformed, which, however, cannot be described only in term of decline or collapse. Some societies became more homogeneous and simpler. The others changed their strategies toward the adaptation to the new environmental (natural, cultural, and social) conditions. In all cases, basic cultural traditions that were stable during the previous centuries changed their appearance as evidenced by the structural regrouping within the whole area under study. Archaeologically, this has found reflection in different types of material culture.

THE SARGARY CULTURE

The end of the Bronze Age in the Eurasian steppes is marked by the formation of the vast cultural occurrence which is known under general term "horizon of cultures of the Valikovaya pottery tradition" (Chernykh 1983, 1992). This cultural occurrence occupied practically of the all steppe and forest-steppe from Altai to eastern Europe. The most western part is constituted by cultures of the Low Danube, eastern Carpathians, and northern coast of the Black Sea. In the east, this formation comprised the cultures of the Don-Volga-Ural area (late Srubnaya culture), southern Urals and Trans-Urals, and Kazakhstan (Sargary, Trushnikovo, Dandybai-Begazy, Amirabad). Their common marker is the poorly ornamented flat-bottomed pottery with clay rollers stuck around the shoulder or neck. There also are some other similarities in metal, economic structure, and funeral ritual.

In the steppe zone, there are a few sites of this period investigated by large-scale excavations. Meanwhile, the number of surveyed site is quite impressive. Therefore, our analysis has to be based mostly on the material coming from surveys.

Compared with the preceding period, the landscape boundaries no longer served as cultural frontiers especially for the widespread of metal objects and specific pottery, which has given the name to the whole cultural zone. One can suppose that this process was accompanied by the movement of some population groups. It is possible that climate change at the turn of the second and first millennia BC (see the Introduction to this book) contributed to this instability.

Traditionally, the final place of the Bronze Age is dated to the period between the twelfth and eleventh centuries BC and the ninth and eighth centuries BC (the transition to the Iron Age). According to new dates, this final phase could have started no later than thirteenth century BC and lasted until the tenth century BC. Some attempts have been made to divide all available material into two chronological groups, but for the steppe zone of the Ural it is not possible because of the lack of material. Beyond the Urals, the materials directly preceding the cultures of early nomads are distinguished: in the Volga area this is the Nur type, in Kazakhstan area – this is the Dongal type. However, in both cases, a relatively small number of finds, mostly pottery, represents this period. It is not easier to single out the latest group from the number of the Final Bronze Age burials (Korenyako 1982).

In the southern Trans-Urals, this period is characterized by sites of the Sargary culture, which is also known by the name of Alexeyevka. The culture that was identified in the 1970s by S. Zdanovich (1983, 2003), occupies quite a large territory, including a part of the forest-steppe between Tobol and Irtysh, northern and central Kazakhstan (Evdokimov 2000; Potyemkina 1979) (Fig. 4.1). In this area, there are "pure" Sargary settlements and funeral sites. Moreover, in central Kazakhstan the sites of the so-called Dandybai-Begazy culture are known (Kuzmina 1994; Margulan 1979). They are represented by big mausoleums containing very elegant and well-manufactured pottery. The pottery is diagnosed by a globular form with very small bottoms and cylindrical necks. The vessels have a black, yellow, or red color and their surfaces are polished. The small-combed decoration is of geometric style. Recent research undertaken in this region has demonstrated that there is such a small quantity of this pottery and it is usually encountered together with pottery of the Sargary culture. This persuaded Varfolomeyev (1991; 2003) to unite both cultures into one – Dandybai-Sargary. Following Korenyako (1990), he states that mausoleums were constructed especially for people of high social status. Hence, central Kazakhstan was the core area of this culture.

In the Trans-Urals, the Sargary (Alexeyevka) pottery is encountered together with some other types, mostly with Mezhovka ceramics. At the same time, the Mezhovka collections often contain Sargary pottery as well. S. Zdanovich (1983) distinguished three chronological groups: the early, middle, and late, within the period between thirteenth and eighth centuries BC.

The Sargary culture is represented by settlements, burial grounds, and some occasional finds. The settlements are of two types, but the temporal position is not yet clear. The first type is characterized by a large habitation territory and the presence of semisubterranean buildings with quite deep basement

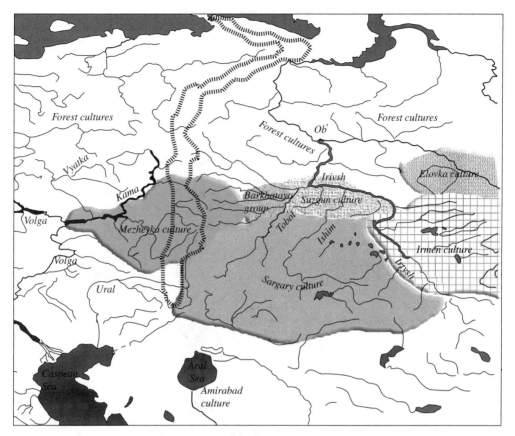

Figure 4.1. Cultures of the Final Bronze Age of the Urals and western Siberia (steppe and forest–steppe zone).

(Fig. 4.2). The house surfaces reach 200 m² and more, and they can be up to several dozen within a settlement (Zdanovich 2003). They cover the area of 20000 m². However, the thickness and saturation of archaeological layers, as a rule, are not high.

The second type unites the smaller settlements (about 1,000–2,500 m²), where house depression are not always visible on the surface. But this type is close to the first type in number and variability of finds. It is likely that people inhabited these settlements periodically but rather briefly, perhaps seasonally.

Alongside the visible tendency of large villages to become small camps, the opposite occurrence took place. Some settlements became bigger. One of these sites excavated on a large scale is Kinzhitai (Vinogradov 1991). This site yielded some material, in particular, pottery of the Kuyusayskaya culture of the southern Aral area that is dated back to the seventh century BC. This settlement occupied the surface of about 9,000 m² and displayed nine big house depressions measuring 0.9 m deep, and 130–350 m².

There is no accuracy in settlement planning. As a rule, the houses were placed freely along the river bank by one row; their transversal walls faced the

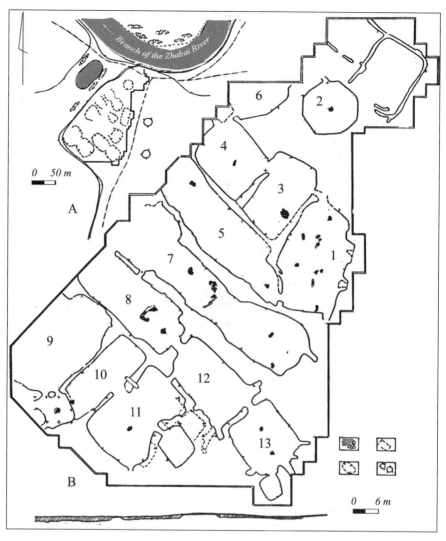

Figure 4.2. The Sargary settlement: **A** – situational plan; **B** – plan of excavated area; (1) hearth and stones; (2) indefinite line; (3) house depression; (4) kurgan (after Zdanovich 1983).

water. Some houses occupied high parts of the flood plain, which are presently often flooded. On average, settlements could host up to fifteen houses. These are usually rectangular and quite similar to structures of previous period. The frame-pillar construction was dominant; a floor was deepened into the ground on 0.7–1.0 m. One could reconstruct the basic features of architecture due to finds of burnt structures. Roofs were of two types: (1) the gabble roof, leaning on a longitudinal row of posts and rafters; and (2) the four sloped roof, leaning on four supporting pillars in the center.

Settlements produce mainly animal bones and flat-bottomed pottery of four basic types, three of which present various forms of a pot and one of a can.

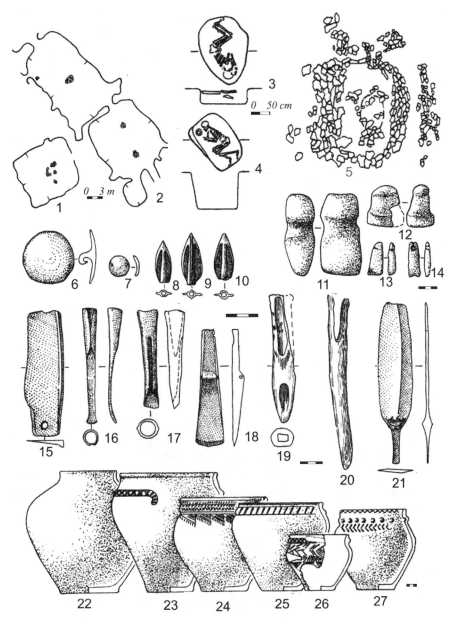

Figure 4.3. Complex of the Sargary material culture: (1) a house of the Petrovka-IV settlement; (2) house of the Sargary settlement; (3–5, 21) burials of the Sargary cemetery; (6) harness plaque from the Petrovka-III settlement; (7–11, 22) plaque, arrowheads, and stone hammers from the Sargary settlement; (12–14, 20, 21, 25) stone tools, bone object, bronze knife, and pot from the Novonikolskoye settlement; (15–16) bronze tools from the Petrovka-II settlement; (19, 27) bone tool, pot from the Ilyinka settlement; (24) pot from the Alekseyevskoye site; (26) pot from the Zhukei cemetery (after Zdanovich 1988).

Well-designed short necks, moderately globular bodies, and small flat bottoms characterize the first type (Fig. 4.3–23). The second type has more stocky general proportions, a large throat and high neck (Fig. 4.3–24). Narrow throats, straight high necks, and high prominent shoulders characterize the third type (Fig. 4.3–22). The last type is represented by a slightly profiled can-shaped vessel. On the whole, the pottery is carelessly made. About 40 percent of the vessels were not decorated at all. The rest were modestly ornamented on the neck and shoulder by curved (incised) zigzag, rhombic netting, and horizontal herringbone, notches. About 10–20 percent of the pottery is decorated with clay girdle (rollers) stacked on a neck (Zdanovich 1984).

Metal tools are quite numerous. These include knives, sickles of the Derbeden type, socketed and wedge-shaped gouges, and flat projectile axes. All of these tools were in common use in the forest-steppe and south forest zone. Weaponry can be connected with bronze bilobed socketed arrowheads and three-lobed bone arrows (Fig. 1.9).

In the Trans-Urals, Sargary funeral monuments are small cemeteries comprising up to three mounds and by solitary kurgans made from earth and stone. Compared with the preceding period, they are located in different topographic situation far from river streams, and on high ground of the initial riverbank. Kurgans are not big and contain one or two inhumations; in single cases, traces of fire use were recorded. The deceased were placed in contracted side positions with unstable orientation. The set of grave goods is quite modest, these are mostly pots, and rarely ornaments (bronze semispherical plaques with back loops and wire pendants).

At the same time, some cemeteries demonstrate a rather complex ritual practice. In particular, burial ground Belokluchovka 7 (Kostukov 1999) comprised several kurgans, one of which produced only one burial with minimal grave goods. However, the stone funeral covering was unusual in form and can be interpreted as the image of a chariot or human (Fig. 4.4).

In northern and central Kazakhstan, funeral sites are represented by burials arranged in stone "boxes" or cists, containing individual inhumations. The deceased were placed variously in a contracted position on the right or left sides, on the back, or in a seating position (Tkachev 2002; Varfolomeyev 1991; Zdanovich & Malutina 1976).

The data collected in Sargary settlements and burial grounds testify to the economic orientation of the population varied depending on environments, but its basis was undoubtedly connected with livestock breeding. The bones of domestic animals are abundantly recorded in all settlements. The first position is occupied by cattle bones, then horse and sheep (Zdanovich 1981; 2003). The cattle from the Sargary settlements belonged to the population of big animals, the distribution of which in the Bronze Age was connected with the steppe area of eastern Europe (Tsalkin 1964). The Sargary horses were determined to be thin-legged and semi-thin-legged type. They were 136–144 cm tall (Makarova 1976).

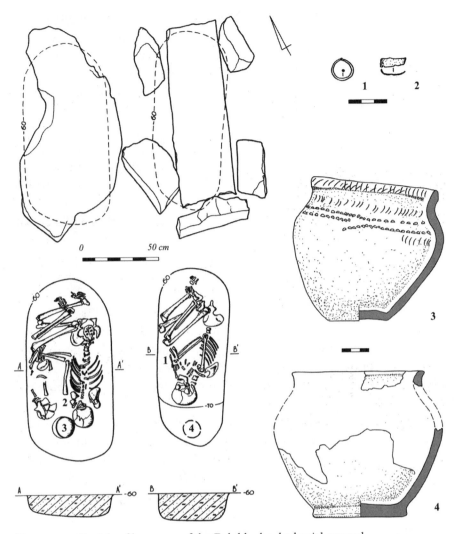

Figure 4.4. Burials of kurgan 7 of the Belokluchovka burial ground.

During the Bronze Age in the Trans-Urals and Kazakhstan as well as in eastern Europe, domestic animals were not greatly evolved. The most significant change that occurred in the final stages of this epoch concerned the notable rise of horse presence. S. Zdanovich (2003: 402) thinks that the Sargary population practiced yearly cycle herding, when one section of the community traveled with the herds in the area around the village, and other section remained stayed in settlement and took care of dairy animals, stored feed and preserved milk products.

The first reliable evidence of agriculture relates to this period and this culture: the carbonized wheatears and corn were found in the Alexeyevka sacred hill (Krivtsova-Grakova 1948). A number of agricultural tools (corn grindings, pestles, knife-choppers, sickles, stone hoes) constitute a substantial part of the Sargary collections (Evdokimov 2000; Zdanovich 2003). However, it is still not enough direct evidence of agriculture, and its place in the structure of the Sargary economy is not clear yet. The correlation between various species of animals was changed compared with the previous period of the Late Bronze Age (Kosintsev & Varov 1995). Archaeozoologists certify to the increase of the horse population in a herd compared with that of cattle. This also testifies to the tendency toward a rise in mobility.

Settlements also produce also some traces of metallurgy: remains of furnaces and casting molds (Evdokimov 1975; Krivtsova-Grakova 1948). The centers of metallurgical production are transferred to other areas, in particular to central Kazakhstan (Atasu, Kent[1]), which supplied the other areas with metal and raw materials on the basis of trade-exchange relations. This conditioned the rise of wealth of this area, expressed in the concentration of very large settlements (with traces of stone architecture), various traces of mining and metallurgical activity (Fig. 1.9), as well as other rich materials (Fig. 4.5), and monumental funeral mausoleums. All this contrasted with the general modest character of the remaining areas of the Sargary culture.

There are no direct materials about social structure of the Sargary groups; however, one can clearly see two tendencies in social development. First – more visible and more largely represented – a society tended to atomization, and some population groups were getting smaller (this is especially visible in the Trans-Urals). Settlement complexes contain a minimum of objects, which might be interpreted as weaponry. Burials do not produce such finds at all. Of course, we should not forget that such a situation could reflect some particular ritual restrictions. There is no doubt that kurgan ritual and inhumation were not used for the entire population of the Southern Trans-Urals, but the criteria for their not being used are not known. In this situation, it is hardly possible to speak of a military way of political genesis, as was suggested for the Volga area (Tsimidanov 1990).

Most of all, we should not interpret the modest character of the Sargary culture as a reflection of lineal degradation. A society in transitional and unstable conditions tried to work out an optimal way of life, which can look simpler to the archaeologist.

The second tendency is reflected by settlement agglomerations such as the Kent example with clear evidence of a regional rise, a mixture of population, and a rise of new local elite (Evdokimov 2000; Varfolomeyev 2003). According to Varfolomeyev, the labor investment for the mausoleum constructions can be counted in dozens and even hundreds of man-hours expended for more than those ordinary burials. Such sharp contrasts in wealth between different territorial groups can serve as evidence of crisis tendencies, which the Sargary society has experienced.

As previously noted, Sargary material culture maintained traces of external contacts from various areas, including quite distant regions of Middle Asia – northwest and south Turkmenistan (Kutimov 1999; Vinogradov 1995b). The

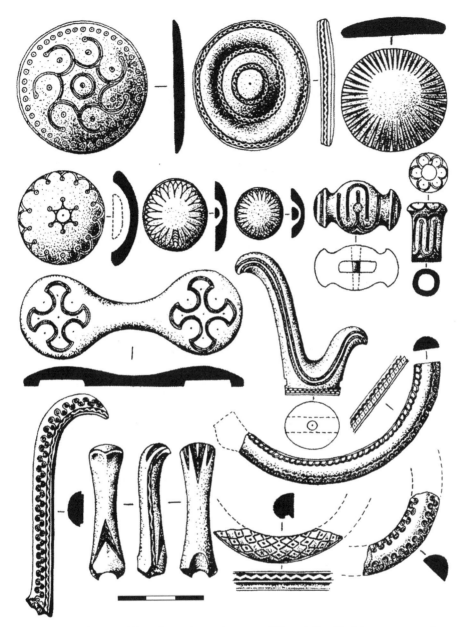

Figure 4.5. Bone artifacts from the settlement of Kent (after Varfolomeyev 2004).

other direction of importance were the areas of eastern Kazakhstan and Altai, where at the turn of the Final Bronze Age and Iron Age the Karasuk culture was developing. So far, these connections are illustrated only by occasional but numerous finds of weaponry. There is a high receptivity to borrowings coming from other cultures. This can be seen particularly in pottery. This period displays cultural similarity within large territories, covering different landscapes.

The origin of the Sargary culture is thought to be a complex genetic process with participation from the Fyodorovo (Bishkul variant) and Cherkaskul traditions, whose penetration into the steppe began during in the Late Bronze Age (Zdanovich 1983). It is also supposed that the Sargary population became a component of the early nomadic culture.

Korenyako (1982: 49) concluded that there was a sharp change of tradition during the Final Bronze Age by the early nomads in the steppe Cis-Urals and Trans-Urals. He pointed out the absence of burials indicating the turn between the Bronze and Iron Ages. However, it cannot be excluded that the descendents of the Sargary population existed in the south Urals up to the Iron Age, keeping their mode of economy and modest culture.

MEZHOVKA-IRMEN CULTURAL HORIZON

Compared to preceding periods, the Final Bronze Age is characterized by a higher cultural similarity of areas situated in different landscape zones on both sides of the Ural Mountains. Because the main cultural marker – ceramics – is very often encountered in settlements deposits in various compositions, there is quite a bit of disagreement between scholars even in the case of cultural attribution of the same sites. This creates many obstacles to the chronological gradation of the period of the Final Bronze Age.

The large group of cultures known under umbrella of "Mezovka-Irmen" horizon completes the Bronze Age in the forest-steppe area. Among them, the Mezhovka and Irmen cultures are better studied and more singnificant (Matveyev 1986; 1993). The sites of this horizon occupy a large territory stretching from the Cis-Urals to the Altai. They demonstrate common stylistic similarities with visible local differences.

These cultures are associated with the end of the Andronovo-like heritage in the forest-steppe and southern forest of western Siberia. In addition, some cultures of forest origin did appear in these areas in the last centuries of the second millennium BC: so-called cultures of the cross-stamped pottery, which we will address later.

The Mezhovka-Irmen horizon united the cultures that were genetically connected with the preceding Andronovo-like formations and had changed under the influence coming from the north (cross-stamped cultures), east (Karasuk culture), and south (Sargary-Alexeyevka cultures). The Karasuk influence was particularly significant. Numerous metal objects of Karasuk metallurgical centers – cranked knives, various socketed axes, two-edged daggers with cut worked handle, decorations – gave special color to this epoch.

The Mezhovka Culture

The Mezhovka culture is one of the biggest cultural formations of the Final Bronze Age. Its sites are situated on both sides of the Ural range (Fig. 4.6), and,

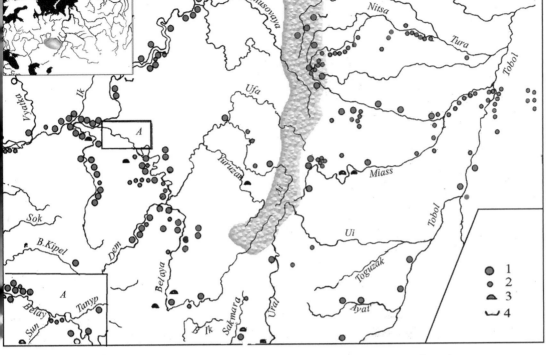

Figure 4.6. Distribution the Mezhovka culture sites: (1) excavated settlements; (2) surveyed settlements; (3) kurgan burial grounds; (4) flat burials.

at the same time, it is a part of the cultural chain of the forest and forest-steppe zone of the Ural and Siberia. This chain includes the sites of the Erzovka (Cis-Urals), Barkhatovo (Trans-Urals), Late Suzgun (Ishim-Irtysh area), and Irmen cultures (Ob-Irtysh forest-steppe).

The Tobol basin can be considered as the eastern limits of Mezhovka pottery distribution, the western one limit be demarcated on the boundary between the forest-steppe and steppe from the Belaya bend to the Middle Kama up to the Chusovaya river (in the Cis-Urals). Mezhovka influence is traceable far to the south in the Sargary settlements.

The chronology is based mainly on pottery typology and a cross-cultural comparison with other areas, in particular a correlation of metal objects. The stratigraphic position of the Mezhovka materials is ascertained for the Trans-Urals area, where one can see the tendency of transition from the Cherkaskul to Mezhovka style. This allows us to consider the late twelfth century BC as the beginning of Mezhovka tradition. The late stage is related to the eighth–seventh centuries BC (Petrin et al. 1993).

The number of "pure" Mezhovka sites is not large. All of them are represented by small or middle-sized open settlements. On the whole, the correlation among stable long-term habitation, short camps, and locations is about 1:2:4 (Obydennov 1998). They are situated on fluvial terraces and on river and lake promontories. The Trans-Urals sites Yazyevo-I and Kamyshoye-II thought to have defensive constructions (ditches and ramparts), but they also contain materials of the Petrovka-Alakul appearance, which might be connected to this fortification (Potyemkina 1985).

The settlement territory, number, and house dimensions vary depending on location in the forest or forest-steppe zone. The Mezhovka pottery is often found in the settlements of the Sargary culture, concentrated in some particular areas. The houses are differed by size and construction. The largest pillar-frame structures are resemble those of the steppe-area, whereas the smaller houses (by about 100 m²) are more peculiar to the forest landscape. However, the bigger dimensions of southern sites could also be conditioned by the Sargary or Late Srubnaya traditions, because these types of pottery are found there together. The houses of maximal size (250–300 m²) are registered in the Tubyak and Yukalikulayevskoye settlements. They were dug into the ground more than one meter. One kind of building tradition is represented by vertical pillar-frame construction; another is manifested by the composition of a deep basement and horizontal frame in its low part. The corridor-like entrance was usually facing to water and situated in the sidewall or in a corner. Fireplaces and storage pits are often found inside houses. There are traces of partitions in big structures.

The pottery and animal bones constitute the largest part of Mezhovka material. The presence of a specific roller on the top part of the pot neck initially determined the eponym pottery marker. However, this feature is found on no more then a quarter of all vessels; stuck on rollers are widely found in the Eurasian steppe and forest steppe in the Final Bronze Age.

Two major types of pottery are distinguished: (1) pots with short straight or turned up necks, globular bodies smoothly passing onto flat bottoms; (2) cans and korchags (large earthenware pots). More important for cultural attribution is the decoration, which usually covers the neck and shoulder. Compared with the preceding period, which saw the total domination of comb-stamped techniques, the carved (fretted) elements are more popular. It is thanks to the latter element that the Mezhovka ceramics are easily recognizable in mixed collections. In general, the ornament patterns are rather simple: herringbone, inclined incisions, horizontal zigzags, grating, and some other patterns.

Bronze objects are represented above all by massive tools – celts-axes of the Cimmerian type, gouges of Derbeden type, sickles of Derbeden and Kataisk types, daggers of Kardashinsky and Cimmerian other types (Fig. 4.7). Double-edged knives with smooth passage to tengue, awls, and needles are quite numberous. The problem is that most of these objects come from either mixed collections or from occasional finds. However, one can think that at least some of these tools are connected to the Mezhovka archaeological context, which is witnessed by casting molds that are yielded by some settlements. The set of stone tools includes a series of pestles, hammers, anvils, and abrasives.

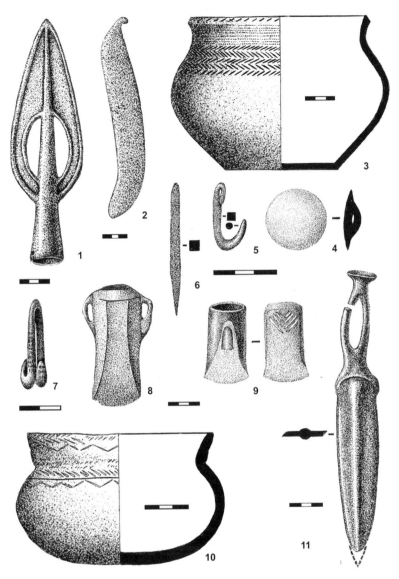

Figure 4.7. Materials of the Mezhovka culture from the Trans-Urals sites (after Shorin, unpublished manuscript, drawing by Timoshek).

Bone and stone arrowheads are numerous. The morphology of the former was determined by the bone form: most of them were a tanged type, there is only one arrowhead with an internal socket. Stone arrowheads are subrectangular with truncated bases. There are finds of three hole cheek-pieces made of horn of Belozersky type, that are used for relative chronology.

Most of funerary sites are concentrated in the Cis-Urals, but these are represented on a very limited scale by separate kurgans and burials. Therefore, we do not have a full image of the mortuary practice of the Mezhovka population. The only fully investigated necropolis, Krasnogorsky-I, yielded material characterizing the kurgan burial tradition, with the use of stone in mound erection. Kurgans contained one to three inhumations, and the deceased were in elongated supine or side position. There are secondary burials, some of which were arranged on the ancient surface. Small depth and modest wooden arrangement are typical features of Mezhovka graves, which were predominantly oriented in a latitudinal direction. Some anthropological definitions showed that individuals of different age groups were buried under kurgans (Obydennov 1998).

Animal bones, belonging mostly to cattle, represent the remains of the funeral feast. Grave good collections included pottery, metal daggers, two spearheads with slated plume, double-edged knives, and ornaments.

The interpretation of the Mezhovka material is quite difficult because of the lacuna in its character. However, we will try to make some inferences using available data.

First of all, it is worth mentioning that the Mezhovka population groups inhabited different ecological niches, and consequently these should have had different economic orientations. But in order to demonstrate this we would need to have at least one site per every local variant, and we do not.

Therefore, the only way to analyze generally the material in general is to relate it to economic activity. There is no data on plant cultivation although in the steppe zone it was already known. The data is better represented by livestock breeding. In faunal collections, the portion of wild species is rather large (in the Cis-Urals Yukalayevo settlement it is up 15 percent), this high percentage accounts for meat animals account and there is a smaller percentage for "fur" animals. Among the domestic species, cattle and horse prevail; there are a few sheep and pig.

For the Trans-Urals, only materials coming from the Berezki–V settlement situated in the area of Argazy Lake can be used. Here, the situation is similar to that of the Cis-Urals: quite important is the portion of wild species, including waterfowl, close to the percentage of horse and cattle (31.25 percent), and a small percentage of sheep (12.5 percent). Pig bones are single (Kosintsev 1988). Fish bones are also found.

Thus, one can conclude that in the Mezhovka territory the role of food appropriating branches was rather important. The aspect of stockbreeding or both sides of the Ural Mountains differed in portion to pig breeding, which finally was conditioned by concrete environments. In particular, the high portion of horses in a herd was dictated by its ability to forge in the winter. There is no doubt that food-producing branches were more significant in southern areas of the Mezhovka territory, and it was reduced in the north.

The problem of the development of metallurgy traditionally excites interest. In this connection, the finds of casting forms, crucibles, and specialized stone tools for ore crushing testify to the local production of bronze implements. So far, traces of local metallurgy have not been discovered, although big copper deposits are situated in the territory of Mezhovka culture. The deposits would function the in later period of the Itkul culture at the beginning of the Iron Age. The question of the sources of Mezhovka metal is still open; it is possible that it was imported from southern regions. The level of other economic branches did not exceed the limits of domestic production.

One can suppose that settlements could accommodate not more than two to three hundred individuals. This number is assessed on the norm of living space per one individual, excluding the possibility of partial use for young cattle. It could be a lineage group, part of which could be dispersed on other smaller habitats, possibly belonging to families.

Burial grounds also do not provide us with material sufficient for a full estimation of the societal organization. A limited number of cemeteries and their modest size bear witness to the large part of the population that should have been buried according to ritual and is not archaeologically visible. The kurgan ritual tradition appeared here from the south and is indirectly confirmed by the fact that almost all Mezhovka settlements are located in the contact zone.

Relative unanimity among researchers on the problem of linguistic definition of the Mezhovka culture is mainly based on the cross-cultural method: its ornamentation is close to ethnographically known ornaments of the Ugrian population of the Urals and western Siberia. However, continuity in material culture does not necessarily reflect language continuity, conversely cultural transformation is not a sufficient argument in favor of language change. Traces of the Mezhovka culture in the steppe world of Iranian speakers are quite numerous. Chlenova (1981) believes that the genesis of the Mezhovka culture is connected with the Karasuk culture, the sites of which are located far east of the Urals in eastern Kazakhstan and the Altai, and which, by all appearances, was related to the Chinese metallurgical tradition. Most other scholars are more careful in their conclusions. They share the hypothesis of a genetic connection between the Mezhovka and Cherkaskul traditions.

Reasonably acceptable is the hypothesis concerning a multicomponent character of all cultural formations of the period under question. There is no doubt that wide interaction existed between south and north that might lead to the mutual adoption of cultural and economic stereotypes.

The end of the Mezhovka tradition is not clear, as the transition to the Iron Age is documented archaeologically on a limited scale, not only in the Urals but in other territories as well. There is some similarity with later Gorokhovo and Itkul antiquities (see Chapter 8), but it requires special research.

The Irmen Culture

The second component of the Mezhovka-Irmen horizon constitutes its eastern part. The numerous materials represent the Irmen culture which was first identified in the mid-1950s (Chlenova 1955; Gryaznov 1956; Matushchenko 1974).

In the Upper Ob' river basin, there are settlements and burial grounds, which are concentrated compactly, forming several local and chronological clusters. This area is considered to be the core zone for the Irmen culture, which is supposed to derive from the interaction between aboriginal and greatly transformed Andronovo-like elements. At the same time, in the Upper Ob' area, the Karasuk influence is very substantial; therefore, Gryaznov (1956) regarded the Irmen antiquities as the variant of Karasuk culture, which is predominantly centerd in southern Siberia. The decreasing Karasuk influence from the east to the west is quite visible. Its western limits are outlined by way of a series of typical Karasuk daggers with cannular handles and mushroomlike tops found in the southern Urals (Chlenova 1981; Vinogradov & Epimakhov 2000).

For western Siberia, the Irmen settlements demonstrate traditional house buildings, and include open villages, small camps, and fortified habitats, which are more characteristic for the later phase. The best studies are for Milovanovo–3, Bystrovka–4, and Chicha–1 settlements. The area of occupation varies from a few hundred to 25,000 m², depending on ecological conditions and period of occupation. House building is represented by pillar-frame and log constructions. The houses are rather big (200–350 m²); they comprise several hearths and preserve traces of various domestic activities including animal stabling during the winter time. Separate houses, a number of structures of economic function are discovered in Irmen villages, as well as extended ash accumulations, some of which reached up to 3.5 m high. The latter always contained a great number of broken tools, pottery sherds, animal bones etc.

Pottery is abundant, and is represented by two basic types: (1) large flat-bottomed massive pots and (2) smaller pots and jars with flat or round bottoms. The first type is characteristic for settlements; the second type is also encountered in the burials. Among ornamental techniques, the incised techique is more commonly seen; it is sometimes accompanied by combed stamps and "pearls." In the decoration of funeral pottery, the Andronovo motifs are clearly traceable: hatched triangles, horizontal rows of rhombuses, zigzags, and so on (Fig. 4.8).

The Irmen funeral ritual is better known than that of other cultures of the Final Bronze Age. Many cemeteries have been almost completely excavated. They yielded rich and impressive material (Bobrov et al. 1993; Matushchenko 1974; Molodin 1985). The Irmen kurgans are of multiburial character and the liner principle of organization of funerary space (Fig. 4.8). The graves contain inhumations in crouched right-sided positions with southern directions of orientation. The graves are rather shallow; wooden frames established on the paleosoil furnish them. Apart from a small number of collective burials, they are in the majority individual. Pottery and some metal goods (nail-like pendants, earrings, sewn plaques) accompany the deceased.

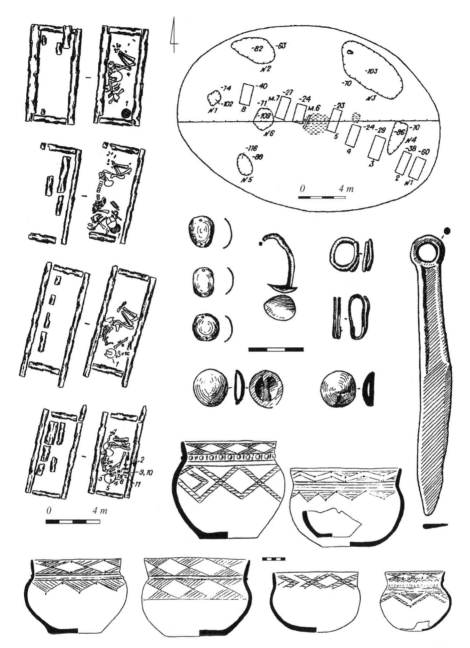

Figure 4.8. Kurgan of the Irmen burial ground of Zhuravlevo-4 (after Bobrov, Chikisheva, and Mikhailov 1993).

As the other "inheritors" of the Andronovo (Fyodorovo) traditions, the Irmen groups have numerous and pronounced pieces of evidence of livestock breeding, and only some traces of cultivation. Osteological collections demonstrate a great predominance of bones of domestic animals compared to wild hunted species. Metallurgy developed on a different scale, depending on the raw material resources.

The chronological position of the Irmen culture is the subject of many disputes. Chlenova (1994), who is brilliant expert in artifact typology and serration, traditionally advocates very late dates (eighth to seventh centuries BC). However, the majority of specialists (Kosarev 1981; Matveyev 1993; Molodin 1985) hold a different opinion, dating the Irmen culture to the eleventh–eighth centuries BC. They also distinguish two phases of its development. Unfortunately, the series of radiocarbon dates obtained for the Chicha-1 fortified settlement has not yet been published.

The Irmen antiquities attract specialists' attention not only because of their mass character but also because of their visible connection to the later cultural formations, relating to the Iron Age, which we will discuss later in this book.

Summary: Bronze Age Trajectory

We have now discussed more than a thousand years of the cultural development in the central part of northern Eurasia. Archaeologically, this is reflected in numerous sites representing a kaleidoscope of local and regional cultural traditions, some of which had a wider spatial distribution than the area under study.

This development is characterized by a significant technoeconomic rise toward the wide introduction of bronze industry and other crafts, strengthening of pastoral stockbreeding, and demographic growth. However, the cultural situation could seem to the reader very intricate. Instead of the rather monotonous Eneolithic cultures that spread over vast territories, we have to deal with dynamic cultural diversity, conditioned by various interplaying factors. Therefore, we will summarize the trajectory of cultural development and emphasize its most significant occurrences. Figure 4.9 gives the approximate image of relationships that might have existed in the Urals and western Siberia during the third and second millennia BC. Several "nodal points" were determinative for the area under study: (1) the spread of bronze metallurgy and animal husbandry associated with expansion of the Yamnaya and Corded Ware cultures; (2) the formation of the Abashevo and Sintashta cultures, stimulated by the decomposition of the Circumpontic technocultural network and expansionist activity of the Catacombnaya population; (3) the formation of the Andronovo and Srubnaya cultural families and development of the Eurasian technocultural network; and (4) the transformation and disintegration of these entities as the background of the collapse of regional economic systems.

The earliest sites with remains of a food-producing economy – livestock-breeding and metallurgy – are attributed to the Yamnaya culture, which appeared in the southern Urals in about 3400/3300 cal BC and developed up to

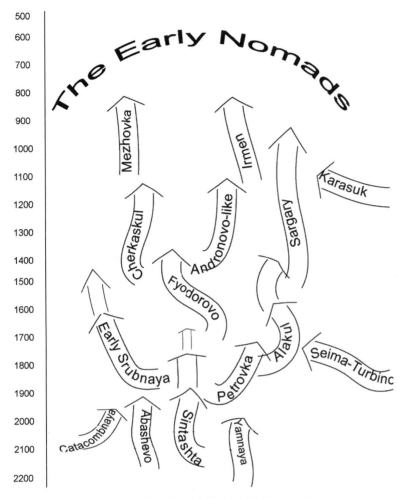

Figure 4.9. Schematic cultural trend during the Bronze Age.

the beginning of the second millennium BC in Poltavka variant. The Yamnaya culture people transformed the monotonous steppe landscape by erecting a great number of earthen mounds above the graves of their tribesmen. The kurgan funeral tradition was established there for many centuries.

According to up-to-date knowledge, the formation of the Yamnaya culture in the Urals resulted from the eastward population movement from the Volga-Caspian steppes. The pastoral economy and possession of wheeled transport could have facilitated this process.

The evidence of specialized metallurgical production in the Yamnaya culture context, which is well represented by the earliest deposits of the Kargaly complex, is very important. It allows us to suppose that one of the push-factors, which conditioned an appearance of the Yamnaya groups in the Urals, was connected with the seeking of new mineral resources. This, in its turn, could reflect the tendency to expand an influence of the Caucasian metallurgical center – one of the most powerful centers within the Circumpontic techno-cultural network. This hypothesis can have two variants. First, the discovery of the Urals copper ores could have resulted from the deliberate movement toward this region. Second, this discovery could have happened accidentally – in the course of its territorial expansion to the east. Yet, it is logical to suggest that in both variants some people familiar with the process of metal production should have been among the newcomers.

The Kargaly metal flowed mainly to the west. Perhaps in the beginning, its production was directed by needs of some powerful groups of the low Volga area. However, later, at the second half of the third millennium BC, to which the greatest number of big kurgans is related, the Yamnaya population in the Urals became more numerous.

Although we said that in the very beginning bronze metallurgy did not play a revolutionary role, we should, however, stress its growing significance. Regions with rich deposits of raw materials became very attractive and dominated surrounding areas, forming the centers of more active development and intensive communication. Such centers were in the Caucasus and Caspian-Pontic steppe, where a great role was played by societies represented by Catcombnaya cultures (2800–1800 cal BC), engaged in a large network of Caucasus–Pontic-Balkan interactions. The Catacomnaya cultural society is characterized as having a strong economic basis, a branching structure of social/professional stratification, and a militarized image (Pustovalov 1992; 1994).

At the turn of the third and second millennia BC, the system of connections within Circumpontic network came to a gradual decline, which was caused by many factors, including an emergence and rise of new productive centers competing for influence, strengthening of new elite, population movements, and the appearance of new cultural traditions. Moreover, we see some indications of technological concurrence, especially at the end of the Middle Bronze Age (early second millennium BC) when two major technological traditions: western (Circumpontic) and eastern (Seima-Turbino) competed for dominance.

In the course of these processes, significant transformations occurred in the eastern European steppe and forest-steppe. Active interrelations between societies with late Yamnaya, Catacombnaya and Corded Ware traditions resulted in formation of the Abashevo cultural intercommunity – one of the key cultural entities of eastern Europe in the Middle Bronze Age. Animal husbandry and bronze metallurgy were introduced into the forest-steppe and transmitted to the forest of north-eastern Europe – into the Eneolithic milieu.

In the southern Trans-Urals, a strong impulse of the cultural process was given by the spontaneous appearance of the Sintashta cultural complex, which dramatically contrasted with the poor archaeological presentation of local Eneolithic background. In particular, this complex pottery and the composition of metal objects found many similarities within the Abashevo and late

Catacombnaya contexts. Yet the nuclear settlement pattern, with its systemic distribution within the compact territory, closed layout, and clustered regular plan, together with the stable architectural tradition (which has no roots in any local culture but finds some parallels in western Anatolia, the Balkans, and Pontic region) alludes to the area of its origin (in a broad sense). There is no doubt that this tradition was brought to the southern Trans-Urals in the course of some migration from the west or southwest, but neither its mechanism nor its form is as yet clear. We will be bold and say that to transmit the settlement tradition in such a canonical form is only possible by a socially organized group of people possessing a strong corporatist ideology. It is possible that this migration was motivated by necessity to find the resources for metallurgy, although this does not deny the other factors. It is worthwhile to remember that ecological conditions in the Sintashta period were arid, but soil, water, and mineral resources were quite rich. All this, together with a picturesque landscape, could possibly correspond to that image that incomers had in their mind. Although this land was poorly populated, incomers had to be in contact with local groups, from which they tried to separate themselves.

At the same time, in the Petrovka culture (the daughter-culture of the Sintashta culture), some elements, especially in pottery design, are explained by the contribution of an indigenous component.

In general, the funeral ritual of the Sintashta population continued the kurgan tradition; small kurgans organized into compact cemeteries are associated with certain settlements. This pattern is typical of a settled mode of life, and an abundant and sophisticated system of animal sacrifices that reflects the ideas of fertility, reproduction and social unity. Animal husbandry in its pastoral variant, supplemented by bronze metallurgy and other crafts, characterises the economic basis of the Sintashta population. The spoked wheeled transport of the southern Urals is one of the earliest discoveries in Eurasia in this field. A chariotry complex spread over the Eurasian steppe, not only in a west–east direction but also to the south. Many scholars believe that the spread of horse, horse harness (bone disc-like cheek pieces), and hand-made pottery indicates the influence of the Sintashta and Petrovka tradition to the Central Asia (Kuzmina 1994; Masson 1999).

It is not easy to estimate the level of the Sintashta society. Obviously, it demonstrates some explosion of complexity, which maybe does not match its classical evolutionist model, which was chiefly developed in the contexts of agricultural societies. What we clearly see that landscape and use of resources were well organized, settlement layout with its emphasis on fortification and cluster planning was systematic, and ritual activity, first of all, in funerary sphere was rather sophisticated and significant. It is difficult to imagine that one or two thousands people, or even five hundreds, dwelt in side-by-side houses, were in egalitarian relations. This society was structured and "knew" some economic specialization, sex-age and status gradations, prestige goods and wealth, but it was conducted by corporatist ideology. The elite played the organizational role, which however was not visibly materialized.

Active cultural interactions, which took place in the beginning of the second millennium BC in the Volga–Ural area, were provoked by and revolved around the Sintashta phenomenon. They have generated a series of new traditions archaeologically represented by a specific combination of cultural attributes. One group of cultures is characterized by a visible genetic link with the Sintashta complex: Petrovka and Alakul cultures. Their territorial and chronological positions partly overlap; they developed on the way of territorial expansion and obliteration of the Sintashta heritage. The nucleated settlement pattern was being replaced by a dispersal model and free standing houses; animal sacrifice became simpler, and pottery became more standard within the corresponding tradition. At the same time, the new form of funeral ritual, cremation, had appeared. The Fyodorovo culture, whose territorial spread was maximal, differs from the forenamed by funeral biritualism: in the west it was cremation under kurgans; in the east, inhumation in the flat and kurgans cemeteries. The process of diversification involved as did the funeral constructions, which varied from simple pit to stone cist. The groups of populations identified with the Alakul and Fyodorovo cultures coexisted in some regions; in other areas, they left mixed complexes.

The formation of the Andronovo family of cultures in the Trans-Urals and western Siberia was paralleled with the development of the Srubnaya cultures in the eastern European steppe and forest-steppe. A large zone of their close interactions covered the southern Urals, where one can find "pure" as well as mixed complexes of both traditions.

These two entities covered a huge area, which, despite the regional and local specifics, was open to mutual contacts stimulated by a significant rise of bronze production and growing needs in metal tools and weapons. Pastoral stock breeding was a common means of subsistence for populations of both the Srubnaya and Andronovo areas. Yet regional ecological conditions and climatic fluctuations conditioned its variations from settled to more mobile forms. Craft production and trade also played an important role in the overall structure of economic life in the Late Bronze Age of Eurasia.

The life was mainly concentrated in river valleys. Drainless open steppes were practically unpopulated. The settlements, predominantly of dispersal model, varied in size: from relatively large village with dozens of houses to small farm or temporary camp. Three to four settlements formed clusters located 5–10 km from each other; these were concentrated along the major rivers (Fig. 3.5). According to paleodemographic reconstructions accomplished by Evdokimov (2002: 87–91), the upper Tobol basin may has been inhabited by 450–550 people lived in eight synchronous Srubnaya and Alakul settlements. The population density in this local region was about 0.008–0.011 individuals per one km². As he estimates, in central and northern Kazakhstan

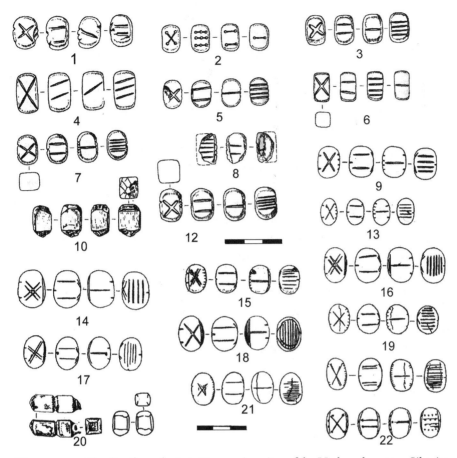

Figure 4.10. The dice from the Late Bronze Age sites of the Urals and western Siberia: (1, 2, 5, 10) the Cherkaskul culture; (4, 7, 11) the Alakul culture; (3, 6, 9, 12–22) the Ural Srubnaya culture (after Stefanov et al. 2001).

(total area – about 400,000 km²), minimally thirty-five hundred to seven thousand people could live simultaneously. Probably they were organized into aggregates of taxonomic segments (tribal formations of different scale), which were linked by real or fictitious affinity, having common territory, name, rituals, culture, and possibly common language dialect.

By the mid-second millennium BC, the area of hunting-fishing economies was greatly reduced and concentrated only in the northern taiga (which covered a huge expanse). This was a result of the Andronovo colonization, which was accompanied with a spread of animal husbandry and metallurgy. The latter together with traditional hunting and fishing composed a diverse economy in the forest-steppe and southern taiga where a series of hybrid cultural traditions came into being. It is interesting to notice that such a cultural paculiarity as the bone dice was in common use in the Urals and western Siberia in the Late Bronze Age (Fig. 4.10).

One more cultural transformation relates to the last centuries of the second millennium BC. It took shape by a gradual deformation of the Alakul and Fyodorovo core-traditions and a growing influence of eastern components (Karasuk culture).

As we promised, we did not delve deeply into the ethnic field because we think there is no much material for this. At the same time, one tendency is visible through the archaeological record – the spread of Indo-European languages, most probably Indo-Iranian, to the east and the rise of cultural diversity and regional and local traditions against the technological unification of metal production.

The western Siberian forest-steppe was the area of active interaction between the Indo-Iranian and Finno-Ugrian groups. It is possible that an Iranian language was the *lingua franca* of communication, just as a Turkic language was in medieval time.

The descendants of the Andronovo heritage met the first millennium BC with a great deal of experience in pastoralism, metallurgy, and with a high ecological and spiritual culture. However, their economic and social potential was not strong enough to resist the growing crisis developing from the combination of many factors, which included ecological deterioration, technological difficulties, demographic decline, and a weakening of interregional connections.

PART TWO

THE IRON AGE – FORMING
EURASIAN INTERACTIONS

CHAPTER 5

THE TRANSITION TO THE IRON AGE
AND NEW TENDENCIES IN ECONOMIC
DEVELOPMENT

This chapter gives an overview of the problem of the introduction of iron and its development in the area that covers the vast space of the forest and forest-steppe of eastern Europe and western Siberia.[1]

In respect to raw materials, throughout the territory in question there are numerous iron ore deposits. However, they differ in quality, mineral composition, and context of deposition. The richest ores are deposited in the mountain regions such as the Ural and Altai, where the content of soluble iron reaches up to 60–70 percent; the poorest ores are in the forest areas of eastern Europe and western Siberia, where the iron concentration does not exceed 45 percent (Kolchin 1953; Zinyakov 1997). When dealing with various types of raw materials, the ancient smelters had to know how to find, extract, and process different types of ores.

The problem of iron introduction has several aspects: (1) chronological, (2) technological, and (3) socioeconomic. We will try to touch on all of these, but, perhaps, not all of them will be fully analyzed.

The epoch of Iron is richly represented by various and numerous archaeological sites, the study of which has allowed scholars to show the extraordinary importance of this period in human history. It is commonly accepted that the historical development was a result of technological advances that were brought about, first of all, by the invention of a ferrous industry. However, we cannot say that this subject was paid systematic attention when compared to the typology and cultural attribution of iron tools and weapons yielded by archaeological sites.

Kolchin (1953), who studied the blacksmiths' work in ancient Russia, is rightly considered to be the founder of physical metallurgy in Russian archaeology. He and his colleague Krug (Kolchin & Krug 1965) pioneered the modeling of the bloomery process, which allowed scholars to understand it much better. The introduction of iron technology in eastern Europe has been well studied by Terekhova and Rozanova (1997), Voznesenskaya (1967, 1978), Khomutova

(1978), Shramko (1962, 1969, 1963, 1977), and Erlikh (2002a, 2002b), whose works are stimulating and helpful. Sunchugashev (1979) has studied metallurgical traditions of eastern and southern Siberia, and Zinyakov (1997; 1988) contributed to our knowledge on iron-making in western Siberia. Various aspects of this topic were studied by other Russian scholars who usually applied methods of metallographic analysis (Zykov 1993).

Several periodizations of iron-use and the development of the ferrous industry have been put forward. According to Snodgrass (1980: 337–8), iron technology passed through three stages: (1) in the first stage, iron was rather rare and had a mostly ceremonial character; (2) in the second stage, it was used in productive processes but on a smaller scale than bronze; and (3) in the third stage, iron dominated all other materials.

Pleiner (2000) suggested the four-stage development of iron-use. This first phase comprises the period when iron made sporadic appearances, was of ritual significance, and quite expensive and valuable. In the second phase, which is determined as an Initial or Proto-Iron Age, iron was produced on a limited scale but on a regular basis. It was accessible only to the upper strata of society. Archaeologically, this phase coincides with the Late or Final Bronze Age. The third phase is considered the Early Iron Age proper, when basic types of implements, knives, chisels, axes and sickles, and weapons were made from iron. The fourth phase is characterized by specialized production on a massive scale of all kinds of tools, which were manufactured using sophisticated techniques.

Despite some nuances, it is commonly accepted that the beginning of the Iron Age is marked by the familiarization of purposeful technology of the carbonization of iron tools and the ousting of bronze from the main (basic) productive process. Keeping this in mind, we will trace how and in what direction iron was introduced into the area in question. We are also interested in understanding the mechanism for the spread of this new technology, and how it manifested itself in social and economic spheres.

THE INTRODUCTION OF IRON TECHNOLOGY INTO EURASIA

Archaeological research in recent decades has provided us with a reasonable amount of data demonstrating that iron was known in the south of eastern Europe, the southern Urals, and southern Siberia thousands of years ago before the beginning of the Iron Age. More then forty-six ironware and four bimetallic wares are known as coming from the sites of the Yamnaya, Afanasyevo, and Catacombnaya cultures[2] (Fig. 5.1). In eastern Europe, these objects are assigned to four groups: tools and weapons, ornaments, objects of cult, and indefinable items, which, most probably, are fragments of some tools. In the Sayan and Altai areas, all of the earliest iron articles fall into the group of ornaments (Fig. 5.1).

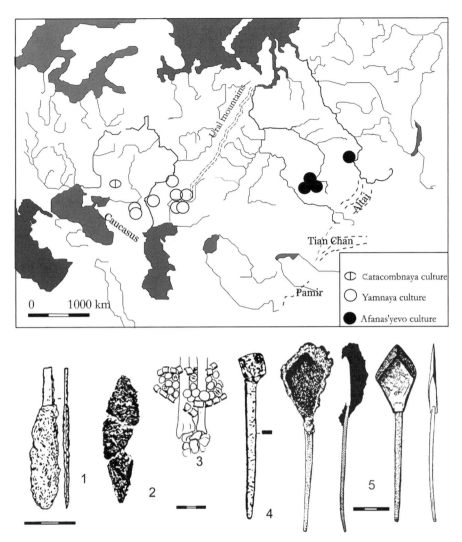

Figure 5.1. Meteoritic iron in Eurasia: **A** – Distribution; **B** – Iron objects of the Early and Middle Bronze Age of Northern Eurasia: (1) Gerasimovka (Catacombnaya culture); (2) Bichkin-Buluk (Yamnaya culture); (3) Afanasyeva Gora, grave 26, construction 2 (Afanasyevo culture); (4) Utevka, kurgan 1, grave 1; (5) Tamar-Utkul'-7, kurgan 8, grave 4 (Yamnaya culture). All items are iron and copper except #2, which is iron only (after Gryaznov 1999; Vasily'ev 1980; Bogdanov 1995; Morgunova and Kravtsov 1994; Shramko 1993; Grakov 1958).

We can clearly see the difference in iron processing between eastern Europe and central Asia. In the first area, iron was used for making tools and some types of weapons: knives, adzes, chisels, and razors. In the Afanasyevo area, only ornaments were manufactured from iron. Morphologically, the iron and bimetallic (bronze-iron) wares of the period under study fully correspond to the basic types of the Circumpontic metallurgical tradition (knives, adzes, chisels). In the kurgan Bolshoye Boldyrevo (southern Cis-Ural) a very interesting object was found – an iron disk, bearing a small chalk cup that contained powdered iron ore (Fig. 2.4). This site also yielded the earliest bimetallic items (Bogdanov 1995; Morgunova 2000; Morgunova & Kravtsov 1994).

We will not dwell on the problem of the meteoritic origin of iron that comes from the kurgans of the Yamnaya culture. Spectral, chemical, and metallographic analyses of early iron provides unambiguous evidence about its meteoritic content. The earliest metallurgists knew how to work meteoritic iron, which was very hard and could be forged in a heated state (Terekhova et al. 1997). Unfortunately, there is no analytical data relating to the Afanasyevo iron items, but we share the conclusion put forward by Terekhova and her coauthors.

All available data testify to the fact that iron was quite a precious metal, and had a place of high status in the society of Yamnaya culture. All iron items come from rich burials located under the big (elite) earthen kurgans (Vasily'ev 1980).

The first wares made of bloomery iron appeared in the south of eastern Europe in the early Middle Bronze Age, recalling the bimetallic knife from the Gerasimovka cemetery. However, the origin of this knife is not clear: it could be imported from the Caucasus.

For the early stage of the Late Bronze Age, we do not have any material that would characterize any attempts of iron processing. It seems the tradition of the Yamnaya and Afanasyevo meteoritic iron technology was discontinued.

The next phase of iron introduction into the life and economy of the Eurasian population can be connected with the end of the Late Bronze Age. It was based on the first experience in receiving bloomery iron (Fig. 5.2-A). It is represented by dozens of items (awls, knives, copying these of bronze) that came from sites of the Srubnaya and Sabatinovka cultures in the eastern European forest-steppe (Bagautdinov et al. 1979; Berezanskaya 1982; Berezanskaya & Gershkovich 1983; Bidzilya et al. 1983; Grakov 1958; Klushintsev 1997; Nikitenko 1998; Podgayevski 1935; Pryakhin 1996). Recent authors have argued that the theory of global ecological and economic crisis, which might have taken place at the close of the second millennium BC. Medvedev (1999a, 1999b) points out the critical situation in the Don forest-steppe area. It was characterized by a crucial shortage of bronze production, which, in turn, was accompanied by the reappearance of archaic stone and bone tools. By contrast, the settlements of the Srubnaya culture steadily produced the remains of iron objects and traces of their production. In the opinion of Grakov (1958) and Pryakhin (1973), the Don forest-steppe can be regarded as one of the early centers of iron emergence in the mid-second millennium BC. Interestingly enough, sites of the local Final Bronze Age do not contain any iron objects; that is to say, the material that has remained here was of secondary importance. Independent assimilation of the bloomery process by inhabitants of the forest-steppe of eastern Europe is also shared by other scholars (Shramko 1987).

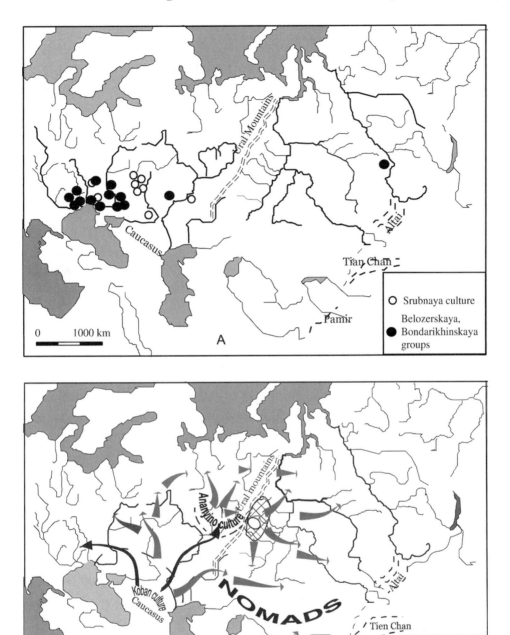

Figure 5.2. A – Distribution of bloomary iron in the Late and Final Bronze Age in Eurasia; **B** – The spread of iron in Eurasia.

Yet, on the whole, for the Final Bronze Age, we can already see more iron objects, yielded by sites of the Valikovaya pottery cultural horizon (Berestenev 1994; Berezanskaya 1982; Buinov 1980; Nikitenko 1998). There are thirty-three objects, among which six knives-daggers are of copper-iron. The greatest number of iron wares (twenty-five), mainly tools and weapons, comes from the Belozyerka and Bondarikhino cultures. These can be compared with the early (Srubnaya) phase, when only the simplest forms dominated. The Belozyersko-Bondarikhino items are marked by the prevalence of knives-daggers and have a more diverse composition of iron wares, including one sword and a fibula, presumably, imported from the Balkan-Danubian area. Yet, morphologically, all objects repeated the forms of the bronze implements. By the end of the Late Bronze Age, two-edged knives had replaced the one-edged ones.

In Terekhova's opinion (1997), the technology of knife and awl production comes from the simple operations of free hot forging. Nevertheless, there is some evidence for the appearance of a technique such as fire-welding, in which the pieces of metal were joined after being heated in the blacksmith's hearth. Some traces of carbonization also have been revealed by metallographic analyses.

The majority of these iron items were produced in local centers, apart from items that were definitely imported, such as the sword and fibulae. We should note that only one item, made from metallurgical iron, has been found in the Asiatic zone of Central-Northern Eurasia.

In the light of this, we have to conclude that the eastern European steppe and forest-steppe was an area of iron production early on. By the end of the second millennium BC, the number of the iron and bimetallic items had gradually increased, reflecting sporadic attempts of the new technology within the old copper and bronze industry. The process of iron-making was not connected with the experience of meteoritic iron processing. It mainly depended on the mastering of the bloomery techniques.

By the tenth–ninth centuries BC, the large Eurasian metallurgical network, which had previously dominated the vast space of the Eurasian continent, began to decline. Nevertheless, it had changed the sociocultural and technological situation in the area under study. Metallurgy expanded to the east and northward into the forest zone, and this expansion did not pass without leaving a trace.

The decline of the Bronze Age cultures partly resulted from climate destabilization in the shape of colder conditions (see the Introduction to this book). This exploded the basis of the settled pastoral economy and followed the economic reorientation to nomadic pastoralism in the steppe area and structural reorganization in the forest-steppe. What is probably most important is that the stable trade-exchange systems of communications, which existed earlier, now broke down. Some traditional raw material sources might have been exhausted and tin supplies became more difficult.

The transition to the widespread use of iron tools and weapons occurred in temperate Eurasia between the eighth and third centuries BC (Fig. 5.2-B).

By the late ninth century BC, the population of eastern Europe had mastered the process of iron production and, in the eighth century BC, they came to make bimetallic swords and learned to make steel (Trans-Caucasus, North Pontic, Middle Volga). In fact, during this short time period, between the eighth and seventh centuries BC, all the basic technological operations were discovered and established there (Grakov 1977; Shramko et al. 1977), namely: production of various types of steel; heat treatment; blacksmith's welding; surface and working part carbonization. According to the latest findings of Russian scholars, one can say, that on the eve of the Iron Age in Eastern Europe there existed two basic technological traditions, dating back to the preceding period:

1. The eastern European or Pontic tradition. This was based on the use of pure iron, the quality of which was much worse than that of bronze. It was centered in the Pontic steppe and forest-steppe, and it emerged as the result of a shortage of the bronze supply.
2. The Trans-Caucasian tradition. This is characterized by the use of carbonization and the heat treatment of steel wares. This tradition is supposed to go back to the ancient center of iron processing of the eastern Mediterranean (Terekhova & Erlikh 2000).

The majority of scholars believe that bimetallic swords and daggers, which were characteristic of the so-called pre-Scythian period, spread through the North Caucasus (Terekhova et al. 1997: 41). However, we can say that the last peak of the bronze industry, which supplied growing military needs mostly in socketed arrowheads and which flooded the Eurasian steppes, coincided with the beginning of the Iron Age. Moreover, the majority of ornaments, horse harness decorations, and cauldrons were cast from bronze.

By the seventh century BC, the people of southeastern Europe already knew all the secrets of iron production except for cast iron (Shramko 1962). In eastern Europe, several centers of the iron industry existed, and they were connected with large fortresses located in the forest-steppe (Shramko 1987: 115). Its inhabitants mastered the iron industry rapidly and effectively became iron suppliers to the Scythians. New material came to be used for making swords and daggers.

THE URAL FERROUS METALLURGY

In the Ural area, nonferrous metallurgy was predominant as long ago as the mid-first millennium BC, although iron objects were known there earlier as imports, particularly bimetallic swords. At this time, iron was valuable and therefore it was rather rare. Beyond the Urals, iron was introduced into widespread practice relatively late (between the fifth and third centuries BC), especially in southern Siberia where rich copper and tin deposits were available.

The end of the Bronze Age of the Urals (ninth to eighth centuries BC) witnessed the appearance of two important metallurgical centers on both sides of the mountains: the Ananyino center in the west, and the Itkul center in the east. They were closely linked and had a common basis, continuing certain traditions of a previous time, but their spheres of influence were different: the first had a western and northern cultural orientation, the second a southern and eastern zone orientation. Both of them functioned during the eighth to third centuries BC (Bel'tikova 1993; 1997; Kuzminykh 1983).

The Ananyino Metallurgy (Cis-Urals Area)

The Cis-Urals metallurgical center was based on the cultural world that was composed of various cultures, which continued the basic traditions of the local Bronze Age. Above all, it involved the Ananyino cultural groups (see Chapter 7, Fig. 7.1).

The Ananyino metallurgical center completed the development of the Volga-Ural non-ferrous metallurgy (Kuzminykh 1983: 171). It is characterized by many revived features of the Seima-Turbino and Eurasian types. Three basic groups of Ananyino copper alloys have been identified: tin, tin-antimony-arsenic, and pure copper, which were in widespread use as long ago as the Bronze Age. This center produced a large number of socketed axes, spearheads, arrowheads, battle hammers, knives-daggers, and plenty of ornaments. The influence of Ananyino metallurgy spread as far as northwest Europe, into central-northern Sweden and Finland (Hjarthner-Holdar & Risberg 1999; Talgren 1937; Zbruyeva 1952). From the outset, Ananyino metallurgists were in close connection with the Caucasian and Pontic centers, from where the so-called Cimmerian bronzes, such as daggers with cross-linked handles, Koban bronze axes, two-ring horse bits, some kinds of plaques, and blades were imported (Terekhova et al. 1997). This fact is of great significance for the problem under study.

The point is that the earliest Ananyino sites (ninth/eighth–sixth centuries BC) produced not only the bronze material but also a number of bronze-iron and iron objects of a high technological level (Fig. 5.3). It is interesting to note that about two-thirds of all known iron items come from the earliest burials dated to the eighth–sixth centuries BC. They are supposed to have been produced locally, although we cannot deny that some of them that were based on this technology were imported from the Caucasus. This technology could be passed on by any migrating metallurgist with knowledge of bloomery iron production. An intriguing point is that the Caucasus is rather far from the Cis-Urals, and

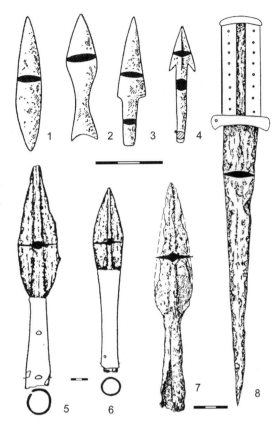

Figure 5.3. Iron and bimetallic objects from the Ananyino culture. (1–5, 8) Starshii (Elder) Akhmylovsky cemetery; (6, 7) Ananyinsky cemetery (after Kahlikov 1977 and Kyzminykh 1983).

there is no early iron found in the cultures that are situated between these two regions.

Later, from the fourth century BC, the local production changed its orientation to that of the Sauromatian needs. However, it should be noted that archaeological sites of the southern variant of the Ananyino culture contain only remains of metalworking without mining. This kind of activity was related to the villages and fortresses, even though the majority of metal is yielded by cemeteries.

What was iron used for? First of all, it was used for mastering tools. Tools number more than seven hundred out of an approximate total of thirteen hundred iron items. The second place is occupied by weapons 520 items (swords, daggers, battle-hammers-axes, spearheads, arrowheads, quiver hooks, etc.). The greater part of a horse harnesses were made from iron. Ornaments (twenty-seven items) are the final items.[3]

How can we describe the technological level of the Ananyino ferrous metallurgy? It can be exemplified by the Starshyi (Elder) Akhmylovsky burial ground, material from which has been technologically well analyzed. About half of all iron items from this cemetery were produced from the, unevenly carbonized steel (wrought iron) and steel with high a percentage of carbon. Surface hardening and tempering also were used. Fourteen percent of the items were made from "pure" iron. Steel of a good quality went to make the battle-axes and sometimes spearheads. The Ananyino people mastered free and hot forging, welding, stamping, burnishing, and carving. Apparently, metallurgists held a special status in society; they were buried with their tools in common cemeteries.

Nevertheless, we should not forget that the general proportion of copper to iron in the Ananyino metallurgy was about 20:1. It was only the beginning of the ferrous industry in the forest zone of eastern Europe and pre-Urals. Since the third-second centuries BC, the territory of its influence extended gradually but constantly. A direct heir of the Ananyino culture, the Pyanobor formation, was completely based on iron production. At the same time, the heavy and rich decorations of Pyanobor women were made of bronze (see Chapter 7).

The Itkul Metallurgy (Trans-Urals Area)

The eastern slopes of the Urals between the eighth and third centuries BC were inhabited by specialized metallurgists, who left their marks upon the culture named Itkulskaya or Itkul (see Chapter 8, Figs. 8.1 and 8.8). They arranged their working places close to living sites. Workshop areas, which today number about forty, were surrounded by ramparts and ditches and situated in high hills. They usually concentrated about two to nine together, forming some kind of local center (Bel'tikova 1997).

The Itkul metallurgy was based on rich natural copper and iron deposits concentrated along the Ural mountains for approximately 270 km. It is represented by various remains, including: furnaces (about one hundred), molds (175), slags, ores, wastes, technical ceramics (tuyers), and tools for ore dressing and metal processing. The furnaces were usually of simple construction, found near the fortifications. The casting molds were made from clay, talc, and copper. The Itkul metallurgists were able to produce a wide assortment of goods: tools (adzes, miner's hacks, awls, chisels), and weapons (arrowheads, spears, swords, daggers, badges for harness). All these were in common use in the steppe and forest-steppe. The vast majority of items produced was made from copper. This is well represented by a general ratio of 600:25 between copper and iron items found in the Itkul settlements.Unlike the Ananyino center, that of the Itkul started to produce iron only in the fifth–third centuries BC. All workshops with remains of iron production are situated on the southeast periphery of the Itkul territory. This can be explained by the differing locations of iron ores, deposits of which are widely spread in western Siberia, whereas copper was mostly deposited in the mountain areas.

At the present stage in our knowledge, it is not possible to distinguish between furnaces for copper and iron production. It is probable that blow-furnaces were of universal construction. There was some novelty in the smelting apparatus, namely, an above-surface furnace, supplemented by a deep chamber and a system consisting of several chambers of different heights.

Iron objects, which are mainly tools and single ornaments are not numerous (about twenty-five), but we should not forget that the Itkul sites are represented only by settlements and no burials. All items copy the copper-bronze forms. Metallographic analyses show that knives were produced from bloomery iron by free forging, but their quality is not high. On the contrary, the pins were forged from unevenly carbonized steel (Fig. 5.4). We also can certify that the technology of bimetallic knife production was laborious. However, in general, the Itkul iron technology was of a primitive character, demonstrating the mastery of the very early stage of the bloomery process.

In the light of all of this, we can conclude that, in the Trans-Uralian (Itkul) metallurgical center, there were existing basic factors for the independent formation of iron production, but that, of course, does not exclude external stimuli. A well-developed mine-metallurgical basis could serve as one such factor. A second factor was connected with the economic orientation (or tributary dependence) to southern Urals nomads, who were major consumers of the Itkul metal as early as the third century BC.

Transition to the Real Ferrous Metal Production

The fifth–third centuries BC constituted the period of formation of the real ferrous metal industry. During this period, iron tools and weapons were made, although bronze continued alongside the latter for many decorative purposes; objects of everyday life and cultic use, and, partly, for the final manufacture of bronze arrowheads, following the ancient steppe patterns. From the third century BC onward, iron tools and weapons were made in greater quantities. The range of goods was extended and new blacksmith techniques appeared.

Beyond the Urals, the best studied and well presented area archaeologically is the Sargat culture (see Chapter 8). Yet strictly speaking, the evidence for Sargat iron smelting is rather scarce until the final centuries BC.

Compared with bronze metallurgy, that of iron developed locally, although we have to think that its origin was connected with some external factors, namely, with involvement into the nomadic sphere of influence and close relationships with the Itkul culture.

The Sargat ferrous metallurgy is evidenced by numerous iron objects, found both in settlements and burial grounds, iron ores, slags, and furnace ruins. Suffice it to say that from the third century BC onward, the majority of tools and weapons were made of iron. Yet, it was rather expensive, especially, in the beginning, when in the graves, bone items usually accompanied those of iron.

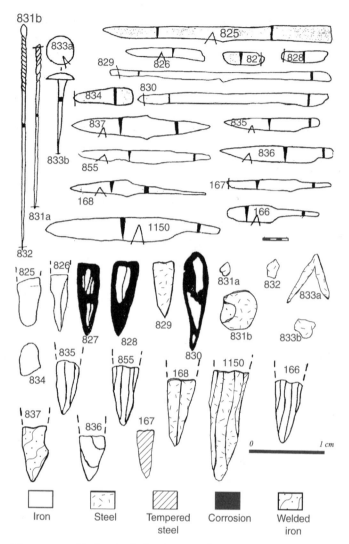

Figure 5.4. Technological scheme of iron objects from the Itkul culture (after Bel'tikova 1991).

Unfortunately, there has not been any special project aimed at studying Sargat metallurgy. However, analyses of some iron items have been accomplished (Zinyakov 1997). Samples have been taken from twelve sites; these represent seventy-two items, including tools (twenty-eight), weapons (twenty-four), horse harness elements (fifteen), clothing accessories (six), and one indefinite item. Iron was used, above all, for making knives, arrowheads, daggers, swords, battle-axes and a panoply of other items. A full assemblage of iron offensive and defensive weapons and horse harnesses come from several unrobbed Sargat graves that also contained numerous Chinese imports.

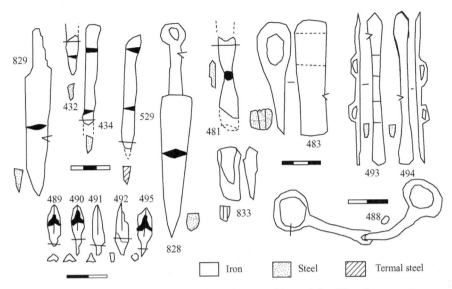

Figure 5.5. Technological schemes of Sargat iron objects (after Zinyakov 1997).

As metallographic analysis shows, among Sargat material, objects made of malleable iron and steel of average and high quality, are prevalent (Fig. 5.5). Unevenly carbonized steel was produced directly in the blast furnace. On average, carbonized steel resulted from a special process of cementation and was used for weapon production. Forging, multilayered welding, and tempering was known as well. For making small decorations, the ferriers employed a brazing technique. Sargat metallurgy is supposed to be of a domestic character; the quality of welding was not high and the temperature regime was rather unstable. The remains of simple blast furnaces and forges have been discovered in some Sargat settlements. As Zinyakov (1997: 114) writes, in the course of metal smelting, the Sargat metallurgists followed the strict regulation of a technological process, starting with the moment of oven construction (type of oven, blowing arrangement, working room parameters), and finishing with metal smelting (proportion of wooden charcoal and ore, moment of furnace charge, blowing force, smelting time, etc.). The Sargat blacksmiths already knew and used carbon steel, which excelled in a soft iron with mechanical qualities.

In other areas of the forest-steppe zone (upper Ob' River – the Bolsherechye culture) the process of iron-making was similar, with some local variations.

Thus, we can say that in the second half of the first millennium BC, the Sargat iron metallurgy was advanced. The increasing production of iron supplied the local population and its nomadic neighbors. This was followed by the spread of iron technology northward to the forest zone, which was occupied by spacious

Ob'-Irtysh cultural communities, one of which is represented by the Kulay culture (Zykov 1993).

The forest inhabitants became acquainted with bloomery iron by the third century BC. They mastered tools, some forms of weaponry, anthropomorphic plaques and ornaments, the number of which had increased by the mid-first millennium CE. Yet, their iron technology was archaic, reflecting an initial stage of the iron industry. Wrought iron, mild steel, and medium steel were in use. Specifics of the Kulay metallurgy consisted in quite a stable tradition of bronze casting, which dominated iron, especially in the production of numerous cultic objects carried out in the Northern Animal Style. However, by the end of the first millennium BC, iron had become predominant, and forced bronze out of tool and weapon production (Chindina 1984: 142–3).

We can draw several conclusions from this chapter.

Iron as a raw material became known in eastern Europe and the southern Urals rather early in the third millennium BC. It was during a stage of meteoritic iron processing, the tradition of which was discontinued.

In the next stage, within proto-Iron Age, coinciding with the end of the Late Bronze Age of archaeological periodization that the bloomery process was tentatively invented in eastern Europe in the areas close to the Caucasus and Pontic zone (second half of the second millennium BC).

Once this process was invented, it was spread from south-east Europe mostly eastward during the period between the eighth and fifth centuries BC (initial stage of the Iron Age). One of the first recipients of the new technology was the Ananyino metallurgical center in the Cis-Urals, which in turn passed it further to the north and west forest. By contrast, the forest Ananyino metallurgy was conservative when compared with that of the forest-steppe of eastern Europe with its early and advanced blacksmith work. This stage comes to the other side of the Urals several centuries later, apparently between 500 cal BC and 300 cal BC. It resulted from the interaction of various internal and external factors, among which political and military ones were of great significance. In the forest area, the beginning of the Iron Age relates to the last centuries BC, but it was characterized by its own variations – long-term preservation of the Bronze Age types.

The real Iron Age began during the final centuries BC and beginning of the first millennium CE for almost all Eurasian zones. Iron was not only domestically produced but also was traded, if we remember the finds of Chinese iron weapons in the western Siberia forest-steppe and Eurasian steppe. In fact, these societies were powerful; they had had a chance to survive, and now they possessed either advanced iron technology or constantly consumed its production.

The irregularity of technological advance is reflected in the different cultures of Eurasia. But there is a common regularity: the transition to the new technology was accompanied by the destruction of the old one and by the

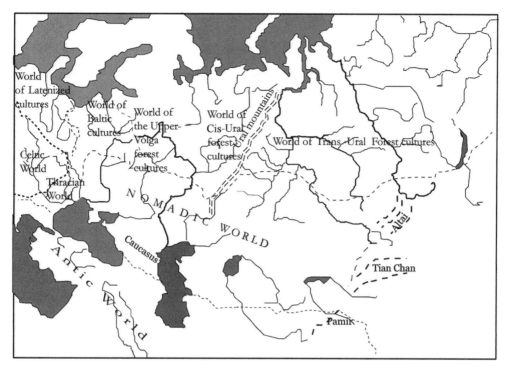

Figure 5.6. The Eurasian worlds of the first millennium BC.

formation of new cultural and social types. Although this process did not have the character of a revolution, as has been noted for western Europe (Kristiansen 1998: 217), their long-term consequences can be regarded as significant.

On a map of the Iron Age (Fig. 5.6), it is relatively easy is to distinguish what we may term "cultural worlds," embracing some regions and groups of cultures, united by intensive interactions, shared cultural models, and historical fate as follows:

1. the world of Classical civilizations.
2. the Celtic world.
3. the world of the cultures of northern Europe.
4. the world of the forest cultures of eastern Europe.
5. the world of the forest cultures of the Cis-Ural and Kama area.
6. the nomadic world.
7. the world of the cultures of the Balkan and Carpathian areas.
8. the world of the forest cultures to the east of the Ural.

Indeed, these worlds were not separated by impassable boundaries. Frontiers changed periodically but, as a whole, they remained more or less stable until the Early Medieval period. These worlds were differentiated not only through their cultural markers and ecological conditions but also by their internal social order. The extreme range of contrasts moves from advanced Classical states as the centers of economic, political, and cultural influence through to unstable social structures of the forest zone of eastern Europe and western Siberia. Most groups in all these worlds shared certain technical and economic developments, yet iron introduction involved all of them in a network of complex interactions.

CHAPTER 6

THE SOUTHERN URALS WITHIN THE NOMADIC WORLD: AT THE CULTURAL CROSSROADS

The first millennium BC was marked by the appearance in the historical arena of new powerful actors, whose "barbarian" image was associated with constant movement, destruction, and horror. The ancient writers characterized them as extremely militant and victorious. From time to time, their groups emerged on the border of "civilizations" under different names, but always with the same look – armed, mounted warriors symbolizing a new epoch. In a relatively short time, the nomadic people adapted to the vast steppe expanse with its extreme climatic conditions and united different areas – either voluntarily or involuntarily – into one economic and cultural zone that greatly enhanced mutual intercommunication. They created the "barbarian periphery" without which the "civilized" states could no longer exist. The birth of this "Nomadic World" in Eurasia was neither easy nor welcomed, but there was no alternative. Before we discuss the Uralian nomadic cultures, we will pause to review some general points of nomadic studies.

GENERAL ASPECTS OF NOMADIC STUDIES

Ecological and Historical Dimensions of Eurasian Nomadism

Eurasian nomadism has long been the focus of attention for travelers, writers, ethnographers, historians, government officials, and military officers of tsarist Russia. Their numerous descriptions and stories are rich in valuable empirical and statistical material. Gathered from these materials, we can see that the character of extensive stockbreeding remained practically unchanged until the early twentieth century. Environments and biological specifics of bred animals, ways of transmigrations, and the forms of use of natural resources determined this nomadism. General specifics of this mode of subsistence, which existed without any great changes over millennia, corresponding to certain ecological conditions, allow scholars to use very rich ethnographic information for reconstruction of basic outlines of ancient nomads (Khazanov 1975, 1984; Tairov 1993).

There are various definitions of nomadism, embracing all its forms from "pure" nomadism to settled stockbreeding (Cribb 1991: 16). In this book, we lean toward the definition suggested by Rudenko (1961) and Khazanov (1975: 5–15; 1984), who define nomadism as a form of food-producing economy with extensive mobile stockbreeding, livestock management all year round with free-range grazing and without stables, and laying fodder for animals when most of the population periodically transmigrates with the flocks. The necessary preconditions of Eurasian nomadism as an economic, cultural, and social phenomenon include: a distinct ecological zone with limited potential for agriculture; a specific herd structure, suitable for arid conditions; the presence of saddles and wheeled draught transport; and a high degree of property differentiation, entailing private (family) ownership of livestock (Khazanov 1975: 9; 2003). It has been repeatedly suggested in the literature that the search for a fully nomadic society should be abandoned in favor of an approach that recognizes nomadic tendencies manifested to varying degrees in a wide range of societies. It is true that nomadic pastoralism consists of pastoralism and nomadism. However, not all pastoralists are nomadic, but the greater the degree of pastoralism, the stronger the tendency toward nomadism (Cribb 1991: 16). According to Khazanov (1984: 19), seminomadic pastoralism is characterized by extensive pastoralism and periodic changing of pastures during the course of the entire, or the greater part of the year, ... but there is also agriculture in a secondary or supplementary capacity. However, in northern Eurasia it is associated with other kinds of activity.

In turn, environment, climate, and landscape can be reflected in various components of human culture and contribute to the formation of a variety of cultural traditions. Similar environmental conditions influence the development of more or less similar cultural attributes. This is reflected in the theory of cultural and economic type, put forward by Russian ethnologists (Andrianov 1968; Cheboksarov & Cheboksarova 1971; Levin & Cheboksarov 1955) and frequently demonstrated in the history of Eurasian nomads.

In particular, this theory can be exemplified by the territory comprising western Kazakhstan and the southern Urals, which was a clearly defined region with its stable summer and winter pastures, which were preserved until the beginning of the twentieth century. Winter pastures were in the low Syr-Darya, near the Aral Sea, and northern Caspian area, and the summer pastures were located along the Ural River and its tributaries as well as in the upper Tobol River (Vostrov 1962). This disposition has not been changed for many centuries despite the ethnically different nomads who occupied this region during different periods (Fig. 6.1).

Nevertheless, the Eurasian steppe is a huge area stretching from Mongolia to the Hungarian "pushta," and, despite some common traits, it is characterized by clear ecological differences. The natural environment into which the Eurasian steppe was transformed by human activity provides conditions for nomadic

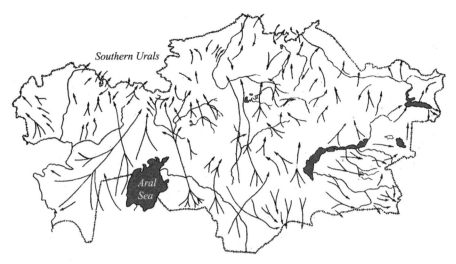

Figure 6.1. Directions of nomadic transmigrations in Kazakhstan at the end of the nineteenth century: arrows show only transmigrations from winter to summer pastures (after Tairov 1993).

stockbreeding. Masanov who has analyzed the materials relating to Kazakh ethnology, designates a "nomadic" space in terms of core and marginal zones. The first covers the ecosystems with the arid, continental climate and seasonal productivity of vegetal assemblages. These are mainly steppes, semideserts, and deserts. A lack of precipitation (usually amounting to a maximum of 200–400 mm per year), high solar radiation, frequent droughts, soil erosions, constant winds, and insufficient water resources are the factors limiting economic activity and requiring special forms of social and cultural adaptation in core zones. Nomadic stockbreeding is the only possible way for human life to survive. The population density is 1.5 individuals per one km². Stable sedentary life is not possible in this core zone (Masanov 1995: 22–4).

Subarid regions with yearly precipitation greater than 400 mm, stable freshwater sources of a natural origin, or rivers of annual water flow are common in marginal zones. These are situated on the boundaries of the landscape-climatic regions, in the periphery of nomadic areas with more stable climatic cycles: in river valleys, near lakes, in the forest-steppe, in the foothills, or around the areas with farming economies. Seminomadic stockbreeding supplemented by other economic resources (hunting, fishing, or farming) is more characteristic for such regions. Thus, the southern Urals and western Siberian steppe and forest-steppe are related to marginal zones, where one can expect to see a smaller degree of mobility. The density of population here was higher than in core regions. In marginal regions, temporal and spatial interconnections between nomadic stockbreeding and other economies varied more than in the arid zone and a tendency to a sedentary life style was stronger. Nomads always competed for holding control over such areas.

In the course of a long history of nomadic studies, there have been many attempts to create a typology of nomadic stockbreeding; however, one cannot say that this issue has common agreement. We can distinguish many types and forms of mobile pastoral stockbreeding both in chronological and structural aspects. There are models based on: (1) house typology (portable, stationary, permanent etc.); (2) herd composition (presence or absence of a cattle in a herd); (3) character of supplemental economic branches (agriculture); and (4) forms of transmigration (Khazanov 1975; Markov 1976; Masanov 1995; Pershits 1994; Shamiladze 1982). A degree of annual mobility determines a type (nomadic, seminomadic, semisettled, etc.); a form is defined by organization of pasturage (steppe-steppe, steppe-mountains, forest-steppe-steppe, etc.). There is a great variety of seasonal pasturing.

According to Tolybekov (1971), seminomadic stockbreeding is characterized by a rather long (about six months) stay in one place; winter houses, haymaking; and limited cultivation. Usually, seminomadic groups have more cattle in herds than nomadic groups, who prefer sheep and horses. We also can distinguish several types of transmigrating: meridional, transmeridional, radial, vertical, ellipsoid, and others (Akishev 1972; Markov 1976; Masanov 1995; Vainshtein 1972, 1980), which depended on particular ecological conditions. The latter, together with sociocultural factors, influenced a herd composition. Each species has its own advantages that should be in balance within the economic structure.

Masanov (1995: 79–84) considers the type of water use very important: preferably natural, which was usual for the forest-steppe and steppe, versus preferably artificial, which developed in the arid desert and semidesert areas, where the water supply comes from wells. Hunting, fishing, and primitive cultivation usually supplements transmigration along the rivers, when winter pasturing in one place was longer, than in the case of transmigration between the wells.

It is worthwhile here to note a description by Raddloff of the Kirghiz (Kazakh) groups:

> Their customs, morals and mode of thinking, in other words, all their lives
> and activity, are closely connected with movement for the sake of animals.
> For mobile stockbreeding groups it is especially important to find suitable
> areas for winter and summer migrations. In general, it is possible to spend at
> least spring and autumn anywhere, because during the springtime, animals
> can find both water and grass quite easily, and in the autumn period, heavy
> precipitation often stimulates the growth of new grass. However, for the
> winter camp, it is necessary to have a place that provides animals with
> shelter from the harsh weather. Suitable areas are typically sought within
> either forests or low river valleys. These places provide shelter from the
> wind, an abundance of water and firewood, and the possibility of pastures
> with shallower snowfall. In contrast, for summer pastures it is desirable to
> have a considerably open space with an ample supply of fresh water supply,
> such as a lake. (Radloff 1989: 253–7)

Plate 6.1. Horses in a pasture.

As to winter pasturing, it was a vitally important part of the nomadic economy. Ethnographic evidence shows that the majority of Eurasian nomads had their winter pastures in the southern part of the nomadic zone, but some groups of northern Kazakhstan wintered in the forest-steppe regions. As Heins wrote: "One part of the Kyrgyz has their pastures in the southern steppe, between sandy hills, as well as along the rivers, full of bulrush and scrub, the another part, approaching the north, spends a winter in dense forests near the rivers" (Heins 1898: 60).

An average nomadic family of south and central Kazakhstan owned about 15–20 camels, 4–5 horses, and 100–150 heads of small cattle (Pershits 1994: 140; Tolybekov 1971: 131) and the extent of their transmigrations was from 1 to 1.5 thousand km. The nomads of northern Kazakhstan had in a family possession about 15 horses, 2 camels, 50 sheep, and 6 head of cattle per family. Correspondingly, the distance of their movement was between 20 and 200 km.

The nomads of the Urals spent about six months in permanent winter camps, which were handed down from one generation to another. The Bashkirs of the Ekaterinburg district in the eighteenth century migrated west toward the Ural Mountains, often forty to seventy kilometers from their settlements (Popov 1813: 16–17). The Bashkirs of the Shadrinsk district transmigrated mostly across the flat Western Siberian Plain (Murzabulatov 1979: 64). In winter, different animals grazed separately, because they ate different kinds of plants or their parts. Horses usually were gathered into separate herds and driven away to distant pastures, where the snow was not more than 30–40 cm deep (although two to five animals often were kept back). At the end of winter, horses were driven back to the camp (Plate 6.1). Sheep could graze only with 10–12 cm of snowfall, and cows grazed near the camps. Conjoint pasturage was practiced only in extreme periods and consisted of successive grazing of different species (Masanov 1995: 95). Russian travelers have described this in the following way: "First, the horses go, they hoof the snow and eat the tops of plants. The cows and camels follow them, eating the middle parts of herbs. They cannot eat the lowest part of the stems. However, sheep can find forge here" (Levshin 1832: 197–8).

All historical and ethnographical materials are witness to the fact that only serious ecological disasters could make nomads change the system of seasonal transmigrations (Kradin 2001a; Shakhmatov 1964).

Specific ecological conditions and the extensive character of stockbreeding in an arid zone determines the dispersal state of nomads. An excessive concentration of animals on the acceptable limits of pasture produced overgrazing, which was succeeded by an ecological crisis and widespread disease. There also were many biological and social factors limiting the potential of such an economy. It could function effectively only in a dynamic balance that was regulated by biologically and socially segmented mechanisms (Masanov 1995: 120–1). The military factor became a point of controversy as a basis of nomadic society, because it required concentrating a large number of animals and people within the armies, which led to the degradation of pastures. This was one of the push factors for their migrations.

Pletneva (1982) suggested that nomadism passes first the stage of total all-year migrating ("tabor"), on irregular routes, then the stage of seasonal regular migration, and finally, limited migrating with constant winter camps and houses (seminomadic). We do not share this opinion, especially concerning the "tabor" migration. A great variety of structural forms of nomadic stockbreeding was not conditioned by evolutionary factors. The total migration of the entire human community with their animals is rather rare. It occurs only in the exclusive conditions of natural, social, or political disaster. The degree of economic mobility was fully dependent on environments, which varied in different parts of Eurasian steppe. In areas with large and stable snowfall, winter mobility was rather low.

Nevertheless, we cannot deny that this type of economy knew no changes over time. These related mostly to techniques of animal breeding, material culture development, military potential, and the role of nomadic societies in political events. In general, nomadism evolved from less mobility in the beginning into greater mobility in the later period; this is evidenced by the development of horse harnessing and the replacement of kibitka-type locomotion with horse and camel saddling, and the gradual disappearance of nontransportable objects from the material culture (Masanov 1995: 42).

Various approaches to stockbreeding cannot be classified as one uniform economic strategy without accounting for specific conditions and respective cultural attributes. One population can simultaneously practice economic patterns characterized as nomadic, seminomadic, and sedentary forms of stockbreeding.

The degree of mobility, herd composition, and amplitude and distance of migration obviously depend on local environment, social, and economic levels of development, and the traditions of any given society.

It is clear that not all pastoral economies are nomadic, but, with an increase in pastoralism from the Bronze Age to the Iron Age, there was a greater tendency for nomadism (Akishev 1972; Evdokimov 2000; Gryaznov 1957; Khabdulina & Zdanovich 1984; Khazanov 1975; Kosarev 1984; Kuzmina 1996a, 1996b; Margulan 1979; Markov 1973; Masanov 1995).

About the Origins of Eurasian Nomadism

This problem has divided the academic community into two major groups: those who are convinced in a rather early emergence (Eneolithic) of pastoral nomadism in Eurasia, and those who support the "later" hypothesis. We discussed the first theory in Chapter 2.

This theory resulted in the belief of some scholars in the nomadic character of the Srubnaya and Andronovo cultures, whereas these groups only tended toward nomadism. In fact, as we saw, the economy of these cultures was mixed and consisted of pastoral stockbreeding, primitive cultivation in the river valleys, metallurgy, hunting, and fishing, and some forms of domestic craft.

According to Vainshtein (1972, 1973, 1980), nomadism could emerge from hunting. Masanov (1995: 35), partly sharing this theory, writes: "Stockbreeders of an arid zone assimilated and cognized geographic environments of this ecological niche in the process of chasing the wild hoofed animals, mixing some stockbreeding and hunting in the form of seasonal migrating."

In this case, only small groups of people might have been involved in such seasonal migrational hunting, but this experience was very important; it helped to better understand animal behavior and to "clean up" the territory of concurrent species. In fact, later, the transmigrations of nomads with their flocks would repeat the routes of natural movements of wild animals. Such hunting-stockbreeding could be one of several transitional forms on the way to nomadism, which become the only possible kind of economy and lifestyle in arid conditions. This process had most likely begun in the Final Bronze Age, as demonstrated by the increase of bones of sheep and horse in contrast with cattle and wild animals.

Recent palaeoenvironmental studies undertaken in different areas of the steppe displayed the heterogeneity of ecological adaptation as a response to the unstable climatic conditions of the arid and semiarid zones. The alternation of pluvial and drought conditions made people change their economic orientation repeatedly. We can suppose that the tendency toward mobile stockbreeding might have been realized several times, depending on which climatic situation was dominant. Yet for this tendency to reach its peak as a nomadic adaptation and a social and economic system, one required not only a specific environment but also an appropriate technological level and long experience in stockbreeding, including bareback riding. Without a doubt, the experience of seasonal alternation of pastures and water sources, which was character- istic for the Eurasian nomadic economy, is definitely rooted in the Bronze Age (Akishev 1972), yet it was realized to a fuller extend only in the first millennium BC.

There is another important and very interesting aspect, to which Khazanov (2003) has directed our attention. Eurasian nomadism as an economic and sociocultural phenomenon could not appear earlier because, in many respects, it depends on the economic and sociopolitical relations with settled statehood societies. This factor seems to be of a secondary character, but it is not; it helps to understand the later establishment of pastoral nomadism in its classical form in the Eurasian steppe. As an extremely specialized type of an economy, it required the products of agricultural societies, as well as metal and wood, which nomads could take from the forest and forest-steppe. In other words, the interregional division of labor or the corresponding level of global economic and political structuring was an extremely important precondition for Eurasian nomadism.

Soil, vegetation, and climate analysis have demonstrated that the general characteristics of modern soils and climate were formed by the first millennium BC (Demkin & Ivanov 1985; Ivanov 1995a, 1996). The biological conditions of the steppe of eastern Europe and western Siberia were influenced either by global or by local climatic cycles. Therefore, their fluctuation was different on both sides of the Ural range and its northern and southern parts. In the east, the fluctuation between extreme humidity and aridity was greater than in eastern Europe, as well as representing a zonal displacement. As a result, in the eastern steppe (Kazakhstan and western Siberia), a migratory type of environ- mental adaptation became more characteristic. It is especially important in an intermediate zone such as the forest-steppe, which was periodically occupied by either hunter-fishers-pastoralists or nomadic and seminomadic populations. The forest-steppe was attractive to nomads because of its stable vegetational and water resources and it was open to all southern influences. In fact, the forest-steppe as a marginal region can serve as a specific indicator of a degree of nomadic power or weakness.

Another issue concerns the mechanism and initial steps of transition to nomadism.[1] One group of scholars states that the reason for the transforma- tion of traditional stockbreeding-farming economies was rooted in the rising imbalance of its two basic branches and the increase of herds. In this situation, the people had to assimilate new territories and intensify the system of grazing. The dominant hypothesis emphasizes the climatic conditionality of transition to nomadism (Gumilev 1966, 1989; Khabdulina & Zdanovich 1984; Kosarev 1991; Medvedev 1999a; Tairov 2003). No less important was the political pressure from the state societies (Khazanov 1975). It seems that the origin of nomadism is a result of many interacting factors: ecological, socioeconomic, political, and cultural (Markov 1973; 1976; Masanov 1995; Shnirelman 1980; 1988).

The long process of domestication of animals, accumulation of knowledge about their breeding in specific conditions, necessary ecological experience (ecological culture), and the formation of a specific complex of material culture had predestined the emergence of pastoral nomadism as a socioeconomic and cultural phenomenon at the turn of the second and first millennia BC. Moreover, various technological advantages and innovations of the Bronze Age had played an essential role in the transition to the new type of economy.

It seems that in the Mongolian steppe and eastern Turkistan (northern and western China) the transition to pastoral nomadism under the influence of ecological factors started earlier than in the western Eurasia steppe. The point is that the Mongolian steppes are characterized by rather extreme environmental conditions and winters with little snow. Because of constant winds, snowfall was not very thick, and this allowed animals easier grazing year round. Yet, this area has clearly pronounced environmental and biological limitations for extensive stockbreeding. In fertile years, nomadic pastoralism could quickly produce a large number of animals that urgently required more pasture and water. Repeated overpopulation above the carrying capacity of the Mongolian steppe to feed a definite number of animals and people caused the effect that is called the "Mongolian generator of peoples" (Kurochkin 1994).

A general warming of the climate marked the second half of the second millennium BC in Eurasia. At about 3100–3000 BP in Mongolia and eastern Turkistan the warm climate changed to an arid phase, which lasted until approximately 2700 BP (Tairov 2003). During this period, we can observe traces of the westward movements of the heterogeneous eastern nomadic groups, which opened the way for their later generations. These segmented groups left Mongolia mainly through the Zungarian gateway and channeled off to the Eurasian steppes.

Almost all important nomadic migrations started in the east. Their model, which was clearly formulated by Gavriluk in her brilliant book (1999), is more or less universal. The first stage of migration (physical movement to different geographical and social environments) is relatively short – lasting only during the life of one generation; rather active military raids mark it. Basic prototypes of new material culture and behavior patterns were forming in the course of this stage. Their expressions are not numerous and were unmatched at that period. They are practically invisible archaeologically.

Next we can see the long process of development in a new place, which is sometimes called "fatherland conquest."[2] It covers the life of about three generations and is characterized by the synthesis of aboriginal and new traditions. The adaptation of an economic system to new environments determines the content of the initial phase of this process. It is poorly reflected in the archaeological record. With the passing of time, the system of seasonal cycles and distribution of pastures among different clans is established. The territorial structure of the nomadic economy occurs within the unchanged economic type. Gradually, if the situation remains stable, the winter camps are transformed to stable habitats that give rise to the tendency of sedentarization. This time is usually well represented in archaeological sites. Yet, the more people and animals are concentrated, the less potential is given by the environment. This leads to the overexploitation of pastures and finally to the collapse of the regional economic system that again increased migrational potential of nomadic society.

Social Organization of Eurasian Nomads

Despite a tremendous number of publications that describe the culture and history of nomadic people, the problem of their social development has not been well represented in world scholarship. It was more popular in the Soviet nomadology than in the West. In the course of several discussions, which took place over a number of years in Soviet Marxist literature, the level of nomadic societies was assessed in a wide range of ways from very primitive egalitarian societies to the developed feudal societies. The attempts to find "a room" for nomads on the "shelves" of social formations theory always met with some difficulties, primarily because of the almost unchangeable character of the basis of nomadic pastoralism and because of the absence of real social classes. By the late 1980s, in Russian literature, the level of nomadic societies was interpreted in terms of several synthetic concepts: (1) preclass nomadic society, (2) early state, (3) some forms of feudalism, and (4) a special nomadic mode of production (Bondarenko et al. 2003; Masanov 1995). Some scholars tended to use the "civilization" approach to the history of Eurasian nomads (Martynov 1989a, 1989b).

Let us now look at the social organization of Eurasian nomads as it is represented in Russian ethnological literature. The specifics and basic controversy of the nomadic mode of production[3] was conditioned by the composition of private property to livestock, the group character of production (organization of flock grazing), and communal property of the land and water sources. The wealth of pastoral nomads is in their flocks, which can be easily alienated by theft, death, from disaster or starvation.

Stockbreeding does not require great human resources and concentration of labor; the system of production is of a dispersal character. Yet, in order to make this system work effectively, one needs to have an effective management structure. The common feature of almost all nomadic societies, on which all specialist agree, is the complex, hierarchical, and ramified clan-tribal structure, which ensured that every individual had a feeling of pride of belonging to the unit.

Reproduction of nomadic societies was a result of several social units: family, group of families, community, and economic and local groups. Among them, a community played a very important role in what determined communal economic activity. In material production, the system of territorial and communal connections was dominant. They ensured the accomplishment of vital productive functions (Masanov 1995: 132–3).

We can distinguish two kinds of nomadic community. The first one, which functioned in winter periods, when forage and water resources were limited, is called minimal or a dispersed community. The communities owned and regulated the autumn pastures and the land around the winter camps. The second type of community, of extended type, is characteristic of warm periods. It consists of several minimal communities, and they owned the spring and summer pastures. The animals were the private property of families (Masanov 1995: 141–3; Shakhmatov 1964).

Another system of social relations acted in noneconomic and military spheres. The primary place here was occupied by a hierarchical organization, based on a vertical genealogical principle, which included some number of patronymic groups (patrilineages). The social status of any individual was determined by the status of his lineage, seniority, and birthright.

A family-kin group that included two or three generations represent the lowest level of patronymic organization defined by its communal works, socialization, heritage transmission, and life rituals (birth, initiations, death) (Masanov 1995: 150–1). The larger organization, which has different names ("lineage," "associative group"), regulate the system of landowning and land use, coordination of intercommunity relations, arbitrage, normative control, and the defense of communal interests. By contrast, some ethnographic reports of the eighteenth century relate that annexation for the right of land use existed in nomadic societies only in the periods of war and discord. In such situations, the chiefs and community leaders were responsible for the regulation of transmigrations.

This system was developed from the free use of pastures, which existed originally when the steppe population was relatively small, and land annexing was a major factor of life (Shakhmatov 1962). The classical system of pastoral seasonal nomadism with a strong regulation of pasture use matured only in medieval times. Hence, we can suppose that competition for pastures, especially for winter pastures, would have been very strong. The communities that were more organized, centralized, and warlike were more successful in exercising control over the land.

The military-potestal relations were in competence with the organization, usually called a "tribe." The tribe regulated contact with other tribes, to resolve political and military problems. The tribe could be of dual (left and right "wings") or triple (left and right wings plus a center), and was militarily organized by the decimal structure (i.e., units of thousands, hundred, and tens with a hierarchy of leaders)[4] (Taskin 1989). In peacetime, the dispersed character of the nomadic society did not require a great central power thus the power of the chiefs was not very significant, but in wartime, a central power was necessary. The amazing ability of nomads to create large armies in case of military danger or political contests is well known. A leader's personality should not be underestimated in the process of sociopolitical consolidation of nomadic societies. The history of the Hsiung-nu tribes is a good example. Cribb (1991: 55) stresses the territorial aspect of a tribe: "The tribe constitutes the operational unit through which units of population are matched to units of territory."

A social stratification in nomadic societies existed in several forms (Pershits 1994: 147–8). The simplest form was based on property differentiation. Another form, which Pershits describes as functional, divided the entire population into the governors (administrators) and the governed. One more form was connected with inherited statuses, as, for example, division of "white bone" and "black bone" in Mongolian and Turkic nomadic societies. The former strata included only the descendants of Chingiz-Khan. The statuses of "forceful" or "elder" tribes were always higher than these of "weak" or "younger" tribes. Social stratification was legislated by customary law.

The genealogical principle determined a hierarchy of all segments of nomadic society and social status of its members, according to the position of their lineages in relation to real or fictitious ancestors. Such a structure had the potential for proprietary and social ranking and stratification, especially in large polities, comprising many tribes and their groups and tended to go a chiefdom's way. A chief could emerge from the free will or forced alliance of several tribes as the head of the most powerful tribe. Depending on concrete historical conditions, this way could lead to various directions: back to a tribal group, or to a complex, or even a supercomplex chiefdom or nomadic empire, some properties of which were not characteristic of agrarian chiefdoms or states (Pershits 1994; Semenov 1994). The nomadic way to a statelike form, usually, passed though conflicts, wars, and expansions. Some scholars stress certain correlations between degrees of consolidation of nomads and political integration in neighboring state societies (Barfield 1991; Bondarenko et al. 2003; Khazanov 1984; Lattimore 1951). The relations between them fall into the category of core/periphery relations, with one exception: the periphery was dependent on the core in some economic aspects (needs in agricultural and artisan production), while at the same time various forms of direct and distant exploitation of state societies were used. Among these forms are plunder, tribute, "gifts" from a conquered land, and unequal trade on the frontiers. This was always very important for nomads and was something over which they fought (Kradin 1992, 2001a, 2002).

All materials so far discovered support the latest theories, according to which Eurasian nomads demonstrated a rather specific way of social development.

Nomadic societies were, without any doubt, complex. It is true that their extensive pastoral economy, low population density, and degree of limited sedentary did not require a legislated hierarchy. This only happened when they were drawn into political units consisting of both agricultural and stock-breeding structures, or when they had to have long and active contacts with advanced urban societies. For example, the Great Steppe Empires produced an impression of highly despotic states. Yet, their internal structure was rather primitive and based on kinship relations. Therefore, Kradin (1992, 1995, 2000, 2001b) characterizes the nomadic empires in terms of super-complex chiefdoms as a prototype of a particular kind of early state.

Three levels of integration and political complexity of pastoral nomads are revealed: (1) acephalous segmentary clans and tribal formations; (2) "secondary" tribes and chiefdoms; and (3) nomadic empires and "quasi-imperial" pastoral polities of smaller size (Kradin 2002).

Material Culture of Nomads

In our efforts to construct a profile of the nomadic material culture, we cannot expect quick and easy results. In fact, herding as a special kind of activity requires virtually no tools (Cribb 1991: 69). Attempts to identify nomadic cultures by using a certain material complex have rarely been successful. Ethnography indicates that pure nomadism is extremely rare. According to Russian scholars, the specifics that indicate a nomadic mode of life are as follows: a portable house, a good saddle with stirrups, light equipment, and extensive animal breeding with annual herding. The basic nomadic markers provided by ethnography, however, do not always find a correlation with the archaeology.

What are the commonly accepted archaeological markers of Eurasian pastoral nomadism? These include a kurgan burial ground (Plate 6.2), a relative absence of permanent settlements and houses or the presence of only camp sites; the absence or a very limited scale of farming; wheeled transport; and the bones of animals capable of traveling long distances and grazing year round, plus devices used for the exploitation of these animals.

Frequently the sedentary population could use many components of so-called nomadic material complex, and vice versa (Cribb 1991: 69). For example, during the Iron Age, the complex of "nomadic" weapons and horse harnesses was widespread over a vast portion of Eurasia, including the forest-steppe and even the forest. The only artifacts that can be used to separate the cultures attached to different landscapes are pottery and settlements. Some of the latter are located in marginal zones that could have served as communication points, and could have been a concentration of various groups of populations, including a nomadic population. The Hsiung-nu, whose "nomadic" reputation is without doubt, had large fortified settlements with rather elaborate internal structures. Kradin (2001a) put forward an interesting hypothesis, that such settlements could accommodate the population of the Hsiung-nu and people working for them (craftsmen, agriculturists).

A nomadic material culture may be ethnographically defined as having three main artifact characteristics: site furniture (fixtures or portable objects), durable or perishable objects, valuables or expendables (Cribb 1991: 66–75). The most characteristic feature of the early Eurasian nomads is the wide use of clay pottery. Almost every grave held some quantity of handmade earthenware. The vessels made on potters' wheels that were usually imported from statehood regions seem to have had more value. As recent research shows, vessels found in graves, could contain ordinary food such as milk, meat broth, and *kasha* (cereal or grain) (Koryakova & Daire 1997).

The bronze cauldron usually associated with elite burials contained animal bones that originally had been pieces of meat placed in the burial. The abundance of pottery in a burial, an item that could easily be broken and was especially vulnerable during movement, raises a question about its place within the nomadic material culture. Indeed, we cannot answer this question fully because we do not know what this material culture was and because a substantial part of this complex was made from organic material and has usually disappeared. Fortunately, we are able to infer from examples provided by the Altai nomadic frozen tombs. As is known, these people produced many utensils made of wood (dishes, mugs, bowls), birch bark (boxes), and leather (some kinds of jar) (Kubarev 1987; Polos'mak 1994, 2000; Rudenko 1961; 1970).

An interesting question that has not yet been discussed relates to the method in which Eurasian nomads organized pottery manufacture and how they preserved it from breakage during transmigration. They could manufacture it either in summer camps or at winter houses although the technology and organization of production could be different. As experiments have demonstrated, it is not difficult to make pottery in the summer, even when there is a scarcity of wood. It takes about 1.5–2 hours to make a pot and an additional 3–10 minutes to decorate it. According to ethnographic material and experiments, dried and pressed dung, which was abundantly available, is more than sufficient fuel to fire ceramics, and wood would be used very minimally. Dried and pressed dung fires up very quickly and maintains the temperature for a long time. Firing occurs without flames with temperatures reaching about 900–950 degrees for a duration of two to three hours (Koryakova & Fedorov 1993: 92–3). Nevertheless, this process requires some stability during a given period. Apart from pot making, the process includes several stages such as clay extraction and preparation as well as preparation of various additives.

It also should be noted that nomads frequently used pottery produced by sedentary populations; for example, the Sarmatians of the Don and Volga areas partially obtained their pottery in this manner. In the eighth–seventh centuries BC, the nomads in this region had only temporary camps in the open steppes, although there were stable settlements in the forest-steppe. Often, the latter

Plate 6.2. Steppe kurgans. **Top**: The Filippovka kurgan; **Below**: Reconstruction of the Temir kurgan in the Arkaim Reserve Museum

were defended by fortifications (Medvedev 1999a) and the forest served as a refuge.

The pastoral nomads of the Eurasian steppe carried out a kurgan funeral ritual that has been described many times in numerous publications. Yet, we still do not have any definitive explanation of its role in the nomadic societies, nor of the processes and circumstances of the mortuary construction. There have been only a few publications devoted to this problem. The huge kurgans of the Scythians, Sarmatians, and other ancient nomads containing the remains of large wooden (sometimes stone) funerary chambers are well known. Obviously, the erection of such constructions required a large labor investment, using a great deal of wood, an item usually not easily accessible in the treeless steppes. Some of the famous Scythian funeral complexes were reused repeatedly and could be considered the permanent houses of nomadic people. As was observed in the Pazyryk culture, some logs from permanent living quarters were reused in the construction of the funerary chamber. For example, a top covering placed above the funeral room in the kurgan 1 of the Ak-Alakha cemetery were the logs from a demolished polygonal house (Polos'mak 1994: 13). This suggests that the nomads had quite solid winter houses where the weather was particularly severe. As Polos'mak writes (1994: 14), the Ukok plateau was treeless, but the Pazyryk people used a great deal of wood in the funerary construction. They could have transported it from the nearest forest in wintertime over the ice with the help of ropes. This device is called *volokusha*, from the word "voloch" (to draw) and this practice is known from recent times. Dendrochronological analysis showed that all the logs used for funerary chambers were cut during the winter, and funerary ceremonies were executed in the spring or early summer. These are all arguments to indicate that the most sophisticated funeral constructions could have been built in advance and would have been possible only in more or less stable ecological and political conditions.

The kurgan was not only a functional mortuary construction; it also was a complex architectural structure, reflecting the specific artistic or cosmological ideas, which could exist in a given society. The organization of cemetery space somehow corresponded to the social order. That is why we can note the typological variety of inner kurgan constructions within the vast steppe and forest-steppe zone (Pyatkin 1987). Many archaeologists focusing on Eurasian kurgans of the Iron Age have pointed out that the large kurgans usually occupy the highest point of the landscape and are visibly connected to other large kurgans forming a chain that can stretch over 5–10 km. Within this complex, smaller kurgans are included (Fig. 6.2).

This system of kurgan location could have played a role in marking points in the nomadic communication system. The single kurgans that occupy the high open positions in a more or less significant distance from a river appear only at the beginning of the Iron Age. They differed from the kurgans of the Bronze Age in that they usually are located in groups along a river terrace. Several groups of archaeologists, particularly in northern Kazakhstan (Zdanovich et al. 1984: 41) and the southern Urals (Tairov & Botalov 1988), undertook some work on the reconstruction of kurgan structures. Detailed paleosoil analyses permitted scholars to conclude that big kurgans such as Kara-Oba and Obaly (northern Kazakhstan) were built from rectangular brick-blocks taken from topsoil. The authors reconstructed the kurgan building process in the following manner:

> Initially, a place suitable for burial was chosen. It should be situated near a pasture, not far from a water source, and certainly on the elevated and forestless steppe ground. Shallow and wide ditches, the soil from which was

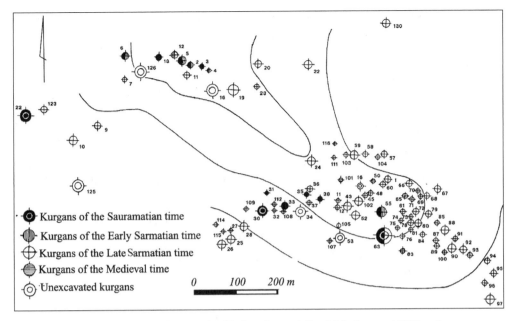

Figure 6.2. Plan of the burial ground of Pokrovka 10 (after Malashev and Yablonsky 2004).

placed on the inner side, outlined the place for the burial mound. Then some ceremonies, the traces of which can be noted by the changed character of paleosoil and the remains of organic materials (grass, brushwood), were performed. After that, a pit grave was dug. The large amount of soil taken from the pit was poured out around it, but some quantity of soil was distributed on the larger ground. A circular moat with a smaller diameter than that of the ditch was constructed from the humus loamy soil. The burial was completed, and part of the soil was returned to the pit. The surface of the inner ground (above the pit) was covered with brushwood and filled with soil. The top level of the construction was covered with topsoil blocks. Finally, this construction was plastered with clay extracted from the ditch. (Zdanovich et al. 1984: 43–4)

The average volume of soil for the kurgan construction removed from the surface of the ground adjacent to the concentric area was about 2,100 m². According to the author's calculations, the labor just for the mound construction required 200–400 individuals for ten days or 70–140 individuals for one month. If we add the necessary work for the funerary chamber (woodcutting, transportation, etc.), digging the ditch, and other operations, it is apparent that the erection of such a big kurgan is very laborious. The Kara Oba kurgan was in the form of a truncated stepped cone, 4 m in height. Mathematical calculations applied to the Varna kurgan in the southern Urals and the results of its experimental reconstruction indicated that the form of this three tiered round construction had a height of 5.7 m and a top diameter of 1.6 m (Tairov &

Botalov 1988: 112–3). These two examples allow us to imagine what a striking impression these constructions would have made (Plate 6.2).

Until recent times, the Kazakhs and Kirgizs buried their people only near winter pastures (Rudenko 1952: 9–10). According to Dyakonova's data, the Tuvinians buried their dead in the areas of traditional transmigration. Therefore, members of a single lineage group could be buried in different cemeteries within a specific clan territory (Dyakonova 1980). If we admit that such a system existed in prehistoric and proto-historic times (which looks quite credible), then we should ask ourselves whether we are able to identify discrete cemeteries with specific clan groups. Archaeologically, we should consider these as separate units within one or another archaeological culture; the problem is to identify them with a specific social group and to move on to the identification of not only the cultural but also the social landscape.

We have indicated some general points relating to the nomadic mode of life; now it is time to look at more concrete subjects.

THE NOMADS OF SOUTHERN URALS

The nomadic world was neither mono-cultural nor mono-ethnic. There are visible differences between its parts (mainly, between eastern and western, but also within both of these geographic areas). Nevertheless, it is united by several common cultural elements, such as general forms of weaponry (swords and arrows), horse harnesses (horse bits), and zoomorphic imagery (cross-legged deer images, stylized animals on utilitarian or cultic objects – Plate 6.3) and funerary practice (barrows of different size and detail but constructed on similar principles). Bronze cauldrons and mirrors are also found everywhere in the Eurasian steppe and forest steppe.

A Short Excursion into the History of Eurasian Nomads

As the nomads began to intrude on the ancient states, they came to the attention of the writers, historians, and geographers of these states (Fig. 6.3). However, very often, the view taken by these authors was quite narrow and unclear. Literary sources, although controversial, inform us about nomadic tribes of the first millennium BC; they are known under various names such as Scythians, Sauromatians, Sarmatians, Saka (Sacians or Sacae), Issedonias, Arimaspians, Massagetians, Dakhi, Wu-sun, Rhoxolani, Siracae, Yazygs, Aorses, Alans, and many others. They relocated from time to time and their motherlands are hard to determine; many of them migrated westward and disappeared there. It is believed that closer connections existed between the Sauromatians and Siracae, Issedonians and Sarmatians, Massagetae-Rhoxolani, and Aorses-Alans. This last group is usually known by the name of "Sarmatians" and were East Iranian–speaking peoples (Machinsky 1971; 1972; Milukova 1989; Shchukin 1994;

Skripkin 1990). Almost all of these tribes are somehow related to the territory of the southern Urals, which lay on the real crossroads between east and west, south and north – in the way of transcontinental movements and migrations. However, because this region was rather far from both western and eastern states, the reports of ancient authors do not reveal much relevant historical information. Researchers have to rely mainly on archaeological material and indirect references to other regions that were closer to ancient civilizations.

The study of nomadic cultures has a long and rich history in Russia, starting at the beginning of the nineteenth century. The analysis of ancient literature, which was brilliantly carried out by Rostovtseff (1922; 1925) and Latyshev (1947a; 1947b; 1947c; 1947d; 1992) in the early twentieth century, still influences Russian Scythian and Sarmatian studies. In search of archaeological equivalents to historically described or just briefly mentioned tribes, scholars have built sophisticated constructs and placed the same tribes in absolutely different and, often, very distant regions. The tradition of giving ethnic names to some archaeological cultures[5] complicates the situation as well. This issue was recently debated

Plate 6.3. Objects in animal style. **Top:** Bone comb from Obruchevka kurgan 2; **Below:** Stone altar from Obruchevka kurgan 2 (late sixth–early fifth centuries BC).

when Yablonsky suggested rejecting the use of historical names for archaeological material of the early nomads and replacing the term "Scythian and Siberian Unity," which is truly illogical but commonly accepted, with the neutral term of "cultural and chronological horizon" (Yablonsky 2000; 2001; Yablonsky & Bashilov 2000). Although sharing Yablonsky's concern, the majority of scholars, have not followed this idea (Medvedev 2002b). Moreover, Yablonsky himself (1996b) does not abandon historical and ethnic terminology.

In this book, we will not dwell on the complicated interpretation of historic written sources; however, we cannot avoid referring to some historically known names traditionally attributed to Eurasian nomads of the Early Iron Age. In Table 6.1, one can see the distribution of some historically known tribes in the area under study. This table reflects the most common interpretations and not some particular theories.

The Scythians, known to the Assyrians under the name of "Ashguzai or Ishkuzai," are the most famous of the Eurasian nomadic peoples. According to Herodotus (IV, 11, 103–105),[6] the beginning of their history is marked by their struggle with the Cimmerians, who inhabited the North Pontic steppe. The Scythians, persecuting the Cimmerians, in the 670s BC came to Asia Minor where, over twenty-eight years, "devastated everything by their violence." In the early sixth century BC, they were ousted by the Medes and returned to the Cis-Caucasus steppe, then moved to the Low Dnepr area. There they created Great Scythia (second Scythian Kingdom), the heyday and decline of which was in the fifth–third centuries BC. Dramatic Macedonian-Scythian relations and the devastating invasion of the Siracaes (Siraks) and Sarmatians caused the downfall of Scythia.

According to the earlier ancient tradition that goes back to Aristeas from Proconessus, in the beginning of their appearance in eastern Europe (the eighth–seventh centuries BC), the Scythians were neighbors of the Issedonians, who might have occupied the south Urals and Trans-Urals steppe. Not far from them, the Ircae (Irks) and "the other Scythians" were placed (Herodotus IV, 21–27). The Sauromatians appeared only in the sixth century BC (Machinsky 1972). Traditionally, after research by Grakov (1947) and Smirnov (1964), the name "Sauromatians" was applied to many nomadic tribes occupying the territory between the Don, Volga, and Ural rivers, to the east of Scythia and behind the Tanais[7] River.

Before the late fifth and early fourth centuries BC, the Sauromatians and Scythians had relatively peaceful relations, but gradually tensions arose between them, and some Sauromatian groups migrated westward to the Scythian lands. The names "Sarmatians" and "Sirmatians," which finally replaced the name "Sauromatians" or became its synonym, first appeared in the fourth century BC, when, as Machinsky (1971) noted, the name Issedonians practically disappeared from the ancient literature. By the third century BC, the Sarmatians crossed the Tanais and then invaded the North Pontic area. Yatsenko (2003) has noted that ancient authors always stressed the greater "barbarity" of the Sarmatians compared with the Scythians but that, in fact, is not true. It is widely accepted that the Sarmatian had a victory over the Scythians, which occurred at the end of the third or beginning of the second century BC. The expansionist politics of Alexander the Great in the Near East is seen as one of the factors that stimulated the rise of the new leading tribes that caused the situation to change (Milukova 1989: 156–7).

From the very beginning, the relations between Sarmatians, who became the most significant political agent in the western part of the nomadic world, Greek

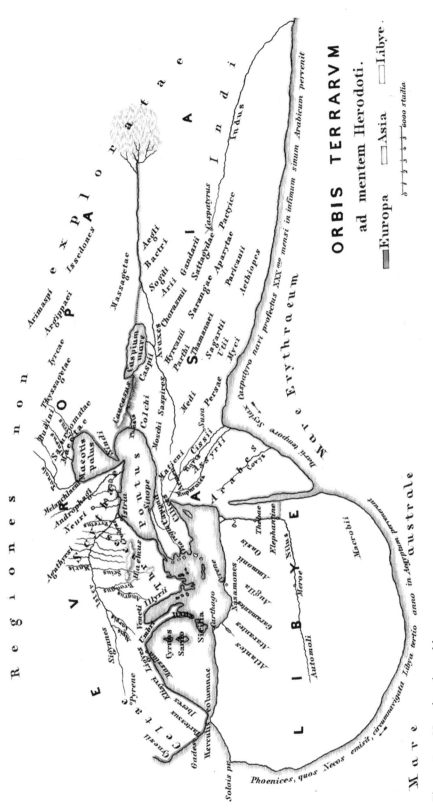

Figure 6.3. Herodotus's world map.

TABLE 6.1. *Schematic disposition of historically known nomadic tribes and major archaeological formations.*

Years, dates	Some historical events	Southern Siberia, Altai, Estern Kazakhstan	Northern and central Kazakhstan	Middle Asia/Aral Sea area	Southern Trans-Urals	Southern Cis-Urals	Low Volga area	Low Don River	Northern Pontic area
800		Sacae (Saka) Arzhan							Cimmerians
770	The end of West Chu				Tasmola-like culture *Issedonians*	Rare archaeological sites *Issedonians ?*	Early Scythians		Scythians
623-594	2nd raid of Scythians to Trans-Caucasus		Sacae	Massagetae *Issedonians ?* Chorasmian state	"Other Scythians" *Sacae*			'Sauromatians' of Herodotus	
600	'Herodotus trade road'					*Issedonians?* Sauromatian culture			Scythians
545	Achaemenid kingdom								
530	Cyrus II against the Massagetae		Tasmola culture		Prokhorovo culture (elite level)	Sauromatian culture	Sauromatians Sauromatian culture	Sauromatians Sauromatian culture	
514-512	Darius campaign		Sacae						Scythians
500		Pazyryk culture				Prokhorovo culture Early Sarmatians			
400	Chorasmia off Persian domination	Yueh-Chih Wu-Suns		*Dahi*	*Dahi?*	Aorces			
330-328	Alexander the Great campaign			Yueh-Chih			Early Sarmatians		
209	Parthian Empire (beginning)	Beginning of Hsiugn-nu state					Prokhorovo culture Sarmatians		
201	Northern raid of shanyu Maodun						Aorces	Sarmatians	
200		Hsiugn-nu		Alans					
160-165	Hsiugn-nu defeated Yueh-Chih			Kang-Ku state Dzhety-asar culture	Middle Sarmatian culture (rare sites)			*Roxolani*	Siraces
100						Middle Sarmatian culture (rare sites)		Alans	Sarmatians
93 AD	Sienbi defeated Hsiugn-nu			Alans		Alans	Middle Sarmatian culture	Alans	Alans
55 AD	Separation of Hsiugn-nu tribes								
155-158	Under the Sienbi pressure Hsiugn-nu moved W and SW				Late Sarmatian culture (rare sites)	Late Sarmatian culture	Sarmatians		

city-states and the Roman Empire, were tense. In the beginning, the Sarmatians were of no concern in Roman politics, but when they began to bother the borders of the empire, the Romans were forced to pay attention to them (Bozi 2002: 8–9). The official map of the Roman Empire, made by Augustus's associate Marcus Agrippa, shows Sarmatia as one of twenty-four districts of the Roman World. In about the first century BC, the geographic and historic manuscripts, in particular, Strabo's *Geography*, contains terms such as "European and Asiatic Sarmatia" (XI, 1–6), separated by the Tanais River. Ptolemy first mapped this division. Strabo's work reflects the situation of the second century BC (Fig. 6.4). The comparison of Starbo's and Pliny's ethnographic maps shows a new westward migration of the Iazygy, Aorces, Rhoxolani, and Siracae tribes (Machinsky 1972), and an increase in the number of Sarmatian sites can be observed west of the Dnepr.

In Asiatic Sarmatia, first the Siracae (Siraks) Aorces and Upper Aorces were dominant and powerful as well as the Roxolani in the west. Schukin (1994) supposes that the westward movement of the Sarmatians resulted in the formation of an independent Sarmatian kingdom between the Dnepr and the Prut Rivers. Another Sarmatian union was centered in the Lower Volga. During the 50–70s BC, the Sarmatians subjugated almost all other tribes to the west of the Urals. However, in the first century CE, written sources emphasize the emergence of the Alans on the historical arena of the Danube and in the Caucasus.

The Greeks did not know much about the eastern nomads, whom they called the Asiatic or Eastern Scythians. It seems this name was merely a synonym for the word "nomad." In this sense, it was later used in the Roman period. The Persians called them the Sacae (Saka), the general name applied to all eastern tribes of the early first millennium BC (eighth–third centuries BC), although among them there were numerous separate groups: Saka-Haomavarga, Saka-Paradarayia, Saka-Tigrakhuada, and so on (Litvinski 1972; Moshkova 1992). Chinese chronicles mention them as the Se, Sai, or Saiki. The Achaemenid rulers had only limited control over the Sacae and from time to time had to send armies to prevent their raids. Conversely, Sacae (Saka) mercenaries sometimes served the Achaemenids.

According to Herodotus (I, 201, 202) the Massagetae, relatives of the Sacae, inhabited a land to the east of the Caspian Sea, or according to Strabo (XI, 6, 7, 8) they settled along the Oxus to the west of Syr-Darya River. Herodotus tells us that the Massagetae were "in front of Issedonians" (Fig. 6.3), who, in this case, should have occupied the south Urals steppe and bordered the Massagetae in northern Kazakhstan. The failure of the last campaign, undertaken by Cyrus II against the Massagetaes in 530 BC, attested to their good military reputation (Moshkova 1992: 15). In 330–328 BC, Alexander the Great conquered Bactria and Sogdiana, but he did not have any success over the nomads. After his death and the long internal conflicts that followed, Middle Asia was included in the Seleucids' state. Yet quite soon, in the mid–third century BC, the eastern provinces such as Greco-Bactria and Parthia became independent (Tolstov 1948: 241–6).

In the late fourth–early third centuries BC, powerful groups of nomads called Dahae (Dahi) came from somewhere in the northeast to the northern Parthian border. Their attacks were the first steps on the way to the great siege of the southern states.

The Dahae and Parnae became known a little later than the Sacae; these two groups seem quite close to each other, as the chronicles mention them together. According to Strabo (IX, 7, 1; 8, 1–3, XI, 511), the Dahae in the third century BC should have had the pastures to the east of the Caspian Sea, next to the Massagetae (Fig. 6.4). It is believed that their leader Archak had founded a new dynasty in Parthia. In a remarkably short period (247–225 BC) the initial core of the future powerful state had been created. Later, the same scenario was repeated in the Kushan state (Moshkova 1992). It seems rather clear that the third century BC was a turning point in the history of Eurasian nomads.

A mixed nomadic population, among which the ancient authors mention such tribes as Asii, Paciani, Tokharians, Sakarauli, relating to Sacae and Massagetae filiations (Strabo XI, VII, 2), gradually was concentrated in south Middle Asia during the third–second centuries BC. This entailed significant relocations in the steppe and was accompanied by the progressing decline of the factious Greco-Bactrian state under the pressure of northern nomads (141–128 BC).

Chinese chronicles provide the basic information about these events mainly because of their connection with the "Northern Barbarians," which constantly bothered the Great State of China and influenced its politics (Fig. 6.5). Among them, the most serious adversaries were the Hsiung-nu, whose power strengthened by the late third century BC when shanyu (chief) Maodun (Mode) came into power. For over twenty-five years (209–174 BC), Maodun managed to conquer many tribes, greatly extend his territory, and transform his tribal union into a powerful political agent acting mainly against China and Yueh-Chih who were hereditary enemies of the Hsiung-nu. Their rivalry had far-reaching effects, which displaced the "Mongolian generator of peoples."

The Yueh-Chih originally lived to the west of the Hsiung-nu somewhere in the mountain province of Gansu (Guangsi). Together with the Wu-sun, they were destined to feel the full weight of the Hunnish inroads (McGovern 1939: 125–9). Initially, the Wu-sun inhabited the territory next to Yueh-Chih and even shared the same pastures; in 176 BC, they reputed their dependence on the Hsiung-nu. In 160–165 BC, the Hsiung-nu after several attempts finally defeated the Yueh-Chih. Their survivors left by the difficult paths of the Tien-Shan Mountains. Moving southwest, the Yueh-Chih came into collision with the Sacae and ousted them from their lands in Zungaria. Later, the Wu-sun,

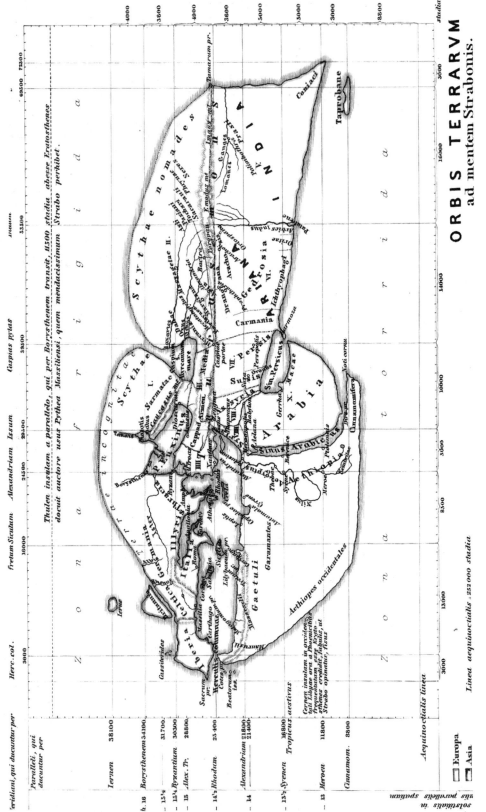

Figure 6.4. Strabo's map.

227

pushed by the Hsiung-nu, conquered the Yueh-Chih, who had gone toward Sogdiana and Bactria.[8] They settled down to the north of Amu-Darya and divided their own lands between five local chiefs. This information goes back to Jang-Kian, first of the Chinese "ambassadors," who in 138 BC had been sent by the Emperor Wu-Di to the west with the purpose of winning over Yueh-Chih to the Chinese side against the Hsiung-nu. He returned to China only in 128 BC (Bichurin 1953a, 1953b; Gumilev 1993a; McGovern 1939).

Because the Chinese chronicles and ancient manuscripts contain rather mixed descriptions, the ethnography, geography, and historical chronology of all these events are vague. One fact, however, is clear: in the second century BC, the situation in Central Asia was far from stable, full of dramatic and even catastrophic actions, entailing great relocations of various nomadic tribes. The Chinese Empire and the Hsiung-nu struggled for supremacy. The eastern Hellenistic Empire had been ruined under attacks of barbarians who deliberately or not became the founders of two great empires of Late Antiquity: the Parthia and Kushan Kingdoms.

Furthermore, Chinese chronicles mention other nomadic states. One of them, the Kang-Ku/Kangha, situated to the north of Chorasmia and in the northwest bordered the Yantsai (Yan-T'sai) chiefdom. Ancient historians noted that the populations of these states were similar to Yueh-Chih. In the first century BC, the Kang-Ku were subject to the Hsiung-nu (Bichurin 1953b; Kuner 1961; Zuyev 1995). After this, the Kang-Ku turned its interests to the north – to the Alanya. The ethnic name Alans first appeared in European manuscripts in the mid-first century CE, together with other tribes of eastern origin. According to Ammianus Marcellinius, the Alans are the same as the Massagetae (Am. Marcel. History. XXXI, 2, 12).

The Kang-Ku state was especially powerful from the first to third centuries CE and controlled a large territory, including the Alanya-state, which inherited the Yantsai. Interestingly enough, according to the chronicles, Kang-Ku and Yantsai (Yan-T'sai) were linked by trade routes going from China, Karashahr, and Fergana (Da-yuan) to the north toward the Urals and the Volga (Bichurin 1953a, 1953b, 1953c; McGovern 1939). Among many hypotheses placing the Kang-Ku in different areas, that of Vainberg seems most credible. She places the lands of this state from the southern Urals, Ural River, and northwest Caspian shore to the northern edges of the Kysyl Kum desert (Vainberg 1999). On all Chinese maps of the "Western Regions," the Kang-Ku state is inalterably placed in the northwest corner (Bichurin 1953c) (Fig. 6.5).

Historically important are the events of the later phase of Hsiung-nu history. In the first century BC, their empire fell on misfortune and disintegration. In the mid-first century CE, under attacks by the Chinese army, they were divided into two groups (two kingdoms): southern and northern. The former remained under the subordination of China; the latter after being defeated by the Sienbi in 93 AD, was divided into four branches: the first went to Semirechye (Middle

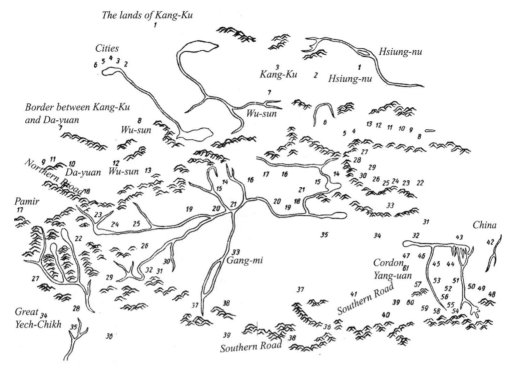

Figure 6.5. Chinese map of "Western Areas" of the Old Han Dynasty. Figures correspond to historical names of states and peoples. N. Kuner translated them from the Chinese language (after Bichurin 1953c).

Asia), the second was assimilated by the Sienbi, the third went to China, and the last branch moved westward (Gumilev 1993a). In 155–158 AD, the raids of the Sienbi headed by their leader Tanshihuai against the Hsiung-nu forced them to leave their home and moved out to the southwest and west (Bichurin 1953a). Information about their further fortune is not clear. There is some mention of their coming to the near–Caspian steppe in about 160 AD and 175–182 AD (Gumilev 1986). Some time later, in the later fourth century CE, the Hsiung-nu tribes invaded Europe, where they became known as the Huns. After having defeated the Alans in 375 AD, they inspired the main stage of the Great Folk Movement in Eurasia.

All conflicts, fights, and tribal relocations occurring in Central Asia recoiled upon other regions, particularly, Europe, where alternate nomadic waves spilled out. In the conflicts with Alexander the Great and his descendents, the nomads (Sacae and Massagetae) created new military tactics and elaborated weaponry, that entailed the birth of a heavy armored cavalry – the cataphracts (Shchukin 1994; Sulimirski 1970; Tolstov 1948). In 53 BC, the Romans first met defeat from the Parthian cataphracts.

Although this review has been quite short and included only those people that directly or indirectly related to the area under question, there is no doubt that Asiatic nomads played a major role in all the political events of the first millennium BC. From time to time, these nomads crossed the Urals, leaving their mark on this territory. They were also active in western Siberia because its forest-steppe landscape was attractive in periods of environmental instability in the steppe. In the following pages, common features shared by most of the nomadic societies will be reviewed and variations, which were more characteristic for the area under study, will be highlighted.

Nomadic Cultures of the Urals

The history of Eurasian nomadic culture is divided into two basic periods, which are determined by the culture of the leading group of tribes. The first period, the Scythian period, is conventionally dated within the interval between the seventh and third centuries BC; the second, the Sarmatian (or Hun-Sarmatian) period, covers the time from the second century BC to the fourth century CE. An earlier period (the ninth–eighth centuries BC) is sometimes called the Cimmerian, pre-Scythian, or Initial Scythian. This last period relates to the origin of the Scythians and their culture, as well as other cultures of the nomadic world.[9]

If we look at the archaeological map of the Eurasian steppe at the beginning at the first millennium BC, we do not see many sites. This is the reason that the origin of Scythian and Saka cultures remains a controversial issue. We do not know their earliest settlements, only kurgans indicate the new epoch. Initially, when the only known sites were of Great Scythia, scholars supposed the western origin of the Scythian culture. However, in the early twentieth century, researchers came to look for its roots in the east – that is, in Siberia (Rostovtseff 1922). The discoveries of the outstanding burial mounds in the Altai, Tuva Khakassia, and a series of C-14 dates gave strength to this theory. The finds from the Arzhan barrow provided evidence that in the east the elements of a developed animal style and elaborate elite burial ritual was already characteristic in the ninth–eighth century BC (Sementsov et al. 1997; Zaitseva et al. 1997b). Moreover, some scholars consider the Sayan and Altai area as the Riphei Mountains – the sacral center of Scythian mythology. This, in our point of view, seems a bit of an exaggeration.

In 1983, Gryaznov put forward the theory that this period, which he called the Arzhan-Chernogorovo stage, corresponded to the process of the formation of the Sacae and Scythian cultures. Despite local variations, some common attributes of material culture characterize the spread of some similar ideological, social and economic patterns in the ninth–eighth centuries BC marked, first of all, by the birth of a new semantic and artistic system – the animal style (Gryaznov 1983; Rayevsky 1985). It means the initial forming of the cultural complex of the early nomads occurred in Central Asia in late tenth–early ninth century BC, and it passed, in Bokovenko's expression (1996), in a hidden form.

What is especially significant is that a new form of funeral ritual reflecting a new concept of the afterlife took shape in the burials of mounted warriors stressing their distinctive social status.

The latest discoveries and research testify to the eastern origin of the initial components of the animal style, which spread westward, enriching and absorbing the novel influences issuing from diverse sources. This is also evidenced by the analysis of stag steles, which first appeared in the south of eastern Europe in the late ninth century BC and had earlier stages in Central Asia and southern Siberia (Mongolia, Tuva, Altai, Xinjang), where there are numerous representations (Bokovenko 2004; Kovalev 2000). This process left its mark in the southern Urals as well. In particular, the Big Gumarovo kurgan contained a burial with a stag stone, which preserved the engraved depictions of weapons (a sword with a straight guard and mushroom-shaped top and Scythian type bow) and a rather specific set of early type of bronze arrowheads (Fig. 6.6) (Ismagilov 1988). Similar finds, as well as specific forms of horse harnesses, swords, daggers, disk shaped mirrors with loops, and archaic arrowheads indicate the westward movement of the so-called proto-Scythians (Murzin 1990) or "Early Scythians of Aristeas and Diodorus" (Alexeyev 2003).

In the course of nomadic studies, researchers have noticed the specificity of the southern Urals, caused by the contact character of this area going back to the Bronze Age. Currently, scholars try to understand the nature of the local culture, which is documented by thousands of sites spread over the Uralian steppe (Fig. 6.7). This steppe area is geographically divided into western (Cis-Urals) and eastern (Trans-Urals) parts, which, as we will see, differed culturally.

Unfortunately, there is no common chronology or interpretation of nomadic material culture. There are, however, some synthesizing works devoted mostly to detailed typology and chronology of basic kinds of artifacts, especially weapons (Khazanov 1971; Smirnov 1961). In 1947, Grakov suggested a periodization, which is still widely used. He divided all materials from the Volga and the Urals into four groups, corresponding to four historical periods that are regarded as separate cultures by some researchers. Grakov's four groups are: (1) Sauromatian, the Blumenfeld culture (sixth to fourth centuries BC), (2) Early Sarmatian, the Prokhorovo culture (fourth to second centuries BC), (3) Middle Sarmatian, the Suslovo culture (second century BC to second century CE), and (4) Late Sarmatian, the Shipovo or Alanian culture (second to fourth centuries CE). All stages were included in one Sarmatian culture. In recent years, however, this has been partly revised. The Shipovo barrows were subsequently attributed to a later period. The chronology of the Prokhorovo (or Early Sarmatian) culture (or phase) was particularly debated, substantially precised for particular locals and broadened to include the fifth and first centuries BC (Skripkin 1990; Tairov 1991). This chronological interval includes the time of its formation in the southern Urals, spreading over the Volga and its latest development in the Northern Pontic area. Consequently, the Middle

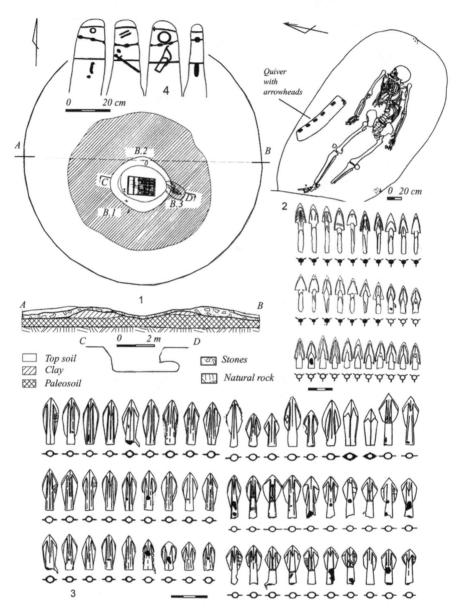

Figure 6.6. Big Gumarovo kurgan: (1) view in plan; (2) burial; (3) set of bronze arrowheads; (4) stag stone (after Ismagilov 1988).

Sarmatian culture was ascribed to the period between the first century BC and first half of the second century CE (Moshkova 2002: 7). We will not delve into the quite complicated and sophisticated Sarmatian chronology, which is based totally on typological seriation of rich artifact collections, cross-cultural analysis, and historical information.

The question of whether or not the Sarmatians and Sauromatians are kindred tribes is unclear. The point is that this time frame, which, in fact, correctly

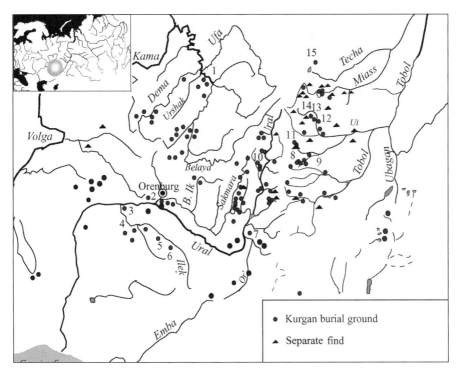

Figure 6.7. Sites of the Early Nomads in the steppe zone of the Southern Urals: (1) Bishungarovo; (2) Chernaya, Kardayilovo; (3) Filippovka; (4) Pokrovka; (5) Pyatimary; (6) Mechet-Sai; (7) Novyi Kumak; (8) Varna; (9) Kesene; (10) Almukhametovo; (11) Temir; (12) Bobrovka; (13) Berezovka; (14) Putilovskaya Zaimka; (15) Irtyash.

detects chronological changes in material culture of European nomads, developed from a theory of cultural evolution and direct reflection of folk history in an archaeological culture. Not all of this is that simple. As we can see from this historical review, nomads were always in the process of movement and fusion. Therefore, it is very hard to determine the limits of their area of inhabitance in terms of archaeological culture in both geographic and chronological terms. That is why the relationships between these two groups of tribes and, correspondingly, between two chronologically different cultures (Sauramatian and Sarmatian) is one of the most disputed issues, along with the vexed question of the many variants of the Sarmatian culture. However, we definitely can understand the meaning of fluid changes in nomadic culture coming out of the prescribed territorial limits of archaeological cultures, using them only as markers of developmental trajectory.

Pre-Sarmatian and Initial Sarmatian Cultural Development

Sites of the transitional period (tenth–eighth century BC) are rare in the southern Urals. Those that do exist are on the northwest periphery of the

Plate 6.4. Burial of the seventh–sixth centuries BC from the Irtyash burial ground.

Ural-Kazakhstan steppes and in the territory between Urals and Volga (Korenyako 1982; Morozov 1995).

The earliest sites of nomads have been discovered to the east of the Urals. Archaeologically, the early nomads, who occupied this area in the seventh to sixth centuries BC, are represented by standard kurgans and some occasional finds. All these remains relate to the Bobrovka stage of the early nomadic culture belonging to the Tasmola cultural tradition emblematic for central and northern Kazakhstan (Tairov 2000). The mounds were constructed from earth or stone or a combination of the two. Sometimes the Bronze Age kurgans were reused. The burials were placed into rectangular or oval pit-graves, some of which were furnished with special niches (podboi) constructed on the longitudinal wall. The deceased were supine, in extended position with their heads oriented to the northwest (Plate 6.4). Signs of organic bedding or a sprinkling

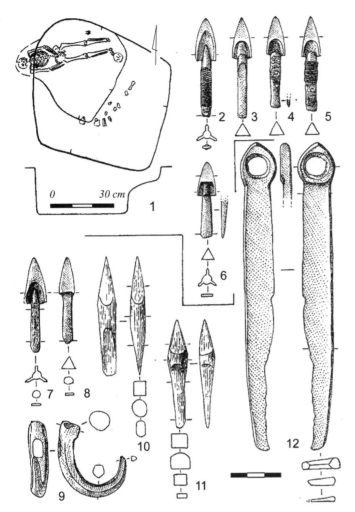

Figure 6.8. Materials of the sixth–second centuries BC from the Southern Urals: (1–6) Kecene cemetery, kurgan 12, grave-pit 1, burial 2; (7–12) Putilovskaya Zaimka cemetery, grave goods (2–9, 12 – bronze; 10–11 – bone) (after Tairov 2000, fig. 34).

of ash were found under the deceased, who were accompanied by traces of meat or a sheep's hind leg and grave goods, including daggers, socketed and tanged, bilobate or trilobate arrowheads, composite belts, mirrors, stone altars, knives of a Central Kazakhstan type, and amulets (Fig. 6.8). The burials differ in number, character, and quality of the grave goods. Male graves contained predominantly weapons, whereas female graves contained chiefly decorations and cult objects. Graves are also distinguished in terms of wealth.

A spectral analysis of bronze artifacts demonstrates a predominance of metal which was in use in the Saka tribal territory. Thus, the early sites of the southern Trans-Uralian nomads definitely belong to the Saka historical and cultural province (Yablonsky et al. 1996), with some specific features conditioned by the environment, transmigration system, and climatic situation. Nomads of the southern Trans-Urals had winter camps near the Aral Sea, where they had contact with other nomads of Middle Asia and southern Kazakhstan, but their summer pastures were situated in the southern Urals, near the forest-steppe of western Siberia. They were closely connected with the Tasmola culture of central Kazakhstan.[10] By contrast, some Scythian (western) elements are also available in this area, as represented in the Big Klimovski kurgan (Gutsalov 1998). These are interpreted as evidence of stable links with European Scythians and the functioning of the so-called Herodotus Trade Route, which is believed to have started in the late sixth century BC (Grakov 1947; Smirnov 1964; Tairov 2000). As we know, the "Other Scythians" occupied some areas around the Ural Mountains. Moreover, the local mineral resources, particularly, gold and copper, could possibly have attracted the western nomads (Tairov 2000). Bartseva (1981) states that from 28 to 36 percent of the metal objects from the Scythian graves of the sixth–fourth centuries BC of the Dnepr's left bank were manufactured from metal of Uralian origin. These needs could have stimulated the formation of the new metallurgical centers in the Urals, one of which (Ananyino) from the very beginning was oriented to the west but gradually turned out to be under the control of local nomadic clans.

In the period from the late sixth to fifth century BC, some changes occurred among the Trans-Uralian nomads, although the basic characteristics of their mortuary practice remained stable. Such details as sporadic cremations, burned wooden roofs, wooden constructions on paleosoil, pit-graves with steps, and corridors (*dromos*) point to the Aral Sea area as the source of their emergence. Additionally, the new types of goods (beaked pots, flat-bottomed pear-shaped pots with small handles, bronze mirrors with flat disk, stone altars with legs) testify to the absorption of new ethnic groups from the south, which were succeeded by ethnic and social consolidation. Tairov (2000) believes that the drift of the southern nomads to the Urals was stimulated by expansionist politics of the Achaemenid rulers in Middle Asia in the sixth century BC. In particular, the famous campaign of Cyrus II against the Massagetae (530 BC), ended in their victory. Next, the Darius raid on the Sacae in 519 BC, which was more successful for the Persians, could not pass without a trace for southern nomads. As it is known, any destabilization in the traditional pasture system entails regrouping in the nomadic environment. Some of these newcomers moved further northwestward – to the Cis-Urals steppe, which was sparsely populated at that time. By Zhelezchkov's (1988) estimation, this process could have lasted about 100–150 years. At the same time, some nomadic groups approached the western Siberian forest-steppe. Archaeological material demonstrates the rising role of the military factor; the presence and number of warrior graves, and the amount and assortment of weapons consisting of eastern and western types dramatically increased (Fig. 6.9).

Thus, in the very late sixth century BC, two large nomadic polities origi-nated in the southern Urals: in the west, chiefly centered on the Ilek River

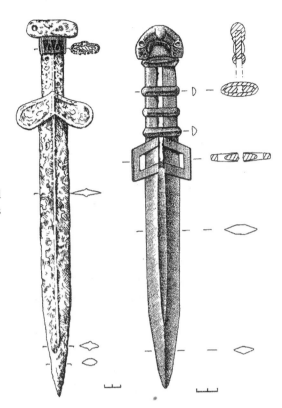

Figure 6.9. Daggers of the sixth–second centuries BC from the southern Trans-Urals (after Tairov 2000).

and, in the east, centered on the southern Trans-Urals. Apparently, they were incorporated into a powerful, hierarchically organized tribal union with the center in the eastern Orenburg area (Tairov 2000). After the late sixth century BC, the influence of nomadic cultures on their northern neighbors constantly increased. The closest forest population, in particular the Itkul culture, experienced intense pressure from the nomads. In the frontier territory along the Sinara River, there is a chain of small fortresses that have yielded insubstantial archaeological deposits but that undoubtedly served as border points. This is also indirectly evidenced by the chemical composition of bronze arrowheads, found in abundance in the burials of the Trans-Uralian nomads. In the fifth century BC, the majority of arrowheads were produced in local Itkul workshops, whereas in the preceding period, as we have seen, graves contained metal objects made of Central Kazakhstan ores.

In the second half of the sixth century BC, ecological conditions of the southern Urals steppe favored nomadic pastoralism. This time was still relatively humid[11]; some years, however, were dry. Paleobotanists reconstruct multigrass steppes, alternating with some forests (Tairov 2003: 35; Khokhlova & Kuznetsov 2003: 70).

A process of transformation in the society of the Uralian nomads, which was provoked by the above mentioned external factors (regrouping of population) and promoted by climatic improvement resulted in their involvement in western (Sauromatian) politics, rather than in the eastern network although traditional connections with their Saka relatives were maintained. This process is reflected in the material culture, which gained a Sauromatian appearance, characteristic of the vast Volga–Ural steppe. By no means do we identify this culture with the historical Sauromatians, who had occupied the lower Don River steppe since the late sixth century BC (Ochir-Goryaeva 2000). The Uralian nomads with a "Sauramatian culture" were obviously of a different ethnic attribution or, more probable, a mixed ethnic composition, if we take the process of adaptation of this territory into account. It is possible that the Issedonians played the leading role in this tribal group. Therefore, the mortuary practice showed great variety that was reflected in many details either of the eastern or western styles. This is also evidenced by the mixed character of metal used for the production of bronze arrowheads and horse harness decorations (Kuznetsova & Kurmankulov 1993). In addition, the elements of Scythian culture are detected in some barrows.

The majority of kurgans contained primary burials, which were predominantly single, being placed into pit-graves with a variety of wooden constructions (Fig. 6.10). However, some burials had a multilayered character serving for the deposition of several persons, most probably relatives, as was recorded in the Tri Mara burial ground (Smirnov 1975). The dead were usually in supine extended position with the head orientation to the west; about 7 percent of the buried lay in a diagonal position (Zhelezchikov 1980). Some funeral sites have a huge distinctive superstructure for the elite. Such large kurgans of between seven and ten meters in height are mainly concentrated in the valleys of the Or' and Ilek rivers (Orenburg district) (Smirnov 1975). Some of them (e.g., Filippovka) produced extremely rich gold objects manufactured in the Saka animal style (Fig. 6.11) and valuable foreign goods (Aruz et al. 2000; Pshenichnuk 1989). These kurgans were funeral monuments of military chiefs but sometimes women were interred in them (Smirnov 1975). Various kinds of weapons, including newly made ones, horse harness items, bronze cauldrons, mainly flat-bottomed clay vessels, ornaments, mirrors with handles, and cult objects, typical for this period, were abundant in these burials. Some scholars explain the presence of rich foreign objects in Sauromatian burials as evidence of stable trade connections with the southern states, but other scholars associate these objects with pay for military service or contributions that some clans could have suggested to Achaemenid kingdom. At the same time, these valuables might have been diplomatic gifts. Whatever the purpose of these objects, their frequency, concentration in separate distinctive burials, together with the complexity of the funeral monuments and abundance of military attributes, do not leave any doubt in the existence of a rather strong social power, which, and this is noteworthy, wanted to emphasize its significance. The Filippovka kurgan fits well into the category of royal or "tsarski" mortuary sites, relating to the very end of that period.

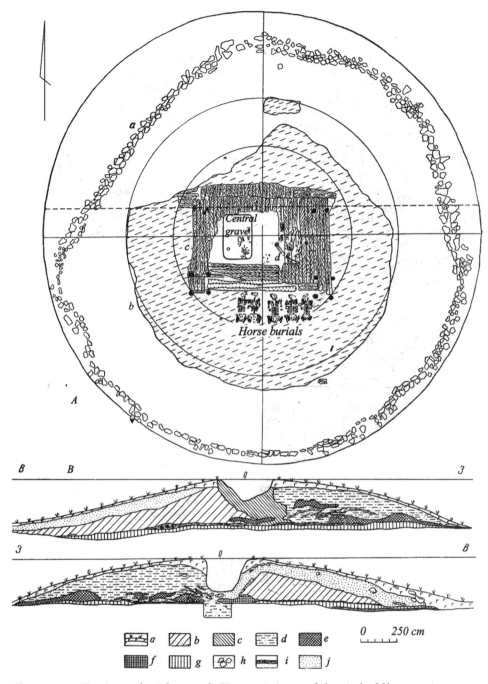

Figure 6.10. Pyatimary burial ground. Kurgan 8 (turn of the sixth–fifth centuries BC): **A** – view in plan: (a) stone circle on paleosoil; (b) layer of wood and plant remains on paleosoil and above the wooden construction and horse burials; (c) wooden construction; (d) burial of guards; **B** – kurgan profiles: (a) top soil; (b) brown-gray sand clay; (c) light brown–gray sand clay; (d) sand clay with gravels; (e) dark-gray sand-clay; (f) sand with small gravel; (g) buried soil; (h) stones; (i) wood; (j) yellow sand (after Smirnov 1964).

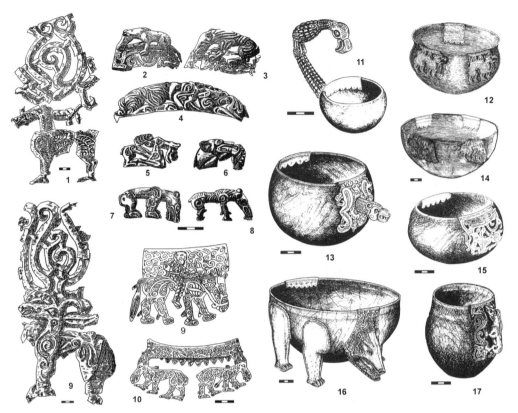

Figure 6.11. Materials from the Filippovka kurgan 1. 1, (2) coverings for wooden stag (treasure (1); 3, (4) feline-shaped plaques (treasure (1); (4) vessel's handle (treasure (1); (5) stag-shaped handle from wooden vessel (treasure (1); (6) handle plaque in form of standing feline predator; (7, 8) handles in form of wolf-like predator; (9, 10) plaques for vessel (treasure 1); (11–17) reconstructed wooden ware (after Pshenichnuk 1989, 2000).

The Early Sarmatian Development (Prokhorovo Culture)

A great deal of research has shown that the major elements of material attributes of the early Sarmatian appearance originated in the southern trans-Urals, where the Prokhorovo (Early Sarmatian) archaeological culture formed during the fifth century BC. New cultural components, particularly round-based pots with talc temper, were introduced by the trans-Uralian forest-steppe population, which had maintained relationships with the nomads for a long time (Moshkova 1974; Tairov 2000). Conversely, some new leading tribal groups had appeared, supposedly the Dahae and Aorsies, which could have brought some elements of their culture and introduced them into the aboriginal milieu (Smirnov 1964).

The early Prokhorovo kurgans were made of either earth or earth and stone. Stones were used as either a mound covering (cairn) or for forming the circles around it. Wooden timber frames or "tents," as well as clay platforms, were frequently discovered under the mounds (Fig. 6.12). Compared with the previous period, secondary burials are much more frequently represented in these

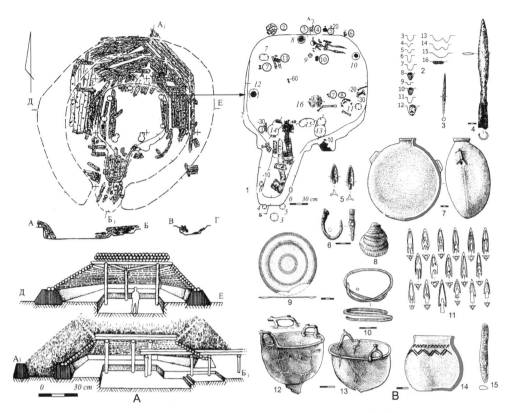

Figure 6.12. Temir kurgan. **A** – Remains of wooden construction and artistic reconstruction of burial chamber. **B** – Plan of burial chamber and grave goods: (1) view in plan; (2) sections of post holes; (3) iron needle; (4) iron spearhead; (5, 11) bronze arrowheads; (6) iron quiver hook; (7) wheel-made flask; (8) shell; (9) bronze mirror; (10) bronze bracelet; (12, 13) bronze cauldrons; (14) clay pot; (15) iron knife (after Tairov 2000).

barrows and were placed concentrically around the central grave (Fig. 6.13). Interesting interpretations have lately been suggested for the circular layout. The greatest percentage of such barrows is found in the Urals, where the climate is colder than in the much warmer western areas of the Volga and Don. If we assume that in cold conditions the nomads buried those who died in wintertime in the spring or early summer, as was detected in the Altai, then we will have to admit that most of the graves situated concentrically were "postponed" burials. Soil and paleobotany analyses have confirmed that the majority of the Early Sarmatian burials of the Urals were arranged in warm periods (Demkin & Demkina 1998). In addition, central and peripheral graves are in the majority synchronic (Zhelezchikov 1980) and thus makes this situation possible. Admitting this, we have to conclude that most of the winter pastures during that period were in the Urals and transmigrations were not very long.

Funeral chambers took various forms: simple, with steps, niches, catacombs, and corridors. They often were furnished with wooden structures, such as wooden frames, a funeral stretcher or coffin, and a wooden or stone roof.

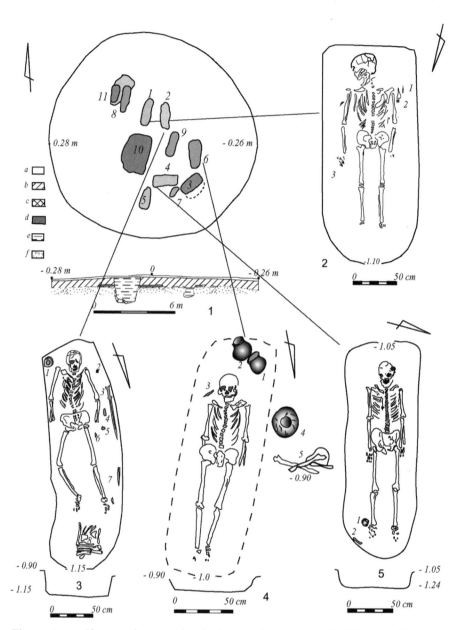

Figure 6.13. Chernaya kurgan (the third–second centuries BC): (1) plan of kurgan; (2) burial 1 (1 – knife; 2 – animal bone; 3 – iron arrowheads); (3) burial 2 (1 – stone mace; 2 – glass bead; 3 – iron sword; 4 – whetstone; 5, 6 – iron buckles; 7 – iron spearhead; 8 – horse bones); (4) burial 6 (1, 2, 4 – pots; 3 – animal bones); (5) burial 4 (1 – spindle; 2 – animal bone).

Sprinkled powdered ochre or chalk, ash, and charcoal pieces occur frequently. The dead were in a supine, extended position, situated along the longitudinal wall; however, diagonal positions were occasionally found. In the fourth to third centuries BC, a southern orientation of the deceased replaced the

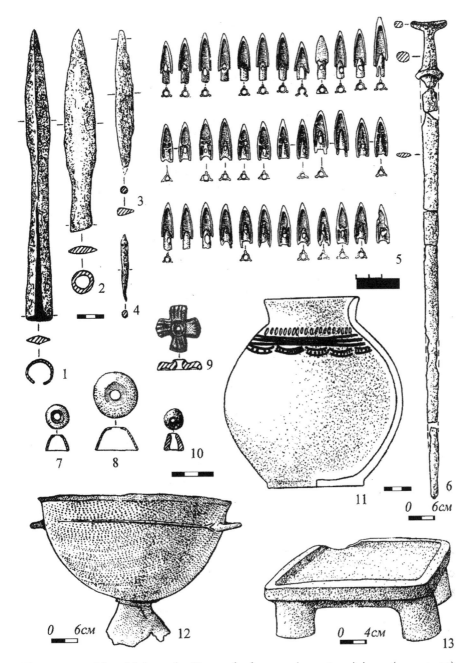

Figure 6.14. Material from the Berezovka kurgan: (1–4, 6, 10) iron, (5, 7, 9, 12) bronze, (8) silver, (11) clay, (13) stone (after Tairov 2000).

western orientation. Evidence of mortuary food offerings includes sheep or horse shoulder blades with the foreleg attached. Compared with the preceding period, the cremation rite had practically died out. During the Prokhorovo phase, new kinds of weaponry appeared. Among them were heavy weapons, including the long sword and dagger, quivers with arrows, spears (Fig. 6.14), helmets, cuirasses, and body armour. Iron, trilobate, tanged arrowheads came into common use (Milukova 1989). This evidence speaks to the change of military tactics toward the use of heavy cavalry and outfighting weapons.

The number of sites of the fourth–third centuries BC in the Urals significantly exceeds those of other periods. For example, according to Zhelzichkov's (1980) work, in the Cis-Urals, 22.1 percent of sites were from the Sauromatian period, 56.5 percent represented the Early Sarmatian period, and 9.2 percent were from the Middle Sarmatian period; and the rest fall into other periods. Some particular areas are characterized in even greater proportion, as was recorded on the left side of the Ilek River, where 80 percent of the 150 burials from 40 barrows were Prokhorovo graves (Demkin & Ryskov 1996; Yablonsky 1996a). Such a large concentration of nomadic population in the South Urals, mainly in the fourth–third centuries BC, is partly explained by ecological factors. Demkin and Ryskov (1996: 51) write that in a large portion of central and southern Kazakhstan, as well as in other regions of Central Asia in the mid-first millennium BC, the desert and semidesert landscapes were predominant, whereas in the southern Urals environmental conditions were more favorable. Therefore, this region served as some sort of "cumulating corridor" or "melting pot" through which various groups of nomads were traveling and spread out in various directions. The original center of the Sarmatian tribal confederation that later moved into the Lower Volga-Don area was here.

During the fourth and third centuries BC, the Prokhorovo cultural complex spread, mainly westward from the Urals. In the fourth century BC, the Uralian nomads migrated, first to the southwest, then, at the turn of the fourth and third centuries BC, they moved to the forest-steppe of the Uralian foothills and further into the Volga basin.

Paleoanthropological data indirectly support this idea. Balabanova (2000: 95–6) states that the anthropological type of population of the early Scythian time differs from that of the preceding period toward the weakening of the Europoid complex. Most of all, this population group was the first wave of migrants from the east to the Volga, who brought a different morphological complex. The latter became widespread in the Sarmatian epoch, when between the Urals and Don area, the brachycranial people with a slight horizontal profile of the face and well-pronounced nasal bones settled.

This broke up former peaceful relations with the Scythians, who could no longer resist such a massive shift. The Uralian nomads also partly migrated to the east (northern Kazakhstan and western Siberia) and to the southeast Aral Sea area. After this, they might have taken part in the frontal nomadic attack on the Greco-Bactrian Kingdom (Mandelshtam 1978). These migrations were caused by various factors, among which have been suggested the overpopulation of the southern Urals, the worsening of climatic conditions, the rise of military activity, incorporation of new ethnic groups, and a change in the general political situation in Middle Asia, near the winter camps of the Trans-Uralian nomads (Tairov 2000). Archaeologically, the rise of Sarmatian influence is reflected in the "sarmatization" of many Eurasian regions, in which only local pottery evidenced the aboriginal presence.

The Middle and Late Sarmatian Developments

Zhelezchikov (1984) attempted on the basis of two thousand excavated burials and the ecological potential of this territory to assess the probable number of nomads that could have inhabited the Pre-Ural and Trans-Volga steppe in the period between the sixth century BC to the first century CE. According to his estimation, about ten thousand people could (on average every year), have lived here in the period from the sixth to fourth century BC, about twenty thousand in the third–second centuries BC, but only about five to seven thousand in the period from the first century BC–first century CE. However, this model did not take into account the wild animals, seasonal use of pastures, and unequal amount of forage eaten by different animals (Khaldeyev 1987). Yet, in general, archaeological data confirm some of its points.

Only about one hundred mortuary sites dating from the second century BC to the first century CE are known in the territory of the southern Trans-Urals and northern Kazakhstan; most of these are related to the beginning of this interval and only single complexes at its end (Botalov 2000). Slightly more than one hundred complexes are recorded in the Cis-Urals area, almost all of them are concentrated on the right bank of the Ural River and in Bashkiria (Fig. 6.15) (Pshenichnuk 1983; Zhelezchikov 1980).

Barrows became simpler and smaller and without any sophisticated constructions. Even stone, a typically Uralian material, was not in great use. Kurgans contained mainly primary graves in narrow elongated pits furnished by parallel stairs or longitudinal niches (podboi) with skeletons oriented to the south (Sergatskov 2002, 94). There is a large number of quadratic pit-graves with the dead placed diagonally (47 percent in the Cis-Urals). All graves had some arrangements such as organic beddings, wooden roofs, or "doors." The complex of grave goods although relatively poor, mainly include iron arrowheads, composite bows, long swords (without pommels), flat-bottomed pots, jars, and knives (Skripkin 1990; 2000). Amongst the funeral "food," sheep legs were absolutely dominant.

The southern Urals in the Middle Sarmatian time looks almost depopulated, especially in the area between the Ilek and Or' rivers, compared with the Lower Volga region, (Pshenichnuk 1983; Skripkin 1990; Zhelezchikov 1983). In the former region, there are also no big kurgans (Sergatskov 2002: 93). It is clear that this region became a periphery of the powerful tribal confederation, Asiatic Sarmatia, which centered in the Lower Volga area. Such a situation is explained by a dramatic climatic deterioration in the area under question (Demkin 1997;

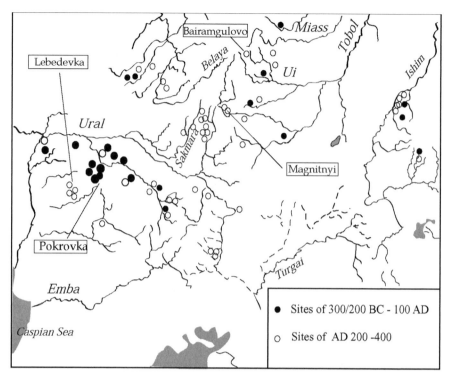

Figure 6.15. Distribution of sites of Late Sarmatian appearance (after Botalov 2000).

Tairov 2003). The Uralian steppe "comes to life" again in the Late Sarmatian period in the second–fourth centuries CE.

In the Late Sarmatian cultural complex, the "podboi"-type graves became more numerous, compared with the preceding period; innovations such as skull deformation and a north-oriented burial rite appeared. The majority of burials produced rather poor material, which includes handmade and wheel thrown pottery, long swords with nephrite or sardonic attachments, mirror-pendants, and rather numerous fibulae that are, however, not known beyond the Urals (Figs. 6.16 and 6.17). Meanwhile, some rich necropolises (e.g., Lebedyevka) relating to the second-third centuries CE have been discovered in the southern Urals. They yielded mainly single burials, containing one or two individuals, accompanied by abundant grave goods, including heavy weapons (long swords), and objects imported from both the east and west: amphorae, fibulae, mirrors (Fig. 6.18), and Roman glass (Moshkova 1982; 1994).

Alongside these typical features, the culture of the southern Urals and northern Kazakhstan of this period show very clear and specific differences with the western variants. The cemeteries are organized in the form of long chains of kurgans lying north to south and are made up of two to five or as many as one hundred kurgans. Together with standard funeral constructions, there are some earthen subrectangular tombs, elongated or "barbell-shaped" kurgans

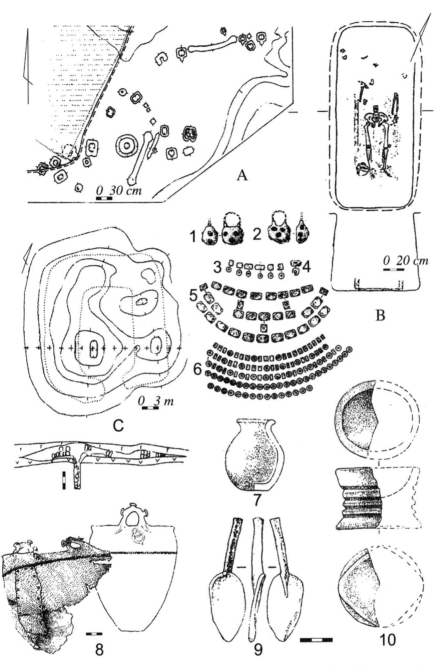

Figure 6.16. Late Sarmatian burial ground of Magnitnyi: **A** – plan of cemetery; **B** – burial 1, kurgan 3; **C** – kurgan 3 in plan; (1, 2) golden beads; (3, 4) golden-glass beads; (5, 6) carnelian and agate beads; (7) clay pot; (8) bronze cauldron; (9) wooden spoon (after Botalov 2000).

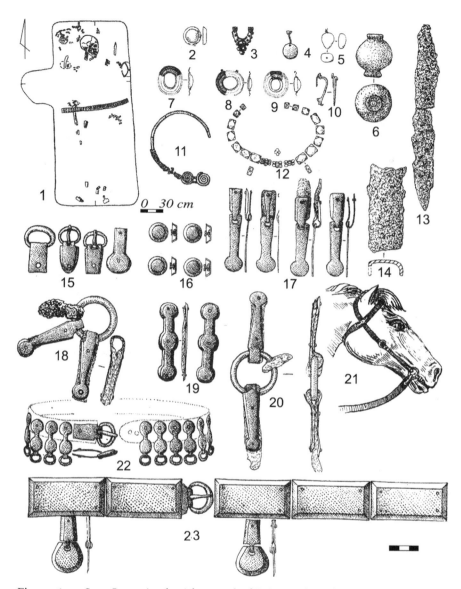

Figure 6.17. Late Sarmatian burial ground of Bairamgulovo, kurgan 2, burial 2: (1) burial 2 in plan; (2, 5, 12) glass beads; (3, 4) golden decorations; (6) clay spindle whorl; (7–9) silver plaques; (10) bronze fibula; (11) silver torque; (13) iron knife; (14) iron object; (15) bronze buckles; (16) bronze belt details; (17–20) bronze plaques of horse harness; (21) artistic reconstruction of harness; (22–23) belts (after Botalov 2000).

(two kurgans linked by an earthen bank). The number of narrow rectangular graves is more than in the Volga region. Chinese mirrors are more abundant as well. In addition to these items, the composite bow and cauldrons of a hunnish type, heavy iron-tanged arrowheads, and new types of horse trappings of an eastern style came into wide use (Bokovenko & Zasetskaya 1994; Botalov 2000). A majority of scholars believe that all these changes resulted from the

Figure 6.18. Late Sarmatians. Lebedevka burial ground: (1, 2) bronze fibulae; (3, 4) bronze mirrors; (5) iron scoop; (6, 7) red-clay and black glossy jars; (1, 4, 5, 7) grave 2, kurgan 23; (2 – grave 1, kurgan 23, 3 – kurgan 19; 6 – kurgan 11) (after Moshkova 1982).

new groups of nomads moving westward. But the question of "Who is behind of these groups?" has led to heated debates. Skipkin (1990) identifies the Early Sarmatian culture with the Aorci and Yagn–Tsai state of Chinese sources. In his opinion, the major creators of the Middle Sarmatian culture were the Alans, who initially were either in the Kang–Ku state or under its political influence.

From the final century BC, a number of objects of an eastern origin appeared in the Eurasian steppe and forest-steppe: turquoise and gold zoomorphic objects, Chinese mirrors, raw opium, nephrite fastenings for sword scabbards, lacquer objects, silk. and other items, and several extremely rich burials date to the first century CE. Such rich material is recorded in some regions, in particular, in Bactria (Tilla-Tepe), western Siberia (Sidorovka and Isakovaka), and the Lower Don area (Khokhlach, Sadovyi, Kobyakovo, Zhutovo, Vysokhino, Dachi, and other areas), which seems to be the center of the powerful nomadic union, supposedly headed by the Alans. These objects may reflect trade along the northern branch of the Silk Route, which began in 36 BC. Some of these objects could have come this way, but it is unlikely that the massive gold sacred decorations of the rich barrows in the Lower Don basin and in the Dnepr region would have been mercantile trade items. Some of the objects have parallels in Siberian collections and among the Hunnish objects. The international (not necessarily ethnic) military aristocracy was the most likely group to disperse the turquoise and gold-style artifacts.

If these objects belong to the Alans, we have to admit that they came to Europe passing the southern Urals. Another question arises: "Who left the sites that have the Late Sarmatian appearance?" Scholars believe in a successive development within the Sarmatian population, among which some new leading tribes arose from time to time. We have to say that the model of perpetual migrations from the east to the west "worked" during the turn of eras. Botalov (2000) unites all sites of the second to fifth centuries CE in the Urals and Kazakhstan steppe into one "Hunnish-Sarmatian" culture and ascribes its creation to the Huns. Archaeological and anthropological materials testify to the new drift of eastern nomads who first stopped at the Urals, from where new groups had already moved westward. Taking into account the dramatic events that took place in Central Asia, we should admit that the Huns might have been among the other dislocated tribal groups looking for their fortune.

As we can see, the southern Ural area was well assimilated by nomadic groups but, depending on climatic conditions and political situation, the number and structure of nomadic tribes were different, fluctuating between accumulation and reduction. However, in all cases, they influenced their neighbors but though different ways, which we will discuss in the following chapters.

CHAPTER 7

THE WORLD OF CULTURES OF CIS-URALS FOREST ZONE OF EASTERN EUROPE: THE MAINTENANCE OF CULTURAL IDENTITIES

This world is composed of various cultures that have continued the basic traditions of the local Bronze Age. The most significant among them are two cultural formations that gave their names to the early (eighth to third centuries BC), and later (second century BC to second century AD) phases of the local Iron Age. These are the Ananyino and the Pyanobor intercommunities, the sites of which are concentrated mainly along the Kama basin (left tributary of the Volga river). Gening (1988) defines this area as the Prikamsky historical and geographical region where the continuous development of economic, social, and cultural processes resulted in the formation of ethnic groups of the western Urals such as: the Komi-Permians, the Udmurts (Votyaks), the Cheremis (Mari), and Mordvins[1] (Goldina 1999; Khalikov 1990). Some Scandinavian scholars regard the northern Fennoscandia as the westernmost component of this world. During the eighth–seventh centuries BC and continuing from that time, the economic and cultural changes that occurred in northern Fenno-Scandia were mainly related to links with the Ananyino culture metallurgical centers (Aronsson & Hedman 2000). Northeastern Europe constituted its part as well.

There has been more then a century of archaeological study of Kama area of the Cis-Urals. In the 1858, the local official Alabin excavated forty-eight graves in the cemetery near the Ananyino village located on the Vyatka River. He collected a large number of bronze artifacts: weaponry, female decorations, implements, and stone anthropomorphic figurines (Alabin 1859; 1860). A few years later, in the 1880s, a collection of splendid bronze objects, heavy bronze belt buckles, hooks, torches, and earrings was found near the village Pyanyi Bor (Kama river). They came from two burial grounds located there and were different from these of the Ananyino site. In 1898, the outstanding Russian archaeologist Spitsin organized a large-scale excavation and after analysis of materials, he introduced new culture, named Pyanoborskaya (Pyanobor), into academic circulation.

These excavations have given rise to intensive fieldwork on the archaeological sites of the Kama area. The Ananyino burial ground attracted many scholars, by the 1890s about two thousand graves were excavated there. Numerous burial grounds and settlements were yet to be discovered in nineteen century. Since that time, the sites of the Ananyino culture and the Pyanobor culture have been in the focus of scientific attention. Their study is associated with scholars such as Aspelin (1877), Spitsin (1893; 1901), Tallgren (1919), Schmidt (1928), Smirnov (1952), Zbruyeva (1952), Gening (1988), and many others. In the course of their research, various problems were discussed and, at the present time, these cultures are considered to have been well studied. We share the commonly accepted idea about the succession of the Ananyino and Pyanobor cultural traditions, and their territorial and chronological variability, mirrored in several local cultural groups.

THE ANANYINO CULTURAL GROUPS

The Ananyino antiquities are represented by numerous burial grounds, open and fortified settlements located on the banks of the Kama River and its tributaries: the Vyatka, the Chusovaya and the Belaya. Ananyino sites also have been discovered in the area situated along the part of Volga near the mouth of the Kama (Fig. 7.1). Additionally, they are registered in the basins of the Pechora, Vychegda, and Mesen' rivers in the northeast of eastern Europe.

In the south, there existed a buffer zone between the Ananyino territory and the area of the South Uralian and Volga "Sauromatian" nomads. In the east, the forest-mountainous area was inhabited by people, who left the sites of the archaic Gamayun culture and the Itkul metal-giving culture (see later).

Chronologically the Ananyino culture covers a period between the eighth and third centuries BC. Its early stage is bounded by the sixth century BC. The late stage is dated to the fourth–third centuries. BC. This periodization is chiefly based on the material coming from funeral sites (Khalikov 1977; Vichtomov 1967; Zbruyeva 1952). Researchers distinguish around eleven territorial variants of this culture, although it appears to be homogeneous from the point of view of ceramics, easily recognizable over all of the inhabited territory. Among them, two interrelated groups (the post-Maklasheyevo and Textile group) occupied in the eighth–sixth centuries BC the broad-leafed forest environments of the Volga-Kama area and look to be more advanced economically, having possessed a quite developed bronze metallurgy. The others, occupying the forests of the Kama, Vyatka, and Vetluga rivers, were more primitive in all economic spheres and were oriented mainly to hunting and fishing.

The Ananyino material culture is specified by the composition of highly developed metalworking and an archaic stone industry rooted in the preceding time. The stone tools are more characteristic for the northern cultural groups (Savelyeva 1984).

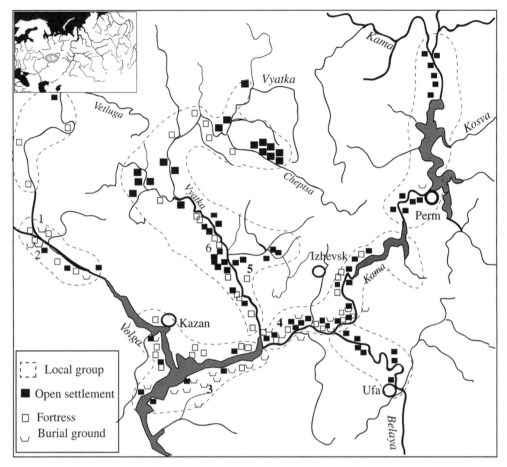

Figure 7.1. Distribution of the Ananyino culture sites; (1) Starshii (Elder) Akhmylovsky burial ground; (2) Akkozinsky burial ground; Novomordovsky burial grounds; (4) Ananyinsky burial ground; (5) Argyzhskoye fortress; (6) Buiskoye fortress (adapted from Khalikov 1977 and Goldina 1999).

Detailed surveys identified a number of open and fortified settlements. The latter are usually situated on the narrow promontories of high riverbanks (about 20–25 m) in 20–40 km from each other (Fig. 7.2). From two sides they are defended by steep slopes; from the third side they are limited by a big earthen moat and ditch (Goldina 1999; Zbruyeva 1952). The size of fortified settlements varies between 2,000 and 30,000 m². Such fortresses are more characteristic of the middle and late stages of the Ananyino culture than of the early one when the settlements were simpler, smaller, and situated in close proximity to water. The fortifications appear first in the south of the Ananyino area as a reaction to the nomadic threat. The same process is traced in other forest-steppe regions of eastern Europe and western Siberia. The Iron Age in the forest zone is sometimes called "the Age of Fortresses." However, an increase of internal social instability can be evidenced by the appearance of fortified sites in the core area of the Ananyino culture. By contrast, Khalikov (1977:18) believed that idea of fortification came to the Volga-Kama population after disintegration of the Finno-Permic linguistic unity[2] in about the middle of the second millennium BC.

Cultural layers of the Ananyino fortified settlements contain many ceramics, animal bones, ash, and river shells. The open settlements are bigger in size but their layers are poorer. Besides the stable residential sites, archaeologists discovered a number of seasonal, temporary hunting camps, which are marked only by assemblages of Ananyino pottery.

Hence, the Ananyino settlement system includes several levels: (1) larger fortified settlements, serving as administrative and ceremonial centers (up to 30,000 m²); (2) small fortified settlements (up to 4,000 m²), which functioned as the subordinated centers; (3) open settlements; and (4) temporary hunting camps.

Settlements accommodated numerous rectangular houses. The tendency of development from small semisubterranean dwellings to larger ones, above-ground pillar or log wooden construction was realized. Sometimes the walls were covered with clay plaster (Malakhai settlement). The hearths were located, as a rule, in the central part of a house floor, and there were either one or two entrances to the dwelling. In the fully excavated Argyzhskoye settlement located in the Vyatka region, the buildings formed three rows (Fig. 7.2) and differed functionally: one row comprised houses 80–100 m², one of two constructions in the middle row served for ritual ceremonies, including some sacrifices. Two entrances led to the house of 52 m². In the central part, there were big fireplaces and a wide trench filled with ashy-charcoal sediments, limestone, raw and burned bones, and pottery fragments. An accumulation of chaotically situated human bones, partly burned, was recovered near the trench. The bones belonged to three men, one woman, and one child. The third row consisted of smaller houses and a workshop, in which a hearth, slag, and debris of molds were found. The storage pits were situated outside the houses – along the promontory edge (Chernykh 1996). Another sanctuary was excavated in the Zuyevy Kluchi settlement. It was represented by huge amount of animal bones – horses, cows, which were sacrificed to idols (Goldina 1999: 175).

More substantial information is provided by the famous Ananyino cemeteries such as Akkozinsky, where 110 graves were excavated, I Novomordovski (twenty-five graves), Zuyevsky, Starshi Akhmylovsky (937 graves- Fig. 7.3), Pershinsky (176 graves), and others. All known graveyards are located near rivers, usually on high banks and terraces and connected to certain villages. They do not have any markers on the surface and comprise, usually, dozens or hundreds of graves, organized into the rows parallel to the river. The major rivers, the Volga and Kama, were of great importance for the local population, which most likely considered running water to be pathways for the dead. The

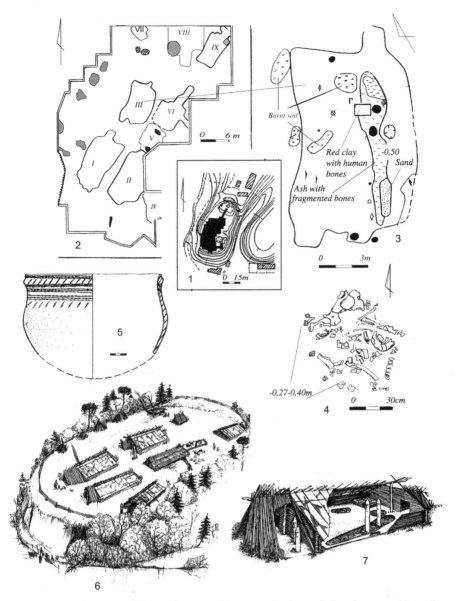

Figure 7.2. The Argyzhskoye fortress: (1) general plan of the fortress; (2) early Ananyino structures (houses); (3) cult building (III); (4) human bones of 3 males, 1 female and 1 child from building III; (5) clay pot; (6) artistic reconstruction of the village; (7) reconstruction of the cult house (after Chernykh 2001; Chernykh et al. 2002a).

deceased were placed in oval or rectangular pits in an extended position, with their legs oriented to the river. Although there were no clearly visible surface constructions above the graves, some traces of burned wooden logs are repeatedly recorded. Scholars have suggested that the Ananyino people constructed a small wooden "mortuary house" above the burial (Khalikov 1977: 91). This

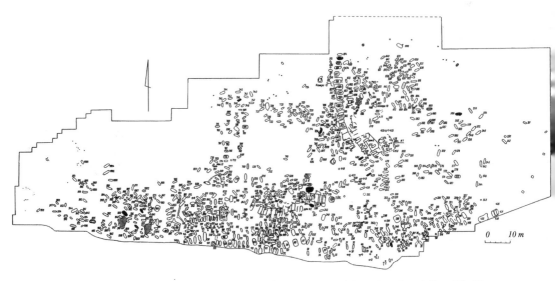

Figure 7.3. Starshii (Elder) Akhmylovsky cemetery: view in plan (after Khalikov 1977).

would account for the shallow (70–80 cm) grave pits. Some burial grounds yielded stone statues erected near the burial. In particular, the famous statue from the Ananyino cemetery comprises a rectangular gravestone with a curved top (Fig. 7.4). A warrior with a dagger, a quiver containing arrowheads, and a battle-axe was depicted on the stone surface (Zbruyeva 1952: 21).

The majority of burials were of individuals, but there is a number of collective and double burials, containing the remains of females and males or one of these and a child (Fig. 7.5). Every cemetery produces some number (between one and five) of secondary burials, containing human bones cleaned of soft tissue or separate skulls only. Male skeletons without skulls also have been discovered in several cases (Goldina 1999: 179; Khalikov 1977: 99). Relatives were buried in one place. Male graves contained, as a rule, horse bones, weapons (spearheads, arrowheads, battle hammer-axes, socketed axes), tools (knives), and some decorations (belts with pendants, torques, bracelets); female burials were furnished with cattle bones, decorations, needles and spindle whorls. Clay pots were given to everybody. The Ananyino people practiced some forms of fire cult, traces of which are represented by charcoal in the grave infilling, possibly from the remains of pyres or sacrificial places with cremation. Interesting remains have been recorded in the Pershino cemetery (cal 800–700 BC) near Perm. Here, together with 176 individuals, double and collective burials, there were three wooden constructions ("houses"), the floors of which were 40–50 cm deep into the soil, and there were preserved the traces of intensive fire use. The remains of round boxes (d = 50 cm) made of birch bark and containing ash, charcoal, and burned bones, were recorded along the walls. Korenuk (1996: 37–9) interprets these as the remains of cremation.

The funerary rituals performed for distinguished persons (e.g., local chiefs) were more complex: their tombs were encircled by stone and covered with an extended wooden roof. Some burials comprised only skulls, accompanied by rich offerings of grave goods (Zbruyeva 1952: 122).

The Ananyino pottery is identified as having ground shell as an admixture to the clay. Pots are usually round bottomed, with a clearly profiled neck; the surface is rather smooth, sometimes polished. Corded and comb decoration combined with holes covers the upper part of a pot.

Despite some regional diversity, the Ananyino societies shared a common economic basis: metalworking, stalled animal husbandry, hunting, and gathering. As to primitive cultivation, it is assumed hypothetically with reference to corresponding tools: bone ends of hoes, iron chisel-knives, and grinding stones which are found in the settlements in a great number (Goldina 1999: 193).

Among the animal bones yielded by settlements, bones of domestic animals are predominant (from 58 to 87 percent). Collections comprise bones of all domestic animal species of the temperate zone: cattle (30–40 percent) horse (30 percent), pig (20–30 percent), sheep (10 percent). Their proportion depended on local environmental conditions. Interestingly enough, in collections of some fortified settlements (Svinogorskoye, Buiskoye, Alten-tau) pig bones took the first position (Bogatkina 1992: 129). Pigs were rather large (83.3 cm at the withers); they were

Figure 7.4. Stone stele from the Ananyino cemetery (after Zbruyeva 1952).

slaughtered under a year old (Andreyeva 1967). The cattle were rather thin-legged, hornless. Cows were 108 cm and bulls 114 cm at the withers – small compared with other forest cultures of eastern Europe (Andreyeva & Petrenko 1976; Petrenko 1984). Cattle were slaughtered chiefly at the age of twenty-eight months, horses around two to three years old. The Ananyino horses were quite strong, yet undersized (122–143 cm at the withers) and used mainly for transportation. There were fewer sheep, but they were in steady use and bred as a source of wool. Dogs were morphologically like modern Siberian huskies and were in everyday service (Bogatkina 1992). The hunting of bear, beaver, squirrel, hare, and deer was aimed predominantly at the acquisition of fur, which was used for commercial exchange with neighbours. The bear also was of great significance as a cult animal. The water and forest birds (duck, goose, swan, black and wood grouses, and heron were hunted as well. The Ananyino

TABLE 7.1. *Representation of domestic animals in the Ananyino culture (Andreyeva & Petrenko 1976)*

Settlements	Horses		Cattle		Sheep/Goats		Pig		Total	
	NISP	percent	NISP	percent	NISP	percent	NISP	percent	NISP	percent
Gremyachanskoye	6,038	44.54	3,827	28.24	1,618	11.94	2,072	15.28	13,555	100
Polovinnoye	956	65.26	335	22.87	98	6.68	76	5.19	1,465	100
Kalinovskoye	112	37.58	135	45.31	10	3.34	41	13.76	298	100
Subbotinskoye	67	56.77	43	36.45	2	1.69	6	5.09	118	100
Skorodum	136	44.59	126	41.31	21	6.88	22	7.22	305	100
Galkinskoye (F)	260	37.35	396	56.89	18	2.59	22	3.17	696	100
Konetsgorskoye (F)	247	30.87	366	45.75	123	15.38	64	8.00	800	100
Altyn-Tau (F)	189	57.79	115	35.17	10	3.06	13	3.98	327	100

(F) – Fortress type settlement.

sites produced about two dozen hollow bone tubes 2.5–9 cm, which emit a high hissing sound. They are interpreted as bird-calls, used for either hunting or some magic actions (Korepanov 1994: 53). The rivers were rich in fish, the remains of which were found in abundance in settlements (sturgeon, starlet, pike, and others).

As described earlier, bronze metallurgy was an advanced branch of the local economy. It promoted the development of other domestic crafts: bone and woodworking and iron production, which gradually replaced bronze production.

The Ananyino groups effectively used natural resources that might give a rise to the local economy and demographic growth, which, if to judge on the number of sites, took place in around the fifth–fourth centuries BC.

There is no doubt that the society of the Ananyino culture was organized in several small tribal groups or simple chiefdoms; it still preserved many egalitarian traditions and a tribal system with vague boundaries between separate units. Nevertheless, the Ananyino society demonstrates the greater degree of militarization compared with other societies of the Eurasian temperate forest zone. The sites produce a great quantity of advanced forms of weaponry. The settlement pattern represents a clear hierarchy and different functions: fortified settlements as administrative centers, watch posts, and open villages of various sizes. An analysis of the composition of grave goods allows the strata in Ananyino society to be distinguished, which appear more visible within the male group (Zbruyeva 1952: 152). Some cemeteries contained graves with rich and distinguished goods: spearheads, battle ax-hammers, numerous arrowheads, and daggers. Special power markers are represented by ceremonial poleaxes coming from various contexts. The back of these were decorated with images of wolf heads with grinning jaws, and sockets with griffin heads. The imported objects

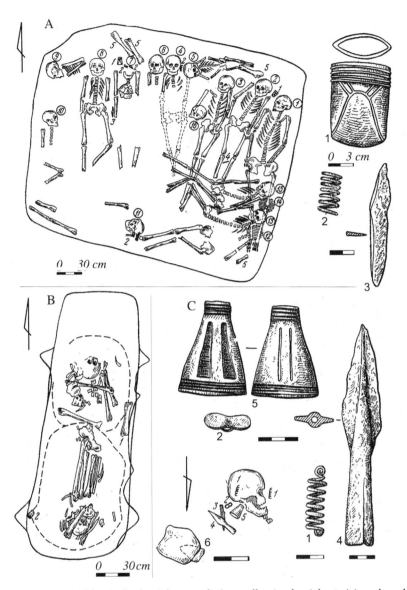

Figure 7.5. Akkozinsky burial ground. **A** – collective burial 46: (1) socketed axe; (2) temple spiral; (3) knife; (4) awl; (5) animal bone. **B** – burial 32: (1) animal bone. **C** – burial 52: (1) temple spiral; (2) paired plaque; (3) knife; (4) spearhead; (5) pendant; (6) stone (1 – silver; 2–5 – bronze; 3–4, – iron) (after Khalikov 1977).

(from Siberia, Kazakhstan, and Middle Asia), which are numerous in the sites of the early stage of the Ananyino culture were concentrated in the possession of local chiefs.

The Ananyino culture is included in the area of the so-called animal style (zoomorphic), the repertoire of which was chiefly represented by animal images. But this style differed from the Scythian style, although, as scholars believe, the latter influenced the former to a great extend. The Ananyino people, in general, preferred to use images of elk, bear, and birds, sometimes deer, snake, pig, but rarely horses (Fig. 7.6). The heads of elk, bearlike animals, and the circled prey animals with bear and wolf characteristics were widely spread within the Ananyino territory. This style serves as the source for the reconstruction of a symbolic system of the Ananyino society.

Scholars for the Ananyino world outlook propose a three-part model. This conclusion derives from the interpretation of numerous art-objects in the context of the Udmurt mythology and folklore. In particular, one of them is the comb-top from the Buiskoye fortified settlement (Fig. 7.6 – left side, below). Ashikhmina (1992), based on ethnographic parallels, interpreted it to be a depiction of the world-tree.

The upper level of the Ananyino cosmological model is connected with the sun, the image of which repeatedly occurs on various objects (round discs with the depiction of the face; round plaques with a concentric design, concentrically decorated spindle-whorls, etc.). Animals such as elk, bear, wolf, and horse are associated with the middle level, and underwater and underground creatures represent the lower one. Communal and tribal ritual centers functioned at some settlements and special places (Zuyevy Kluchi, Svinogor, Zaosinnovskoye, Gremyachanskoye, Glyadenovskoye). These are evidenced by remains of fire surrounded by posts, and various offerings: animal bones, anthropomorphic and zoomorphic figurines, clay troches ("cakes"), and various objects with solar signs. Tribal centers are usually situated on high elevated grounds and marked by a great accumulation of ash, charcoal, crushed bones, votive objects, thousands of arrowheads, hundreds of anthropomorphic, ornithomorphic, zoomorphic figurines, dogs, flies, and bees. Scholars believe that animal bones are connected with collective immolations during calendar ceremonies, and votive objects are more likely individual offerings. The Ananyino societies practiced a ritual of human sacrifice as well (Goldina 1999: 203).

It is commonly accepted by archaeology, ethnography, and linguistics that the ancestors of the Permian peoples (Udmurts, Komi-Permians, and Komi-Zyryans) left the sites of Ananyino cultural intercommunity.[3] In the west, in the middle Volga basin, the Ananyino groups were neighbors of the groups that produced textile ceramics, these were ancestors of the Volga Finns (Goldina 1999; Napolskikh 1997). As Napolskikh states (1997: 196–7), in the Iron Age the penetration of the bearers of the Finnish languages from the Volga area to northwest Europe was completed. Archaeologically, this is well evidenced by the spread of metal and textile pottery from the Volga and Kama regions. He explains this shift by series of factors: climatic change (cooling and moistening at the turn of the second and first millennia BC), active functioning of the Cis-Ural metallurgy, and the highly adaptive potential of the forest population.

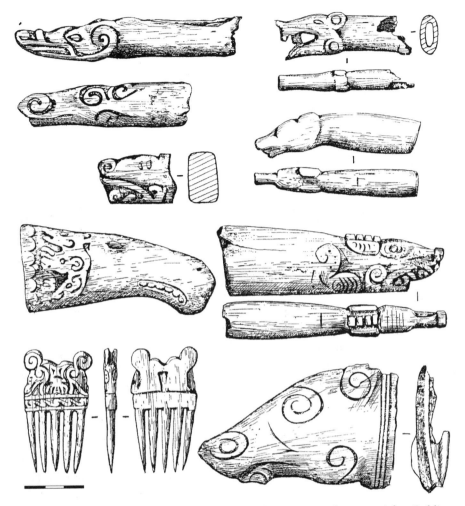

Figure 7.6. Bone objects in animal style from the Ananyino fortresses (after Goldina 1999).

THE PYANOBOR CULTURAL GROUPS

In the third and second centuries BC, the more or less homogenous Ananyino unity split into several new groups archaeologically represented by cultures, which inherited many of the Ananyino traditions but developed in different social and economic conditions (Fig. 7.7-A). This separation occurred on the basis of local cultural variants experiencing growing internal tension and pressure from the southern nomadic societies. Technologically, the new cultures almost completely depended on iron production, and socially they were at a more advanced level. All of the new cultures belonged to the period between the third century BC and the fifth century AD. They formed the Pyanobor cultural or pan-tribal union (Gening 1988: 28–9). It embraced the area of middle and low Kama, low Belaya, and Vyatka rivers. Another union that also derived from the Ananyino basis was the Glyadenovo union, which occupied the Upper Kama area. These corresponded to two parts of the bisected Permian basis: proto-Udmurts and proto-Komi (Goldina 1999: 209).

The southern part of the Pyanobor cultural union, was represented by the Kara-Abyz subculture, and occupied a region the broad-leafed forest and forest-steppe, along the Middle Belaya river (north-west of Bashkiria). It is characterised by vast open and fortified settlements and flat burial fields (except during the early part of the Shipovo necropolis), composed of thousands of shallow graves. The fortresses, which are spaced between 5,000 m² and 50,000 m² apart, occupy high promontories and have two or three defensive lines consisting of ditches and ramparts. The biggest, Okhlebinino-II fortified settlement, occupies 25,000 m². The open villages are sided to the low riverbanks, and they have rather poor archaeological deposits, compared to the fortresses. Unfortunately, these are excavated only on a very limited scale.

In the cemeteries, the dead were placed on or wrapped in baste, laid on their backs in extended position, were oriented to a river by their legs, and were accompanied by clothing ornaments, particularly relating to the belt (Fig. 7.8-A). Male and female burials differed in grave goods, according to their social status: men's graves yielded a number of weapons – iron swords, daggers, spears, and horse harnesses (Fig. 7.8-B); women's graves contained mostly ornaments (various kinds of earrings and temporal pendants, necklaces, breast plaques, and pendants), utensils and pottery. Ethnographic detail of women's costume was stressed by leather belts crossed on the breast and decorated by numerous metal clips, round plaques, and ended with lyrelike open-work plaques. The deceased were given a piece of meat: a leg of mutton or pork. Craniological analysis undertaken by some Russian anthropologists characterizes the Kara-Abyz population in term of Europoid anthropological type: mesocranial skulls with a little Mongoloid admixture (Efimova 1991).

This culture continued along Ananyino lines but with some Sarmatian (Prokhorovo) influence and with inclusions of population groups coming from beyond the Urals. Nomadic presence here was not limited only by influence; it was more substantial. Some scholars interpret this influence as a result of the process of sedenterization when some part of the nomads passed to a more stable economic and life regime. Researchers distinguish four tribal groups concentrated around the biggest fortified settlements. The Kara-Abyz population was numerous and more heavily armed compared with other cultures of the Pyanobor pan-tribal union. The culture is generally dated to the period between the third century BC and third century AD.

The best studied group is the Cheganda subculture, also known as the Pyanobor culture itself (Ageyev 1992). It is located along the Kama River near the confluence with the Belaya River, in a zone of coniferous and broad-leafed

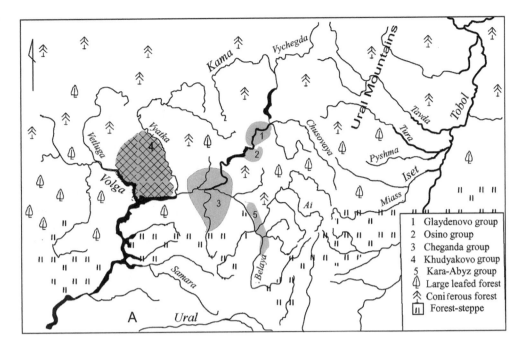

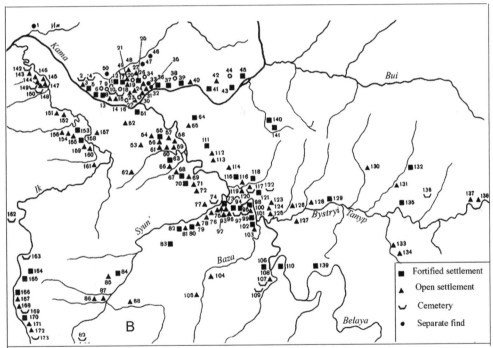

Figure 7.7. A – Map of the Pyanobor groups. B – Distribution of sites of the Cheganda group in the Kama River basin (after Gening 1988).

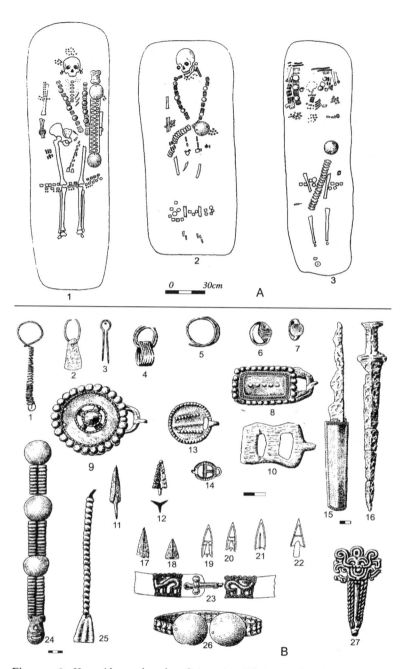

Figure 7.8. Kara-Abyz cultural tradition. **A** – Biktimirovsky I burial ground: (1) grave 46; (2) grave 1; (3) grave 3 (After Gening 1988.); **B** – Materails from Kara-Abyz cemeteries: (1) temple pendant; 2, (4) earrings; (3) clip; (5–7) finger rings; (8–10, 13, 14) belt buckles; (11, 12, 17–22) arrowheads; (15, 16) swords; (23, 24, 26) belts; (25) belt pendant; (27) quiver hook (after Bader 1976).

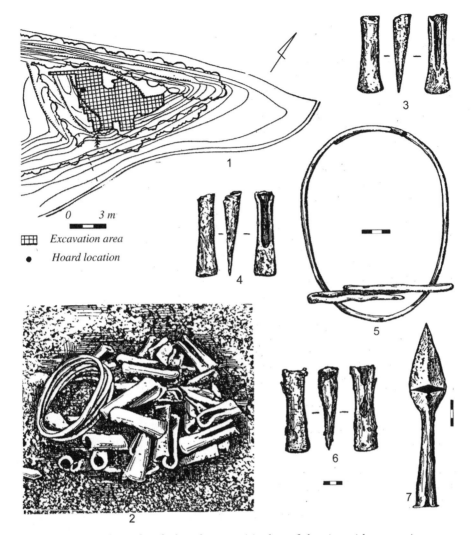

Figure 7.9. Buiskoye fortified settlement: (1) plan of the site with excavation area; (2) hoard 2; 3, 4, (6) iron socketed axes; (5) bronze torque; (7) iron spearhead (after Goldina 1999).

forest (Fig. 7.7-B). The settlements are located in the vast Kama-Belaya valley, with its extremely rich meadows used for cattle grazing. Low terraces were used for agriculture. Fortified villages of more than 5,000 (30,000 -50,000) m² in size served for permanent inhabitancy, whereas those of 500–2,000 m² were refuge sites or outposts (Fig. 7.9). The big fortresses were surrounded by a vast inhabitancy area 4,000–10,000 m² in size. The sites are grouped into several clusters separated by 20–30 km of free space. Each cluster covers a territory of 90–100 km² and corresponds to a certain tribal group (Ageyev 1992; Gening 1988).

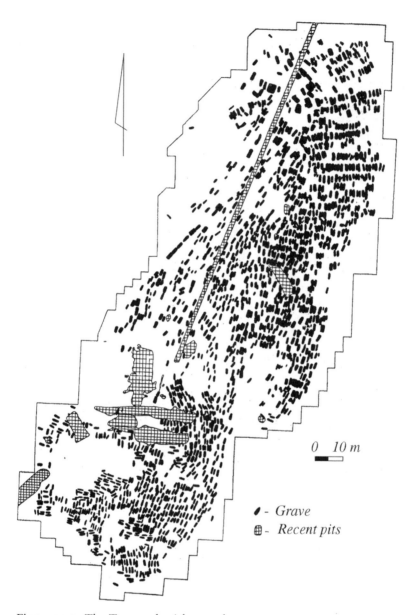

Figure 7.10. The Tarasovo burial ground.

The wooden houses, all of which, with small variations, measuring ten by five meters, had a central hearth and walls covered with clay plaster. The houses stand 10–15 m away from each other forming streets. The storage pits and summer hearths were arranged in between the houses. There also were big common public houses in some settlements (Goldina 1999: 212).

Funeral sites, located not far from the settlements, have some common features with those of the Kara-Abyz culture. At present more than forty burial grounds with around five thousand burials have been excavated. They vary in size. For example, Tarasovo burial field comprised 1879 graves (Fig. 7.10), and only 224 graves composed the Cheganda-II necropolis.

The cemeteries were located on the riverbanks. The graves do not have any markers on the surface, except the remains of memorial ceremonies (food, pottery, bones, pyre traces), but the fact that the graves do not overlap each other, can be interpreted as evidence in favor of the graves originally having identification. The fully excavated Tarasovo cemetery studied by Izhevsk archaeologists provides valuable information about burial ritual, social structure, and demographic structure of the Cheganda population. Scholars believe two lineages, each of which oriented their dead differently, founded that cemetery (Goldina 1999: 212–16).

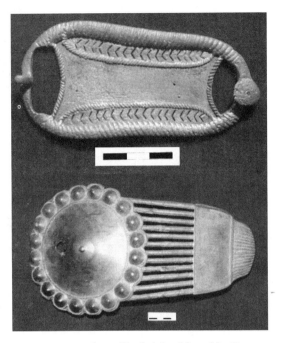

Plate 7.1. Epaulette-like belt buckles of the Pyanobor style.

Close relatives, members of three generation families, were buried in one row, consisting of local groups, which belonged to the small families. The wooden coffins made of and covered by boards contained the remains of individuals placed in extended supine position. About 80 percent of the burials are of an individual character, a small but steady percentage fall into collective graves (up to eight skeletons in one pit). In one part of the Tarasovo cemetery there was a concentration of such burials that probably resulted from some disease, which may have ravaged the population. In two graves, the dead had severed left hands, which were placed at the right of the head.

Objects of everyday life were very rarely placed in the pit grave. The deceased were dressed in their best clothing, decorated with many bronze ornaments. So-called epaulette-like belt clasps (Plate 7.1), temple pendants shaped in a question mark, and round breast badges and torques constitute the most characteristic part of the Cheganda (Pyanobor) material complex (Fig. 7.11). Heavy decorative bronze brooches also were frequently found in the burials. The total weight of bronzes sometimes reached several kilograms and represented very few everyday objects. The clothes and shoes of the Pyanobor women were richly decorated (Fig. 7.12). Two customs were apparent: first, to place a belt along the dead body and second, to put some additional ornaments and small instruments (gift set) into wooden boxes or vessels. These originated in the third century BC and were widespread in the third–fifth centuries AD accounted for up to 20–30 percent of total number of

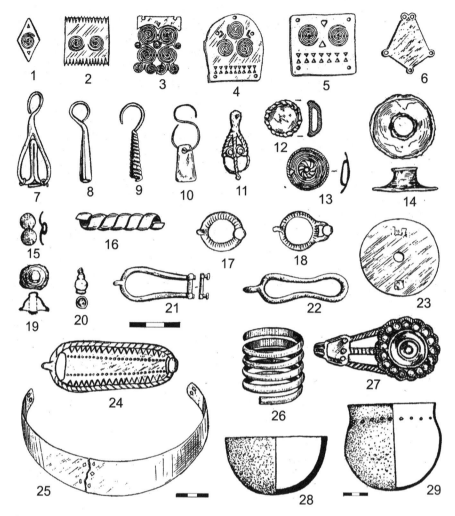

Figure 7.11. Materials from Cheganda burial grounds: (1–5, 15) dress decorations; (6, 20) temple pendants; (12–14, 19, 23) plaques; (16) spiral; (17, 18, 21, 22, 24) clasps with fixed hook; (25) headdress; (26) bracelet; (28) epaulette-like buckle; (28, 29) pots (after Goldina 1999).

graves. Such gift sets were more characteristic for female graves. The men were accompanied with iron knives, bone and iron arrowheads, swords, and horse harness elements (Fig. 7.13). The pottery is represented by round-based bowls, poorly decorated and made of local clay with crushed shell, ceramics, dry clay, calcified bones, and bird dung temper.

The common opinion is that the Cheganda (Pyanobor) society was stratified and consisted of several units, ruled by local chiefs and united into a politically organized polity. This is evidenced by the systematic and hierarchic territorial distribution of fortresses, the high density of population and the standardization of material culture, which strikes us by its richness and sophistication. Detailed

Figure 7.12. Artistic reconstructions of the Pyanobor female decorations, by V. Gening (after Goldina 1999).

statistical analysis of grave goods composition allowed Ostanina (1997: 134–6) to distinguish four groups of female graves, and three of male graves in the late cemeteries. She concluded that richness and power were concentrated in several lineages, which determined property and social status of individuals. Social position of a member of such a group depended on age and contribution to the economic or military function of society.

Most of the men were unmounted archers, but about 20 percent of them were horse riders. They also could have an ax and a sword. Distinctive persons of high social status owned a cuirass and a helmet (Goldina 1999: 219). Ethnically, it was part of a differentiated proto-Permian grouping (Gening 1988). We will not discuss the disputed periodization of this culture. At the time of writing, it is accepted that this culture had three periods: formative (third–first centuries BC); middle or classical (first–second centuries CE), and conclusive (third–fifth centuries CE).[4]

Another variant of the Pyanobor confederation is represented by the Khudyakovo variant the sites of which are recorded along the Vyatka River (a tributary of the Kama).[5] Some biritualism: inhumation and partial or full cremation is an attribute of its mortuary practice, in which fire played a more significant role than in the Cheganda groups. The Khudyakovo graves are also full

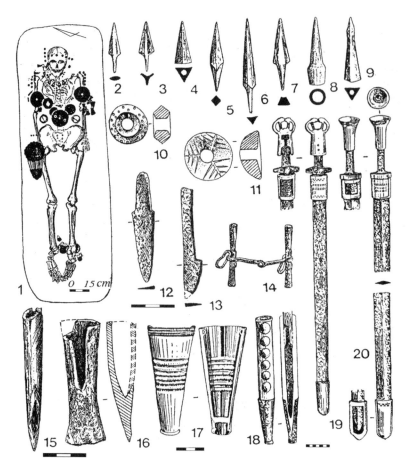

Figure 7.13. Materials from the Cheganda cemetery: (1) burial 15; (2–9) arrowheads; (10, 11) spindles; (12, 13) knives; (14) horse bits; (15) hoe-head; (16) hoe; (17, 18) scabbards; (19, 20) swords; (2, 9–13, 15) bone; (3, 12–14, 16) iron; (10, 11) clay; (17, 18) bronze; (19, 29) iron/bronze (after Goldina 1999).

of goods numbering up to three to four hundred items in one grave. Together with various forms of epaulette-like clasps the inhabitants of the Vyatka basin favoured the use horselike pendants; they invented the shaky pendants, which will be very popular in the Cis-Urals in the medieval period. A highly artistic style of bronze casting was characteristic for this area. This is well reflected in the female costume with leather belts decorated by numerous appliqués, three-part buckles, and long composite hollow festoons attached to the belt. Big bronze breast plates, torques, bracelets, special hats of the "taky'a" type, sewn from the wool and covered with copper appliqués, small tubes, and beads also decorated the costumes (Leshchinskaya 1995). In the Buiskoye and Argyzh-skoye settlements, several hoards of metal objects have been found (Fig. 7.14). One of them consisted of 900 iron spears, 186 socketed axes, and 5 bronze torques (Ashikhmina 1987). This fact elucidates the mass craft production of

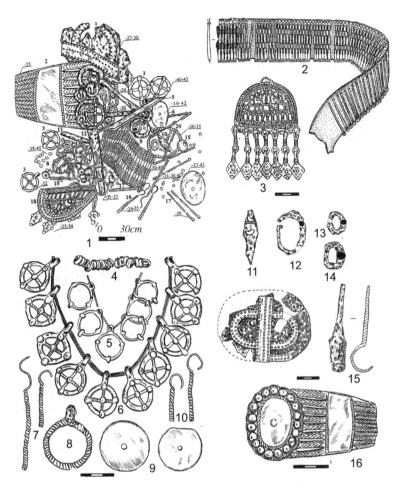

Figure 7.14. The hoard from the Argyzhskoye fortified settlement: (1) general plan; (2) leather belt with bronze plaques; (3) arched pendant; (4) bronze ring-like beads; (5–6) bronze ring-shaped pendants; (7, 10) bronze temporal pendants in the shape of a question mark; (8) iron pendant; (11, 12) fragments of iron bits; (13, 14) iron buckles; (15) iron spoon; (16) epaulet-shaped buckle; (17) butterfly shaped fibula (after Chernykh, Vanchikov and Shatalov 2002).

iron goods and throws light on the fact that these goods were of great value and worth fighting for.

The materials yielded by all Pyanobor sites are evidence to the relative prosperity and economic rise of the Pyanobor societies, which steadily occupied practically the whole Kama region, including the small river valleys in the forest zone. Alongside the clustered system of settlement when the population accumulated at the big fortified settlements, there also existed dispersed settlements in small villages which emerged in cleared grounds. Interestingly enough, smaller cemeteries and villages are more characteristic for the deeper forested areas and small rivers.

Scholars studying the demography believe that the Pyanobor society was structured. That is, extended families consisting of several generations numbering twenty to twenty-five persons could be basic social and economic unit. They formed the larger communities based on kinship relations (lineages). This is well documented by cemeteries: small (thirty to seventy graves), belonging to families or a group of kin families (Zhuravleva 1995) and large (about two thousand graves) belonging to several patronymic groups. According to demographic analysis undertaken for the later cemeteries, the average life of men was about thirty-seven years, women (Plate 7.2) thirty-one years (Ostanina 1997: 138). Social stratification, which was already visible in the Ananyino groups, became stronger in the Pyanobor society especially at the beginning of the first millennium CE. The social structure evolved from dominancy of extended family in the early period to the smaller one in late period.

Metal production, primarily iron, became specialized and self-inclusive branch of an economy. Complex technical operations such as soldering and casting which are used in the manufacture of ornaments and a rather standard character of artifacts attest to an existence of specialized craftsmen working for intertribal exchange. The Pyanobor decorations, specifically female decorations, (these are symbols of local identity) sometimes are encountered beyond the cultural territory, marking the ways of intercultural contacts, possibly, at the marriage level.

As Gening stated (1980: 131), by the fourth–fifth centuries CE the local craftsmen could receive up to 5 kg of iron in the bloomers. Their burials differed from other people as their graves were supplied with smithy and jeweler instruments. One hundred eighty-six iron hoes, nine iron spears, and six bronze torques were hoarded in the Buyskoye settlement of the second century CE. There is no doubt that slash-and-burn arable farming tended to be more important in the life of the late Pyanobor communities. The grains of amelcorn (*Triticum vulgare dicoccum*), barley, wheat, and oats were encountered in the Osinskoye fortified settlement (Goldina 1999: 255). At the same time, fishing and hunting supplemented the subsistence economy. Fur hunting seems to have been of great significance: the bones of fur-bearing animals (sobol, marten, squirrel, and beaver) prevail among the bones of wild animals found in settlements. Animal husbandry also developed. Horse, cattle, and pig were the preferred animals for breeding. Only the sites of the Kara-Abyz groups demonstrate the prevalence of sheep, then horse bones, indicating the more mobile character of their pastoralism as compared with the settled mode of life of the majority of population. Animal husbandry with a meat-milk orientation was based on the rich grass resources of the Kama-Belaya valley. The age characteristics of butchered animals attest to the rational use of all breeding animals. Cows younger than three years of age and horses younger than nine to twelve years were not slaughtered. Pigs and sheep were kept until they were 1.5 years old; rarely, they could be kept until they were three years old. The age analysis of animal bones shows that cattle, pig, and sheep were bred for meat, milk, and wool, and horses were used for transportation needs. Petrenko has related them to the forest type (Ostanina 1997: 146–7). The predominantly forest environments determined an organization of animal husbandry, which existed in a form of free grazing without a herder. This form is well known from local ethnographic data when animals being organized in separate herds (pigs and sheep – one herd; horses and cows – another herd) freely roamed in the nearby forest and meadows (Tsalkin 1966: 92–3). For example, in the Udmurt villages, the pigs were kept in the enclosed forest from spring to late autumn when they were along with their offspring gathered together (Ostanina 1997: 148). Stabling continued for five to six months. During the cold period, young animals were stabled in the houses until they have been stronger.

Plate 7.2. The Pyanobor woman: sculptural reconstruction by G. Lebedinskaya.

The Pyanobor sites have produced a number of imported objects, which tend to be more numerous in the late period (second–third centuries CE). These are the silver items that arrived from the Mediterranean and Central Asia. Beads imported from the Caucasus, Egypt, and Syria were of wide popularity.

Ageyev (1992: 86) supposes that the Kama population was organized into a confederation of different chiefdoms sharing a common origin, language, ideology, territory, and one level of social and economic development.

The Glyadenovo groups occupied the upper Kama, southern taiga, where hunting was of prime importance. In 1896–1897, the richest Glyadenovo bone producing site (kostishche) was discovered (Novokreshchennykh 1914), then published by Spitsin (1914). This site also produced a large number of votive objects. From the beginning, it was interpreted as a sacrificial place of the Pyanobor culture. Later, other similar sites were discovered. These sites were described in terms of a special archaeological culture Glyadenovskaya culture (Gening 1988: 131). "Kostishche" are usually situated on the grounds of earlier fortresses and represented by several alternating stratigraphic layers. In particular, basic components of the Glyadenovo "kostishche" are the following: (1) a layer of burned bones and ash, concentrated in the central part of an area, (2) a layer of unburned bones, deposited in a continuous mass around the first concentration, (3) great number of artifacts including ceramic vessels, bone, iron, and copper tools, arms (mostly arrowheads), knives, glass beads, small buckles, miniature copies of tools, and cult figurines of humans, animals, and birds. In Yugo-Kamskoye kostishche, there was a similar structure. It comprised a layer of burned bones and ash 50–150 cm thick, underlain by a layer, 15–20 cm, of unburned animal bones. Cleft long animal bones, ribs, and teeth banded this concentration (Polyakov 2001).

Unfortunately, no proper zoological analysis was carried out on this material. Some general examination of the faunal collection demonstrates the total predominance of bones of wild animals: bear, elk, reindeer, lynx, and boar.

Twelve thousand nine hundred glass beads with internal gilding were found in the Glayedenovo kostishche. About one thousand anthropomorphic figurines cut from a copper sheet also come from this site (Fig. 7.15). These are simple schematic figures, riders, archers, humans with serpents, and humans on dragons. Zoomorphic images include dogs (about 460 items), hare, squirrel, boar, bear, and sometimes horse and cow. Birds are represented with outspread wings. There are also insects (bees) and snakes. These objects are considered as offerings to the local gods of hunting. Gening (1988), who found numerous parallels in Ob-Ugrian mythology and religion, interprets the figurines as the "soul containers."

The numismatic material from the Glyadenovo "kostishche" is of particular interest. It is represented by five copper coins of the Kushan ruler Kundzhula Kadfiz (20 BC–30 AD) (Novokreshchennykh 1914), of Tsar Khuvishka (106–133 AD), and the coins of the Chinese Emperor Guan of the Young Han Dynasty (25–56 AD) (Vildanov & Melnichuk 1999).

There are two basic interpretations of such sites: (1) these were burial grounds with the remains of cremation and animal sacrifices (Gening 1988:155); or (2), these were tribal sanctuaries (Polyakov 2001; Spitsin 1914). Recently discovered flat burial grounds with Glaydenovo pottery made the second hypothesis more favorable. The latter differed in size, consisting of ten–twelve or as many as several hundred inhumations or cremations, arranged in standard pits. The complete absence of grave goods, except some pottery, is a specific trait of the Glyadenovo burial ritual.

Eight clusters of settlements, burial grounds and sanctuaries, separated by 15–50 km, are distinguished within the Glyadenovo territory, which was isolated from the nomad invasions by the Kara-Abyz and Cheganda chiefdoms. Each cluster contains two to seven sites, including one fortified settlement and some open villages, and according to Polyakov (2001), corresponds to certain small tribal groups. The culture was more archaic, but it preserved rather unusual and unique type of sites – communal sanctuaries.

Figure 7.15. Cult copper figurines from the Glyadenovo bone-producing site (after Gening 1988).

In the conclusion, we can say that the world of the described cultures demonstrates the unity and progression of economic and cultural evolution. Comprehensive statistical analysis aiming to compare them on basic characteristics of funeral practice has shown their substantial closeness: during almost thousand years, local people practiced mainly inhumation in flat cemeteries (Ivanov 1999). A steady development is noticeable in settlement pattern, pottery design and belief system. These cultures produced distinctive objects of decorative art, some elements of which are preserved in the folk art of the Permian peoples (so-called Perm Animal Style).

The subsistence system was based on stabled cattle breeding and primitive farming which developed into slash-and-burn arable farming by the end of the first millennium BC. Both of these required considerable labor investment. Hunting and fishing also were essential, although they played different roles depending on the local environment. The different crafts, especially metallurgy, which the Ananyino groups pioneered, were very important. By the end of the first millennium BC, iron production became a specialized professional craft. The Pyanobor society displayed visible features of prosperity, compared with contemporaneous groups of the forest inhabitants.

The diversified economy enabled local the population a stable reserve of food. This entailed a population growth, that was reflected in a remarkable quantitative increase of Ananyino, and then Pyanobor settlements. In particular, around five to seven thousand people appear to have inhabited the Cheganda area (one person per square kilometer [Gening 1988: 204]).

We can say that this type of economy ensured a substantial surplus production in the form of cattle, fur, metal, weapons, valuable decorations, and other prestige goods, which could be plundered, exchanged or stored in a fortress. The fortresses, which appear not only on the border with nomads but in all regions of the Ananyino and Pyanobor areas, testify to a rise in tensions between different groups. The settlement hierarchy, which emerged in the Ananyino cultural intercommunity, tended to develop in the Pyanobor groups, which in turn, displayed the growth of the size of the fortresses.

Social development tended to deepen social stratification, raising the role of local chiefs, and forming territorial units sharing common origin, language, and ideology. Progressive development in stable economic and political conditions, which existed in the forested Cis-Urals until the mid-first millennium CE, should have been promoted ethnic consolidation and maintenance of cultural identity.

Until the second century CE, the Kama populations did not experience any great invasions. However, in the second century, the impact of Sarmatian groups on the Kara–Abyz territory can be seen in the archaeological record. The local population moved northward and mixed with the Cheganda groups. This is evidenced by mixed archaeological sites. This movement led to a chain reaction of internal migrations within the Pyanobor world. At the end of the fourth century CE, some new groups invaded the area of the Cis-Urals, apparently coming from east of the Urals beginning the process of the Great Folk Movement.[6] Because of a very active process of interaction between the aboriginal population and the newcomers, the cultural makeup was changed and new cultures appeared in the area in question. Yet, despite these invasions, traditions of the Iron Age were preserved here for another several hundred years.

CHAPTER 8

THE FOREST-STEPPE CULTURES OF
THE URALS AND WESTERN SIBERIA:
ON THE NORTHERN PERIPHERY
OF THE NOMADIC WORLD

CULTURAL GROUPS OF THE FOREST-MOUNTAIN AREA
OF THE MIDDLE AND SOUTHERN URALS

When we discussed the Urals metallurgy earlier in this book, we referred in
particular to the Itkul culture, which is the basis of the Trans-Uralian metallurgical center of the Iron Age. Now we will discuss this in more detail, as well
as look at other groups of the forest-mountain area of the Urals known by the
name of Gamayun. These cultural formations are not so large compared with
those we have discussed earlier, but they represent a rather interesting example
of coexistence in the same environment, adapting to it in different ways and
with different economic strategies.

The territory occupied by sites of the Itkul and Gamayun cultures extends
in a narrow band (about 150 km wide) along the eastern slope of the Ural
Mountains from the Vagil, Tura, and Rezh rivers in the north to Chelyabinsk
city in the south (Fig. 8.1). The local environments include the dendritical
system of fresh water mountain lakes and rivers of the Ob' River basin, a
continental climate favorable for hunting and fishing, and containing unlimited
forest and mineral resources.

Both cultures are dated to the period between the eighth and third centuries
BC, with some differences in internal chronology (Bel'tikova 1993; Borzunov
1992). Both of them lack archaeological burials with a few exceptions in the
Itkul culture.

The Gamayun culture is rather archaic in appearance. At the beginning of
its study, some scholars placed it in the Bronze Age (Borzunov 1992). Open or
fortified settlements and fortified houses represent the Gamayun culture. The
latter are considered as house-refuges, having solid wooden walls with a ditch
and strengthened by an earthen bank (Fig. 8.2). The average total area of such
a construction is about 600 m², from which the living space varies between
40 and 400 m². These houses were characteristic of the earlier period than the
later one. Among the open settlements, there are small stable villages consisting

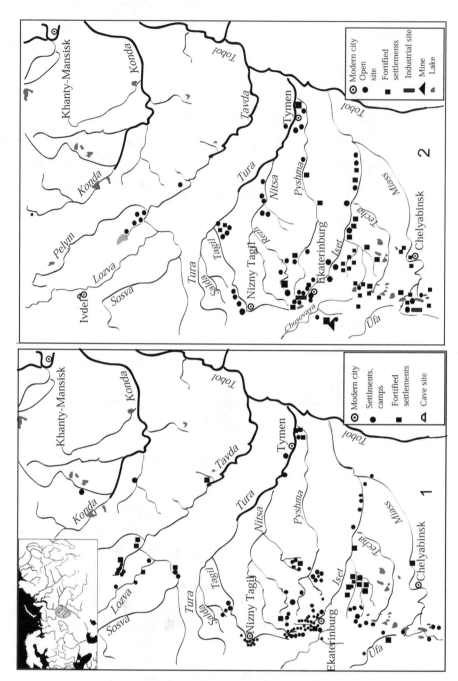

Figure 8.1. Distribution of sites of the Gamayun culture (1) and the Itkul culture (2).

278

of several houses, and seasonal short-time hunting-fishing camps. The typical Gamayun habitat consists of one or two houses.

Fortified villages range in relative scale: small (96–1,000 m²), medium (1,100–2,000 m²), and larger (3,200–5,300 m²), and occupy the low hills and promontories along riverbanks and promontories (Fig. 8.3). The larger villages served for constant habitation and are more characteristic for the later phase; the smaller ones were mainly frontier-guard stations. According to Borzunov's observation (1992), the fortified settlements are chiefly concentrated on the periphery of the occupied territory. Overall, the Gamayun fortifications are quite simple, consisting of ditches and ramparts built of earth and wood. The houses vary from small hovels and *chums* (portable houses of conic form) to stable pillar-framed wooden houses with one or two sections. The

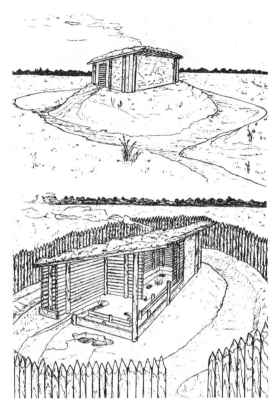

Figure 8.2. Artistic reconstruction of the Gamayun fortified houses (after Borzunov 1992).

houses served not only for living needs but also for some domestic activities.

The excavated sites yielded a great quantity of stone tools, a number of bone objects, and a few copper and iron items. The pottery, which distinguishes the Gamayum groups from the other groups, traditionally has talc, quartzite, and chamotte additives in the clay. The round-bottomed, low, and large open bowls are completely decorated with hole-crossed, hole-hatched, and wavy-rolling stamps arranged in rather standard zones and design patterns (Fig. 8.4–1). The "visiting card" of the Gamayun ornamentation is the crosslike stamp; the major area in which it is found is western Siberia, covering its southernmost taiga zone and northern forest-steppe stretching from the Trans-Urals up to the Middle Ob' (the so-called massive of cultures with stamped crosslike ornaments). These cultures are rooted in the Late Bronze Age of the Lower Ob' River forest area, from which some population groups moved southward because of overly humid conditions that occurred there at the turn of the second and first millennia BC (Borzunov 1992; Kosarev 1991). Archaeological and paleoenvironmental materials unambiguously testify to the crisis which occurred during the Late Bronze Age in the Lower Ob' basin. The cooling and humidification in the taiga always reduced the potential for hunting and

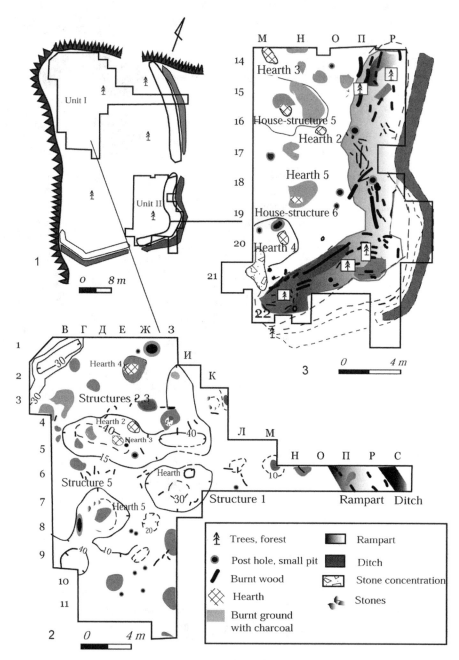

Figure 8.3. The Zotinskoye 2 fortified settlement: (1) general plan; (2) excavation area I; (3) excavation area II (after Borzunov 1992).

fishing economies: lakes became swamps and animals left for better ecological niches. The populations moved along the rivers. In the beginning (tenth–ninth centuries BC), migrations and resettling were directed to the north and north-west; the sites with pottery, decorated with typical figured stamps, appeared

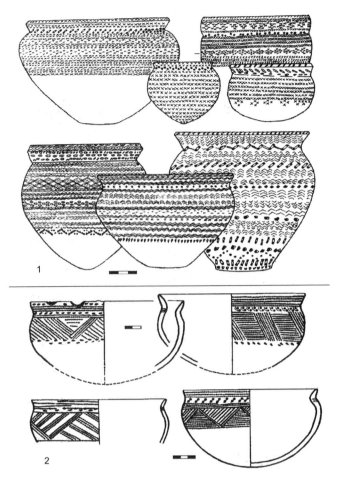

Figure 8.4. 1 – Gamayun pottery; 2 – Itkul pottery (after Borzunov 1992).

in the tundra zone. The small size of the Late Bronze Age and Gamyun sites show that the migrating communities were rather small: not more than twenty or thirty people, perhaps clan groups or extended families (Borzunov 1992).

One of the groups came to the Urals in the late ninth century BC. It brought its culture and subsistence economy, which was typical for the taiga, zone and based on hunting, fishing, and gathering. During the period of adaptation, the Gamayun population became acquainted with and adopted some elements of stockbreeding and metalworking. The bones of wild animals (elk, roe deer, and reindeer) amount to 80–90 percent of the osteological collections in the middle Urals, and 50 percent in the southern Urals. Meanwhile, what is striking in this culture is the great variety of stone tools and minerals that were used for these tools. There is a large variety of granite, sand-rock, argillite, jasper, sardonyx, chalcedony, quartzite, talc, and rock crystal. The majority of Gamayun stone tools are multifunctional and used in hunting, slaughtering, and fell (hide) processing.

The Gamayun newcomers came to the Urals where the aboriginal population – the early Itkul groups, descendents of the Mezhovka cultural tradition of the Final Bronze Age – had harnessed the local mineral resources for metal production. By all appearances, the relations between the early Itkul and Gamayun groups were rather tense from the very beginning. This is witnessed by the number of Gamayun fortified houses and traces of destruction of Gamayun villages (Borzunov 1992). With the passage of time, the new and aboriginal populations came to a consensus and formed some sort of symbiotic system based on a division of labor and specialization.

Archaeologically, the habitation sites and metallurgical workshops represent the Itkul culture. All materials from the Itkul sites explicitly point to the metallurgical specialization of local communities. Yet, in the eighteenth and nineteenth centuries, the rich collections of bronzes, which later would be assigned to the Itkul culture, were assembled by amateurs and professionals. A certain number of these objects collected during that time was deposited in some European museums. In particular, a rather large collection is in the National Museum of Finland in Helsinki. Because of special research undertaken by Bel'tikova in the 1960s–1990s, we now have a relatively comprehensive notion of the Itkul materials.

About 115 Itkul sites are located in the area of major concentration of mineral deposits, including copper ore and talc deposits (Bel'tikova 2002). The sites form seven clusters, comprising from two to nine sites are located 30–50 km from one another, rarely as much as 90 km. Several sites are situated at a distance of 300 km from the mainland. These sites are in western Siberia, and they do not have any trace of metallurgy.

The majority of the Itkul sites are fortified villages or fortified metallurgical workshops, 80 percent of which occupy the high topographic positions (10–40 m) of rivers or lake terraces (Fig. 8.5). These are hill plateaux, rock grounds, or parts of promontories and riverbanks with windy areas. Occupied space varies between 250–3,800 m². Some of these sites have simple fortifications, consisting of a wall, moat, ditch, or groove. The walls were constructed with horizontally placed wooden logs, strengthened by additional clay and/or stone pitching. Earth and stone were the infill between double walls. Earthen moats (2.8–5 m wide) followed the wall circuit. The typical layout for the small and middle-sized fortified villages was a closed circular, rectangular, or oval layout and occupied ground that was more vulnerable. The bigger settlements (1,400–3,800 m²), took up very high topographic positions usually with an open-order defensive line and were confined to rectangular-, semioval-, or trapezoid-shaped grounds.

The Itkul cultural deposits are distinctive. As a rule, they are not thick (not more than 80–90 cm), with specific traces of metallurgical activity – crumbly dark-brown humus with cherry or black-colored nuances, containing crumbs of ore, burned bones, technical ceramics, slag, fragments of pine or birch bark, and a great deal of ash. The living areas do not have such features.

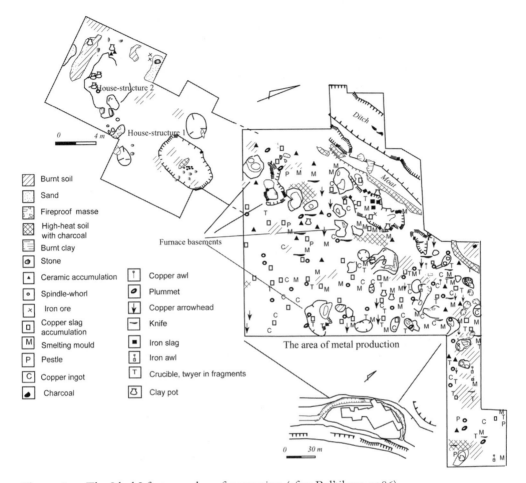

Burnt soil

Sand

Fireproof masse

High-heat soil with charcoal

Burnt clay

Stone

Ceramic accumulation

Spindle-whorl

Iron ore

Copper slag accumulation

Smelting mould

Pestle

Copper ingot

Charcoal

Copper awl

Plummet

Copper arrowhead

Knife

Iron slag

Iron awl

Crucible, twyer in fragments

Clay pot

Figure 8.5. The Itkul I fortress: plan of excavation (after Bel'tikova 1986).

There are a range of structures discovered in the Itkul settlements. They fall into three groups: living houses, living houses with remains of metal production, and a variety of structures connected with special productive functions. Rectangular semisubterranean and surface-based houses are of a pillar-framed construction and are rather small (25–58 m²) with a simple interior – one or two hearths, wooden plank-beds, and shallow floor pits with clay plastering (Bel'tikova 1997; Borzunov 1992). In small working areas, people smelted copper, sometimes worked with iron, but, more often, they served for just metal processing (without mining and ore processing). The mass production of metal was either in larger dwellings or outdoors. The remains of numerous structures connected with this kind of activity are registered in the Itkul settlements.

All dwellings and workspaces are usually located along the fortifications or in open villages along the ground edges. The metal production was a well-run process, which included mining (sulphide and oxide copper ores), ore processing and transportation, metal smelting, and object manufacturing. Eliquation

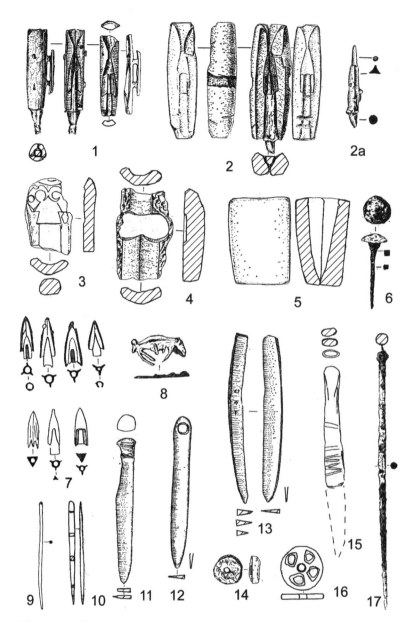

Figure 8.6. Materials from Itkul sites (after Bel'tikova 1986).

(melting) was executed on nonnatural blowing in furnaces and ovens. These were of the simplest constructions, made of stone, wood, and clay with inside plastering.

Numerous artifacts attesting the metallurgical process come from the Itkul sites. Among them are diverse closed molds, of single or multiple usage, for flat and three-dimensional casting, made of clay, talcum stone, or copper. A large series of worked-pieces, wasters (arrowheads, knives, awls), and ore- and metal-processing instruments are included in the collections (Fig. 8.6).

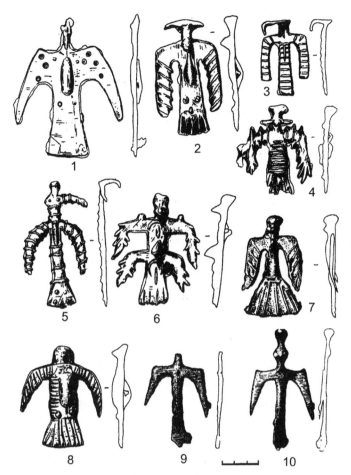

Figure 8.7. Bird-shaped idols from the Middle Trans-Urals, smelted in the Itkul workshops: (1–5, 6.8) from Azov-gora; (4) Sukhorechenskaya cave; (9, 10) Palatki – I site (after Viktorova 2002).

The Itkul metallurgists specialized mainly in bronze production based on local mineral deposits. Spectral analysis has revealed several chemical groups, among which pure copper is dominant (88.46 percent). This is a marker of Itkul production.

Tin bronze is only 6 percent, and tin-arsenic, arsenic, and lead-arsenic bronzes constitute the remainder (Bel'tikova 1997). The lack of natural hardeners in the Urals, in particular tin, is said to account for the small amount of bronze production. Tin was most likely imported from the Altai Mountains (Bel'tikova 1993). The assortment of Itkul production completely corresponds to the needs of that period: socketed bronze arrowheads of Scythian and Saka types, spearheads, daggers, knives, various tools, ornaments, amulets, and cast cult objects – birdlike idols (Fig. 8.7).

Scholars have ascertained several levels of intercultural specialization. Bel'tikova (1997) states that metal smelting and casting was carried out mainly in mountain clusters, and metalworking was concentrated in the periphery. Inside the clusters, there also were some operational divisions; there are sites with either full or a limited cycle of production (Borzunov 1981).

The yield of animal bones in the sites gives evidence about the Itkul life support subsystem. A large proportion (30–40 percent) of bones is from wild animals (elk, roe deer, bear, fox, and beaver) correspond with the forest environment. Among the domestic animals, horse and cattle constitute the largest number of bones in the osteological collections. It should be noted, however, that these collections are not very rich when compared to forest-steppe and steppe areas. On the contrary, in Bel'tikova's opinion, the bones of domestic animals do not necessarily testify to their local origin. They could have been the result of exchange operations with forest-steppe populations.

The Itkul pottery is quite recognizable. It is made of local clays with additives of talc, crushed stone, sand, chamotte, and some organic matter. The round-bottomed pots, of chiefly horizontal proportions, are decorated with rather standard comb-stamped patterns, covering only the pot's upper third (Fig. 8.4–2). In the northern regions, the ornaments are more complex, than in the south.

Bel'tikova used the large amount of data, stratigraphy, artifact chronology, and synchronization of external connections, to explore the territorial and chronological dynamics of the Itkul metallurgical center (Bel'tikova 1986, 1993, 1997). By 700–600 cal BC, metal production was concentrated in the narrow foothill area between the Isetskoye and Itkul lakes (about 80 km distance). All sites of this period combined living and production functions to produce a full cycle of base metal (from ore dressing to manufacturing of ready objects).

By 500 cal BC, the industrial activity covered an area of 270 km long from south to north. An interesting selectivity of sites is noticeable for this time: some of the sites did not present easy living conditions but were optimal for metal production (high rocky ground with steep slopes). In the piedmont clusters, the workshops with large-scale metal production and functional specialization emerged. Not only was bronze produced there but also some amount of iron. A division of labor between metallurgist and blacksmith is supposed to have existed in that period. Additionally, iron production stimulated the changes in Itkul metallurgy (Bel'tikova 1997: 20). The new production points emerged on the periphery of the Itkul territory, beyond the major ore deposits. This presupposes a certain level of regional specialization (Bel'tikova 1993).

These changes also resulted from regional economic situations and relations with neighboring societies. As we know, rather powerful nomadic groups that needed metal, in general, and weapons, in particular, occupied the southern Urals. These needs conditioned a dramatic increase in the metal production in the Itkul territory that is well attested archaeologically. The new workshops as well as the exchange points have emerged mainly in its southern part in proximity to the nomadic frontier. Furthermore, Itkul metal has been found in forest-steppe sites left by people who inhabited the Iset and Tobol river valleys. From these valleys, the Vorobyevo, Baitovo, and Nosilovo groups[1] were stylistically close to the Itkul. Altogether, they formed a so-called Iset association (Koryakova 1991a, 1994b), which was based on congenial relations and division of labor. In the seventh–fifth centuries BC, the Itkul center practically had a monopoly providing copper and copper items to this area (Bel'tikova 1997, 2002).

Some sites of the fifth–fourth centuries BC contain both Itkul and Gamayum artifacts (Bel'tikova 1993) that are regarded as evidence of close relationships between these two cultural groups, which complemented each other economically. Whereas the Itkul society was completely focused on metal production, the Gamayun groups were hunters, fishers, and some of them were most likely miners (if we remember their good skills in stone processing) as well as perhaps transporters of ore and charcoal-burners. It was not by chance that both cultures ended at the same time – by the end of the third century BC.

The Itkul external economic connections were rather large. They are traced four ways: (1) the chemical composition of metal, (2) the production technology of metal objects, (3) the morphology of objects, and (4) finds of corresponding types of pottery in contacting regions (Bel'tikova 1997). The Itkul metallurgists supplied metal not only to villages of the Iset association, but also to the Gorokhovo and Sargat groups (see later) and partly their production went to northern Kazakhstan and the forest regions. They had close relations with the Ananyino populations, which partly used Trans-Uralian ores for manufacturing various objects that were chiefly diffused westward. Some connections, perhaps less regular, existed with more remote areas: southern Siberia (Tagar culture), Upper Ob' region (Bolsherechye culture), and southern Kazakhstan (Saka cultures).

In the meanwhile, by the end of the third century BC, the Itkul metallurgical centers as a working system began to decline. This was caused by the wide use of iron, which did not require specialized production as did bronze.

THE FOREST-STEPPE CULTURES OF THE TRANS-URALS AND WESTERN SIBERIA

These cultures have only been outlined relatively recently, although their remains were first discovered here as early as the sixteenth century. Treasure seekers (*bugrovshdiks*) were at work at this time, and their activities were particularly destructive in the Trans-Urals and western Siberia.

Fortunately, not only robbers were interested in western Siberian graves. During recent years, notable advances have been made in our understanding of the cultural situation in the Trans-Urals and the western Siberian region. The pronounced intermediate positions, an intensity of influence of steppe and forest traditions, and a degree of their integration determine the specifics of the Trans-Uralian forest-steppe.

Current research indicates that, in the first part of the Iron Age, the Sargat culture played a major role in the development not only of the Tobol and Irtysh forest-steppe but also over a much wider area (Fig. 8.8). The sites are registered in the forest-steppe and partly in the northern steppe between the Urals in the west and the Baraba lowland in the east (Middle Irtysh River). The specific "veil" of the Sargat influence was formed around its core area. Its density varied depending on which cultures were covered by it.

The Sargat culture was a multicomponent system. For this reason, we distinguish two concepts: the Sargat culture as a narrowly defined archaeological assemblage, and a greater formation – the Sargat intercommunity, comprising all cultural groups between the Tobol and Irtysh rivers (Koryakova 1991b, 1997). It covers the period lasting about a thousand years: from the fifth century bc to the third century CE.

Since the 1920s, when the Sargat culture was first distinguished, the number of newly discovered sites has increased greatly. We should mention the names of the Russian archaeologists who made a great contribution to the study of western Siberian Iron Age: V. Levasheva, K. Salnikov, V. Chernetsov, V. Stoyanov, V. Gening, V. Mogil'nikov, M. Kosarev, L. Chindina, and others. A series of research reports, relating to different aspects of Sargat archaeology, has been carried out (Daire & Koryakova 2002; Koryakova 1994a, 1994b; Koryakova & Daire 1997, 2000; Matveyeva 1993, 1994, 2000). Several chronological models have been suggested. All of them are similar and are based on the typological development of material culture and funeral ritual with reference to Sarmatian archaeology. The database of radiocarbon dates is in the process of being filled out, and many new dates are not as yet systematically published. However, one can say that these absolute dates have not shaken the general chronological scheme suggested for the Sargat intercommunity formation. This scheme includes four phases reflecting basic changes, which are visible in archaeological records: (1) the formative phase (seventh–sixth centuries BC); (2) the phase of rising development (fifth–third centuries BC), (3) the developed or classical phase (second century BC–second century CE), and (4) the decline and transformational phase (third–fourth centuries CE). The boundaries between phases are not strict but, rather, conventional along a clear cultural continuity. The weakest points of Sargat chronology are its beginning and ending because of the transitional character of these periods. We suggest a general model of cultural development, which might have taken place in the Tobol-Irtysh forest-steppe during the Iron Age. This model is based on numerous analytical works, involving a great quantity of archaeological collections and other materials coming from hundreds of archaeological sites.

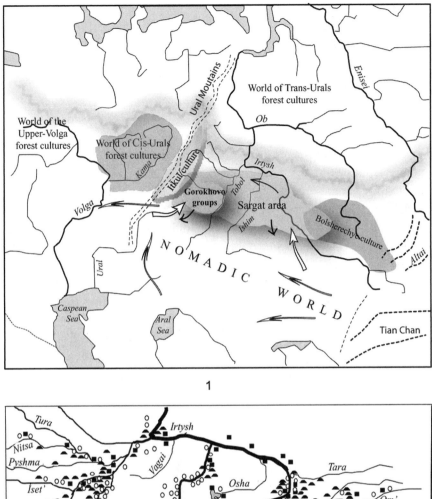

Figure 8.8. Cultural groups of the Iron Age in the forest-steppe zone of western Siberia. (1) general disposition; (2) distribution of the Sargat culture sites.

Pre-Sargat (Formative) Phase

We have already shown that on the eve of the Iron Age, the population, which had left its traces in the Mezhovka-Irmen cultural horizon of the Final Bronze Age, now inhabited the forest-steppe of the Urals and Siberia. In the steppe area of Kazakhstan and Middle Asia, the last centuries of the second millennium BC were represented archaeologically by the eastern variants of the Valikovaya pottery cultural horizon: the Sargary culture or Dandybai-Sargary, according to Varfolomeyev (northern and central Kazakhstan) and the Amirabad culture (Chorasmia). Archaeological material of Dandybai-Sargary settlements, where the forest-steppe pottery and Chorasmian wheel-made ware are embedded together in the same layer with local ceramics, provide us with evidence about active contacts between these regions.

In the ninth–eighth centuries BC, the western Siberian forest-steppe had quite weak links with the forming nomadic world. Additionally, it experienced pressure from the cultures of forest origin. The increasing number of sites with "forest" attributes evidences it, in particular, appearance in the forest-steppe of "cross-stamped" pottery ornamentation and increasing presence of bones of wild animals. The Gamayun cultural groups described earlier exemplify this process. Traditionally, this "wave" is explained by an overly wet period in the southern taiga and a southward shift of the forest biocenoses (Kosarev 1984). It is also possible that this process was preceded by rather good conditions in the taiga, stimulating some demographic growth and segmentation of communities. The steppe experienced an opposite reaction and was in some sort of crisis and transitional process toward greater pastoral mobility.

Thus, on the eve of the transition to the Iron Age, north–central Eurasia displayed the following cultural zones that differed by economic specialization and cultural appearance:

- The Steppe Eurasian zone, represented by elements of the latest occurrences of the Valikovaya pottery horizon and the Arzhan phase of the Scythian and Saka cultures (Chapters 4, 6);
- The Forest-steppe zone represented by the Mezhovka-Irmen horizon of the Final Bronze Age (Chapter 4);
- The Taiga zone represented by the Lozva-Atlym phase of the Late Bronze Age.[2]

These zones were not tightly bounded. Because of climatic instability, their outlines were unstable as well, activating internal migrational tendencies. From the north toward the forest-steppe, the Lozva-Atlym cultural groups penetrated moving chiefly along the forest landscapes. They changed the cultural appearance of the southern taiga and northern forest-steppe, forming up a short-lived but clearly expressed series of cultures stylistically united by cross-stamped ornamentation, one of which was described earlier (Gamayun culture).

At the same time, separate groups of people with Valikovaya pottery tradition settled in some of the lands of the southern forest-steppe. For example, in the Middle Irtysh area, one can see a chronological and territorial superpositioning of late Irmen, late Sargary, and late Suzgun traditions, as it was well represented in the material of the beautifully investigated Chicha settlement (Molodin & Parzinger 2001).

Because of the interactions and exchange by people, their achievements and ideas, the preconditions for the emergence of new cultural groups may have been shaped. Most probably, these nonuniform processes lasted until the seventh–sixth centuries BC (Koryakova 1991a).

As we know from Chapter 6, by the eighth century BC, the Saka tribal unions occupied the steppe area between the Urals and southern Siberia. The Uralian nomads tended to dominate the Itkul-culture populations, whose specialization in mining and metallurgy was of great significance to the neighboring societies.

In the Middle Iset and Middle Tobol basin, the cultural groups differed only by pottery traditions, representing various lines of cultural development going back to the local Bronze Age. They formed the Iset association dating to the period from the eighth to third centuries BC. The mortuary ritual of these cultures is hardly known. The inhabitants lived in semisubterranean and surface dwellings. Open and fortified settlements are characteristic. Unfortunately, these sites are poorly studied and not to any great extent; therefore, it is difficult to see in more detail the situation that came around in the eighth–early seventh centuries BC in the Middle Trans-Urals. However, it is indisputable that the processes revolving around the functioning of Itkul metallurgy played the decisive role. Itkul ceramics are encountered together with local types.

In addition to the cultural groups named earlier in the Middle Trans-Urals in the heart of the Pre-Sargatian phase (by the fifth century bc), the Gorokhovo cultural tradition emerged (Fig. 8.8). This process was stimulated by the growing influence coming from the south. As we saw earlier, the nomads of the southern Urals traveled along the pastures between Central Asia and the Urals. In the summer, they usually migrated toward the southern forest-steppe. This accounts for the funeral rituals of the Trans-Uralian population having much in common with nomadic rituals; both share northern orientations of bodies, wooden funeral tentlike constructions, and an almost identical suite of grave goods (see Chapter 6).

It is believed that the Gorokhovo cultural group resulted from a process in which several components took part. A part of the population of the Iset association, with Sargary-Mezovka roots, under the influence of various factors (climatic, economic, and political) gradually accepted mobile forms of pastoral herding. Nomads accelerated this process. As they were familiar with the cultural world of Central Asia, they could bring its elements (architecture, fortification system, and pottery) to the Trans-Uralian forest-steppe.[3] According to recent research (Tairov 2000), in the seventh–fifth centuries BC, the nomads of the southern Urals were linked culturally and probably, politically, to the Saka tribal confederation. Then, the funeral ritual of the Gorokhovo population appeared in an almost ready-made package, and many attributes of the Gorokhovo funeral ritual have some Saka "flavor." This is exemplified by the Skaty burial ground – a cemetery of the Gorokhovo culture aristocracy (Fig. 8.9) (Daire & Koryakova 2002).

Because it was formed under the influence and with the direct participation of South Urals nomads, the Gorokhovo culture became an organic part of the system of "steppe–forest-steppe," maintaining a balance of interactions within it. We believe that the formation of this system was speeded by the social rise of nomadic society, demonstrating clear evidence of far reaching social stratification. By the fifth century BC, huge kurgans sharply contrasting with numerous middle- and small-size mounds appeared in the southern forest-steppe. Unfortunately, they have been studied only on a limited scale because of clear markers of ancient robbery and the very high price of excavation.

The Gorokhovo culture initiated a cultural synthesis in the Iset and Tobol area, but it did not destroy the system of relations existing around the Itkul metallurgical center. Therefore, the Trans-Uralian sites demonstrate, on the one hand, the diversity of ceramic traditions, and, on the other, the stability of interrelations between them.

An analogous process occurred in the eastern part of the Tobol and Irtysh forest-steppe, where it developed on the basis of late Irmen culture with participation of a nomadic component as well. A great number of sites distributed across a vast territory including the upper Ob' forest steppe, Altai, Baraba, and Irtish River valley, represented the late Irmen culture. Researchers believe that the Irmen culture was responsible for the emergence of the Sargat cultural core-tradition. In the middle Irtysh area, as in the west, this process occurred in conditions of growing dispersal and weakening of internal connections that caused the destruction of traditional informational links between population groups and generations of the Final Bronze Age. The irregularity of cultural evolution, conditioned by the transition to new economic orientation and new relations, determined the intermixture of new and old traditions.

Gorokhovo-Sargat Phase

It would not be an exaggeration to say that the second half of the first millennium BC was a "Golden Age" of the western Siberian forest-steppe. Archaeologically, the greatest number of sites compared with preceding and subsequent periods represents this time.

By the early fifth century BC, the situation became stable and the forest-steppe conclusively came under the strong influence of steppe societies. In the Middle Trans-Urals the Gorokhovo cultural complex reached its peak. Here we find both open and fortified settlements demonstrating a rather high level of architecture, and burial grounds with clear features of nomadic burial practices, for example, tent-shaped wooden constructions and pit-graves with "podboi" (niches in the longitudinal wall). The Gorokhovo fortresses were implanted on strategically suitable grounds along the rivers of the Tobol basin. These are

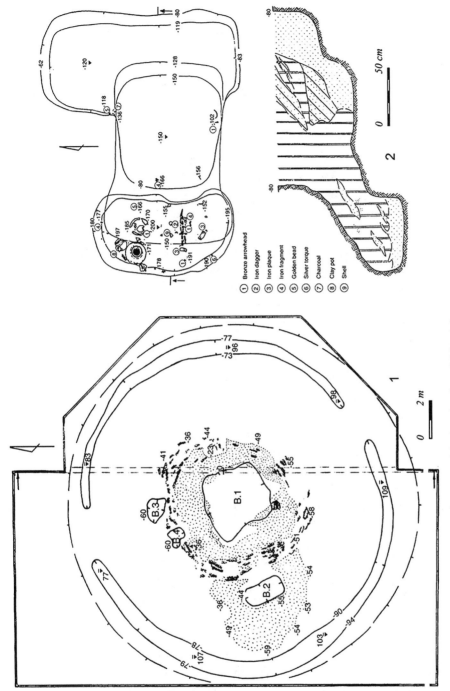

Figure 8.9. The Skaty cemetery, kurgan 4:(1) view in plan; (2) burial 3.

① Bronze arrowhead
② Iron dagger
③ Iron plaque
④ Iron fragment
⑤ Golden bead
⑥ Silver torque
⑦ Clay pot
⑧ Charcoal
⑨ Shell

of two types: frontier forts, characteristic for the southern part of the tribal territory (Fig. 8.10), and middle and large composite settlements consisting of fortified ground and open inhabitancy areas. There are also smaller or larger open villages. Gorokhovo houses are rather interesting. The leading type is a combined building, comprising living and economic rooms linked by a long corridor. This standard was reproduced all over the territory, as evidence of a stable architectural tradition. The level of architecture of the Gorokhovo population was relatively high for that time.

Large elite barrows, including very big kurgans, became an organic part of the local landscapes. Their construction was analogous to the ones found on the steppe, and they were furnished with rich grave goods placed in complex burial chambers. Burial grounds are of the kurgan type, predominantly with one to three graves. The graves are usually individual or (rarely) collective inhumations, accompanied by pieces of meat, liquid food, and some goods, corresponding to the status of the dead. Some pits showed evidence of vertical wood pillars supporting an upper covering, in particular, a tent-shaped daylight surface construction; these are especially characteristic of western areas close to the South Urals. In the mountain areas, there are some modest burials of herdsmen, without visible markers, almost without any offerings. Gorokhovo pottery, made of clay with the essential admixture of talc, morphologically and ornamentally resemble Sarmatian pottery, on the one hand, and the Sargat ware, on the other.

Abundant archeozoological material clearly testifies to a stockbreeding economic basis of the Gorokhovo society. The closest historical parallel can be found in the Bashkir model of a seminomadic economy.

Consolidation of the Gorokhovo groups, which reached its peak in the fourth century BC, was stimulated by political influence and the direct impact of southern nomadic groups to the Itkul association area. Remember that in about the fifth century BC, because of the destabilization of the political situation in the steppe, some Saka groups who usually travelled between the Chorasmia and southern Urals had to change their traditional routes, transfer their center to the north, and establish their encampments near the forest-steppe (Tairov 1991, 2000). Climatic change also may have stimulated the amount of activity found on the steppe. By the mid-first millennium BC, desert and semidesert landscape conditions had formed over most of Central Asia and Kazakhstan. But in the southern Urals and western Siberian steppe, conditions more propitious for the pastoral economy continued. At that time, the forest-steppe had good plant and water resources and segments of the steppe population repeatedly poured into the region.

Some visual image of these processes can be seen in so-called Sapogovo hoards (Fig. 8.11). They were found along the Karbolka river (southern Urals), on the border between the southern nomads and Gorokhovo lands, and composed of eighteen metal anthropomorphic objects, made in a treelike style

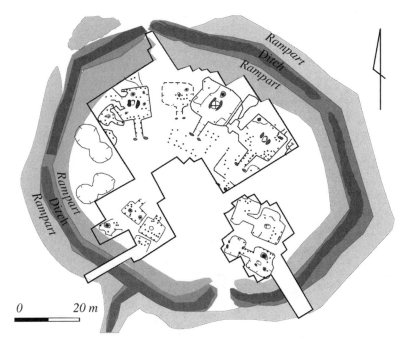

● Pit, depression   ☉ Hearth

Figure 8.10. The Gorokhovo fortress.

(Tolmachev 1912). The figurines had various armor images (daggers and swords). Stylistic analysis of the armor allows scholars to relate the hoard to the fourth–third centuries BC. Technologically, these figures are close to the flat cult figure-castings, which were widely spread in the forest zone between the fifth century BC and twelfth century CE. They are likely of Itkul production.

The Gorokhovo culture, which has been studied systematically in recent years, demonstrates the following attributes: (1) clear core-territory and its spatial extension; (2) pronounced settlement and burial hierarchy; (3) monumental and ordinary funeral architecture, and (4) military makeup. These allow us to interpret its society in terms of a tribal union or chiefdom of a nomadic model.[4]

The process of Gorokhovo consolidation ran in parallel with the strengthening of Sargat dominance coming from the east. From the fifth century BC onward, the Sargat culture spread its influence all over the western Siberian forest-steppe, from the Irtysh area to the Urals, to the territory that was controlled by Gorokhovo policy.

The strength of the Sargat culture also resulted from the inclusion of several components. Its substratum was the local ancestral population; the superstratum was presumably composed of nomadic and seminomadic groups coming from the northern Kazakhstan area. The earliest kurgans with Sargat pottery are discovered there. There probably was not a mass invasion but just a gradual

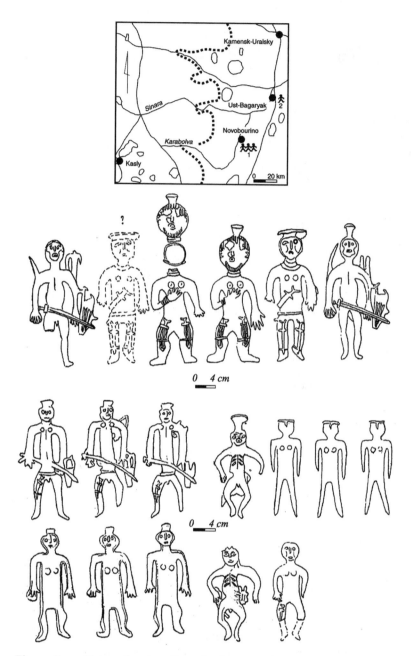

Figure 8.11. Bronze figurines from the Sapogovo hoards (Trans-Urals).

northward movement. These groups were probably not numerous, but more active and militant, possessing stronger ideological power in which the rising aristocracy played a consolidating role.

To support the hypothesis about the Ugrian affinity of the local component of the forest-steppe culture, which is probable because of cultural continuity there, we shall have to suppose the introduction of an Iranian linguistic

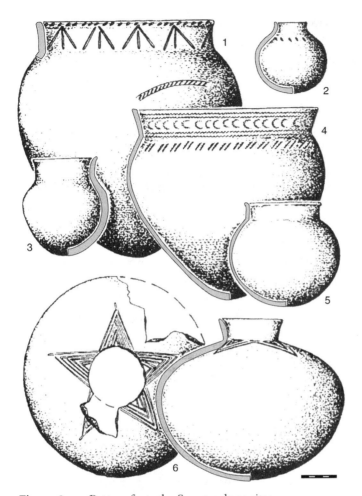

Figure 8.12. Pottery from the Sargat culture sites.

component (southern nomads) into the Ugrian surroundings (Koryakova 1994c, 1998). This does not contradict the model of a later cultural process occurring in the territory during the course of the formation of the Siberian Tatars. For example, Tomilov (1986) writes that in the thirteenth century CE the Turks[5] came to settle in the Tura region (Trans-Urals), which was originally occupied by the Ugrians. In about three hundred years, historical documents tell of a predominantly Turkic-speaking population in this region. The nomads of different clans very often competed for control over forest-steppe and forest areas, from where it was possible to obtain fur, undoubtedly valuable at all times.

By the fourth centuries BC, the number of sites increased and the Sargat cultural complex had become clearly dominant all over the territory between the Urals and Baraba lowland. This is manifested by a significant presence of Sargat ceramics (Fig. 8.12), which are found together with other ceramic types; this is especially characteristic for the westerly (Trans-Uralian) area. In burials there, the Sargat vessels were often accompanied by pots of Gorokhovo type. Many vessels, having a Sargat profile are decorated in the Itkul fashion, or they have a talc temper as found in the Gorokhovo culture. The interrelationship was mainly realized among the Gorokhovo, Itkul, and Sargat cultural core-traditions. The Pavlinovo archaeological complex (Fig. 8.14), which was systematically studied during the last decade, is a good example of Gorokhovo-Sargat interrelationship (Koryakova et al. 2004).

The strengthening of Sargat influence was accompanied by a cultural levelling over a vast area. It was expressed in common principles of funeral ritual, common ornamental canons, in particular, such as the "star" motive (Fig. 8.12), common forms of architecture and house building. At the same time, the active inclusion of groups that were different in origin and economic orientation, created ethnographic specifics of separate variants of the Sargat entity; these were not less than seven in number.

We have no evidence, which would points to tension between the Gorokhovo and Sargat groups. However, it is quite probable that the westward incursion of Gorokhovo elements and their impact on the Prokhorovo (Early Sarmatian) cultural complex might have been a consequence of the Sargat domination of the Trans-Urals. But the time from the fifth to the third centuries BC was likely marked by a certain balance between the two main components of the Sargat policy. Moreover, the Gorokhovo tradition existed in the late period as well, in ritual, in house building, and in pottery making.

As mentioned earlier, the first impact from the nomadic area was assigned to the Pre-Sargat phase, it was rather long but not of an expansionist character. However, at the end of the third century BC, a new cycle of nomadic shift began to be associated with the Sarmatians. From the end of the fourth century BC onward, the Early Sarmatian nomads had begun gradually to leave the southern Ural steppe and move partly westward, partly southward to where their descendants would later take part in campaigns against the Greco-Bactrian state.

Complexes with typically Sarmatian fire remains, chalk dust, and latitudinal body orientations appeared, and the number of warriors' graves increased. Moreover, the place and role of wooden tent constructions was modified. They were gradually transformed into flat extended platforms.

Nevertheless, the process of internal consolidation and integration was clearly associated with the forest-steppe. The latter has never been empty. Despite whatever environmental or political "storms" ran over it, some aboriginal component, flexibly reacting to all external impulses, was always preserved.

Classic Sargat Phase

At the end of the third century BC, one can see clear features of cultural stabilization. The Sargat phase represented an amplification of a process begun during the preceding period among the elite. The population of the western

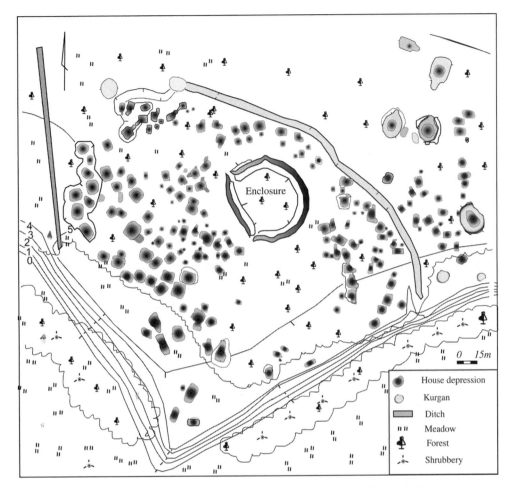

Figure 8.13. The Sargat culture, Batakovo archaeological complex on the Irtysh River.

Siberian forest-steppe followed the steppe societies in terms of their social and cultural development. This came about because of the rise in iron technology, weapon production, and an involvement in long-distance exchange networks (see later), especially between the nomadic chiefdoms of Europe, the Urals and the Altai and state-organized societies of Central Asia.

The notion of population growth is evidenced by a large number of archaeological sites dated between the second century BC and the late second century CE (in contrast, the number of simultaneous steppe sites in the South Urals was reduced). Classical attributes of the Sargat archaeological complex relate to this period.

The settlement pattern was represented by small and large open and fortified sites, forming territorial clusters on riverbanks at a distance of 30–40 km from each other. According to this pattern, and an almost epidemic presence of Sargat pottery in the settlements together with other types of pottery, internal social interactions were rather active. A cluster consisting of several open villages

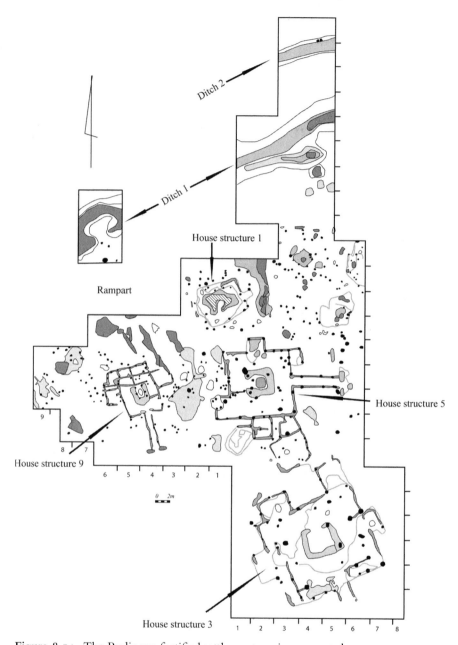

Figure 8.14. The Pavlinovo fortified settlement: major excavated area.

usually centered around one large fortified settlement was marked by attributes of long-term habitation (Fig. 8.13). A concentration of aristocratic cemeteries in some given areas indicates tribal territories.

Large timber-built houses have been studied in the villages. Dwellings consisted of one or several rooms, which were differentiated by size and interior structure. In the Trans-Urals, the Sargat architectural pattern was based on

1

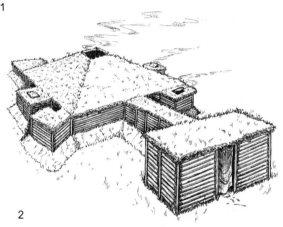

2

Figure 8.15. The Pavlinovo settlement. House no. 5: (1) general view of the floor level; (2) artistic reconstruction (drawing by A. Kovrigin).

the Gorokhovo principle of one-row linked between rooms, but here it was expanded by the addition of more rooms, the number of which could be three or four. Together with these, there are small semisubterranean dwellings or houses used for some economic purpose. This was seen particularly in the series of various buildings excavated in fortified settlements (Fig. 8.14; 8.15).

All kinds of funeral rituals were preserved, but several new features appeared. As a rule, every barrow contained more than one body – from two to twenty bodies. Burial grounds, as a rule, were collective-grave barrows, belonging to family groups. The funeral rite and grave goods were standardized. One or two ditches surrounded the kurgans. As a rule, one or two graves in the center were the primary burials, and later burials were arranged around the periphery. There were several types of grave pits some with straight vertical walls and others with benched walls. Burial chambers displayed some elements of house design. The

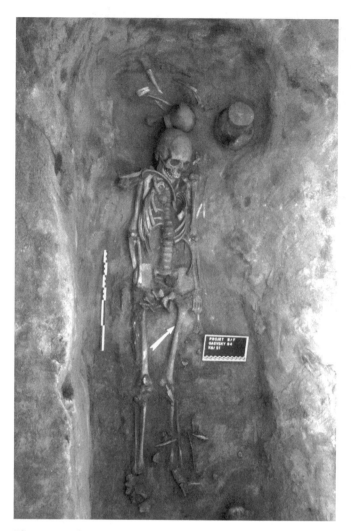

Plate 8.1. The Sargat type burial from the Gayevo cemetery (photo by P. Courtaud).

funeral ceremony included animal sacrifices and food offerings (Plate 8.1). Some ethnographic details such as the methods of constructing the roof and the erection of vertical posts within funeral chamber become apparent.

The late 1980s was marked by several discoveries of unrobbed wealthy graves whose gold and silver objects can be compared to those in the Peter the Great Collection as well as to those collected by Witsen (Rudenko 1962). These graves were excavated in the Tobol and Irtysh areas and in particular in the Tutrino (Matveyev & Matveyeva 1987, 1992; Matveyeva 1993), Isakovka (Pogodin 1998a; Pogodin & Trufanov 1991), and Sidorovka cemeteries (Matushchenko 1989; Matushchenko & Tataurova 1997). The graves were similar to those in many Sargat cemeteries: many graves had been robbed, but some held wheel-made pottery fragments, remains of weapons, and gold appliqués. One interesting discovery was at Sidorovka kurgan 1, which had,

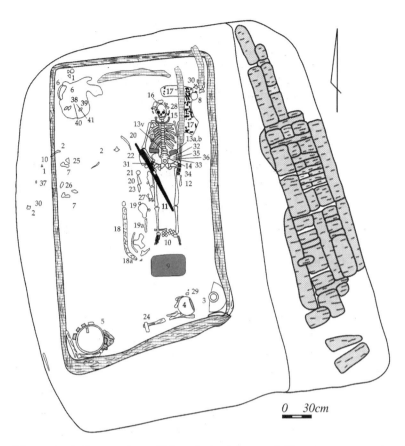

Figure 8.16. Sargat culture. Sidorovka burial ground. Kurgan 1, grave 2: (1, 2) animal bones; (3) big imported pot; (4–5) small and large bronze cauldrons; (6) silver phaleras; (6a) iron armoury; (7) silver buckles; (8) silver bowl; (9) piece of leather (vessel); (10) 2 gold-turquoise buckles; (11) iron sword; (12) iron knife; (13a.b)- 2 gold plaques; (13c) gold belt plaque; (14) silver belt buckle; (15) gold torque; (16) gold ornaments; (17) remains of gold-silver brocade; (18) remains of quiver decorated by brocade; (18a) 3 gold appliqués; (19) horse bones; (19a) 20 iron arrowheads; (20) 4 end bow plaques; (21) iron dagger; (22) big bead; (23) 6 small gold plaques; (24) iron axe; (25) big iron buckle; (26) small silver buckle; (27) remains of bone object; (28) gold earring; (29) silver decoration; (30) handmade pot; (31) 9 silver rivets; (32) piece of leather belt; (33) bronze ring; (34) silver chibouk of smoking pipe; (35) piece of felt; (36) small silver bottle; (37) iron shank; (38) iron bits; (39) iron shank; (40) remains of iron spear; (41) gold bell (after Matushchenko & Tataurova 1997).

apart from the destroyed central burial, a well-preserved peripheral burial. Its large pit held two interments; the upper grave was destroyed, but it protected a lower well-preserved one. It is difficult to say whether this burial was deliberately or accidentally preserved, but its contents were intact and rich (Fig. 8.16).

Another elite burial was excavated by Pogodin in 1989 in the Isakovka cemetery, Omsk oblast. Especially rich was grave 6 in kurgan 3. It lay at the periphery of the kurgan and overlapped its circular outer ditch. The grave was covered with a massive three-layer wooden roof. The bottom covering rested on a wooden frame forming a fairly large funeral chamber. A wooden bed (2.2 × 1 m) held the remains of a man wrapped in golden textiles; his head was oriented to the northwest. Outside the chamber, between its wall and the northern wall of the pit, were two large bronze cauldrons holding a wooden spoon and the remains of horse meat and bones. A closed clay pot with five tubes and white powder inside, used for smoking, hung by an iron chain on the north wall. A large vessel of Central Asian origin and a leather vessel stood in the southwest corner, and a small handmade Sargat-type pot was placed near the head of the deceased. Near the skull, a large silver phiale, identical to one found in the Kazanluk district in Bulgaria (Marazov 1998), held remnants of silk, another silver phiale with a lotus decoration and a silver bowl adorned with dolphins and swimming ducks were placed near the feet of the dead man (Fig. 8.17). Alongside his right knee was a bronze kettle or wine container. The deceased wore a massive gold torque around his neck and one gold earring. Two gold plaques decorated his wide red belt, to which was attached by a stone staple a lacquer-covered scabbard holding a long iron sword; the scabbard had been placed across the body from right to left. An iron dagger adorned with stone-inlaid gold plaques hung from the belt as well. Beside the western wall were iron armor and a large iron belt (Pogodin 1989; 1996; 1998a; b).

These graves and other graves in the Isakovka cemetery produced rich material, including heavy weapons (Fig. 8.18), gold objects decorated with turquoise (Plate 8.2), silver phaleras (Plate 8.2), bowls or phialae (Plate 8.3) (Livshits 2002), and beautiful bronze cattle and vessels of the Han dynasty period in excellent preservation (Pogodin 1989).

One can dwell on three inscribed silver bowls coming from the Isakovka 1 burial ground (kurgan 3) excavated by Pogodin in 1989. Two bowls carry Chorasmian inscriptions, and one has a Parthian inscription.

On silver phiale 1 (Plate 8.3), the inscription is engraved smoothly on its plain everted rim. According to Livshits (2002: 43–6), this inscription marks the earliest stage of Chorasmian writing, which derives from the Aramaic alphabet of the Achaemenid epoch. He provides an almost complete translation: "This banquet bowl is for Barzavan, son of Takhumak ... His Majesty, king Amurzham, son of the king Wardan, (this bowl) is made for him as a gift ... on the third (of the month) frawarin."

The second Isakovka bowl is conical-shaped (Fig. 8.17). The composition, three dolphins alternating with three flowers, is depicted in the center of the interior. The natant dolphins and ducks are also depicted along the bowl's interior rim; the inscription is engraved rather deeply on the exterior. Livshits (2002: 53) could decipher only part of the inscription: "This bowl, of the weight (?) by 120 staters ... to the sovereign Wardak ... the gift to him. ... Through mediation of Ruman (?) Tir."

Figure 8.17. Silver bowl # 2 from the Isakovka 1 kurgan 3, grave 6. The composition from three dolphins alternating with three flowers was depicted in its central part from inside. The natant dolphins and ducks are also depicted along the bowl's rim form inside; the inscription was engraved rather deeply on its external side. Livshits decoded it partially: "This bowl, of the weight (?) by 120 staters... to the sovereign Wardak... the gift to him... Through mediation of Ruman (?) Tir" (after Livshits 2002, Pogodin 1989).

The third silver bowl carries the Parthian inscription, rendered in pointillé on the exterior. It gives the bowl weight: "5 karshes, 2 staters, 1 drachma" (Lifshits 2002: 54). The interior center of the bowl is decorated in octofoil along with a gilt garland and narrow fillet. Stylistically, the first phiale relates to the Achaemenid metalwork tradition (Ozcen & Osturk 1996: 38–41); the two others find their closest parallels among the bowls in the collection of

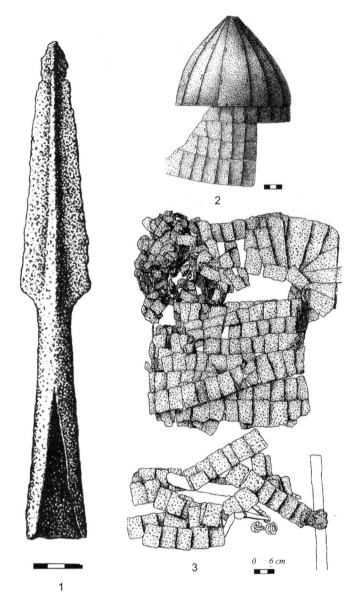

Figure 8.18. Sargat heavy weaponry: (1) iron spear; (2) iron helmet; (3) iron armor and belt (after Pogodin 1998b).

the Getty Museum (treasures I, II, III) (Pfrommer 1993: 24) and in Thracian treasures (Marazov 1998).

At present, many vessels with Aramaic inscriptions come from the Sargat territory, among which should be included objects published by Trever (1940).

All of these valuable objects, found together with Chinese and Hunnic materials in the same grave, probably were either diplomatic gifts or trophies taken in raids to the southern lands.

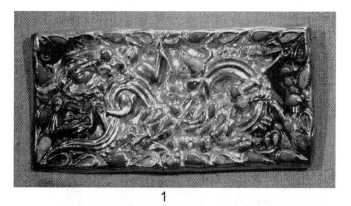

1

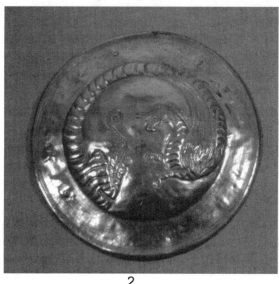

2

Plate 8.2. Objects from Sidorovka kurgan 1, grave 2: 1 (top) – Gold and turquoise belt plaque. Two gold belt plaques inlaid with semiprecious stones and decorated with a combat scene of two tigers and a wolf-headed serpent were found at the waist of the buried man. The tigers' bodies and the border were marked by tear-shaped cells. 2 (below) – Silver phalera (after Matushchenko and Tataurova 199).

The classification and distribution of grave goods together with an analysis of the constructional complexity testifies to the existence of several social strata (Berseneva 2005; Koryakova 1988; 1997; Matveyeva 2000). The high social status of people (Plate 8.4) is marked not so much by the grand mortuary constructions as by the character of the grave goods – the most prestigious were foreign objects. Another marked social statement was the luxury of the burial chamber, made of a wooden box with a couch and timber covering. Such burials can be arranged in the peripheral part of a barrow, and therefore the contrast between barrows is not striking.

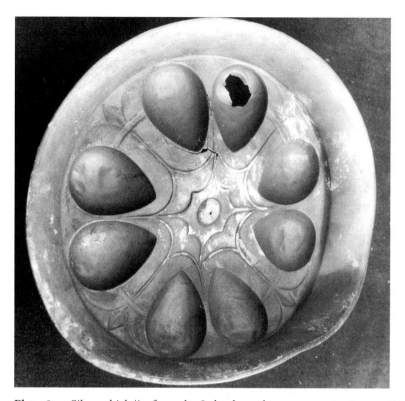

Plate 8.3. Silver phial #1 from the Isakovka 1, kurgan 3, grave 6, excavated by L. Pogodin. It weighs 612.2 g and has a plain averted rim. The inscription is engraved smoothly on its rim. According to Livshits, this inscription marks the earliest stage of Chorasmian writing, which derives from the Aramaic alphabet of the Achaemenid epoch. He translated it almost completely: "This banquet bowl is of Barzavan, son of Takhumak. His Majesty, king Amurzham, son of the king Wardan, (this bowl) is made for him as a gift... on the third (of the month) frawarin (after Livshits 2002; original photo by L. Pogodin).

All research reveals the age and gender gradations within Sargat society and symbolism corresponding to them. Archaeologically are visible two age levels: adult and subadult separated by an age of twelve to fourteen years. The *adulthood* was indicated by these artifacts, which never accompanied children (weapon, horse bridle, cult objects). However, if we remember the burials of small children with rather rich personal belongings discovered in the Skaty cemetery, we can assume social status was inherited. Special analysis of Sargat burials recently undertaken by Berseneva (2005) has shown that weapons, horse harness, and ornaments marked rather gender than merely biological sex. Subadults composed a separate gender close to the status of women. Vertical status relations were determinative in Sargat funeral practice (Berseneva 2005: 20).

By contrast, there is an evident disparity between the number of buried people and the potential number of people that could be accommodated by

Plate 8.4. Sculptural reconstruction of people from the Sargat-culture elite burials (by G. Lebedinskaya).

settlements (Daire & Koryakova 2002; Koryakova 1997), Additionally, demographic parameters of the buried population are not normal (Razhev 2001); this can point to some selection the criteria of which we do not know. In this case, we have to suppose some alternative burial rituals, which did not leave traces in the archaeological record or at least have not yet been found.

Undoubtedly, at first the forest-steppe inhabitants adopted many military inventions from the southern nomads. However, in the second half of the first millennium BC, they made their own contribution to the general development of warfare. It seems likely, that the big composite (so-called Hunnic) bow[6] appeared in the Sargat area earlier than in the Sarmatian territory. Most probably, the Sarmatians adopted it from their northeastern neighbors. The bow of the Hunnic type was the best bow of the late first millennium BC (Khudyakov 1986).

Sargat burials of the third century BC have yielded bone plaques of a big bow, which coexisted with the small bows of the Scythian type. The latter was used for shooting small bronze arrowheads, manufactured by the Itkul metallurgists. The iron arrowheads, which appeared in mass in the third–second centuries BC, were assigned to the larger bow.

The complex of Sargat elite armament included a bow, dagger, long sword, and in special cases, a shield, helmet, and lamellar armor, initially fashioned from bone and leather, and then later from iron. The complex of elite weaponry, recovered from unrobbed graves in Sidorovka and Isakovka, belonged to the catafractarian type of heavily armed mounted warrior, which became widely known in Eurasia from the last centuries BC (Fig. 8.18). Horse harnesses are also very frequent finds, as are arrows. As the faunal analysis shows, the horse was the most respected animal, and judging by paleanthropological observations, the Sargat people spent some time on horseback (Razhev 2001). The elite graves described earlier are related to the end of the period in question. They yielded a number of objects with gold-turquoise ornament identical, on the one hand, to part of the Siberian Collection and, on the other hand, to those from Sarmatian tombs of the first-second centuries CE. This style, which is also known as the Sarmatian style, replaced the Scythian Animal Style in Eurasian steppe.

In Eurasia, there were eight regions of dissemination of items made in the "gold-turquoise" style: (1) Mongolia and Ordos, (2) the Sayan and Altai mountains, (3) the forest-steppe and steppe between the Ob' and Irtysh rivers, (4) the Seven Rivers basin (Semirechye), (5) Iran, (6) Bactria, (7) the Lower Syrdarya basin; and (8) Sarmatia (Treister & Yatsenko 1997/98: 53).

According to Rostovtseff (1929: 100–6), the creators and carriers of this new animal style were the Yueh-Chih who brought it to southern Russia. Tolstov (1948: 220) connected it to the Massagetae. Sarinaidi (1987) suggested that "gold-turquoise" objects were manufactured in Bactria alone. Some scholars believe that this style emerged in China in the third to second centuries BC, came into use among the Saka, and only after that became known in Bactria. Later, the style appeared in Sarmatia and then diffused westward as a symbol of aristocratic status (Yatsenko 1993).

According to Skripkin (1996: 164–5) and Yatsenko (Treister & Yatsenko 1997/98: 59), diffusion of the new style was connected with the westward migration of the Alans, who later would play a consolidating role in the formation of a strong military and political union in the east European steppe. One can suppose that the forest-steppe of western Siberia probably became acquainted with this style around the second to first centuries BC. The scenes depicted on Sargat finds are closer to the Chinese and Hunnic traditions. We consequently have to consider the hypothesis that there were stable contacts between the Sargat polity and the east and south, especially with Chorasmia and the Kang-Ku state. Among the imports into the Sargat territory, the objects deriving from Fergana, Bactria, and Chorasmia are dominant, about 15 percent come from the eastern (Hunnic) world and about 10 percent from the Cis-Urals area (Matveyeva 1995; 1997).

We can again refer to the large number of objects with Aramaic inscriptions and early Chorasmian inscriptions, which are generally rare, from the Sargat territory. Coins found by Siberian grave robbers and discussed in Rudenko's book (1962) suggest that their number might have been even greater. Some Roman coins were found in the Tobol area and near Omsk (Mogilñikov 1992: 304), and Chinese coins were discovered in the Baraba area (Polos'mak 1987).

Some scholars (Bokovenko & Zasetskaya 1993: 86) have concluded that the northern periphery of the Silk Road trade system embraced the distant lands of the western Siberian forest-steppe. Pogodin (1998a: 38) investigated the remains of lacquer objects from the Sargat burials and found about twelve belts and around twenty daggers and swords with lacquer coverings. Additionally, Pogodin (1996) collected a database of remains of silk fabric with golden stitching; these fabrics are rather numerous in the Sargat graves. All this bears witness to a rather strong power within Sargat society which should have been played as part of some agent participating in long-distance interactions.

We believe that the Sargat society was organized into a chiefdom consisting of several regional units (Koryakova 1996, 1997). Matveyeva (2000) shares this interpretation. Gumilev (1993a), referring to one Chinese map (Bichurin 1953c), mentions the Northern Ugrian Kingdom (Ui-Beigo), which was presumably located between the Tobol and Irtysh rivers and had peaceful relations with the Hsiung-nu. Unfortunately, we do not have any other literary evidence concerning the western Siberian forest-steppe. Meanwhile, the connections with the Hsiung-nu are archaeologically documented.

In about the third century BC, objects of Hunnic origin appeared in the eastern part of the Tobol and Irtysh area. These are bronze belt buckles and some types of iron arrowheads. Chinese written sources inform us about the Khan-Ku state, which became powerful after the collapse of Greco-Bactria and the dissolution of the Yueh-Chih tribal union. But later it was ruled by the Kushan kings and acted against the northern tribes, subjugating the Yantsai kingdom. Thus, its frontiers could have reached the southern Urals and western Siberia (Kuner 1961).

From the third century BC, the Sargat union was put under pressure by the gradual shift of the Kulay culture,[7] which dwelled in the forest zone. This is well evidenced by the appearance of the Kulay-culture sites in the forest-steppe. They are especially numerous in the Valley of the Irtysh River. This movement, which began first in the Irtysh area, had caused the eastern part of the population to depart from the Irtysh River towards the Trans-Urals and, partly, to the Altai area, where the sites with Sargat ceramics are recorded.

Late Sargat Phase

The late phase of the Sargat development (the third to fourth centuries CE) is represented by a much smaller quantity of archaeological material, most of which comes from the western (Trans-Urals) region. Recorded sites are in the form of burials under smaller barrows, sometimes encircled by a ditch suggesting that the main principles of the mortuary practice remained. On the one hand, we can see some very clear elements of nomadic funeral rituals presented in the burials; on the other hand, one can note the growing influence of the cultures originating in the forest. Although the number of Sargat sites decreased, those of the forest cultures increased. Archaeological material indicates evidence of certain depopulation and, obviously, political disintegration. A culture again passed to a state of dispersal.

The period of the third to fifth centuries CE, known as the period of the Great Folk Movement, was not, of course, the first in the chain of such events. Its progress had been signaled within previous processes. Iron technology had made the social and economic development of different regions of Eurasia relatively uniform, even if these regions were remote from the great states of that time. By the middle of the first millennium BC, the adoption of iron metallurgy was complete in the forest-steppe and now advanced to the forest zone of western Siberia.

Meanwhile, everywhere in Eurasia, cultural changes occurred during the second quarter of the first millennium CE. In the Kama basin, to the west of the Urals the Pyanobor union gradually disintegrated. In the southern Urals, the number of late Sarmatian sites greatly decreased. The general cultural degradation and transformation of these times were stimulated by climatic changes, the increasing of the Hsiung-nu influence and the rupture of a stable trade network.

SUMMARY: INTERACTIONS BETWEEN NOMADS AND FOREST POPULATIONS

In previous sections we have viewed three culturally different groups of societies, which by dint of their location had to interact. At the core of these contacts were nomadic societies, which periodically occupied the southern Ural and western Siberian steppe.

Mapping the nomadic sites demonstrates that, during the early period (the seventh to fifth centuries BC), their territory was limited to only the steppe landscapes (Ivanov 1995b). However, in the west, by the fourth century BC, the forest-steppe area of the Don and Dnepr basins was included culturally and politically into the Scythian kingdom (the so-called Scythoid cultures). To the east of the Volga River, the sites of the "Sauromatians" (Cis-Uralian nomads) are mostly situated in the steppe area rather than in the forest-steppe. There was no direct contact between them and the Volga Finno-Volgaic population of the Diyakovo and Gorodetskaya cultures. The Ananyino culture occupied the forest area and was open to association with the Cimmerians and Scythians but was almost closed for the south Uralian nomads. Additionally, the early Ananyino metallurgical centers were linked to Scythian polities. This is a very interesting observation, because the latter were more distant geographically than the south Uralian nomads. That is to say, material culture presents here the evidence about political preferences, which could exist between different Eurasian societies.

We also can see that at least a part of the forest-steppe was not populated during some time between the eighth and seventh centuries BC. The south Uralian nomads who were more involved in relations with the Saka tribal groups, used metalwork made in Trans-Uralian (Itkul culture) workshops. That is why we can see the evidence of a direct nomadic shift to the southwest forest-steppe as far as the Itkul territory. Of particular interest is that these two participants of interaction remained culturally different, as is seen in their absolutely different archaeological material culture, sign system, and funeral rituals.

It follows from the general theory of nomadism that this kind of economy and mode of life is very dependent on the environment and corresponding ecological conditions. The theory of ecological stress explains an alternation of periods of high nomadic activity and their periodic migrations (Zhelezchikov 1986). Because of the different climatic changes in different regions of the Eurasian steppe, some parts experienced conditions that were either overly arid or overly humid. During such conditions, the nomads were concentrated in highly productive regions. However, at other times, conditions were such that animal and human population growth forced nomads to migrate to other areas in search of better pastures and free lands. A high concentration of sites during the fifth to third centuries BC in the southern Urals indicates that this area was one such center in Eurasia.

However, not just ecological factors determined nomadic activity. It was important to have access to sources of metal, the closest of which was located within the Itkul territory. The new metallurgical centers, situated on both slopes of the Urals, were oriented to nomadic needs, supplying them with weaponry. The division of labor between different societies connected with different landscapes maintained mutual exchange relationships. Nevertheless, military and political factors, conditioned by nomadic activity and expansion, reinforced the tendency to internal integration.

As we have seen, until the late sixth century BC, the forest-steppe of western Siberia was relatively free of nomadic (Saka) influence. Initially, some individual objects of harnesses and weaponry indicated their presence; later, kurgan burials, including large barrows, appeared on the southern margin of the forest-steppe. Western Siberia, together with the Kazakhstan steppe, became a part of the same cultural and economic system, which centered on Central and Middle Asian states.

By the fifth century BC, a turning point for north–central Eurasia and the western Siberian forest steppe experienced the direct impact of the nomadic population. The new synthesis of cultures is represented by numerous sites displaying a settlement hierarchy and burial grounds which show an almost completely nomadic model of mortuary practice. It gives us a clear example of relationships between different economic systems and social structures.

This culture has been formed through interaction between nomads and the aboriginal population. The model of such interaction can be based on relations between settled herders, hunters, and pastoral nomads (Koryakova 1994c).

Reciprocal influence from the forest-steppe cultures, however, is traced in the Prokhorovo aspect of the Early Sarmatian culture. We see Prokhorovo sites spreading westward, some of them into the forest-steppe of eastern Europe. The southern part of the forest cultures of the Volga-Kama basin provides the evidence for strong Sarmatian influence; maybe even political domination. However, this influence is found mostly in the material culture and weaponry, but it absolutely did not touch any ideological sphere as there were strong differences in mortuary practice, art style, and sign system during the same period.

In the Cis-Urals, the forest population and nomads had to interact because of various factors, but they remained culturally and ethnically separated and never mixed. As has been described previously, the opposite situation was characteristic for the western Siberian forest-steppe, where the process of interaction with the nomadic population was much deeper.

In conclusion, we can note different forms of interactions that existed in the area under study.

The exchange of material goods appears quite inherent to all contacting societies, and it is evidenced by everyday objects. Ornaments and luxury goods (glass beads, female decorations, horse harnesses, and distinctive forms of weaponry), which at the beginning were not so numerous, were concentrated in the possession of the tribal elites of the forest population. There were several levels of exchange: from simple interclan and intercommunity barters to long-distance core/periphery relations. States could trade luxury goods with the intermediary of nomads to exchange of service, employ, horses, fur, leather, and even women. Core/periphery relations became of great importance in the second half of the first millennium BC. For the Uralian nomads, the states of Central Asia played the same role as the Greek cities of the Northern Pont for the Scythians, who regarded them as a source of wealth and luxury, coming both from robbery and from frontier trade.

With reference to nineteenth- to twentieth-century ethnographic examples from the same area, it is possible to suppose that some forms of tributary dependence of some forest societies on their nomadic neighbors may have existed. This can be seen through the traces of specialized production of the Ananyino and Itkul cultures, which were discovered in nomadic graves. Yet, most probably, it was distant exploitation, and nomads did not occupy the territory of these cultures.

Social interactions can be traced through the structural modifications of a culture. Changes in the funerary practices of the forest-steppe population toward the adoption of nomadic social and ideological models are visible only in the Trans-Ural forest-steppe. A necessary condition of this process is a readiness to accept new ideas and a new social order, a development usually occurring initially at the elite level.

Finally, direct invasion of nomads into the forest and forest-steppe was limited by environmental factors. However, in the event of this happening, its impact led to major cultural change and the formation of a new social network.

CHAPTER 9

SOCIAL TRENDS IN NORTH-CENTRAL EURASIA DURING THE SECOND AND FIRST MILLENNIA BC

This concluding chapter will summarize the material presented in the preceding chapters and highlight the basic events that occurred in the area under study during the second and first millennia BC.

It would be presumptuous to hope that we could present the course of social development with all its details. We will only try to indicate some features of this process. As mentioned earlier, thirty years ago, the social level of cultures situated on the "barbarian periphery" of the classical civilizations in north-central Eurasia was defined as primitive, and as having evolved gradually in a linear progression from collective to feudal relations. Today, we would suggest that social development in temperate Eurasia occurred cyclically. This territory "knew" both great highs and great lows, glory and declines, technological inventions and adoptions, social consolidations and disintegrations. Perhaps the most important consequence of its development was that this area organically evolved into large networks of Eurasian interactions.

Looking at Eurasian archaeology of the Bronze Age through the "eyes" of the Iron Age, one can see the difference between these two epochs. The latter is more understandable for our modern rational vision. Such notions as value, wealth, prestige, and status are quite close to our estimations. One cannot say the same about the Bronze Age.

The notable rise of complexity characterizes the current situation in Bronze Age archaeology. On the one hand, we see an incredible rise of data deriving from recent discoveries. New cultural types, sequences, and models are introduced into the old concepts, some elements of which either changed or precised. Thus far, perhaps the most notable issue concerns the redating of either many if not all cultures of that epoch toward an earlier time. All this makes the cultural landscape of the Eurasian Bronze Age rather complicated.

In examining the literature since the late 1980s, several dominant trends emerge. In recent publications, one can find terms applying to the Bronze Age cultures of the second millennium BC such as "Indo-European non-urban civilization of Eurasian stockbreeding province" (Malov 1995), "proto-urban," "quasi-urban civilization" (Zdanovich 1997a), "frustrated civilization" (Zdanovich 1995), or "early complex societies of the nonurban way of development" (Masson 1998), and so on. These sociological innovations indicate somewhat of a change of paradigms: from primitivism to modernism in social interpretations.

At the same time, traditional Marxist evolutionary models ascended to the stage theory: savagery, military democracy, and slavery was still in use. According to this model, the Bronze Age cultures were in the early stage of decomposition of the primordial society. Meanwhile, schematism of this model in the context of early periods and falseness in the context of later periods are now evident (Gei 2001: 84). A large number of archaeologists who share dissatisfaction with old theories are, however, skeptical about the potential of the archaeological record to reconstruct past social realities (moderate scepticism). According to them, the only certainty we can find is an age-sex structure, which is well reflected in the funeral ritual.

Nevertheless, in Russia general interest in social archaeology has gradually deepened. Yet, up to the present, some key positions on the interpretation of reasons and forms of long-term processes occurring in such an important area as the Urals are still not well formulated. This is because scholars usually deal chiefly with the problems of concrete cultures and do not often address the larger subjects.

By contrast, we would say that by force of some objective and subjective reasons, the greater part of the Eurasian territory is still out of the range of the theoretical vision of Western archaeologists. Therefore, many problems remain to be seen and looked at only within regional discussions.

We will attempt to look at the social landscape of central-northern Eurasia and its development and discuss some questions that appear interesting and important to us.

SOCIAL STRATEGIES OF THE SECOND MILLENNIUM BC

We hope that in previous chapters we have convinced the reader that steppe cultures of the Bronze Age are of key significance for understanding the long-term processes that occurred in the vast Eurasian space.

There is no doubt that during this period the area was neither primeval society nor a state. Consequently, we can operate only within the category of tribal organization from its simple to complex (chiefdom) level if we consider the latter as the highest expression of tribalism.

The features of the rise in social complexity appear in the Eneolithic period and become much more visible by the Early and Middle Bronze Age. However, we are not able to clearly answer the question "How does the social landscape of Central Eurasia appear at that time?" Comparing the material with various models, we inevitably run up against contradictions, which we indicated in previous chapters and which we will emphasize here.

There is no doubt that the turning point in the Ural development was the beginning of the Bronze Age, which was inaugurated by the formation of a principally new economic and social situation. From this time, the difference between the more advanced southern zone and northern zone, which remained essentially Eneolithic or Neolithic, takes on a pronounced appearance. In the Early Bronze Age the area of productive economy covered only a part of the southern zone of the area under study (the Cis-Urals), but its influence went much further (both territorially and chronologically), and deeper, than it seems at first glance. It provided a relatively stable subsistence for local communities that in turn had the advantage of the emergence of such specialized skills as metallurgy. Parallel with livestock breeding specialization, the formation of major mining-metallurgical centers was very important.

Historically speaking, bronze metallurgy, without any doubt, advanced the efficiency of human labor. It stimulated the process of specialization and changed the character of exchange between societies. The growing needs in metal and components of its production, particularly, in tin, the deposits of which were relatively rare, inspired the emergence of regular exchange/trade networks. The introduction of metallurgy, therefore, can be regarded as one of a number of very significant stimuli for interactions between different areas and the formation of dependency relations. Generalizing this thesis, one can note that the bronze industry, with its reliance on raw material deposits, was the first to promote a centripetal cultural development.

Social strategies of the Yamnaya culture populations were of an expanding character, and the needs in metal played the role of push-factor. It is, therefore, not surprising that Yamnaya sites have been discovered in the Trans-Urals and central Kazakhstan. We also should not forget about technological innovations such as wheeled transport, the evidence for which is more abundant. Nobody doubts that the Yamnaya culture was a product of migration in the area under study, yet specialists debate the mechanisms and time of this (or these) migrations. Tkachev (2000) emphasizes in detail the southwest connections, referring to the Cis-Caucasus area as one of the probable sources of various cultural traditions and their elements. Kuznetsov (1996a) speaks about direct migrations from that area in the mid-third millennium BC.

We think that not only did migrations take place but also that there was gradual settling into new territories, which usually followed the initial migrational movement of small population groups. One of the necessary conditions of such a process is the existence of a relatively good informational flow in and between societies. We would not be right in thinking that such a movement could flow spontaneously, without any organizing structure, the role of which might have been played by the new elite buried under the big kurgans (in contrast with the mass of smaller buriel barrows). Nevertheless, it is difficult to imagine that the miners who were coming seasonally to Kargaly, who worked and lived there in marginal conditions (Chernykh 2002), were of an elite status. Possibly, the metal producers and consumers were of a different status. In this case, we can think at least about two socially unequal groups within the Yamnaya communities (not a numerous elite and a mass of ordinary population). Taking many examples of ritual variability within mortuary practice into account, however, we can suggest greater social heterogeneity.

Unfortunately, it is not easy to detail this statement on the basis of the data available. The limited and asymmetrical amount of material has made us unable to reconstruct the demographic and social structure in detail. However, we assume that the rise of social complexity went on the way of personal status accretion that was realized in the variability of funeral rituals and the individual character of the majority of burials. One can logically suggest that there was a social leadership whose power was greatly ritualized. We know that ritual, rank, and coercion are attributes of rising social complexity.

The Yamnaya culture was responsible for dissemination of technical advantages of the Circumpontic complex in an easterly and northerly direction. Social consequences of economic, spiritual and informational "revolutions" were essential. They "prepared" the next generations for serious changes, which opened the period of the "Great Eurasian Discoveries and Transformations" that took place in the first third of the second millennium BC. These events started from the decomposition of the Circumpontic technoeconomic network, when traditional exchange links between steppe societies were broken, and old metallurgical centers lost their monopoly. Environmental factors and some archaeologically invisible forces animated the mechanism of migrations, the consequences of which were realized to the full extent at the beginning of the second millennium BC in cultural diversification and a specific rise of cultural complexity characteristic for the steppe and forest-steppe zones. The forest zone was still preserving the archaic order, and at this time, we cannot see any substantial influences coming there from the south.[1]

As we indicated in previous chapters, the first centuries of the second millennium BC, in the Volga – Ural – Kazakhstan area, were "colored" by the Abashevo and Sintashta traditions. By this time, we can see that the Sintashta and Abashevo technological and cultural complexes played a central and generating role for surrounding groups, forming regional systems of relations "center-periphery." This became a special marker of the Urals Bronze Age. This appears undoubted against the background of other synchronic or later cultures of the Bronze Age, compared to which the Sintashta society remains the outstanding example of complexity. In order to support this idea, we can refer to anthropological examples, collected by Kosarev, who wrote (1991: 90–2), that complex social structures can periodically appear at moments of crisis or when communities need to consolidate for some economic or political purpose.

The Sintashta phenomenon at present resists any distinct definition within existing social concepts. The Sintashta society has been interpreted as (1) a middle-scale society, based on a proto-city structure and strong territorial community (Zdanovich 1997a); (2) a specialized metal-producing society; (3) a simple chiefdom (Berezkin 1995); (4) a complex chiefdom (Koryakova 1996, 2002); (5) an early complex society (Masson 1998); and (6) an early urban or proto-urban society (Kyzlasov 1999; Zdanovich & Zdanovich 1995).

The greater part of the research thus far acknowledges the alien nature of this culture in the southern Trans-Urals, resulting from either an eastward or northward migration. It originated from various components in the course of migrational movements that resulted from the collapse of the Circumpontic network. Migrations and new territory assimilation not only entailed the transformation of the initial cultural elements, but they also generated some traits that earlier had not functioned as integral parts of the system. During the time of migrations and further consolidation within the new territory, the degree of social integration increased, and this was reflected in the mythology and funeral rituals. All this may bear witness to the Sintashta funeral ritual, which probably reflected an ideal societal structure that did not necessarily correspond to their current reality but existed as a remnant of the period when the culture was forming and territory was being assimilated. However, the question about dynamics of ritual transformation and its connection to the change of social relations is disputable.

The economic basis of the Sintashta society was composed of pastoral stock-breeding, metallurgy, and farming, and its technological potential was quite high. The full extent of this structure is yet not yet evaluated, but it would certainly not be wrong to state that this society possessed surplus product. However, it appears to have been invested mostly within the residential architecture and to the very sophisticated ritual system. The extremely lavish and sophisticated animal sacrifices can be interpreted as a reflection of a specific redistribution system, used by the living part of the community for the sake of wealth augmentation and more probably for its corporate consolidation. Additionally, the surplus products that could be formed as a result of the production process and exchange operation was invested into livestock breeding and metallurgy in the periods of ecological and other crises (Saenz 1991).

We cannot answer with one voice the question about the form of that social complexity. Without any doubt, it was not at the state level, as some scholars admit. The other models, chiefdom and protopolis, are accompanied by a whole series of limitations. Furthermore, we can see clear traces of coordinational activity directed to the organization of masses of people: a high concentration of population within a relatively small territory is evidenced by the archaeology.

By some external attributes, this complex can be correlated with the structure of the chiefdom, having at least two hierarchical levels, if the hypothesis pertaining to a "village" periphery is grounded by further excavations. If, however, a detailed analysis of all cultural components, in particular the funeral rite, does not distinguish strong internal stratification, corresponding to our understanding of wealth systems within prehistoric societies, we may then doubt the degree of social inequality within the representative communities (although it is clear that this criteria is not self-evident). However, the cases when the social leaders shared the same life conditions with other members are not exclusive. Additionally, the number and sex-age characteristics of the deceased people appear to contradict the settlement size, which may in turn relate to the existence of alternative burial rituals for societal groups not being related to the elite strata of the society. One can stress that this cultural complex testifies to a high degree of social integration within the Sintashta groups.

Regarding economic specialization, again it is not clearly evident. Yet, if one were to consider the domestic and communal character of the metallurgical production (the remains of metal production were found in almost every excavated dwelling structure), then we should ask, "Who raised the cattle?" These two branches themselves appear to be specialized, even in the need to supply some separate community. Domestic animals were of high material and symbolic value for the Sintashta population. In addition to their own sources, cattle might be obtained from exchange with, or be forcibly withdrawn from, other societies, which were of a lower economic and social level.

The more we work with the material, the stronger we believe that some sort of sacral knowledge was the conducting force in Sintashta society. The ritualistic aspect of its culture is expressed in its main components: regularly organized animal sacrifices in settlements and burial grounds, creating an impression of "plentifulness," typical for fertility cults (Zdanovich 1997a). People who possessed the sacral knowledge were organizers and rulers. However, their power was not externally exhibited. All this forces us to think that the rise of complexity did not go hand-in-hand with personal leadership, aggrandizement, and social hierarchization, which appears to have been limited by democratic ideology. The available materials do not allow us to think there was a very strong separation of the elite from the population buried under the kurgans. It also is difficult to fully reconstruct the social structure, because the kurgan funeral ritual was used only for that part of the population who lived in and around the fortresses. We think that Sintashta society was reproduced as far as sacral knowledge (or ideology) was preserved in societal memory.

Two opposite social strategies are visible through analysis. The first is a corporate strategy, which served for internal social integration, consolidation, and social reproduction. This strategy is evidenced by settlement patterns that did not spread out of limited areas and contrasted with aboriginal patterns; in landscape domestication, which focused on these settlements; and in group-oriented funeral ceremonies. As Kowalevski (2000: 175) notes:

"Corporate strategies build political-economic power collectively, and power may be occluded or ideologically anonymous."

The second strategy – network strategy – reflects the spread of Sintashta influence: the charioteer funeral complex and some funeral traditions far beyond the core-area: in Kazakhstan, the Cis-Urals, and in the Volga area.

The Sintashta phenomenon existed for rather a short time (2100/2000–1700 cal BC), but served as a nucleus, generating new cultural prototypes, which gave rise to other cultures of the Bronze Age that constituted the Andronovo family of cultures. It is possible that these strategies were concurrent, and the second one was more successful. It was responsible for dissolving and branching out the classic Sintashta core-tradition. This tradition is visible in the Petrovka society, the level of which is quite close to that described earlier, but it can be seen to contain certain eroded and obliterated characteristics of the Sintashta complex. Some traces of the Sintashta heritage are seen in the Alakul and Fyodorovo traditions.

The factors that initiated the processes of consolidation in the beginning had ceased to operate. A metal-producing zone extended to the Cis- and Trans-Urals territories. Fortified centers also were losing their dominant positions. This tradition of building complex systems of fortification gradually ceased to exist. The funeral ritual demonstrates the decline of the military level in that the number of finds relating to weaponry is decreased. The system of long-distance connections also changed; interregional relations became equal, and this brought about the process by which the significance of the traditional Sintashta elite complex decreased as well. This is reflected in the funeral ritual in which burial diversity and stratification becomes less and less visible archaeologically.

Broadly speaking, one can describe the time of the early second millennium BC in the Urals as unstable, with sharp cultural and social contrasts and competing social strategies.

We think that the main development in the social process at the beginning of the second millennium BC was the appearance of the new forms of social organization against the background of some revolutionary technological inventions.

A wide distribution of similar cultural norms conditioned by influence of the Sintashta traditions of the Late Bronze Age are found in the territory between the Volga area and central Kazakhstan. Such a strong similarity can be explained, in particular, by far-ranging connections, which could accompany the distribution of metal objects from one productive center.

The Late Bronze Age can be identified as the period of stabilization that is associated with classical Srubnaya and Alakul core-traditions. The whole series of common attributes in economy and material culture was conditioned not only by similar ecological conditions but also by close cultural background and the distribution of Iranian languages. We do not regard the genesis of the Late

Bronze Age cultures as a process of linear evolution; however, we can see that already in the Middle Bronze Age this territory functioned as a united system, based on the relations connected with metal production, as well as with raw material, metal goods distribution, and regional economic specialization.

Meanwhile, in relation to the Andronovo cultural family, this time can be called the period of great colonization and expansion. In the beginning of the Late Bronze Age, the area of productive economy was greatly extended. It occurred not only because the populations subdued new forms of activity but also as a result of direct expansion of the bearers of the Petrovka-Alakul traditions. The extensive way of economic development became ascendant; therefore, we see an incredible spatial outspread of these cultural stereotypes. Through external archaeological attributes, a social simplification was accompanied at the same time by the rise of cultural diversity, reflected in the styles of the Alakul and Fyodorovo traditions and in an almost endless series of their variations, which can be seen to have taken place over a vast territory. In this vast inhabited space, wich enjoyed favorable ecological conditions (Table 0.1), the successful maintenance of a subsystem economy was achieved and the Andronovo populations entered into extensive development against the background of a gradual but constant technological rise.

The introduction of tin bronze and widespread use of the technique of thin-walled casting caused a shortage of of raw materials. The Altai and Kazakhstan tin became an important factor of communication for a number of societies. The Great Tin and Nephrite Road linked many Eurasian regions. The influence of the Seima-Turbino metallurgy, the sites of which are located along the northern limits of the forest-steppe, were far out of this area.

In the Trans-Ural region, there are no brilliant sites such as the Rostovka, Seima, or Turbino cemeteries; however, the typical objects of the Seima type are known in the steppe area. The Seima-Turbino impulse together with Sintashta and Abashevo technological heritage became an essential component of Eurasian metallurgy, which synthesized technological accomplishments of the northern and southern zones. This facilitated contacts and population movements within Eurasian space. Materials demonstrate long-distance connections (the best example is the Borodino hoard), and some displacement of the northern (forest) groups to the south (steppe)[2] as, for example, in case of Cherkaskul culture, which was not typical of the earlier time.

The extensive development obviously had its limits. These limits were determined not only by regional ecological conditions and climatic fluctuations, which is quite evident, but also by a degree of social organization, which has regrettably still not been studied in great detail.

Visibly, the egalitarian character of burial sites, relatively small settlements, which with few exceptions did not have any fortifications, and homogeneous settlement patterns force us to conclude that the Late Bronze society was not very stratified. It was, rather, based on a kinship structure. Such a statement does not deny the existence of specialized villages and aggregations of villages. However, it was not enough to speak about high social complexity. It is also worthwhile to mention that burial sites of the Late Bronze Age are much larger than those of the preceding period. This fact can indirectly give evidence about the predominance of egalitarian tendencies in social strategies.[3] A major part of the population was buried in these cemeteries. One can suggest that the basis of the kin-tribal structure, which would later be realized to the full extent in nomadic societies, might have been forming during the second half of the second millennium BC.

As follows from Chapter 3, the Alakul sites are characterized by a high standardization of material culture and an almost complete absence of military features. Mortuary sites do not produce clear evidence of social stratification; sophisticated architecture disappears, settlement patterns move toward the dispersal model, and the number of social material markers (weaponry, chariots) sharply decreases. However, there is no evidence suggesting any external invasion or conquest. Thus, the culture evolved gradually and constantly under the action of internal factors. Funerary rituals do not provide evidence of unquestionable social stratification, although the diversity of funerary rituals, reflected in burial grounds also can correspond to certain social rules, the meaning of which we are not able to read.

The reduction of complexity in the post-Sintashta period could be explained in terms of three models. First, this reduction could have resulted from the natural process of cultural adaptation to local natural and cultural environments. We cannot exclude, however, the fact that the social system that was brought to the Trans-Urals in the beginning of the second millennium BC had been formed in different conditions and turned out to be unadjusted to the local conditions. As a result, it was simplified. The second model is based on the assumption that the formation of the Sintashta complex was a result of "metallurgical" factors. At the turn of the third and second millennia BC, the Trans-Ural area was included in a large network, where it played a part of an integrating core area. In this case, social devolution might have been connected with this network's destruction and general decentralization. The third explanation can rely on the thesis about "loss" or deformation of the above mentioned sacral knowledge – ideology of the elite.

These models are not alternatives but, rather, mutually complementary. Overall, simplification of a social system is not surprising, because within any complex society comprising some potentially independent structures, there is a tendency toward simplification and decentralization.

Such a social "devolution" also could have resulted from the impossibility of maintaining demographic concentration within the relatively small territory, as we saw for the preceding period. By all appearances, the potential of intensification of livestock-breeding (and probably some agriculture), limited by a corresponding technological level and climatic conditions, were practically exhausted by the beginning of the Late Bronze Age. The way was found, not in the intensification of labor, but in the external expansion. Migrational potential was realized as a result of several factors. During the Middle and early Late Bronze Age, the population of the steppe area had the advantage in some social domains. Its possession of new economic strategies that could consolidate rather large groups of people can be emphasized. A high level of technology and accumulated experience in long-distance connections played a very important role as well. These connections served as the means of informational exchange: they facilitated the flow of new ideas and their penetration into new regions. It is also not accidental that expansion started from colonization of the forest-steppe, which, by that time, was occupied by societies of a lower social level. This colonization resulted in formation of synthetic or symbiotic Andronovo-like societies that, in turn, brought their traditions to the southern taiga zone, where some elements of the Andronovo (Fyodorovo) heritage (sophisticated geometric motifs of the "carpet-type" ornamentation) were preserved up to modern times.

When seeking explanations of a principally new situation, which was formed in the Late Bronze Age, it is not enough to appeal to an ecological factor.[4] More significant is the factor of transformation of interrelations between societies and an extensive way of development. As a result, a society rejects the sumptuous ways of its functioning, such as magnificent funeral ceremonies and complex architecture. An extension of the metal-producing area reduced the opportunities to exploit metal-consuming societies. This extension, in turn, should have reduced the income of societies that had held a monopoly on metal production. Consequently, the investments in the "irrational" (ceremonial) sphere of social life also should have been reduced.

Material cultures reacted to such changes by simplification and lose of features, which are usually interpreted as evidence of complexity. When speaking about social devolution, we should stress that we do not mean social degradation. In particular, all technological achievements were maintained.[5]

Nevertheless, one can see that, in spite of some social simplification, contrasting first the preceding period together with population growth, the accompanying segmentation of communities and their mutual absorption, the ethnic mixture and formation of relatively large entities, it can be said that in a general sense society in the Andronovo area moved toward the rise of heterogeneity, which was more horizontal than vertical. By the end of the Bronze Age in some parts of this vast area, the big settlements with features of urban organization had appeared (Kent, Chicha). Interregional specialization became more stable and was dependent on mineral deposits. All this speaks in favour of global and dramatic changes that occurred in the outcome of the Bronze Age in the central part of northern Eurasia.

Generally speaking, the Eurasian world of the second millennium BC demonstrates at least four structural zones: (1) the small urban area (eastern

Mediterranean and Mesopotamia), (2) a close periphery of moderate size (Trans-Caucasus, Iran, and Central Asian oases, which we did not consider in this book); (3) the distant (second) periphery, which extended over most of the temperate belt including the great Eurasian steppes; and, (4) the furthest periphery trapped in the Eneolithic and Neolithic economy of the remote north. Within the second periphery, as we saw, several independent centers such as Caucasian, Uralian, and Altaian had been formed, which shaped the social landscape of that huge area.

These zones were as significant socially as economically. Close by, especially near the oases of Middle Asia, the preconditions existed for the development of prestate organizations and proto-cities. Materials of southern cultures, in particular that of Sapally, illuminate intensive and constant contacts with the population of the northern steppe origin (Masson 1999). Conversely, according to Pyankova (1989) and Masson (1999), the Vakhsh culture of southwestern Turkmenia was greatly contributed to by the steppe substratum.

The most significant social and economic changes occurred in the steppe and forest-steppe, through the establishment of a mixed economy based on pastoral cattle breeding, primitive agriculture,[6] and crafts, including metallurgy and carpentry.

In the southern forest, the diversified economy consisted of hunting and fishing, supplemented by livestock breeding. In the taiga and tundra zones, methods of intensive hunting and fishing were developed. Four basic types of economic specialization are distinguished here: (1) mobile hunting of reindeer (in the tundra), (2) collective hunting of hoofed forest animals during their transmigrations (in the northern forest),[7] (3) a seasonal hunting and fishing economy,[8] and (4) settled fishing.[9]

All of these successes allowed population growth and social restructuring in many areas. An increase in production and economic differentiation, as much as the influence of advanced societies, stimulated long-distance and regional exchange contacts. However, all these processes were interrupted by local, regional, and interregional collapses.

In particular, by the end of the Bronze Age, in the Urals, we see the traces of depopulation and social degradation. The principal innovation was expressed in the rise of mobility in the pastoral economy. What is noticeable is that burials became chiefly individual. We can hypothesize that the small density of sites (not only burials but also settlements[10]) in the Urals area may have resulted from seasonal use of this area, which was exploited mostly in the summer period. This could mean that the pastoral-nomadic system, which would be typical of the next epoch, might have been forming at this time.

SOCIAL STRATEGIES IN THE IRON AGE

The transition to the wide use of iron tools and weapons occurred in temperate Eurasia between 800 and 300 BC. As we saw, iron was known in the southern

Urals one thousand years before, when it was used for prestige goods in the Yamnaya culture. Despite this, iron seems not to have been used for this purpose for a long period after its actual introduction. The beginning of the Iron Age is marked by the last "explosion" of the bronze industry, which supplied growing military needs. At this time, iron was valuable, and therefore it was not put into graves, but later it became a common metal. Gold and silver, and also imported objects, were used as criteria for nobility and wealth in this epoch. Very soon, bronze was in short supply.

The broad decline of the Bronze Age cultures resulted partly from climatic deterioration, followed by an economic reorientation to nomadism. This event itself cannot be seen as having only one implication. On the one hand, nomadism made it possible to assimilate such a huge space and to create a partial solution to demographic problems. On the other hand, it had no great potential resources for urbanization. Yet, because a nomadic economy cannot exist without links with settled civilizations, even if such contacts are not always peaceful, nomadism helped them spread their achievements and thus participate in the general historical process. Our understanding of social and cultural trends in Eurasia in the Iron Age depends on how we understand the nomadic world. As has been demonstrated in earlier research, the tendency toward nomadism always existed within the societies inhabiting the Eurasian steppe. It took a considerable amount of time and experience in stock breeding before proper mechanisms of natural adaptation could be worked out. In the archaeological record, the transition to nomadism seems to have happened relatively quickly, but we should not forget that the development of animal husbandry during the Late Bronze Age, when horses were trained to be ridden, may have been an unintentional preparation for this shift in the subsistence economy (Kuzmina 1996a, 1996b).

In the ninth–seventh centuries BC the earliest kurgans of a nomadic elite appeared – first in the east, in Siberia, and then they became a part of the steppe landscape in the west. The largest of these barrows demonstrating a great investment of labor are not common. They are known in Siberia (Arzhan and Salbyk), in the northern Caucasus (Kelermes and Ul'skiye), and in Chorasmia (Tagisken). It is true that many steppe barrows have either not yet been excavated, or have been destroyed. The large elite barrows that have been studied in the most detail relate to the fifth–second centuries BC. Some of them were about 100 m in diameter and have been interpreted as royal funeral sites. They also performed the function of ceremonial centers (Grach 1980; Gryaznov 1980; Murzin 1990). It is not necessary to discuss high levels of social differentiation in early nomadic cultures, which are well known. More crucial is the question of how and why Eurasian society reached such levels so quickly. We broached this issue in Chapter 6 and will now continue this discussion.

It is reasonable to take as a model the territory of northern Kazakhstan that provides an archaeological sequence from the Bronze Age to the epoch of nomads. Khabdulina (1994; Khabdulina & Zdanovich 1984) and other researchers explained the social change in this area with reference to economic reasons, largely stemming, from the local pluvial conditions of the tenth to ninth centuries BC, when the weather gradually became cooler. The impact of the forest ecosystems to the south made some groups of the Sargary culture population leave their settlements. Traces of flooding has been discovered at many settlements in northern Kazakhstan (Khabdulina & Zdanovich 1984; Zdanovich 1970). In some places, the population tried to maintain itsr traditional economy based on pastoral cattle-breeding and land cultivation as long as possible. However, in new conditions, that system of material production had exhausted its potential. Archaeologically, this time period is characterized by small, short-term camps, and only rarely by settlements with traces of craft production. The latter were employed as centers of small communities. At the same time, some rare settlements situated in more or less good climatic conditions became centers of population growth (e.g., the Kent settlement in Central Kazakhstan). Yet, the more nomadism spread, the more settled elements moved out of the steppe area.

One can see that the cemeteries also were transformed. Instead of the compactly arranged burial grounds of the Bronze Age, there appeared separate solitary barrows out of river valleys and usually located on watersheds. Burials acquired a more individual character. The most characteristic feature in the eighth–sixth centuries BC was the above-ground architectural construction, which was the most elaborate and sophisticated part of the funeral complex, and which reflected an idea of distinctiveness and served to establish the new ideology. Undoubtedly, at this time the size and complexity of funeral construction as indicators of social status and prestige were of paramount significance. As has been demonstrated by recent research, a barrow might originally be erected as a stepped pyramidal construction of topsoil bricks placed on a base of an imposing wooden funeral chamber. Such barrows were usually situated on high ground and dominated chains of other barrows. With regard to the early period, we can assume that changes came into being earlier at the elite level of barrows, which contrasted sharply with the majority of the ordinary population buried in extremely modest graves. The material culture associated with the new barrows demonstrated a significant military character.

Similar transformations took place in many parts of the Eurasian steppe, but because of cultural and social asymmetry, they did not coincide in time. Medvedev (1999a) noticed that the transition to nomadism in the eastern European steppe was inspired by the collapse of the mixed economy of the late Srubnaya society, which could not preserve itself in conditions of cooling and aridity. The anthropogenic factor played its negative role as well.

Hence, in this divergence process, society was definitely separated into groups differentiated according to economic orientation (Koryakova 1996). These groups occupying different ecological niches had to adapt to the new ecological conditions. In addition, some new groups of mobile populations came here from the east.

Fierce competition for pastures is supposed to have been of great importance. It is logical to suggest that these communities were successful in exercising control over the land, that they were socially organized, centralized, and more militant. Their strategies potentially could have led to war. Migrations involved different groups of people in active interaction. As Murzin (1990: 78) has demonstrated, the formation of the Scythian ethnos (in the Pontic area) at the beginning of the seventh century BC can be considered as one of the results of this process. The ethnic and social structure of the Scythian union at the time of its campaign in Trans-Caucasus stemmed from the conquest of the Cimmerians by the proto-Scythians who arrived from the east. The exploitation of conquered people was effected within the framework of the early three-part political structure.

A similar model serves to describe the origin of the Hsiung-nu tribes, who were descendants of the Hsiung-nu tribes that had come to northern Mongolia from the south, and of aboriginal people. In the fourth century BC, they were organized into an early political union, consisting of twenty-four clans. It was ruled by a hereditary chief and by tribal leaders interacting with him in hierarchical early relations (Gumilev 1993b: 462). The stability of this social structure was promoted by a political and military organization based on the three-part principle: "left side," "center," and "right side." As usual, the left side clans were less significant with respect to the most powerful center than the right side clans. The left side provided the ordinary militia, the right side the army, and the center wielded political and administrative power. Later, in the medieval period, this structure was known among the Kazakh tribes.

Hence, during the early stage of the Iron Age the social landscape of Eurasia tended toward a great structural transformation. Traditionally, this has been explained by economic transformations, and that is so. We would, however, suggest that the establishment of a new means of subsistence and a new mode of life, in which livestock was used as moveable wealth, depended on how communities were socially organized in order to adapt to new ecological and political conditions.

The main distinction of the Iron Age from the preceding epoch lies in technological changes and the political field. This situation was closely connected with a militarization of society. The beginning of the first millennium BC is represented by a clear rise of influence coming from the statehood area. New World empires, which were not known in the second millennium BC, extended their interests toward the forest zone of Eurasia. In fact, they divided northern Eurasia into several spheres of influence and formed their own close peripheries, the size of which were determined by the level of social maturity of its populations. First the steppe (nomadic) population, then the forest-steppe, and finally the forest groups were involved in this system of core/periphery relationships.

The stable trade system with the participation of nomadic societies was established by the fifth century BC and developed later. The second source of the nomadic population's wealth was their control of trade routes. This period is marked by an increase in warfare that led to advances in weaponry but that initially still continued in the early tradition. Still, the growing demand for iron brought the marginal societies of the forest steppe, where wood was available, into the sphere of the nomads' interest. The northern periphery of the nomadic world very soon become an additional source of wealth, provided by the tributary dependent population. It is not surprising that the Early Iron Age is characterized by an increase of fortified settlements in this area, some of which were designed as military camps. Degrees of resistance varied: it was stronger in the forest-steppe of eastern Europe, where well-defended fortresses appeared, and less noticeable beyond the Urals (the pre-Sargat phase of the Sargat culture).

Strictly speaking, the appearance of fortresses in the forest zone indicate the beginning of a new social order there. Yet some communal traditions as represented by large flat cemeteries of the Ananyino culture and by open settlements concentrated around small fortresses were preserved. Undoubtedly, this region was drawn into Scythian politics. Its metal-working was oriented to their needs. The Trans-Ural cultures had no visible cemeteries. The part of the aboriginal population changed their mortuary practices only after the fifth century BC, when this territory had become part of the nomadic world.

We would like to stress that, during the early Scythian period, the Eurasian temperate zone was drawn into a large interregional network, accompanied by growing militarization and social complexity. By the sixth–fifth centuries BC in the steppe and the forest-steppe, a specific system of chiefly organized societies had been established. The closer these were to the states, the more centralized they were. The second factor that we should not forget is that the nomads reached the empire level when they included the agricultural or other more settled population territorially and economically. As an example, one can note that the Scythian Kingdom, which existed from the sixth to the fourth centuries BC in the northern Pontic region, was involved into regional politics and controlled forest-steppe societies of eastern Europe (Artamonov 1972; Khazanov 1975; Murzin 1990). Such a system was quite vulnerable to many internal and external violations. From time to time, the leadership passed to new more powerful tribes, which changed the contours of the areas under their control.

The second half of the first millennium BC is better represented archaeologically compared to the preceding period. The sites are numerous throughout Eurasia. Unfortunately, we do not have sufficiently effective methods to help us understand all the diverse information hidden in countless barrows and settlements of the Sarmatian epoch, which can be called the "Golden Age" of Eurasian late prehistory. We are not, however, pessimistic with regard to prospects for tracing basic tendencies and long-term patterns. There also are written sources that report the names of some peoples and some states in the historical arena.

From this point of view, we shall only dwell on certain aspects of social development as represented in archaeological material from the area under study. Primarily, this material provides evidence of new demographic growth and a general increase in wealth in many societies. Almost all cultures were completely based on iron technology, whereas bronze became a metal used for manufacturing certain prestigious or cult objects. The conclusive introduction of iron and its wide proliferation had leveled the social and economic background in vast portions of Eurasia. In the last centuries of the first millennium BC, even the societies of the northern forest zone demonstrated the indication of social stratification, militarization, and the rise of an elite. In conditions of total predominance of the mythological world outlook, social orders and stratification were primarily reflected in funerary rituals. Comparison with the preceding period reveals new elements in their archaeological representation.

The analysis of funerary sites undertaken in different regions and different cultures demonstrates a more clearly expressed heterogeneity than was found before. For example, Grach (1980) classified the burial grounds discovered beyond the Urals. He distinguished several basic categories of sites presumably corresponding to different social strata, brilliantly argued by Khazanov (1975):

1. Royal burials. Royal burials have been found in the Altai mountains (the Pasyryk culture), large barrows in Tuva (Arzhan), in the Minussinsk depression (Tagar culture), and in Kazakhstan (Beschatyr, Chilikty). We can extend this list through reference to royal barrows in the Urals left by the Saka and Sarmatians (Filippovka), and, of course, to the famous Scythian burials, most of which date from the fourth–third centuries BC. All royal barrows are not identical to each other in size and complexity. Unfortunately, they have been plundered almost totally and only some lucky exceptions to the rule enable us to imagine how rich and imposing these must have been. Sometimes it is hard to distinguish true royal burials from those of local chiefs.

2. Elite burials. These are indicated either by complex burial constructions, or by rich and unusual grave goods. In this connection, we need to refer to the new "glacial" barrows recently excavated in the Altai region, which have yielded extraordinary finds, representing the culture of the middle rank of the military aristocracy: in the fifth–third centuries BC (Polos'mak 1994; 2000). These were not large in size but were furnished with objects associated with funeral repasts, and contained complex funeral chambers with double wooden walls. The dead also were accompanied by many sacrificed harnessed horses, but the burials did not

contain imported objects and the deceased were dressed quite simply. Most of these people's wealth was contained in their horses. Therefore, the splendid wooden decoration belonged to them (Polos'mak 1994: 60–80). It is interesting that the described burials produced virtually no gold objects. Meanwhile, there was a great deal of decoration made from wood in the Animal Style and only covered by thin gold foil.

Burials or their remains presenting extremely valuable objects made from gold or silver are particularly well known in different areas. The famous Animal Style usually indicates high social status. The prestige goods system of the fifth–fourth centuries BC was oriented predominantly to the local nomadic culture, the main feature of which was the Animal Style. During close relationships, first with classical civilizations, then also with Parthia and China, distinctive status came to be indicated by foreign objects of luxury. This tendency became rather noticeable in the last centuries BC and at the beginning of the first millennium CE, when the interregional trade system was fully established. Interestingly, the elite burials of this time were located not only in the center as was traditionally accepted, but often on the periphery of the funerary space. Sometimes they were arranged at the bottom of a deep hole, under a second burial, which was destined to distract the robbers' attention. After several discoveries of rich graves between the Urals and the Irtysh river one can be sure that part of the Siberian Collection (Rudenko 1962) comes from this area. It is precisely the Sargat culture that must have had considerable demographic and military resources in order to compete successfully with the Sarmatians and to maintain trade links with Central Asia and China. The elite of this society was mainly responsible for assuming control over the trade routes, passing through western Siberia. This is why rich burials of this time contained many imported objects: decorative objects from Central Asia and Iran, pottery from Chorasmia, mirrors, silk, and bronze utensils from China of the Han dynasty.

The cavalry was recruited mainly from the elite. As has been clearly demonstrated by many researchers, statistical analysis always bears out this pattern. In particular, analysis of the large database of graves of the forest-steppe beyond the Urals has demonstrated that about 20 percent of graves contained a "horse bit-sword-bow" set (Koryakova 1988; Matveyeva 2000). A similar proportion was recorded in connection with materials from other regions. Bunatyan (1985), for example, established statistically the number of such graves in Scythia as 15–20 percent. She also distinguished several smaller groups within this category. As a rule, the elite included several levels of nobility.

3. Burials of the ordinary population. These are most numerous in all cultures (60–70 percent), and usually they yielded a restricted range of

tools, arrowheads, personal jewelry, vessels, animal bones. Quite often, however, female graves contained beads that had been imported from India, the Mediterranean, and Iran. There was no local bead production in temperate Eurasia. The fact that they were encountered in almost every female grave gives evidence about the large bead trade market.

The group of people, which were designated as "foot archers" and who were found buried in 23 percent of graves, may constitute the highest level of this stratum.

4. Burials of the dependent population (3–5 percent) are the graves of people without any property. Sometimes they are laid out in unusual positions, sometimes in a ditch, surrounding a barrow mound, and sometimes they manifest traces of a violent death.

Indeed, the groups described here do not exhaust the variety found in the social structure. Certain combinations were at the same time both the reflection of specific regional characteristics and the expression of general patterns. A high percentage of the elite that had concentrated the biggest part of the financial wealth in their own hands needed to make every effort to keep this position, but in competitive conditions this might be done via active expansionist politics. In order to have access to wealth, demonstrated by prestigious luxury, the elite would have made every effort to organize the population under its control. This obviously resulted in an increase in various forms of tribute and an increase in administrative functions. We should not forget that at this time there existed a number of fortresses that were centers of craft specialization, of population, and communication. If we recall the complexity of the spatial structure and fortification of some fortresses such as those in the forest-steppe, which have been discovered in all regions, we cannot doubt that they had an administrative role. There is no doubt that Eurasian society of the Iron Age tended toward hierarchical structures. Nevertheless, the extremely unstable political situation against an unstable ecological background time and time again turned society back to simpler chiefdoms or some kind of tribal groups.

The new links were established when new social and ideological relations together with economic changes were being introduced into the historical process. In the second half of the first millennium BC, the economic and cultural zones of Eurasia could not develop separately but only interdependently. By the end of the first millennium BC, the world was already divided into spheres of influence between the Roman and Parthian empires and the Han Dynasty of China. The cultures of the temperate Eurasian zone as their close periphery were much influenced by them economically, socially, politically, and ideologically. We are convinced that the formation of the first steppe empires occurred in the first millennium BC, and it was a reaction to the growing power of classical states.

The nomads competed not only for pastures but also for trade routes which crossed these pastures. They conquered the forest population in order to gain access to fur because it was in demand in the states. The Chinese chronicles mention that in Han China sable fur was highly valued: this fur came from the "Yan' land," situated in the Southern Urals to the north of Yantzai. The share of the fur that reached Turkistan was thereafter transported to India and the Roman Empire (Lubo-Lesnichenko 1994: 243). In particular, nomads actively traded livestock, especially horses, with China (Fig. 9.1).

By force of various factors (environmental, political, economic, and some others that we cannot determine at this time), some Eurasian societies became highly organized within the regional economic system. A good example of such relations is found in the territory of Central Asia – Kazakhstan and western Siberia. Recent research has shown that around the Silk Road there was a system of trade routes that partly coincided with paths of traditional nomadic transmigrations (Tairov 1995). Which goods were used for commercial exchange? As mentioned earlier, luxury objects, found in Trans-Uralian graves, come from advanced southern centers, including China and Iran. Some European goods such as bracelets and fibulae also reached the Urals. Late written documents report which goods were exported to Central Asia. Except fur, referred to earlier, these included treated horse leather, honey, nuts, birch bark, fish glue, and fish teeth (Tairov 1995: 34). In the fourth–third centuries BC, trade links among the southern Chinese state of Chu, Central Asia, and Siberia existed. There was a great number of long Chinese iron swords found in the Eurasian steppe and Trans-Uralian forest-steppe in the last centuries BC when there was a state monopoly on the production of iron and weaponry trade in Han Dynasty China. The finds from the Pazyryk culture and other Eurasian cultures reveal that the Chinese supplied silk, bronze mirrors, and jewelry, and that these were not rare (Lubo-Lesnichenko 1985, 1987; Polos'mak 1994). Chinese objects penetrated Europe by the southern route via Persia and further via the Mediterranean. There is no doubt that Chinese goods were available before the Silk Road officially began to function. Without this early commercial foundation, the system of long-distance trade could not have been formed so quickly. Unfortunately, the northern direction of this trade is not well studied, except for the "steppe" route, which led from China and probably Mongolia to the west around the Caspian Sea (Stavisky 1997: 22). One portion of this route led from eastern Turkistan across the Pamir and then along the middle Syr-Darya to the northwest (Fig. 6.5). It is thought that the Great Silk Road in the early phases may not have run in an unbroken line. Trade may have been conducted by stages (Gorbunova 1993/94: 7).

Tairov (1995) supposes that the most effective trade routes were established in the late first millennium BC and existed without any major changes up until the nineteenth century CE. The main trade centers of central Eurasia were situated in the states of Central Asia through which the main branches of the Silk Road

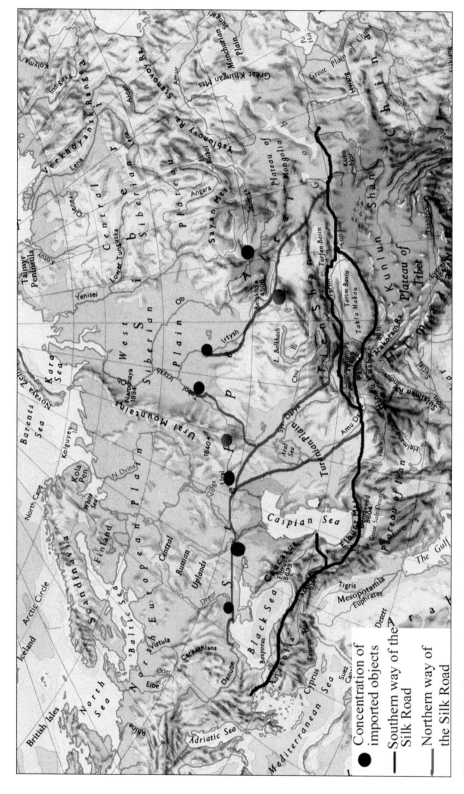

Figure 9.1. Trade routes in central-northern Eurasia connected to the Great Silk Route system.

335

passed. In the sixth–third centuries BC, their northern trade was oriented to southeastern Europe, but after the second century BC, caravans went to western Siberia, where the Sargat culture constituted the most powerful ethnic and political union. It is quite probable that this is a reflection of the competition for control over the northern branch of the Silk Road, which led to the Volga River. Later, in 700–800 AD, the more significant stretches connected Central Asia and eastern Europe (Volgan Bulgaria); in 1400–1500 AD, when new states appeared in western Siberia (the Siberian Tatar Kingdom), the trade routes led there again. Organized trade, therefore, was established when the main partners attained the level of statehood or at least complex chiefdom. Kristiansen (1991: 25) was absolutely right when he said, "After the emergence of state systems, it is no longer possible to talk about independent developments."

However, in the middle of the first millennium CE, this system collapsed under the influence of many factors, which it had created itself. Its destructive factor was again connected with large-scale movement of eastern nomads known as the Great Migration of Peoples. One cycle was over and a new one was to begin.

We have attempted to construct the direction of social trends in the Urals, in light of these concepts (Koryakova 2002). We have aimed to identify some regularities in the archaeological record that correspond to a number of basic social and economic strategies vertically in terms of degree of internal structural change, and horizontally in terms of cultural and chronological distribution.

Reflecting on the specifics of archaeological information, and not having direct anthropological parallels to vanished societies, we cannot be assured about the possibility of reconstructing them in full, even possessing literary sources. However, we are able to explore the tendency on the relative scale of social complexity, after agreeing on the necessary criteria. This tendency can be described through some trajectory, in that some local, regional, and interregional levels can be reflected within it (Fig. 9.2).

Taken as a preliminary view, it can therefore be – and perhaps should be – criticized and developed further. When we draw such a curve, covering several centuries and even millennia, we can distinguish a much-summarized tendency, consisting of many concrete "histories." These "histories" are reflected in various ceramic types and styles, architectural traditions, burial combinations, and other forms of material culture, which we cannot always easily coordinate.

Evidently, social trends within a given time period are often far from a progressive step forward in evolution. As many areas of research have shown, it can be of a cyclical nature, conditioned by many factors: environmental, economic, demographic, social, political, ethnic, and so on, and can be reflected in the alternation of periods of rise and decline, collapse and stability, and the consolidation and fragmentation of social systems.

The processes of cultural and social change during the second and first millennia BC were not linear in their evolution and fluctuated between rise and

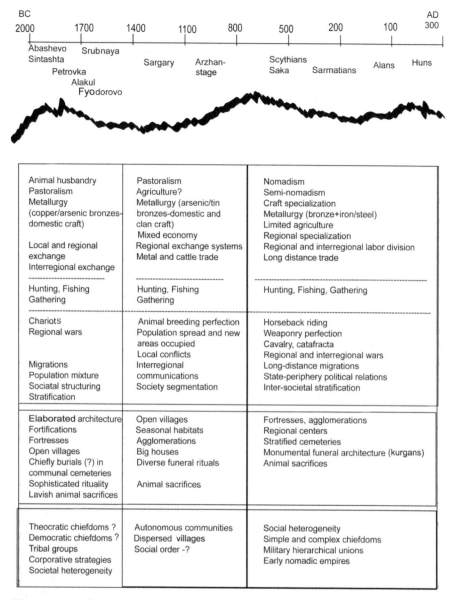

Figure 9.2. Schematic trend of social development during the second and first millennia BC.

decline. The main long-term trends were characteristic for all the Eurasian territory, although they developed cyclically and were shaped differently in different regions and periods.

We can see moments of advance to clearly expressed complex structures and then a return to simple extensive patterns. The stimulating factors forcing society to develop its organization were ecological and technological crises, which conditioned the search for the most effective forms of social adaptation.

The geographical environment dictated specific forms of behavior, which were mirrored in different cultures.

If we compare the outline of social trends in the territory in question and in central Europe, presented by Kristiansen (1998), we will discern some similarities and some differences.

The beginning of the second millennia BC was a time of extreme activity in search of technological and military fields accompanied by a progression toward sociocultural complexity. The appearance of new cultures resulted from the combination of internal and external factors, including prevailing eastward migrations. The social landscape of the temperate zone was represented by early complex societies that differed in size, scale, and activity, and interacted with tribal structures of most of the forest zone, on the one hand, and the aboriginal population of the steppe, on the other. We think that the Sintashta culture, with its complex ideological and cosmological system, manifests the highpoint of development in the second millennium BC.

It was succeeded by the large extensive diffusion of the descendant population and the colonization of new landscapes. As social heterogeneity increased, opposing elements of communality become more visible. Yet technological evolution involves a great deal of population expansion and the discovery of new mineral resources. At this stage of social development in the temperate zone of Eurasia, many more-or-less autonomous communities regionally organized in tribal units are supposed to have been in existence.

The transition to the Iron Age is marked by the disintegration of these societies and by an increased incidence of their collapse. Against a background of ecological stress, the Eurasian population changed the basic thrust of its economic activity. One can say that this time (1000–800 BC) was probably the most dramatic moment in the prehistory of Eurasia. It set in motion a chain of recurrent westward migrations that continually disrupted the cultural sequences in Central Eurasia. Thus, the social evolution that had peaked here needed to return to the point where it had begun.

NOTES

Introduction

1. The Udmurts and the Komi form the Permic branch of Finno-Ugric–speaking peoples. The Udmurts occupy the Kama-Vyatka interfluve to the west of the Urals. The Komi occupy the area from the upper reaches of the Kama up to Pechora river. The Khanty and Manci (Ob-Ugric peoples) live in the area in northwestern Siberia between the Urals and the river Ob'. Until the early twentieth century, their former habitats included areas west of the Urals. Proto-Ugric is thought to have been spoken in the forest and forest-steppe of the southern Urals and western Siberia (Hajdu 1985; Carpelan & Parpola 2001).

2. Until the second half of the eighteenth century, this river was called Yayik. The government of Catherine the Second renamed it because it was associated with the great peasant revolt under the leadership of E. Pugachev.

3. It is interesting to refer to historic information collected by Russian travellers in the eighteenth and nineteenth centuries. "Around the Krivino village – in the Kurgan district – there were 6 lakes until 1854, after that time, there were 30. Some of lakes of the Kyrgyz (Kazakh) steppe area are characterized by specific physical occurrence. Some days they disappear, and then fill with water again. Some years they are deep and full of fish, then the water goes away, and their bottoms are covered by thick grass. Local people say that such phenomena occur every twenty years" (Kosarev 1984: 27).

4. However, the palinological data are not so univocal (Khotinsky et al. 1982: 151). Reliable records testifying to the penetration of steppe flora into the forest zone have only recently been published (Ryabogina et al. 2001a; Semochkina & Ryabogina 2001).

5. Even at the present time, some large forests are preserved in the steppe zone, and in the taiga one can find steppe landscapes.

6. In dry periods, the risk of forest brush fires is rather high. It takes about ninety years for natural reforestation, the first stage of which is usually represented by the forest-steppe (Kosarev 1984: 40).

7. At present, the series of dates issued from the C-14 Laboratory of the Institute for History of Material Culture (St. Petersburg) are periodically published in its yearbook *Archaeology and Radiocarbon*.

8. This means that some sites, containing objects, typologically and technologically relating to the earlier phase, are dated to the same period (2800–2500 cal BC) as these, which are related to the later phase.

9. This period will be not be regarded in our book, as it is the beginning of the medieval time, according to historical periodization.

10. The ethnography detects a gross diversity of spatially conditioned systems, which fall into two groups depending on given principles of their analysis: (1) economic and cultural types (for instance, Arctic hunters to sea animals; forest hunters and fishers; steppe nomads, etc.); and (2) historical and ethnographic regional intercommunities (for instance, the western-Siberian intercommunity, which includes forest populations; and the south-Siberian intercommunity, which includes the Sayan and Altai peoples, Siberian Tatars, Chulym Turks, Northern Kazakhs, and some others).

1. The Development of Bronze Metallurgy

1. In a metallurgical center, the full cycle of metal production was realized: mining, ore processing, smelting, and metalworking. A metalworking center worked on imported raw material or scrap metal; the productive cycle is confined to operations with metal.

2. The database on Circumpontic network comprises more than eighty-four thousand objects (Chernykh et al. 2002b: 5–23).

3. In terms of metallurgical development, the boundary between the Early and Middle Bronze Age is more visible in the technology of the production of the elite weapon – socketed axes (Chernykh et al. 2000a: 6–7).

4. Northern Eurasia comprised several mining-metallurgical zones: (1) Balkan – Carpathian, (2) Caucasus, (3) Urals, (4) Kazakhstan, (5) Pamir – Tien-Shan, (6) Sayan – Altai, and (7) eastern Siberia (Trans-Baikal).

5. Within the Urals mining-metallurgical zone, more than one thousand large copper deposits are known. Among them are Elenovka and Ush-Katta (northern Mugodzhares), Kichiginskoye, Mednaya Gora, Polaykovskoye, Voznesenskoye, Kamenskij, Ust-Kabanskij, and others. Smaller deposits are more numerous, for example, in the Cis-Urals, in the basin of the Dema and Ilek rivers, and about twenty-eight hundred sandstone deposits are known (Morozov 1981).

6. According to Grigory'ev (2000b: 459), the total number of such complex furnaces is about twenty-two. At the same time, there also were some other types of furnaces (i.e., ovens).

7. The invention of the chimney was conditioned by the necessity to remove the sulphurous gas, which derived from the smelting of sulphide ore (Grigory'ev 2000b: 468).

8. Specialists from the Institute of Mineralogy and the Institute of Geology and Geochemistry (Ural Division of RAS) distinguish the following types of metal: (A) Types of copper: (1) pure (where As, Sn, Ag < 0.1 wt%); (2) arsenical (where As contents are in the range 0.1– 1 wt%); (3) argentian (content of Ag 0.1–1 wt%). (B) Types of bronze: (1) arseniferrous (content of As 1–4 wt%); (2) stanniferrous (content of Sn 1–7 wt%); (3) nikeliferrous (content of Ni 1– 5 wt%) (Zaikov et al. 2002:430).

9. These zones were associated correspondingly with the Srubnaya and Andronovo cultural formations (Chernykh et al. 1989: 8; Chernykh et al. 2004) (see Chapter 3).

10. For example, we can refer to burials of metalworkers in the steppe of northern Caucasus (Gei 1986) and Don-Dnepr area (Pustovalov 1994); Utyevka-6 and Potapovka burial grounds in the Volga area (Vasily'ev 1980;Vasily'ev et al. 1994;); Pepkino kurgan in the Cis-Urals (Bader 1964, Khalikov et al. 1966); Rostovka and Sopka-2 burial grounds in Siberia (Matushchenko & Sinitsina 1988; Molodin 1983); and others.

2. The Achievements and Collisions of the Early and Middle Bronze Age

1. The child burials are extremely rare in the Cis-Urals, as well as in other areas.

2. The Repin culture (originated in the Middle Eneolithic, 3000/2900 cal. BC) was revealed by Sinuk (1981) in the Middle Don region, from where it was dispersed to the Volga and Dnepr areas. It is characterized by open settlements and kurgan and flat burials with supine inhumations. Pottery is round-bottomed, decorated with incised lines and combed impressions, combined with pits at the base of a neck; corded decoration and bosses at the base of a neck (Sinuk 1981).

3. The first Abashevo site, the cemetery near the village of Abashevo in the Chuvashia (on the Volga) was excavated in the 1920s by V. F. Smolin (1927). In the 1950s and 1960s, K. V. Salnikov (1967) distinguished the following variants: in the Middle Volga, in Bashkiria (Stelitamak), in the Trans-Urals (Magnitogorsk), and in the Middle and Lower Don. In the 1970s, A. D. Pryakhin (1971; 1976; 1977) described the Abashevo cultural and historical inercommunity with several subcultures (Fig. 2.5-B).

4. A complete review of the history of study of the Sintashta culture can be seen in the introductory article of D. Zdanovich (2002b).

5. Only information about the Sintashta settlement is published; information about two other sites have been published on a limited scale.

6. According to G. Zdanovich (verbal communication), the soil that was used for building the walls had been enriched by some additional components; this statement was inferred from chemical analysis of the natural soil and "soil" used for the wall construction.

7. Full-scale field investigation of the Olginskoye fortified settlement began in the summer 2005, under the authors' direction.

8. In the summer of 2005, G. B. Zdanovich recommended the work on the Big Sintashta Kurgan aiming to explore unexcavated parts of the site.

9. At the time of writing, the earliest finds of the disklike (shield) cheek-pieces come from Trans-Uralian and Cis-Uralian Sintashta sites, the Potapovka sites of the Volga area, and the Abashevo burials of the Volga and Don region.

10. There are some graves in which the "wheel impressions" were clearly not parallel; also, some graves have only one "wheel impression." In the Sintashta cemetery, in one grave there were four "impressions," and only two of them preserved the traces of felloe and spokes. We do not see any controversy here, because it comes to the sacral sphere, in which the principle "pars pro toto" is common. It also is important to consider possible symbolic (partial or temporary) chariot placement.

11. A. A. Tkachev names the sites of central Kazakhstan with the term of "Nurtai type," emphasizing by this its specific features, although he does not deny its affiliation to the Petrovka culture.

12. This size is determined only within fortifications; in some settlements, traces of occupation are recorded in a wider area. However, because these settlements have been insufficiently investigated, it is not easy to determine their precise size.

13. In particular, this is well documented in the excavation of the Usty'e site.

14. One can speak about the difference in house architecture between the Urals and northern Kazakhstan. The latter are usually smaller and preferably built of wood, whereas the former have a wooden-earthen construction.

15. Unfortunately, this statement is based on a single published example of the complex analysis of metal coming from the Kulevchy-III site. Although based on the scholars' opinion, such a situation is very similar to other Petrovka sites (Degtyareva et al. 2001; Grigory'ev 2000b).

16. It is possible that in other cases the settlements were destroyed by modern construction.

17. In this case, the deceased were placed across the grave's long axes and oriented to the north.

18. Apparently, in most cases this was an imitation, although in the Nikolayevka burial ground in the "wheel pit" a bronze nail has been discovered.

19. Millet grain scales have been discovered at Alandskoye in the floor depression in one of the houses. Pieces of millet also were found in the food remains from pots of Arkaim and Alandskoye (Gaiduchenko 2002a: 403).

20. The channels that are visible on aerial photos around the site are interpreted by specialists as the traces of some sort of irrigation or drainage system (Zdanovich 1995). However, in order to prove or confute this argument, a special project should be organized.

21. For the Indo-Iranians, Yima/Yama is the primordial ancestor and the king of the beyond (Pyankov 2002: 42).

22. G. Zdanovich thinks that people abandoning the settlement set them on fire deliberately. It is also probable that the fire traces could be from wildfire.

23. In Bolshekaragansky kurgan 25, only 50 percent of the dead were children.

24. In the Eneolithic (the third millennium BC), the southern Urals was included into the Trans-Uralian and northern Kazakhstan Eneolithic subarea (Zaibert 1993), which was a part of large area of cultures with geometrical pottery ornamentation. This area stretched from the Ob' River and Aral Sea up to the Baltic Sea. Large permanent settlements and small seasonal camps, occupied by the horse-hunters and fishers, characterize the Trans-Uralian Eneolithic culture.

25. The burial pottery appears to be of a standard type, perhaps because of a rigid selection required by ritual prescriptions.

26. There are single complexes of the Yamnaya culture, but they are currently seen as very modest.

27. The linguistic-paleontological approach employs the names of trees and animals to delineate the homeland territory – the ecological area of proto-language (Hajdu 1985; Napolskikh 1997).

28. This is documented by accumulations of shells and baked molluscs found in some settlements near the hearths (Goldina 1999)

29. This is partly confirmed by paleoantropological material. Craniological analysis showed that people buried in the Balanovo cemetery were almost completely of the Middle Mediterranean craniological type, which was not known earlier (Akimova 1963).

30. In the Vyatka basin, the Balanovo pottery was found on the floor of houses together

with the Eneolithic Garinskaya pottery (Goldina 1999:130).

31. In the east, these are paralleled with the Samus-Okunevo cultures.

32. Traditionally, in Russian archaeology, the main criteria of archaeological culture identification is the ceramic style. The Seima-Turbino metal objects did not have clear pottery accompaniments, and therefore it has been difficult to find a concept that would correspond to accepted categories.

3. Stabilization, Colonization, and Expansion in the Late Bronze Age

1. This review does not consider the Srubnaya materials of the Trans-Urals sites: Spasskoye and Tavlykayevo (Gorbunov 1989: 54–5), which are, so far, not numerous. However, they do contain Alakul and Fyodorovo materials. Different local variants of the Srubnaya culture are characterized by some heterogeneity in terms of correlation between different types of sites. If, in the Cis-Urals, most sites are settlements, then in the Low Volga area the situation is reversed and burial grounds prevail (Kachalova 1993).

2. The Iranian hypothesis with regard to the Scythian language is considered to be well grounded. Scythian words and names as well as the elements of the Scythian mythology became known thanks to close contacts with Greeks in the northern Pontic area. The epic poetry of the Ossetians and other peoples of the Caucasus-speaking languages of the Iranian group date back to the Scythian time (Abayev 1949; Rayevsky 1985).

3. The term "Andronovo cultural and historical community" was introduced by Formozov (1951)

4. In central Kazakhstan, the sites of the Alakul affiliations with a mixture of the Fyodorovo are known under the name of Atasu (Kuzmina 1994).

5. Here, as earlier, we do not describe numerous mining sites, which, as a rule, are difficult to attribute culturally and chronologically.

6. In some sites of central Kazakhstan, stone was not used for house building. Stone use tended to rise gradually from west to east. It was used basically to reinforce the foundation walls, not the house walls.

7. In the northern periphery of the Alakul area, small houses that were excavated

(Koryakova et al. 1991) are possibly connected with the conditions of the forest zone.

8. It is interesting to refer to the situation that was described by Matveyev with relation to the Alakul burials of the Trans-Urals. He noticed that in all cases when it was possible to identify sex of cremated persons, they were women (1998: 199).

9. For the Minusinsk depression, a rather substantial series of C-14 dates has recently been received. The Andronovo (Fyodorovo) sites are related to the period between 1800 cal BC and 1500 cal BC, and they are succeeded by the Karasuk culture (Corsdorf et al. 2004).

10. This inventory is taken from the review relating to western Kazakhstan (Evdokimov & Usmanova 1990: 77–80). As for the Trans-Urals, the picture is more modest.

11. In the late nineteenth century, in order to facilitate an assessment of property of the Kazaks, the Russian administration introduced the system of value of different kinds of livestock. A horse was considered a principle unit of calculation. Thus, a colt $= 1/6$ of a horse; cow $= 5/6$ of a horse; a calf $= 1/6$ of a cow. A camel was equal to 2 horses; young camel (two-year-old) $= 1$ horse; one-year-old $= 1/2$ of a horse; goat and sheep $= 1/6$ of a horse (Kosarev 1991: 37).

12. Kuzmina's arguments: (1) genetic connection between some elements of the Andronovo cultural complex and some elements of culture of the Iranian speaking Saka and Sauromatians; (2) the Andronovo tradition can be traced in the culture of some Iranian, Indic, and relict peoples (type of big house in Ossetia, Hindu-Kush, and Hindustan, pottery handmade pottery etc.); (3) cultural and economic type of the ancient Indo-Iranians reconstructed on the data from written sources, historical tradition, linguistic and ethnographic material finds a correspondence in Central-Eurasian zone.

13. The Novo-Shadrino VII settlement was excavated by Korochkova in the 1980s. Together with several houses, two large ash accumulations have been discovered there. They contained many ceramic sherds, clay pieces, animal bones, and separated human bones. One of two ash accumulations produced the remains of thirteen fractioned human skeletons, which were deposited by several groups together with rubbish in the center of ash pit. Dogs had nibbled some of the bones. By the time of the bones deposition into the ash pit, they were not yet free

of soft tissue and had been put into some covering. This settlement burial may reflect some stage of the funeral ritual connected with partial cremation or freeing of bones of the soft tissue (Korochkova 1999).

4. On the Eve of a New Epoch: Final Bronze Age

1. The Kent site is situated in the Kent mountain-forest massive near Karaganda town (central Kazakhstan). Covering a territory of 150,000 m², about one hundred ruined buildings have been discovered. Cultural deposits reach 1.20 m. The settlement has a rather large district consisting of numerous smaller villages. The excavated area is about 2,632 m², where eight dwelling structures and one "big enclosure" have been revealed. A rich collection of artifacts represents various activities of the local population (Varfolomeyev 2003).

5. The Transition to the Iron Age and New Tendencies in Economic Development

1. This chapter is based on the paper "Introduction of iron in Central-Northern Eurasia," prepared with the participation of G. Bel'tikova and S. Kuzminykh for the conference *Introduction of Iron in Eurasia*, Uppsala, October 2000.

2. These figures are based on the following publications: the Yamnaya culture – Bogdanov (1995); Grakov (1958); Morgunova (2000); Morgunova and Kravtsov (1994); Porokh (1999); Vasily'ev (1980); the Catacombnaya culture – Shramko and Mashkarov (1993); the Afanasyevo culture – Gryaznov (1999); Stepanova (1997).

3. These figures are provided by the following publications: Bolshov (1988); Kakhovski (1983); Kazakov (1994); Khalikov (1977); and Patrushev (1984, 1990).

6. The Southern Ural within the Nomadic World: At the Cultural Crossroads

1. The process of evolutional development of nomadism was intensively studied in Russia in the 1950–1980s in terms of stadial theory (Akishev 1972; Gryaznov 1957; Rudenko 1961). Three basic stages of livestock breeding were distinguished: (1) pridomnaya (herding nearby village), (2) pastoral (as a form of driving herds from one part of a pasture to another), and (3) yailazh-naya (when herds were grazing on seasonal pastures). Later research showed that in reality there were many different types and forms of stock-breeding and the transition to nomadism was far from a stadial development (Masanov 1995; Shamiladze 1982).

2. This term is known from the early Hungarian history. The period of the occupation of the Carpathian Basin by the nomadic Hungarians or Magyars is called in the Hungarian genesis legend "the Conquest period" or " the Conquest of new fatherland" (the end of the ninth century CE). Historically known are some stages of their ancestors' "journey" from the ancient homeland (in the Trans-Urals) to the new one. These are following: (1) "Magna Hungaria" – in the western side of the Southern Urals and low Kama river (500–700 CE); (2) "Levedia" – somewhere in the Don river area among the Khazars (700–850 CE); (3) "Etelkoze" – in the low Dnepr and Dniester rivers area (850–890 CE) from where they made repeated raids westward and that completed by the formation of the early Hungarian kingdom (Fodor 1975).

3. The concept of a nomadic mode of production goes back to Markov's works. He characterized it as the following: (1) natural-self-sufficient character of production; (2) craft and trade are not specialized within society; (3) division of labor exists only on the level of cooperation, mutual aid, and communal work; (4) the cycle of material production is totally realized by the households or their groups; (5) close connection (synthesis) of individual with a community, environments, animals, mode of life, labor cycle, material culture, and spiritual culture; (6) correspondence between labor expanses and "caring capacity" of environment; (7) universal but spontaneous character of social stratification; (8) domination of economic forms of property, dependency, and exploitation; and (9) the underdevelopment of social-administrative institutions (Markov 1976).

4. The first historical evidence about such a system relates to the Hsiung-nu – nomadic tribes that occupied the Mongolian and Trans-Baikal steppes from the third to the first centuries BC. Their empire was divided into three parts: center, left wing, and right wing. They were commanded by highest chief (the Shan-yu) and his closest relatives; in particular, the left wing was commanded by elder sun of the Shan-yu – the heir to the throne. Shan-yu had

supreme power. The next level in the Hsiung-nu hierarchy was occupied by the tribal chiefs and elders. The army was based on the decimal principle: it was divided into "thousands," which were headed by tribal chiefs. "Thousands" were divided into "hundreds," and "tens," which were commanded by clan leaders of different ranks. The systems of military and civil hierarchy existed in parallel (Kradin 2001). The same system was recorded for the Mongolian society.

5. For example, the Early Sarmatian culture has its archaeological equivalent in the Prokhorovo culture. The sites of the large area between the Volga and Trans-Urals were united under the name of the Sauromatian culture, which appeared homogeneous twenty years ago, but now several local subcultures have been revealed that are not necessarily connected to the historical Sauromatians. This has caused a detailed discussion about the subordination of the concepts "archaeological culture," "epoch" (there are the terms such as "Sarmatian Epoch"), "cultural and historical entity," and so on (Moshkova 1988).

6. We are aware that Herodotus's *History*, especially in the part relating to "barbarians," is very controversial and that it contains earlier historical tradition and folklore materials, which can be far from the historical reality.

7. The Tanais River is commonly identified with the River Don. However, there are some other interpretations.

8. Tolstov (1948) interpreted these events as the results of the deliberate politics of the Hsiung-nu cooperating with Bactrian kings who aimed to be secure from the powerful Yueh-Chih.

9. The Scythian epoch is also internally divided into two periods: (1) the Early Scythian (seventh–sixth centuries BC) and (2) the Classical Scythian period (fifth–fourth centuries BC). Additionally, more detailed chronology and historical periodization of European Scythia is suggested (Alexeyev 2004).

10. With respect to the Tasmola culture, one has to be precise about its definition. Traditionally, the kurgans with so-called moustaches (stone patches branching from the kurgan), were regarded as the main marker of this culture (Davis-Kimball et al. 1995). The latest large-scale excavations of such kurgans have demonstrated that those constructions relate to the late first mil-

lennium CE. They belong to the later nomadic culture of so-called Selentashskii type. The material of the seventh–third centuries BC, which attests the Tasmola culture, is connected with the standard kurgans, which were reused in medieval times (Botalov 2000; Tairov 1999).

11. In northern Kazakhstan and southern Trans-Urals, the average temperatures of July were on $1–1.5°C$ lower than the norm in present times (Tairov 2003: 51).

7. The World of Cultures of Cis-Urals Forest Zone of Eastern Europe: The Maintenance of Cultural Identities

1. The two latter groups constitute the Volga Finns.

2. It was divided into Permic languages in the east and Finno-Volgaic in the west.

3. The history of the Finno-Ugric peoples has long been the focus of interest of archaeologists, ethnographers, and linguists of the former USSR. Numerous studies have resulted about the general line of cultural continuity in the forest zone of the Cis-Urals, at least from the Bronze Age to historical timed. (An extended bibliography can be found in Goldina 1999; Hajdu 1985; and Napolskikh 1997.)

4. According to Ostanina (1997), following Gening (1967), the conclusive stage of the Cheganda subculture corresponds to a separate culture known as Mazuninskaya. The number of its sites is 3.3 times more than those of the Cheganda and Kara-Abyz (Ostanina 1997: 85).

5. This group of sites is also known under the name of the Azelino culture (third–fifth centuries BC), fully described by Gening (1963).

6. The Great Folk Movement is the conditional term characterizing a large series of ethnic displacements and migrations in Eurasia in the fourth–eighth centuries CE. It was finalized by frontal shift of barbarian tribes (Samarians, Goths, Huns, Germans) to the Roman Empire.

8. The Forest-Steppe Cultures of the Urals and Western Siberia: On the Northern Periphery of the Nomadic World

1. More detailed characteristics of Trans-Uralian pottery traditions can be found in Sharapova 2004.

2. These cultures of the taiga zone are not included in our review.

3. We should stress that such a model of cultural interactions between Central Asia and western Siberia was realized repeatedly in historical times.

4. For a long time, in Marxist archaeology, the development of late prehistoric societies was regarded within the concept of *military democracy*, which, however, could not embrace all varieties of transitional forms preceding an early state. In search of various forms of social evolution in late prehistory (pre–state level) in the 1970s, some Russian scholars accepted and developed the concept of chiefdom (Khazanov 1979; Vasilyev 1981; Kradin 1992; Berezkin 1995) as an intermediate sociopolitical organization, which emerges when there are stable conditions of surplus product growth. Chiefdom is based on social ranking, but its structure is conditioned by clan relationships. Typologically, a "chiefdom" can be seen to correspond with the "military-hierarchical" society, following military *democracy*, or "ehtnopotestal unions," which are common within Russian classificatory nomenclature (Kubbel 1988). Some research, however, correlates it with a stage of military democracy (Gulyaev 1987).

5. It is historically known that the ancient Turks (*Tuku* and *Tele* of Chinese chronicles) were connected with northern Hsiung-nu tribes. The *Tuku* tribes were united into the first state (the first Turkic khanate) in the early sixth century CE. Since that time, the Turkic-speaking people largely occupied western Siberia, Kazakhstan, and Central Asia. However, scholars relate the early appearance of Turks here to the last centuries of the first millennium BC/beginning of the first millennium CE (Okladnikov 1968).

6. The big composite bow is usually represented by two pairs of bone plaques, which were used for strengthening its central part and two shoulders. Such a bow was about 1.30 m in length.

7. We have not reviewed the Kulay culture, because it is outside the geographical framework of this book. The Kulay-culture sites are distributed in the northern taiga zone of the Ob' River basin. Its cultural marker is very specific pottery with sophisticated stamped decoration.

9. Social Trends in North-Central Eurasia during the Second and First Millennia BC

1. There are some facts confirming the penetration of the Abashevo population into the forest-mountain zone, but they are more sporadic than constant.

2. Despite many unsolved problems in the study of the Cherkaskul culture itself, its southward spread is well documented archaeologically and cannot be doubted.

3. We use the term "egalitarian" in a relative meaning, because we are convinced that an inequality is an attribute of human social life. Olga Artemova (1993), based on extensive ethnographic study and analysis, concluded that there is no early, or initial, egalitarian form of life. There is evidence of inequality in the Palaeolithic and among the most seemingly noncomplex living peoples.

4. As we pointed out earlier, paleoclimatologists have not found any serious ecological changes between the third and fourth quarters of the second millennium BC.

5. The only exclusion is monumental architecture, the utilitarian meaning of which is still under question.

6. The Irmen culture has produced a series of clay vessels from the Milovanovo settlement (Upper Ob') with imprints of cereal and millet. Grinding stones are also well represented.

7. Research of ethnographic materials characterizing the forest populations of western Siberia provide information about such a form of collective hunting (*pokoluga* – a local term). Groups of hunters waited for the animals in places where they crossed a river (Matushchenko 1999a: 113). Archaeologically, this form of hunting is represented on petroglyphs and on a series of hunting devices.

8. In addition to the animal and fish bones, various hunting and fishing tools are usual in the taiga settlements.

9. Fishing specialization is well documented by the Tukh-Emtor IV site, which has yielded a great quantity of river fish bones and net weights (Matushchenko 1999a: 104).

10. The archaeological layer in these sites is very modest in artifacts.

REFERENCES

Abyaev, V. I. 1949. *Osetinsky yazyk i folklore*. Moscow-Leningrad: AN SSSR.

Agapov, S. A., I. B. Vasily'ev, O. V. Kuzmina, & A. P. Semenova. 1983. Srubnaya kultura lesostepnogo Povolzhy'a. In *Bronze Age cultures of eastern Europe*, ed. S. A. Agapov. Kuibyshev: Kuibyshev Pedagogical University: 6–58

Ageyev, B. B. 1992. *Pyanoborskaya kultura*. Ufa: Nauka.

Akimova, M. S. 1963. Paleoantropologicheskiye materialy iz Balanovskogo mogilnika. In *Balanovski mogilnik. Iz istoriyi lesnogo Povolzhy'a v epokhu bronzy*, ed. O. N. Bader. Moscow: Academy of Science Press: 322–362.

Akishev, K. A. 1972. K probleme proiskhozhdeniya nomadisma v aridnoi zone drevnego Kazakhstana. In *Poiski i raskopki v Kazakhstane*, ed. K. A. Akishev. Alma-Ata: Nauka: 31–46.

Alabin, P. V. 1859. Ananyinski mogilnik. *Vyatskiye gubernskiye vedomosti* 27–30.

———. 1860 Ananyinski mogilnik. *Vestnik Imperatorskogo Russkogo geograficheskogo obshchestva* 29.

Alexeyev, A. Y. 2003. *Khronologiya Evropeiskoi Skifiyi*. St. Petersburg: The Hermitage Publishing House.

———. 2004. Some chronological problems of European Scythia: archaeology and radiocarbon. In *Impact of the Environment on Human Migration in Eursaia*, ed. E. Marian Scott, A. Y. Alekseyev, A. Y., & G. Zaitseva. London: Kluwer Academic Publishers: 9–20.

Alexeyev, V. A., & E. F. Kuznetsova. 1983. Kenkazgan – drevniy rudnik Tsentralnogo Kazakhstana. In *Sovetskaya arkheologoya* 2: 203–12.

Alexandrovsky, A. L. 2003. *Paleoklimaty golotsena po dannym izucheniya pogrebennykh pochv stepnoi zony*. Paper presented to the Chteniya, posvyashchennyie 100-letiyu deyatelnosti V. A. Gorodtsova v Gosudarstvennom Istoricheskom Muzeye, Moscow, 2003: 192–3.

Andreyeva, E. G., & A. G. Petrenko. 1976. Drevniye mlekopitayushchiye po arkheologicheskim materialam Srednego Povolzh'ya i Verkhnego Prikamy'a. In *Iz arkheologiyi Volgo-Kamy'a*, ed. A. K. Khalikov. Kazan: Institute of Language, Literature and History: 176–90.

Andreyeva, T. G. 1967. Zhivotnye Prikamy'a anannyinskogo vremeni po ostatkam iz arkheologocheskikh pamyatnikov. *Uchenye zapiski Permskogo Gosudarstvennogo Universiteta* 148: 171–86.

Andrianov, B. V. 1968. Khozyaistevenno-kulturnyje tipy i istorieskii protsess. *Sovetskaya etnografiya* 2: 5–20.

Anthony, D. V., & D. R. Brown. 2003. Eneolithic Horse Rituals and Riding in the Steppe: New Evidences. In *Prehistoric Steppe Adaptation and the Horse*, ed. M. G. Levin, C. Renfrew, & K. Boyle. Oxford: McDonald Institute for Archaeological Research: 55–65.

Antipina, E., & A. Morales. 2003. Srubnaya Faunas and Beyond: a Critical Assesment of the Archaeozoological Information from the East European Steppe. In *Prehistoric Steppe Adaptation and the Horse*, ed. M. G. Levin, C. Renfrew, & K. Boyle. Oxford: McDonald Institute for Archaeological Research: 329–51.

Aronsson, K., & S.-D. Hedman. 2000. Intercultural contacts among Eurasian Pastoral Nomads. The Case of Northern Fennoscandia. In *Kurgans, Ritual Sites, and Settlements:*

Eurasian Bronze and Iron Age, ed. J. Davis-Kimball, E. M. Murphy, L. Koryakova, & L. T. Yablonsky. BAR International Series 890. Oxford: Archaeopress: 185–93.

Artamonov, M. I. 1972. Skifskoje tsarstvo. *Sovetskaya arkheologiya* 3: 56–67.

Artemova, O. Yu. 1993. Pervobytnyi egalitarizm I ranniye formy sotsialnoi differentsitsiyi. In *Ranniye formy sotsialnoi differentsiatsiyi*, ed. V. A. Popov. Moscow: Nauka: 40–70.

Arutyunov, S. A. 1989. *Narody i kultury: razvitiye i vzaimodeistviye*. Moscow: Nauka.

Aruz, J., A. Farkas, A. Alexeyev, & E. Korolkova. (eds.) 2000. *The Golden Deer of Eurasia*. New York: The Metropolitan Museum of Art and Yale University Press.

Ashikhmina, L. I. 1987. Klad s Buiskogo gorodishcha. In *Novyje arkheologicheskiye issledovaniya na territoriyi Urala*, ed. R. D. Goldina. Izhevsk: Udmurt University: 25–50.

———. 1992. *Rekonstruktsiya predstavlenij o mirovom dereve u naseleniya Severnogo Priuraly'a v epokhu bronzy i rannego zheleza*. Syktyvkar: Komi center of RAS.

Aspelin, J. 1877. Antiquitès du Nord Finno-ougrien. *Travaux de la 3-e-session du Congres Intern. Des Orientalistes* II.

Avanesova, N. A. 1979. Problema istoriyi andronovskogo kulturnogo yedinstva. Ph.D. dissertation: Moscow: Moscow State University.

———. 1991. *Kultura pastusheskikh plemen epokhi bronzy Asiatskoi chasti SSSR (po metallicheskim izdeliyam)*. Taskent: Fan.

Bader, O. N. 1964. *Drevneishiye metallurgi Priuraly'a*. Moscow: Nauka.

Bader, O. N., & A. K. Khalikov. 1987. Balanovskaya kultura. In *Epokha bronzy lesnoi polosy SSSR*, ed. O. N. Bader, D. A. Krainov, & M. F. Kosarev (Arkheologiya SSSR). Moscow: Nauka: 76–83.

Bader, O. N., D. A. Krainov, & M. F. Kosarev. (eds.) 1987. *Epokha bronzy lesnoi polosy SSSR* (Arkheologiya SSSR). Moscow: Nauka.

Bagautdinov, R. S., L. N. Zhigulina, L. V. Kuznetsova, N. P. Salugina, & V. A. Skarabovenko. 1979. Raboty Kuibyshevskogo universiteta na novostroikakh Srednego Povolzhy'a. In *Arkheologicheskiye otkrytiya 1978 g.*, ed. B. A. Rybakov. Moscow: Nauka: 156–7.

Baiburin, A. K. 1981. Semioticheskij status veshchei i mifologiya. *Sbornik muzeya antropologiyi i etnografiyi ANSSSR* XXXVII: 200–20.

———. 1983. *Zhilishche v obryadakh i predstaveniyakh vostochnykh slavyan*. Leningrad: Nauka.

Balabanova, M. A. 2000. Dinamika kraniologiyi kochevnikov Yuzhnogo Priuraly'a i Niznego Povolzhy'a v VI-I vv. do n.e. In *Rannesarmatskaya kultura: formirovaniye, razvitiye, khronologiya*, ed. V. N. Myshkin. Samara: Samarski Nauchnyi Tsentr RAN: 95–104.

Barfield, T. J. 1991. Inner Asia and Cycles of Power in China's Imperial Dynastic History. In *Rulers from the Steppe: State Formations on the Eurasian Periphery*, ed. G. Seamon, & D. Marks. Los Angeles: Ethnographic Press: 21–62.

Bartseva, T. I. 1981. *Tsvetnaya metalloobrabotka skifskogo vremeni*. Moskow: Nauka.

Bel'tikova, G. V. 1986. Itkulskoye I gorodishche – mesto drevenego metallurgicheskogo proizvodstva. In *Problemy Uralo-Sibirskoi arkheologiyi*, ed. V. Kovaleva. Sverdlovsk: Ural State University: 63–79.

———. 1993. Razvitiye itkulskogo ochaga metallurgii. In *Voprosy arkheologiyi Urala*, ed. V. Kovaleva. Ekaterinburg: Ural State University: 93–108.

———. 1997. Zauralskii ochag metallurgiyi: Ph.D. dissertation: Moscow, Institute of Archaeology RAS.

———. 2002. Itkulskij ochag metallurgiyi: orientatsiyi, svyazi. *Uralski istoricheskj vestnik* 8: 142–63.

Benecke, N., & v.d. Driesch. 2003. Horse Exploitation in the Kazakh Steppes during the Eneolithic and Bronze Age. In *Prehistoric Steppe Adaptation and the Horse*, ed. M. G. Levin, C. Renfrew, & K. Boyle. Oxford: McDonald Institute for Archaeological Research: 69–82.

Berestenev, S. I. 1994. Poseleniye Tarantsevo i vopros o naseleniyi Dneprovskogo lesostepnogo mezhdurechy'a v nachale rannego zheleznogo veka. *Rossijskaya arkheologiya* 3: 121–9.

Berezanskaya, S. S. 1982. *Severnaya Ukraina v epokhu bronzy*. Kiev: Naukova Dumka.

Berezanskaya, S. S., & Y. P. Gershkovich. 1983. Andronovskie elementy v srubnoi kul'ture na Ukraine. In *Bronzovyi vek stepnoi polosy Uralo-Irtyshskogo mezhdurech'ya*, ed. G. B. Zdanovich. Chelyabinsk: Chelyabinsk State University: 100–10.

Berezkin, Y. E. 1995. *Arkaim kak tseremonial'nyi tsentr: vzglyad amerikanista*. Paper presented to the Konvergetsiya i divergentsiya v razvitiyi kultur epokhi eneolita – bronnzy Srednei i Voctochnoi Evropy, Saratov, 1995: 29–39.

Berseneva, N. 2005. *Pogrebalnaya obryadnost naseleniya srednego Priirtyshy'a v epokhu rannego zheleza: sotsialnye aspecty*. Ekaterinburg: Institite of history and Archaeology of RAS.

Besedin, V. I. 1995. O khronologiyi Pepkinskogo kurgana. *Rossijskaya archeologiya* 3: 197–200.

Bichurin, N. Y. 1953a. *Sobraniye svedenij o narodakh, obitavshikh v Srednei Aziyi v drevniye vremena* I. Moscow-Leningrad: Academy of Science Press.

———. 1953b. *Sobraniye svedenij o narodakh, obitavshikh v Srednei Aziyi v drevniye vremena* II. Moscow: Academy of Science Press.

———. 1953c. *Sobraniye svedenij o narodakh, obitavshikh v Srednei Aziyi v drevniye vremena* III. Moscow-Leningrad: Academy of Science Press.

Bidzilya, V. I., G. A. Voznesenskaya, D. P. Nedopako, & S. V. Pan'kov. 1983. *Istoriya chernoi metallurgiyi na terripotoriyi USSR*. Kiev: Naukova Dumka.

Bobrov, V. V., T. A. Chikisheva, & Y. A. Mikhailov. 1993. *Mogilnik epokhi pozdnei bronzy Zhuravlevo-4*. Novosibirsk: Nauka.

Bochkarev, V. S. 1978. Pogrebeniya liteishchikov epokhi bronzy. In *Problemy arkheologiyi 2*. Leningrad: Leningrad State University: 30–52.

———. 1991. Volgo-Uralskij ochag kulturogeneza epokhi pozdnei bronzy. In *Sotsiogenez i kulturogenez v istoricheskom aspekte*, ed. V. M. Masson. St. Petersburg: Institute for History of Material Culture: 24–7.

———. 1995a. Karpato-dunaiskii i Volgo-Ural'skii ochag kul'turogeneza epokhi bronzy. In *Konvergetsija i divergentsija v razvitii kul'tur epohi eneolita – bronnzy Sredney i Voctochnoi Evropy*, ed. V. S. Bochkarev. St. Petersburg: Institute for History of Material Culture: 18–29.

———. 1995b. Kulturogenez i razvitiye metalloproizvodstva v epokhu pozdnei bronzy (po materialam yuzhnoi poloviny Vostochnoi Evropy). In *Drevniye indoiranskiye kultury Volgo-Uraly'a*, ed. I. B. Vasily'ev. Samara: Samara Pedagogical University: 114–23.

Bogatkina, O. G. 1992. Ostatki mlekopitaushchikh iz raskopok gorodishcha Sorochyi Gory. In *Arkheologicheskiye pamyatniki zony vodokhranilishch Volgo-Kamskogo kaskada*. Kazan: Kazan State University: 76–85.

Bogdanov, S. V. 1990. Parnye pogrebeniya drevneyamnoy kultury s raschlenyonnymi kostyakami. In *Arheologiya Volgo-Uralskikh stepei*, ed. G. Zdanovich. Chelyabinsk: Chelyabinsk University: 48–60.

———. 1995. *Otchet ob okhrannykh raskopkakh v Orenburgskoi oblasti v 1995 g.* Arkhiv Instituta arkheologiyi. Manuskript.

———. 1998. Bol'shoy Dedurovskiy Mar. In *Arheologicheskie pamyatniki Orenburzhya*, ed. N. L. Morgunova. Orenburg: DIMUR: 48–60.

———. 1999. Drevneishiye kurgannyje kultury stepnogo Priuraly'a: problemy kulturogeneza. Ph.D. dissertation: Ufa, Institute of History, Language and Literature.

———. 2000a. Drevneyamnyj nekropol v okrestnostyakh s. Grachevka. In *Arkheologicheskiye pamyatniki Orenburzhy'a* V, ed. N. L. Morgunova. Orenburg: "Orenburgskaya guberniya": 11–26.

———. 2000b. Materialy tipa Kasimcha-Suvorovo iz okrestnostej Novoorska v sisteme eneoloticheskikh drevnostej Vostochnoi Evropy. In *Kulturnoye naslediye stepei*, ed. S. V. Bogdanov. Orenburg: "Orenburgskaya guberniya": 8–28

———. 2000c. Problemy formirovaniya drevneishikh kurgannykh kultur vostoka Yuzhno-Russkikh stepei. In *Problemy izucheniya eneolita i bronzovogo veka Urala*, ed. S. Zasedateleva. Orsk: Institute for Studies of Eurasian Steppe: 10–6.

———. 2001. *Pershinski kurgannyi mogilnik*. Paper presented to the XV Uralskoye arkheologicheskoye soveshchaniye, Orenburg, 2001: 64–7.

———. 2004. *Epokha medi stepnogo Priuraly'a*. Ekaterinburg: Ural Branch of Russian Academy of Sciences.

Bogdanov, S. V., & M. F. Khalyapin. 2000. Pogrebalnye pamyatniki pokrovskoi epokhi v stepnom Priuraly'e. In *Kulturnoye naslediye stepei severnoi Evraziyi*, ed. A. L. Chibilyev. Orenburg: The Institute of Steppe Studies: 44–56.

Bogdanov, S. V., A. U. Kravtsov, & N. L. Morgunova. 1992. Kurgany drevneyamnoi kultury v levoberezhye r. Ural. In *Drevnaya istoria naseleniya Volgo-Uralskikh stepei*, ed. A. Sinyuk. Orenburg: Orenburg Pedagogical Institute: 80–91.

Bokovenko, N., & I. Zasetskaya. 1994. *The Origin of Hunnish cauldrons in East-Europe*. Paper presented to the The Archaeology of the Steppes: Methods and Strategies. Naples, 1994: 701–24.

Bokovenko, N. A. 1996. Asian Influence on European Scythia. *Ancient Civilizations from Scythia to Siberia* III (1): 97–122.

———. 2004. Migrations of early nomads of the Eurasain steppe in the context of climatic changes. In *Impact of the Environment on Human Migration in Eursaia*, ed. G. Zaitseva. London: Kluwer Academic Publishers: 21–34.

Bokovenko, N. A., & I. P. Zasetskaya. 1993. Proiskhozhdeniye kotlov "gunnskogo" tipa Vostochnoi Evropy v svete problemy khunno-gunnskikh svyazei. *Peterburgskii arkheologicheski vestnik* 3: 80–9.

Bolshov, S. V. 1988. *Mogilnik na ostrove Mol'-bishchenski: Katalog arkheologicheskikh kollektsii.* Yoshkar-Ola: Marijski Muzei.

Bondarenko, D. M., A. V. Korotayev, & N. N. Kradin. 2003. Introduction: Social Evolution, Alternatives, and Nomadism. In *Nomadic Pathways in Social Evolution*, ed. T. J. Barfield, D. M. Bondarenko, & N. N. Kradin. Moscow: Center for Civilizational and Regional Studies RAS.

Borzunov, V. A. 1992. *Zauraly'e na rubezhe bronzovogo i zheleznogo vekov (gamayunskaya kultura).* Ekaterinburg: Ural State University.

Borzunov, V. A., & G. V. Bel'tikova. 1999. Stoyanka abashevskikh metallurgov v gorno-lesnom Zauraly'e. In *120 let arkheologiyi vostochnogo sklona Urala*, ed. V. T. Kovaleva. Ekaterinburg: Ural State University: 43–52.

Botalov, S. V. 2000. Pozdnyaya drevnost i srednevekovy'e. In *Drevnyaya istoriya Yuzhnogo Zaural'ya*, ed. N. O. Ivanova Chelyabinsk: South Urals State University: 208–88.

Botalov, S. V., S. A. Grigory'ev, & G. B. Zdanovich. 1996. Pogrebalnyje kompleksy epokhi bronzy Bolshekaraganskogo mogilnika. In *Materialy po arkheologiyi i etnografiji Yuzhnogo Urala*, ed. A. D. Tairov. Chelyabinsk: Kamennyi Poyas: 64–88.

Bozi, F. 2002. Sarmaty v I v. do n.e. – II v. n.e. po dannym antichnykh istochnikov. In *Statisticheskaya obrabotka porebalnykh pamyatnikov Aziatskoi Sarmatiyi. Srednesarmatskaya kultura*, ed. M. G. Moshkova. Moscow: Institute of Archaeology RAS: 8–12.

Bradley, R. 1991. The pattern of change in British prehistory. In *Chiefdoms: Power, Economy and Ideology*. Cambridge: Cambridge University Press: 44–70.

Bromlei, Y. V., L. S. Kubbel, & V. A. Shnirelman (eds.) 1988. *Istoriya pervobytnogo obshchestva. E-pokha klassoobrazovaniya* (3). Moscow: Nauka.

Buinov, Y. V. 1980. O khozyaistve plemen bondarikhinskoi kultury. *Vestnik Kharkovskogo universiteta* 201: 94–100.

Bunatyan, E. P. 1985. *Metodika sotsialnykh reconstructsii v arheologiyi po materialam skifskikh mogilnikov 4–3 vekov do n.e.* Kiev: Naukova Dumka.

Bytkovski, O. F., & V. V. Tkachev. 1996. Pogrebalnyje kompleksy srednego bronzovogo veka iz Vostochnogo Orenburzhy'a. In *Arkheologicheskiye pamyatniki Orenburgy'a*, ed. N. L. Morgunova. Orenburg: Orenburg Pedagogical Institute: 68–84.

Carneiro, R. 1981. The Chiefdom: Precursor to the State. In *The transition to Statehood in the New World*, ed. G. Jones, & R. Kautz. Cambridge: Cambridge University Press: 37–79.

Carpelan, C., & A. Parpola. 2001. Emergence, Contacts and Dispersal of Proto-Indo-European, Proto-Uralic and Proto-Aryan in Archaeological perspective. In *Early Contacts Between Uralic and Indo-European: Linguistic and Archaeological Considerations*, ed. C. Carpelan, A. Parpola & P. Koskikallio. Helsinki: Soumalais-Ugrilainen Seura: 55–150.

Cheboksarov, N. N., & I. A. Cheboksarova. 1971. *Narody, Rasy, Kultury*. Moscow: Nauka.

Chemyakin, Yu. P. 2000. Poselenie Korkino. In *Uralskaya istoricheskaya entsiklopediya*. Ekaterinburg: Akademkniga: 281–2.

Chernai, I. L. 1985. Tekstilnoye delo i keramika po materialam iz pamyatnikov eneolita-bronzy Yuzhnogo Zauraly'a i Severnogo Kazakhstana. In *Eneolit i bronzovyi vek Uralo-Irtyshskogo mezhdurechy'a*, ed. S. Y. Zdanovich. Chelyabinsk: Chelyabinsk State University: 93–109.

Chernikov, S. S. 1949. *Drevnaya metallurgija i gornoye delo Zapadnogo Altaya*. Moscow: Nauka.

———. 1960. *Vostochnyi Kazakhstan v epokhu bronzy* (Materialy i issledovaniya po arkheologii SSSR 88). Moscow-Leningrad: Academy of Science Press.

Chernykh, E. N. 1966. *Istoriya dreveneishei metallurgiyi Vostochnoi Evropy*. Moscow: Nauka.

———. 1970. *Drevneishaya metallurgiya Urala i Povolzhya*. Moscow: Nauka.

———. 1978. Metallurgicheskiye provintsiyi i periodizatsiya epokhi rannego metalla na territoriyi SSSR. *Sovetskaya arkheologiya* 4: 53–81.

———. 1983. Problema obshchnosti kultur valikovoi keramiki v stepyakh Evrazii. In *Bronzovyi vek stepnoi polosy Uralo-Irtyshskogo mezhdurechy'a*, ed. G. B. Zdanovich. Chekyabinsk: Chelyabinsk State University: 81–99.

———. 1989. Metall i drevniye kultury: uzlovyje problemy issledovaniya. In *Estestvennonauchnyje metody i arkheologiya*, ed. E. Chernykh. Moscow: Nauka: 14–30.

———. 1992. *Ancient Metallurgy in the USSR. The Early Metal Age.* Cambridge: Cambridge University Press.

———. 1997a. *Kargaly – zabytyi mir.* Moscow: Nox.

———. 1997b. Kargaly-krupneishii gornometallurgicheskii tsentr Severnoi Evraziyi. *Rossijskaya arkheologiya* 1: 21–36.

Chernykh, E. N. (ed.) 2002. *Kargaly* (1). Moscow: Languages of Slavonic cultures.

Chernykh, E. N., S. A. Agapov, & S. V. Kuzminykh. 1989. Evraziiskaya metallurgicheskaya provintsiya kak sistema. In *Tekhnicheskii i sotzialnyi progress v epokhu pervobytno-obshchinnogo stroya*, ed. V. D. Viktorova. Sverdlovsk: Ural Division of RAS: 5–10.

Chernykh, E. N., L. I. Avilova, & L. B. Orlovskaya. 2000. *Metallurgicheskiye provintsiji i rediouglerodnaya khronologiya.* Moscow: Institute of Archaeology of RAS.

Chernykh, E. N., L. I. Avilova, L. B. Orlovskaya, & S. V. Kuzminykh. 2002b. Ancient metallurgy in the Circumpontic area: from unity to desintegration. *Rossijskaya arkheologiya* 1: 5–23.

Chernykh, E. N., & C. J. Easteo. 2002. The beginning of exploitation of Kargaly center: Radiocarbon dates. *Rossijskaya arkheologiya* 2: 44–53.

Chernykh, E. N., & S. V. Kuzminykh. 1987. Pamyatniki seiminsko-turbinskogo tipa v Evraziyi. In *Epokha bronzy lesnoi polosy SSSR*, ed. O. N. Bader. Archeologiya. SSSR. Moscow: Nauka: 84–105.

———. 1989. *Drevnyaya metallurgiya Severnoi Evraziyi (seiminsko-turbinskij fenomen).* Moscow: Nauka.

Chernykh, E. N., S. V. Kuzminykh, E. Y. Lebedeva, S. A. Agapov, V. Y. Lun'ko, L. B. Orlovskaya, T. O. Teneishvili, & D. V. Val'kov. 1999. Arkheologicheskiye pamyatniki epokhi bronzy na Kargalakh (poseleniye Gornyi i drugiye). *Rossijskaya arkheologiya* 1: 77–102.

Chernykh, E. N., S. V. Kuzminykh, E. Y. Lebedeva, & V. Y. Lunkov. 2000b. Issledovaniye kurgannogo mogilnika u s. Pershino. In *Arkheologicheskye pamyatniki Orenburzhy'a* IV, ed. N. L. Morgunova. Orenburg: "Orenburgskaya guberniya": 63–75.

Chernykh, E. N., S. V. Kuzminykh, & L. B. Orlovskaya. 2004. Ancient Metallurgy of Northern Eurasia: From the Urals to the Sayano-Altai. In *Metallurgy in Ancient Eirasia from The Urals to the Yellow River*, ed. K. M. Linduff. Chinese Studies. Lewiston, Queenston, Lampeter: The Edwin Mellen Press: 15–36.

Chernykh, E. N., E. Y. Lebedeva, & S. V. Kuzminyh. 1997. K probleme istokov zemledeliya v Vostochnoi Evrope. In *Sabatinovskaya i Srubnaya Kultury: Problemy Vzaimosvyazei Vostoka*, ed. V. N. Klushintsev. Kiev-Nikolayev-Yuznoukrainsk: 27–8.

Chernykh, E. N., & L. B. Orlovskaya. 2004. Radiouglerodnaya khronologiya yamnoi obshchnosti i istoki kurgannykh kultur. *Rossijskaya arkheologiya* 1: 84–99.

Chernykh, E. M. 1996. Kultovyi komplex Argyzhskogo gorodishcha na r. Vyatke. In *Svyatilishcha i zhertvennye mesta finno-ugorskogo naseleniya Evrazii*. Perm: 58–70.

Chernykh, E. M., V. V. Vanchikov, & V. A. Shatalov. 2002a. *Argyzskoye gorodishche na reke Vyatke.* Moscow: Institut komputernykh issledovanij.

Childe, V. G. 1927. *The Dawn of European Civilization.* London: Kegan, Paul, Trench, Trubner.

———. 1929. *The Danube in Prehistory.* Oxford: Oxford University Press.

Chindina, L. A. 1984. *Drevnaya istoriya Srednego Prioby'a v epokhu zheleza.* Tomsk: Tomsk State University.

Chlenova, N. L. 1955. O kulturakh bronzovoi epokhi lesostepnoi zony Zapadnoi Sibiri. *Sovetskaya arkheologiya* XXIII: 38–57.

———. 1981. Svyazi kultur Zapadnoi Sibiri s kulturami Priuraly'a i Severnogo Povolzhy'a. In *Problemy zapadnosibirskoi arkheologiyi. Epokha zheleza*, ed. T. N. Troitskaya. Novosibirsk: Nauka: 4–42.

———. 1994. *Pamyatniki kontsa epokhi bronzy v Zapadnoi Sibiri.* Moscow: Institute of Archaeology RAS.

————. 1997. *Tsentralnaya Azia i skify*. Moscow: Institute of archaeology RAS.

Corsdorf, J., H. Parzinger, & A. Nagler. 2004. C-14 dating of the Siberian steppe zone from Bronze Age to Scythian time. In *Impact of the Environment on Human Migration in Eurasia*, ed. E. Marian Scott, A. Y. Alexeyev, & G. Zaitseva. London: Kluwer Academic Publishers: 83–89.

Cribb, R. 1991. *Nomads in Archaeology* (New Studies in Archaeology). Cambridge: Cambridge University Press.

Daire, M.-Y., & L. N. Koryakova, ed. 2002. *Habitats et nécropoles de l'Age du Fer au carrefour de l'Eurasie*. Paris: Broccard.

Danilenko, V. N. 1974. *Eneolit Ukrainy: etnoistoricheskoe issledovanie*. Kiev: Naukova Dumka.

Davis-Kimball, J., V. Bashilov, & L. Yablonsky. (eds.) 1995. *Nomads of the Eurasian Steppe in the Early Iron Age*. Berkeley, CA: Zinat Press.

Degtyareva, A. D., S. V. Kuzminykh, & L. B. Orlovskaya. 2001. Metalloproizvodstvo petrovskikh plemen (po materialam poseleniya Kulevchi III). *Voprosy arkheologiyi, antropologiyi i etnografiyi* 3: 23–54.

Demkin, V. A., & T. S. Demkina. 1998. *Rol' prirodnoi sredy v zhizni rannikh kochenikov evraziiskikh stepei*. Paper presented to the Antichnaya tsivilizatsiya i varvarski mir, Krasnodar, 1998: 3–6.

————. 1999. O chem mogut povedat' stepnyie kurgany? *Donskaya arkheologiya* 1: 24–31.

Demkin, V. A., & I. V. Ivanov. 1985. *Razvitie pochv Prikaspiiskoi nizmennosty v golotsene*. Puchino: Nauchnyi tsentr biologicheskikh issledovanii.

Demkin, V. A., & Y. G. Ryskov. 1996. Paleoekologicheskiye usloviya sukhostepnogo Preduraly'a vo II tys. do n.e. – I tys. n.e. i ikh rol' v zhizni naseleniya bronzovogo i rannezheleznogo vekov. In *Kurgany levoberezhnogo Ileka*, ed. L. T. Yablonsky. Moscow: Institute of Archaeology RAS: 49–53.

Demkin, V. F. 1997. *Paleopochvovedeniye i arkheologiya: Integratsiya v izuchenii prirody i obshestva*. Pushchino: Nauchnyi tsentr biologicheskikh issledovanii.

Dergachev, V. A., G. I. Zaitseva, V. I. Timofeyev, A. A. Sementsov, & L. M. Lebedeva. 1996. Izmeneniya prirodnykh protsessov i radiouglerodnaya khronologiya arkheologicheskikh pamyatnikov. In *Arkheologiya i Radiouglerod*, ed. G. I. Zaitseva, V. V. Der-

gachev, & V. M. Masson. St. Petersburg: Institute for History of Material Culture: 7–17.

Dryomov, I. I. 2002. The Regional Differences in the Prestige Bronze Age Burials (Peculiarities of the Pokrovsk Group). In *Complex Societies of Central Eurasia from the 3rd to the 1st Millennium BC (Regional Specifics in Light of Global Models*, ed. K. Jones-Bley, & D. Zdanovich. Journal of Indo-European Studies Monograph Series 45. Washington, D.C.: Institute for Study of Man: 296–313.

Duryagin, V. V. 1999. Ozernyje geosistemy vostochnogo sklona Yuzhnogo Urala i ikh izmeneniye v zone tekhnogennogo vozdeistviya. Ph.D. dissertation: Perm, Perm University.

Dyakonova, V. P. 1980. Tuvintsy. In *Semeinaya obryadnost' narodov Sibiri*, ed. C. M. Gurvich. Moscow: Nauka: 113–19.

Efimova, S. G. 1991. *Paleoanthropogiya Povolzhy'a i Priuraly'a*. Moscow: Nauka.

Epimachov, A., & L. Korjakova. 2004. Streitwagen der eurasien Steppe in der Bronzezeit: Das Volga-Uralgebirge und Kasachstan. In *Rad und Wagen: Der Ursprung einer Innovation Wagen im Vorderen Orient und Europa*, ed. M. Fanca, & S. Burmeister. Oldenburg: 221–36.

Epimakhov, A. V. 1993. O khronologicheskom sootnosheniyi sintashtinskikh i abashevskikh pamyatnikov. In *Arkheologicheskiye kultury i kulturno-istoricheskiye obshchnosti Bolshogo Urala*, ed. I. B. Vasily'ev. Ekaterinburg: Nauka: 57–8.

————. 1995. Pogrebalnyje pamyatniki sintashtinskogo vremeni (arkhitekturno-planirovochnoye resheniye). In *Rossia i Vostok: Problemy vzaimodeistviya*, ed. G. B. Zdanovich. Chelyabinsk: Chelyabinsk State University: 43–7.

————. 1996. Demograficheskije aspekty sotsiologicheskikh rekonstruktsij (po materialam sintashtinsko-petrovskikh pamyatnikov). In *XIII Uralskoe arheologicheskoye soveshchaniye*, ed. V. A. Ivanov. Ufa: Vostochnyi Universitet: 58–60.

————. 2002a. Complex Societies and the Possibilities to Diagnoze them on the Basis of Archaeological Data: Sintashta type Sites of the Middle Bronze Age. In *Complex Societies of Central Eurasia from the 3rd to the 1st Millennium BC: Regional Specifics in Light of Global Models*, ed. K. Jones-Bley, & D. Zdanovich. Journal of Indo-European Studies Monograph Series 45. Washington, D.C.: Institute for Study of Man: 139–48.

———. 2002b. *Yuzhnoye Zauralye v period srednei bronzy.* Chelyabinsk: Southern Urals State University.

Erlikh, V. R. 2002a. The transition from the Bronze to the Iron Age in the North-West Caucasus (Raising a Problem) Part I. *Rossijskaya arkheologiya* 3: 26–38.

———. 2002b. The Transition from the Bronze to the Iron Age in the North-West Caucasus (Raising a Problem) Part II. *Rossijskaya arkheologiya* 4: 40–9.

Evdokimov, V. V. 1975. Novyje raskopki Alekseyevskogo poseleniya na r. Tobol. *Sovetskaya arkheologiya* 4: 163–72.

———. 1983. Khronologiya i periodizatsiya pamyatnikov Kustanaiskogo Pritoboly'a. In *Bronzovyi vek stepnoi polosy Uralo-Irtyshskogo mezhdurechy'a,* ed. G. B. Zdanovich. Chelyabinsk: Bashkir State University: 35–47.

———. 2000. *Istoricheskaya sreda epokhi bronzy stepej Tsentralnogo i Severnogo Kazakhstana.* Almaty: Institute of Archaeology of Kasakh Academy of Sciences.

Evdokimov, V. V., & V. G. Loman. 1989. Raskopki yamnogo kurgana v Karagandinskoi oblasti. In *Voprosy arkheologiyi severnogo i tsentpalnogo Kazakhstana,* ed. V. V. Evdokimov. Karaganda: Karaganda University: 34–46.

Evdokimov, V. V., & E. R. Usmanova. 1990. Znakovyi status ukrashenii v pogrebal'nom obryade (po materialam mogilnikov andronovskoi kulturno-istoricheskoi obshchnjsti is Tsentralnogo Kazakhstana). In *Arkheologiya Volgo-Uralskikh stepei,* ed. G. B. Zdanovich. Chelyabinsk: Chelyabinsk State University: 66–80.

Fedorova-Davydova, E. A. 1964. K voprosu o periodizatsiyi pamyatnikov epokhi bronzy v Yuzhnom Priuraly'e. In *Arkheologiya i etnografiya Bashkiriyi* II, ed. R. G. Kuzeyev. Ufa: Baskirskii Tsentr RAS: 84–92.

———. 1973. K probleme andronovskoi kultury. In *Problemy arkheologiyi Urala i Sibiri,* ed. V. N. Chernetsov. Moscow: Nauka: 125–64.

Fodor, I. 1975. *In Search of a New Homeland: The prehistory of the Hungarian people and the Conquest.* Budapest: Corvina Kiado.

Formozov, A. A. 1951. K voprosu o proiskhozhdeniyi andronovskoi kultury. *Kratkiye soobshcheniya Instituta istoriyi materialnoi kultury* XXXIX: 3–15.

Gaiduchenko, L. L. 1993. Sootnosheniye ostatkov domashnikh i dikikh zhivotnykh iz kazakhskikh poselenij raznogo tipa XVIII–XX vv. In *Kochevniki Uralo-Kazakhstanskikh stepei,* ed. A. D. Tairov. Ekaterinburg: Nauka: 193–6.

———. 2002a. The Biological Remains from the Forified Settlements of the Country of Towns of the Trans-Urals. In *Complex Societies of Central Eurasia from the 3rd to the 1st Millennium BC: Regional Specifics in Light of Global Models,* ed. K. Jones-Bley & D. Zdanovich. Journal of Indo-European Studies Monograph Series 45. Washington, D.C.: Institute for Study of Man: 400–16.

———. 2002b. Nekotoryje biologicheskiye kharakteristiki zhivotnykh iz zhertvennykh komplexov kurgana 25 Bolshekaraganskogo mogilnika. In *Arkaim: Nekropolis,* ed. D. Zdanovich. Chelyabinsk: South Ural Press: 173–95.

———. 2002c. Opredeleniye konstitutsionnogo i khozyaistvennogo typa loshadi po arkheozoologicheskim ostankam. In *Arkaim: Nekropolis,* ed. D. Zdanovich. Chelyabinsk: South Ural Press: 189–95.

Gaiduchenko, L. L., & D. G. Zdanovich. 2000. Raschet velichiny biomassy I poyedayemoi massy tela kopytnykh v arkheoekologicheskikh issledovaniyakh. In *Arkeologicheski istochnik I modelirovaniye drevnikh tekhnologii,* ed. G. B. Zdanovich. Chelyabinsk: Arkaim-Chelyabinsk State University: 45–72.

Gavriluk, N. A. 1999. *Ekonomika Stepnoi Skifiyi. VI -III vv. do n. e.* Kharkov: Izdatelstvo PTF.

Gei, A. N. 1999. O nekotorykh simvolicheskikh momentakh pogrebalnoi obryadnosti stepnykh skotovodov Predkavkazy'a v epokhu bronzy. In *Pogrebalnyi obryad: rekonstruktsiya i interpretatsiya drevnikh ideologicheskikh predstavlenii.* Moscow: Vostochnaya Literatura: 78–113.

———. 2001. K voprosu ob urovne sotsialnogo razvitiya stepnykh skotovodov bronzovogo veka. In *Bronzobyi vek Vostochnoi Evropy: kharakteristika kultur, khronologiya i periodizatsiya,* ed. Yu. I. Kolev, P. F. Kuznetsov, & O. V. Kuzmina. Samara: Samara State Pedagogical University: 82–4.

Gening, V. F. 1963. *Azelinskaya kultura* (Voprosy arkheologii Urala 5). Izhevsk: Ural State University.

———. 1967. Gorodishche Cheganda-I v mazuninskoye vremya. *Voprosy arkheologiyi Urala* 7: 141–63.

———. 1977. Mogilnik Sintashta i problema rannikh indoiranskikh plemen. *Sovetskaya arkheologiya* 4: 53–73.

———. 1980. Oputyatskoye gorodishche – metallurgicheski tsentr kharinskogo vremeni v Prikamy'e. In *Pamyatniki epokhi srednevekovy'a v Verkhnem Prikamy'e*, ed. R. D. Goldina. Izhevsk: Izhevsk State University: 102–39.

———. 1988. *Etnicheskaya istoriya Zapadnovo Priuraly'a na rubezhe nashei ery*. Moscow: Nauka.

Gening, V. F., G. B. Zdanovich, & V. V. Gening. 1992. *Sintashta: arheologicheskiye pamyatniki ariyskikh plemen Uralo-Kazahstanskikh stepei*. Chelyabinsk: South Ural Press.

Gershkovich, Y. P. 1998. Etnokulturnyje svyazi v epokhu pozdnei bronzy v svete khronologichekogo sootnosheniya pamyatnikov. *Arkheologicheskij almanakh* 7: 61–92.

Gimbutas, M. 1965. *Bronze Age Cultures in Central and Eastern Europe*. The Hague: Mouton, & Co.

———. 1997. *The Kurgan Culture and the Indo-Europeanization of Europe: Selected Papers from 1952 to 1993*. In M. R. Dexter & K. Jones-Bley (eds.), Journal of Indo-European Studies Monograph Series 18. Washington, D.C.: Institute for the Study of Man.

Goldina, R. D. 1999. *Drevnyaya i srednevekovaya istoriya udmurtskogo naroda*. Izhevsk: Udmurt State University.

Gorbunov, V. S. 1986. *Abashevskaya kultura Yuzhnogo Priuraly'a*. Ufa: Bashkir State University.

———. 1992. *Bronzovyi vek Volgo-Uraliskoi lesostepi*. Ufa: Baskir Pedagogical Institute.

———. 1996. *Srubnaya kulturno-istoricheskaya obshchnost' – itogi i perspektivy isucheniya*. Paper presented at the XIII Ural'skoje arheologicheskoje soveshchanije, Ufa, 1996: 80–1.

Gorbunov, V. S., & Y. A. Morozov. 1991. *Nekropol epokhi bronzy Yuznogo Priuraly'a*. Ufa: Bashkirskoye kniznoye izdatelstvo.

Gorbunova, N. 1993/94. Traditional Movements of Nomadic Pastoralists and the Role of Seasonal Migrations in the Formation of Antient Trade Routes in Central Asia. *Silk Road Art and Archaeology*: 5–10.

Gorodtsov, V. A. 1916. *Kultury bronzovoi epokhi v Srednei Rossiyi*. Moscow.

Gosden, C. 1999. The organization of society. In *Companion Encyclopedia of Archaeology*, ed.

G. Barker. London and New York: Routledge: 470–503.

Grach, A. D. 1980. *Drevniye kochevniki v tsentre Aziyi*. Moscow: Nauka.

Grakov, B. N. 1947. NAIKOKRATO MENOI (Perezhitki matriarkhata u sarmatov). *Vestnik drevnei istoriyi* 3: 100–21.

———. 1958. Stareishiye nakhodki zheleznykh veshchei v Evropeiskoi chasti SSSR. *Sovetskaya arkheologiya* 4: 3–9.

———. 1977. *Rannii zheleznyi vek*. Moscow: Moscow State University.

Grigory'ev, S. A. 2000a. Epokha bronzy. In *Drevnaya istoriya Yuzhnogo Zauraly'a. Kamennyi vek. Epokha bronzy*, ed. N. O. Iovavan. Chelyabinsk: Southern Urals State University: 222–442.

———. 2000b. Metallurgicheskoye proizvodstvo na yuzhnom Urale v epokhu srednei bronzy. In *Drevnaya istoriya Yuzhnogo Urala*, ed. N. O. Iovavan Chelyabinsk: Southern Urals State University: 444–600.

———. 2002. The Sintashta Culture and Indo-European Problem. In *Complex Societies of Central Eurasia from the 3rd to the 1st Millennium BC: Regional Specifics in Light of Global Models*, ed. K. Jones-Bley, & D. Zdanovich. Journal of Indo-European Studies Monograph Series 45. Washington, D.C.: Institute for Study of Man: 148–60.

Grigory'ev, S. A., & I. A. Rusanov. 1995. Experimentalnaya rekonstruktsiya drevnego metallurgicheskogo proizvodstva. In *Arkaim: Issledovaniya, poiski, otkrytiya*, ed. G. B. Zdanovich. Chelyabinsk: Center Arkaim: 147–58.

Gryaznov, M. P. 1927. *Pogrebeniya bronzovoi epokhi v Zapadnom Kazakhstane*. (Kazaki, V. 1). Leningrad: 179–221.

———. 1956. *Istoriya drevnikh plemen Verkhnei Obi* (Materialy i issledovaniya po arkheologiyi SSSR 48). Moscow: Nauka.

———. 1957. Etapy razvitiya khozyaistva skotovodcheskikh plemen Kazakhstana i Yuzhnoi Sibiri v epokhu bronzy. *Kratkie soobshcheniya Instituta Arkheologii SSSR XXVI*: 23–8.

———. 1980. *Arzhan – tsarskij kurgan ranneskifskogo vremeni*. Leningrad: Nauka.

———. 1983. Nachalnaya faza razvitiya skifo-sibirskikh kultur. In *Arkheologiya Yuznoi Sibiri*, ed. A. I. Martynov. Kemerovo: Kemerovo State University: 3–20.

———. 1999. *Afanasyevskaya kultura na Yenisee*. St. Petersburg: Dmitry Bulanin.

Gumilev, L. N. 1966. Istoki ritma kochevoi kultury Sredinnoi Aziyi:opyt istoriko-geographicheskogo sinteza. *Narody Aziji i Afriki* 4: 25–46.

———. 1986. Hunny v Aziyi i Evrope. *Voprosy istoriyi* 6: 67–78.

———. 1989. *Etnogenez i biosfera zemli.* Leningrad: Leningrad State University.

———. 1993a. *Hunnu: stepnaya trilogiya.* St. Petersburg: Taim-Aut – Compass.

———. 1993b. *Ritmy Evraziyi. Epokhi i tsivilizatsiyi.* St. Petersburg: Ekopros.

Gutsalov, S. Y. 1998. Kurgan ranneskifskogo vremeni na Ileke. In *Arkheologicheskiye pamyatniki Orenburzhy'a* II, ed. N. L. Morgunova. Orenburg: Demer: 136–42.

Hajdu, P. 1985. *Uralskiye yazyki I narody.* Moscow: Progress.

Hall, M. 1997. Towards an absolute chronology for the Iron Age of Inner Asia. *Antiquity* 71: 863–74.

Harding, A. 2000. *European Societies in the Bronze Age* (Cambridge World Archaeology). Cambridge: Cambridge University Press.

Heins, A. K. 1898. *Sobraniye literaturnykh trudov* II. St. Petersburg.

Herodotus. 1972. *History.* Leningrad: Nauka.

Hjarthner-Holdar, E., & C. Risberg. 1999. *Interaction between Different Regions in Sweden and Russia during the Late Bronze Age in the Light of the Introduction Iron Technology.* Paper presented to the Complex Societies of Central Eurasia in the Third to the First Millennia BC, Chelyabinsk-Arkaim, 1999: 300–02.

Ismagilov, R. 1988. Pogrebeniye Bolshogo Gumarovskogo kurgana v Yuzhnom Priuraly'e i problema proiskhozhdeniya skifskoi kultury. *Archeologicheski Sbornik Gosudarstvennogo Ermitazha* 29: 28–46.

Itina, M. A. 1961. Raskopki mogilnika tazabagy'abskoi kultury Kokcha 3. In *Mogilnik bronzovogo veka Kokcha 3*, ed. S. P. Tolstov. Materialy Khorezmskoi Expeditsiyi. Moscow: Academy of Science Press: 3–97.

———. 1963. Poseleniye Yakke-Parsan 2 In *Polevye issledovanoya Khorezmskoi expeditsiyi v 1958–1961 gg.*, ed. S. P. Tolstov. Materialy Khorezmskoi Expeditsiyi. Moscow: Academy of Science Press: 107–29.

———. 1977. *Istoriya stepnykh plemen Yuzhnogo Priaraly'a.* Moscow: Nauka.

Ivanov, I. V. 1992. *Evolutsiya pochv stepnoi zony v Golotsene.* Moscow: Nauka.

———. 1995a. Mesto sarmatskoi epokhi v sisteme landshaftno-klimaticheskilh izmenenij golotsena. In *Problemy istoriyi i kultury sarmatov*, ed. A. S. Skripkin. Volgograd: Institute of Archaeology: 85–7.

———. 1996. *Osobennosti vzaimodeistviya prirody i obshchestva na granitse Evropy i Aziyi.* Paper presented to the Vzaimodeistviye cheloveka i prirody na granitse Evropy i Aziyi, Samara, 1996: 4–6.

Ivanov, I. V., & S. S. Chernyansky. 1996. Obshchiye zakonomernosti razvitiya chernozemov.

———. 2000. Voprosy arkheologicheskogo pochvovedeniya i nelotoryje rezultaty paleopochvennykh isledovanyi v zapovednike "Arkaim." In *Arkheologicheskyi istochnik i modelirovaniye drevnikh tekhnologyi*, ed. S. Y. Zdanovich. Chelyabinsk: Center "Arkaim," Institute of History and Archaeology of RAS: 3–16.

Ivanov, V. A. 1995b. Dinamika "kochevoi stepi" v Uralo-Volzhskom regione v epokhu drevnosty i sredenvekovy'a. In *Kurgany kochevnikov Yuzhnogo Urala*, ed. B. B. Ageyev. Ufa: Gilem: 20–37.

———. 1999. *Drevniye ugro-mady'ary v Vostochnoi Evrope.* Ufa: Gimen.

Ivanova, S. V. 2001. *Sotsialnaya struktura naseleniya yamnoi kultury Severo-Zapadnogo Prichernomorya.* Odessa: Odessa Pedagogical University.

Jones-Bley, K. 2002. Indo-European Burial, the "Rig Veda" and "Avesta". In *Complex Societies of Central Eurasia from the 3rd to the 1st Millennium BC: Regional Specifics in Light of Global Models*, ed. K. Jones-Bley, & D. Zdanovich. Journal of Indo-European Studies Monograph Series 45. Washington, D.C.: Institute for Study of Man: 68–81.

Kachalova, M. K. (ed.) 1993. *Pamyatniki srubnoi kultury. Volgo-Uralskoye mezhdurechy'e.* (Arkheologiya Rossiyi. Svod arkheologicheskikh istochnikov. B 1–10. I). Saratov: Saratov State University.

Kadyrbayev, M. K., & Z. Kurmankulov. 1992. *Kultura drevnikh skotovodov i metallurgov Sary-Arki.* Alma-Ata: Gylem.

Kakhovski, B. V. 1983. Issledovaniya arkheologicheskikh pamyatnikov Chuvashii. In *Novye issledovaniya po arkheologii i etnografii Chuvashii*, ed. V. P. Ivanov, & V. A.

Prokhorova. Cheboksary: Chuvash State University: 3–25.

Kaliyeva, S. S., G. V. Kolbin, & V. N. Logvin. 1992. Mogilnik i poseleniye Bestamak. In *Margulanovskiye chteniya*, ed. V. F. Zaibert. Petropavlovsk: Petropavlovsk Pedagogical Institute: 57–9.

Kazakov, E. P. 1994. Izmerski VII mogilnik. In *Pamyatniki drevnei istoriyi Volgo-Kamy'a*, ed. P. N. Starostin. Kazan: IYaLI ANT: 20–39.

Khabarova, S. V. 1993. K voprosu ob obryade sozhzheniya v alakulskoi pogrebalnoi traditsiyi (po materialam mogilnika Ermak-4). In *Kulturnogeneticheskiye protsessy v Zapadnoi Sibiri*. Tomsk: Tomsk State University: 47–9.

Khabdulina, M. K. 1994. *Stepnoye Priishimye v epokhu rannego zheleza*. Almaty: Gylym-Rakurs.

Khabdulina, M. K., & G. B. Zdanovich. 1984. Landchaftno-klimaticheskiye kolebaniya golotsena i voprosy kulturno-istoricheskoi situatsiyi v Severnom Kazakhstane. In *Bronzovyi vek Uralo-Irtyshskogo mezhdurechy'a*, ed. G. Zdanovich. Chelyabinsk: Chelyabinsk State University: 136–58.

Khaldeyev, V. V. 1987. Skol'ko bylo sarmatov?. *Sovetskaya arkheologiya* 3: 230–31.

Khalikov, A. K. 1977. *Volgo-Kamy'e v nachale epohi zheleza*. Moscow: Nauka.

———. 1990. K probleme preyemstvennosti archeologicheskikh kultur. In *Vzaimodeistviye drevnikh kultur Urala*, ed. V. A. Oborin. Perm: Perm State University: 4–8.

Khalikov, A. K., G. V. Lebedinskaya, & M. M. Gerasimova. 1966. *Pepkinski kurgan (abashevski kurgan)*. Yoshkar-Ola: Mari Press.

Khazanov, A. M. 1971. *Ocherki voennogo dela sarmatov*. Moscow: Nauka.

———. 1975. *Sotsianaya istoriya skifov: Osnovnye problemy razvitiya drevnikh kochevnikov Evraziiskikh stepei*. Moscow: Nauka.

———. 1979. Klassoobrazovaniye: faktory i mekhanizmy. In *Issledovaniya po obshchei ethnografiyi*. ed. Yu. V. Bromley, S. I. Bruk, A. I. Pershits, S. Ya. Serov. Moscow: Nauka: 125–77.

———. 1984. *The Nomads and the Outside World*. Cambridge: Cambridge Univerity Press.

———. 2003. Nomads of the Eurasian Steppes in Historical Retrospective. In *Nomadic Pathways in Social Evolution*, ed. D. M. Bondarenko, A. V. Korotayev, & N. N. Kradin. Moscow: Russian State University of Humanities.

Khlobystin, L. S. 1976. *Poselenie Lipovaya Kur'ya*. Leningrad: Nauka.

Khokhlova, O. S., & A. M. Kuznetsova. 2003. *Morphologiya pedogennykh karbonatnykh akkumulatsij v paleopochvakh Yuznogo Priuraly'a v svyazi s usloviyami sredy raznykh epoch golotsena*. Paper presented to the *Problemy evolutsiyi pochv*, Pushchino, 2003: 66–71.

Khomutova, K. S. 1978. Metalloobrabotka na poseleniyakh diyakovskoi kultury. *Sovetskaya arkheologiya* 2: 62–77.

Khotinsky, N. A. 1977. *Golotsen Severnoi Evrazii*. Moscow: Nauka.

Khotinsky, N. A., V. K. Nemkova, & T. G. Surova. 1982. Glavnye etapy razvitiya rastitelnosti i klimata Urala v Golotsene. In *Arkheologicheskiye issledovaniya severa Evraziyi*, ed. V. E. Stoyanov. Sverdlovsk: Ural State University: 145–53.

Kirushin, Y. F. 1992. O phenomene seiminsko-turbinskikh bronz i vremeni formirovaniya kultur rannei bronzy v Zapadnoi Sibiri. In *Severnaya Evraziya ot drevnosti do srednevekovy'a*. St. Petersburg: Institute for History of Material Culture: 66–9.

———. 2002. *Eneolit i rannaya bronza yuga Zapadnoi Sibiri*. Barnaul: Altai University Press.

Klein, L. S. 2000. Arkheologicheskaya periodizatsiya. *Stratum plus* 1: 485–513.

Klimanov, V. A. 2002. Klimat Severnoi Evraziyi v neoglatsiale (okolo 2500 let nazad). *Doklady Akademiyi Nauk* 5: 676–80.

Klimenko, V. V. 1998. Klimat i istoriya v epokhu pervykh vysokikh kultur (3500–500 gg. do n.e.). *Vostok [Oriens]*: 5–41.

———. 2000. Klimat i istoriya ot Konfutsiya do Mukhammeda. *Vostok [Oriens]*, 5–32.

———. 2003. Klimat i istoriya v sredniye veka. *Vostok [Oriens]* 4: 5–41.

Klushintsev, V. N. 1997. Yuznoukrainsk: klad s poseleniya Bugskoye IV i aspekty sabatinovskoi metalloobrabotki. In *Sabatinovskaya i srubnaya kultury: problemy vzaimosvyazei Vostoka i Zapada v epokhu pozdnei bronzy*, ed. V. N. Klushintsev. Kiev-Nikolayev-Yuzhnoukrainsk: Institute of archaeology NAS of Ukraine: 12–7.

Kolchin, B. A. 1953. *Chernaya metallurgiya i metalloobrabotka v Drevnei Rusi* (Materialy i issledovaniya po archeologii SSSR 32). Moscow: Academy of Science Press.

Kolchin, B. A., & O. Y. Krug. 1965. Fizicheskoye modelirovaniye syrodutnogo protsessa. *Materialy i issledovaniya po archeologii SSSR* 129. Moscow: Nauka: 196–215.

Kolev, Y. I. 1991. Novyi tip pamyatnikov kontsa epokhi bronzy v lesostepnom Povolzhy'e. In *Drevnosti vostochno-evropeiskoi lesostepi*, ed. N. Y. Merpert. Samara: Samara State University: 162–206.

Korenuk, S. N. 1996. Novyi tip sooruzhenyi Pershinskogo moguilnika. In *Svyatilishcha i kultovye mesta Finno-Ugorskogo naseleniya Evrazii*, ed. A. F. Melnichuk. Perm: Perm University: 40–3.

Korenyako, V. A. 1982. O pogrebeniyakh vremeni perekhoda ot bronzy k rannemu zhelezu v priuralskikh stepyakh. In *Priuraly'e v epokhu bronzy i rannego zheleza*, ed. V. A. Ivanov & A. H. Pshenichnuk. Ufa: Institut hisroriyi, yasyka i literatury Bashkirskogo otdeleniya AN SSSR: 35–81.

———. 1990. O sotsialnoi interepretatsiyi pamayatnikov bronzovogo veka. *Sovetskaya arkheologiya* 2: 28–40.

Korepanov, K. I. 1994. K izucheniyu muzykalnogo tvorchestva naseleniya Volgo-Kamyia epokhi rannego zheleza. In *Istoriya i kultura Volgo-Vyatskogo kraya*, ed. V. V. Nizov. Kirov: Volgo-Vyatskoe knizhnoe izdatel'stvo: 53–5.

Korfmann, M. 1983. *Demircihuyuk. Die Ergebnosse der Ausgrabungen 1975–1978. Architectur, Stratigraphie und Befunde*. 1. Mainz-am-Rhein: Verlag Philipp von Zaben.

Korochkova, O. N. 1993. O fedorovskoi kulture. In *Problemy kulturogeneza i kulturnoye naslediye. Arkheologiya i izucheniye kulturnykh protsessov i yavlenij*, ed. Y. Y. Piotrovskyi. St. Petersburg: Institute for History of Material Culture: 84–7.

———. 1999. Novoye v izucheniyi zolnikov i pogrebalnykh kompleksov epokhi pozdnei bronzy Zapadnoi Sibiri. Paper presented to the 120 let arkheologiyi vostochnogo sklona Urala. Pervyje chteniya pamyati V. F. Geninga, Ekaterinburg, 1999: 57–63.

Korochkova, O. N., & V. I. Stefanov. 2004. The Trans-Ural Federovo Complexes in Relation to the Andronovo. In *Metallurgy in Ancient Eastren Euarasia from the Urals to yellow River*, ed. K. M. Linduff. Lewiston, Queenston, Lampeter: The Edwin Mellen Press, Ltd: 85–107.

Korochkova, O. N., V. I. Stefanov, & N. K. Stefanova. 1991. Kultury bronzovogo veka predtaezhnogo Tobolo-Irtysh'ya (po materialam rabot UAE). In *Voprosy arkeologiyi Urala*, ed. V. T. Kovaleva. Sverdlovsk: Ural State University: 70–92.

Koryakova, L. N. 1988. *Rannii zheleznyi vek Zaurlaya i Zapadnoi Sibiri*. Sverdlovsk: Ural State University.

———. 1991a. *Kulturno-istoricheskiye obshchnosti Urala i Zapadnoi Sibiri (Tobolo-Irtyshskaya provintsiya v nachale zheleznogo veka)*. Ekaterinburg: Institute of History and Archaeology of RAS.

———. 1991b. Sargatskaya kultura ili obshchnost? In *Problemy izucheniya sargatskoi kultury*, ed. L. I. Pogodin. Omsk: Omsk State University, 3–8.

———. 1994a. Pogrebalnaya obryadnost' lesostepnogo naseleniya Tobolo-Irtyshskogo mezhdurechya. In *Ocherki ethnogeneza narodov Zapadnoi Sibiri (Essays on ethnogenesis of the peoples of western Siberia)*, ed. V. M. Kulemzin & N. V. Lukina. Tomsk: Tomsk State University: 113–70.

———. 1994b. Poseleniya i zhilishcha Tobolo-Irtyshskoi lesostepi. In *Ocherki kulturogeneza narodov Zapadnoi Sibiri*, ed. L. M. Pletneva. Tomsk: Tomsk State University: 259–74.

———. 1994c. Zametki k voprosu ob ugorskom etnogeneze v svete vzaimodeistviya arkheologicheskiklh kultur Zauraly'a i Zapadnoi Sibiri. *Problemy istoriyi, filologiyi, kultury* 1: 6–15.

———. 1996. Social Trend in Temperate Eurasia during the Second and First millennia BC. *Journal of European Archaeology* 4: 243–80.

———. 1997. Gayevski mogilnik v kontekste evolutsiyi sargatskoi kulturnoi obshchnosti. In *Culture of Trans-Uralian Cattle and Horse Breeders (Gayevsky mogilnik sargatskoi obshchnosti)*, ed. L. N. Koryakova & M.-Y. Daire. Ekaterinburg: Ekaterinburg Press: 130–7.

———. 1998. Cultural Relationships in North-Central Eurasia. In *Archaeology and Language II: Correlating Archaeological and Linguistic Hypotheses*, ed. R. Blench & M. Spriggs. London: Routlege: 209–19.

———. 2002. Social Landscape of central Eurasia in the Bronze and Iron Ages: Tendences, Factors and Limits of Transformation. In *Complex Societies of Central Eurasia from the 3rd to the 1st Millennium BC: Regional Specifics in Light of Global Models*, ed. K. Jones-Bley

& D. Zdanovich. Journal of Indo-European Studies Monograph Series 45. Washington, D.C.: Institute for Study of Man: 97–118.

Koryakova, L. N., & M.-Y. Daire, ed. 1997. *The Culture of Trans-Uralian Cattle and Horse Breeders on the Turn of Erae.* Ekaterinburg: Ekaterinburg Press.

Koryakova, L. N. 2000. Burial and Settlements at the Eurasian Crossroads: Joint Franco-Russian project. In *Kurgans, Ritual Sites and Settlements: Eurasian Bronze and Iron Age,* ed. J. Davis-Kimball, E. Murphy, L. Koryakova, & L. Yablonsky. BAR. Interntional Series, 890. Oxford: 63–75.

———. 2003. Present-day Russian Archaeology and the Outside World. In *Archaologien Europas/Archaeologies of Europe. History, Methods and Theories,* ed. P. Beil, A. Gramsch and A. Marciniak. New York, Munchen, Berlin: Waxmann: 239–54

Koryakova, L. N., & R. O. Fedorov. 1993. Goncharniye navyki zauralskogo naseleniya v rannem zheleznom veke. In *Znaniya i navyki uralskogo naseleniya v drevnosti i srednevekovye,* ed. L. N. Koryakova. Ekaterinburg: Ural Division of RAS: 76–96.

Koryakova, L. N., Daire, M.-Y., L. Langouet, E. Gonsalez, D. Marguerie, P. Courtaud, P. Kosintsev, A. Kovrigin, D. Razhev, N. Berseneva, S. Panteleyeva, S. Sharapova, B. Hanks, A. Kazdym, O. Mikrukova & E. Efimova. 2004. Iron Age societies and Environment: Multi-Disciplinary Research in the Iset River Valley (Russia). In *The Archaeology of River Valleys,* ed. H. Dobrzanska, E. Jerem, & T. Kalicki. Budapest: Archeolingua: 185–214.

Koryakova, L. N. & A. Sergeev. 1986. Geographicheskyi aspekt khozyaistvennoi deyatelnosti plemen sargatskoi kultury. In *Voprosy archeologii Urala* 18, ed. V. Stoyanov. Sverdlovsk: Ural State University: 90–8.

Koryakova, L. N., V. I. Stefanov, & N. K. Stefanova. 1991. *Problemy metodiki issledovanij drevnikh pamyatnikov i kul'turno-khronologicheskaya stratigrafiya poseleniya Uk III.* Sverdlovsk: Ural Division of RAS.

Kosarev, M. F. 1981. *Bronzovyi vek Zapadnoi Sibiri.* Moscow: Nauka.

———. 1984. *Zapadnaya Sibir' v drevnosti.* Moscow: Nauka.

———. 1991. *Drevnyaya istoriya Zapadnoi Sibiri: chelovek i prirodnaya sreda.* Moscow: Nauka.

Kosintsev, P. A. 1988. Golotsenovye ostatki krupnykh mlekopitaushchikh Zapadnoi Sibiri. In *Sovremennoye sostoyaniye i istoriya zhivotnogo mira Zapadno-Sibirskoi nizmennosti,* ed. N. Smirnov. Sverdlovsk: Institute of Plant and Animal Ecology: 32–51.

———. 1989. Okhota i skotovodstvo u naseleniya lesostepnogo Zauraly'a v epokhu bronzy. In *Stanovleniye i razvitiye proizvodyashchego khozyaistva na Urale,* ed. V. D. Viktorova & N. G. Smirnov. Sverdlovsk: Ural Division of RAS: 84–104.

———. 2000. Kostnye ostatki zhivotnykh iz ukreplennogo poseleniya Arkaim. In *Arkheologicheski istochnik i modelorovaniye drevnikh tekhnologii,* ed. S. Y. Zdanovich. Chelyabinsk: Tsentr "Arkaim," Institute of History and Archaeology of RAS: 17–44.

Kosintsev, P. A., & A. I. Varov. 1995. Kostnye ostatki is raskopok dvukh poseleniy pozdnego bronzovogo veka v Uzhnom Zauraly'e. In *Problemy istorii, filologii, kul'tury,* ed. M. Abramzon. Magnitogorsk: 29–34.

Kostukov, V. P., & A. V. Epimakhov. 1999. Predvaritelnyje rezultaty issledovanija mogilnika epokhi bronzy Troitsk-7. In *120 let arkheologiyi vostochnogo sklona Urala.,* ed. V. T. Kovaleva. Ekaterinburg: Ural State University: 66–70.

Kostukov, V. P., & D. I. Razhev. 2004. Pogrebeniya iz kurgannoi gruppy Verblyuzh'i gorki i nekotorye problemy perekhoda ot epokhi bronzy k rannemu zheleznomu veku v Yuzhnom Zauraly'e. In *Vestnik Chelyabinskogo Gosudarstvennogo Pedagogicheskogo Universiteta.* Seriya 1, Istoricheskie nauki 2: 129–49.

Kovalev, A. A. 2000. O proiskhozhedeniyi olennykh kamnei zapadnogo regiona. In *Arkheologiya, paleoekologiya i paleodemografiya Evraziyi,* ed. V. S. Olkhovsky. Moscow: Nauka: 138–79.

Kovaleva, V. T. 1997. *Vzaimodeistviye kultur i etnosov po materialam arkheologii: poseleniye Tashkovo II.* Ekaterinburg: Ural State University.

Kovaleva, V. T., O. V. Ryzhkova, & A. V. Shamanayev. 2000. *Tashkovskaya kultura: poseleniye Andreyevskoye Ozero XIII.* Ekaterinburg: Ural State University.

Kowalewski, S. 2000. Tsiklicheskiye transformatsiyi v severo-amerikanskoi arkheologiyi.

In *Alternativnye puti k tsivilizatsiyi*, ed. N. N. Kradin, A. V. Korotayev, D. M. Bondarenko, & V. A. Lynsha. Moscow: Logos: 171–185.

Kradin, N. N. 1992. *Kochevye obshchestva*. Vladivostok: Dalnauka.

———. 1995. Vozhdestvo: sovremennoye sostoyaniye i problemy izucherniya. In *Ranniye formy politicheskoi organizatsiyi*, ed. V. P. Popov. Moscow: Vostochnaya literatura: 11–6.

———. 2000. Nomadic Empires in Evolutionary Perspectives. In *Aletrantives of Social Evolution*, ed. N. N. Kradin, A. V. Korotayev, D. M. Bondarenko, V. De Munk, & P. Wason. Vladivostok: Far Eastern Branch of RAS.

———. 2001a. *Imperiya Hunnu*. Moscow: Logos.

———. 2001b. *Politicheskaya antropologiya*. Moscow: Ladomir.

———. 2002. Nomadism, Evolution and World-System: Pastoral Societies in Theories of Historical Development. *Journal of Wold-System Research* III: 368–88.

Krasnov, Y. A. 1971. *Ranneye zemledeliye i zhivotnovodstvo v lesnoi polose Vostochnoi Evropy*. Moscow: Nauka.

Kremenetsky, K. 2003. Steppe and Forest-steppe Belt of Eurasia: Holocene Environmental History (trans.) C. Scarre. In *Prehistoric Steppe Adaptation and the Horse*, ed. M. G. Levin, C. Renfrew, & K. Boyle. McDonald Institute. Monographs. Cambridge: McDonald Institute for Archaeological Research: 11–28.

Kristiansen, K. 1991. Chiefdom, state, and system of social evolution. In *Chiefdoms: Power, Economy and Ideology*, ed. T. Earle. Cambridge: Cambridge University Press: 16–43.

———. 1998. *Europe before History* (New Studies in Archaeology). Cambridge: Cambridge University Press.

Krivtsova-Grakova, O. A. 1948. Alexeyevskoye poselenie i mogilnik. *Arheologicheskii sbornik. Trudy Gosudarstevennogo Istoricheskogo Muzeya* XVII: 59–172.

Kubarev, V. D. 1987. *Kurgany Ulandryka*. Novosibirsk: Nauka.

Kuner, N. 1961. *Kitaiskiye izvestia o narodakh Yuzhnoi Sibiri, Tsentral'noi Asiyi i Dal'nevo Vostoka*. Moskva: Vostochaya Literatura.

Kurochkin, G. N. 1994. Generator kochevykh narodov v Tsentralnoi Aziyi i mekhanizm ego funktionirovaniya. In *Paleodemografiya i migrationnye protsessy v Zapadni Sibiri v drevnosti i srednevekovy'e*, ed. V. V. Bobrov. Barnaul: Altai State University: 89–92.

Kutimov, Y. G. 1999. Kulturnaya atribitsiya keramiki stepnogo oblika epokhi pozdnei bronzy. *STRATUM plus* 2: 314–25.

Kuzmina, E. E. 1962. Arkheologicheskoye obsledovaniye pamyatnikov Elenovskogo mikroraiona andronovskoi kultury. *Kratkiye soobshcheniya Instituta Arkheologiyi SSSR* 88: 84–92.

———. 1974. Kolesnyi transport i problema etnicheskoi i sotsialnoi istoriyi. *Vestinik drevnei istoriyi* 4: 68–87.

———. 1981. Slozheniye skotovodcheskogo khozyaistva v stepyakh Evrasiyi i rekonstruktsiya sotsialnoi struktury obshchestva drevneishikh pastusheskikh plemen. In *Materialy po khozyaistvu i obshchestvennomu stroyu plemyen Yuzhnogo Urala*, ed. N. Mazhitov & A. Pshenichnuk. Ufa: Institut Istoriyi, Yazyka i Literatury: 23–43.

———. 1994. Otkuda prishli indo-ariyi. *Materialnaja kultura plemen andronovskoi obshchnosti i proiskhozhdenije indoirantsev*. Moscow: Nauka.

———. 1996a. Ekologia stepei Evrasii i problema proiskhozhdenia nomadisma (1). *Vestnik drevnei istoriyi* 2: 73–94.

———. 1996b. Ekologia stepei Evrasiyi i problema proiskhozhdenia nomadisma (2). *Vestnik drevnei istoriyi* 3: 81–94.

———. 2001. Contacts between Finno-Ugric and Indo-Iranian speakers in the light of archaeological, linguistic and mythological data. In *Early Contacts between Uralic and Indo-European: Linguistic and Archaeological Considerations*, ed. C. Carpelan, A. Parpola and P. Koskikallio. Helsinki: Suomalais-Ugrilainen Seura: 289–300.

———. 2004. Historical representatives on the Andronovo and metal use in eastern Asia. In *Metallurgy in Ancient Eastren Eurasia from the Urals to yellow River*, ed. K. M. Linduff. Lewiston, Queenston, Lampeter: The Edwin Mellen Press, Ltd: 38–84.

Kuzmina, O. V. 1992. *Abashevskaya kultura v lesostepnom Volgo-Uraly'e*. Samara: Samara State Pedagogical University.

———. 2001. Abashevskaya kultura v sisteme kultur bronzovogo veka Vostochnoi Evropy. In *Bronzovyi vek Vostochnoi Evropy: kharakteristika kultur, khronologiya i periodizatsiya*, ed. Yu. I. Kolev, P. F. Kuznetsov & O. V. Kuzmina. Samara: Samara State Pedagogical University: 153–160.

Kuzminykh, S. V. 1977. K voprosu o volosovskoi i garinsko-borskoi metallurgiyi. *Sovetskaya arkheologiya* 2: 20–34.

———. 1983. *Metallurgiya Volgo-Kamya v rannem zheleznom veke*. Moscow: Nauka.

Kuznetsov, P. F. 1996a. Kavkazskii ochag i kultury bronzobogo veka Volgo-Uraly'a. In *Mezdu Aziyei i Evropoi. Kavkaz v 4–1 tys. do n.e.*, ed. V. Bochkarev. St. Petersburg: Institute for History of Material Culture: 64–6.

———. 1996b. Novyje radiouglerodnyje daty dlya khronologiyi kultur eneolita-bronzovogo veka yuga lesostepnogo Povolzhy'a. *Radiouglerod i arkheologiya. Arkheologicheskiye izyskaniya* 37: 56–60.

———. 1996c. Problemy migratsij v razvitom bronzovom veke Volgo-Uraly'a. In *Drevnosti Volgo-Donskikh stepei v sisteme vostochno-evropeiskogo bronzovogo veka*, ed. A. V. Kiyashko. Volgograd: Peremena: 40–3.

Kuznetsova, E. F., & Z. K. Kurmankulov. 1993. Bronzovyje izdeliya iz pamyatnikov savromatskoi kutury Zapadnogo Kazakhstana (dannye spectralnogo sostava). In *Kochevniki Uralo-Kazakhstanskikh stepei*, ed. A. D. Tairov. Ekaterinburg: Nauka: 44–51.

Kyzlasov, L. P. 1999. Pervogoroda drevnei Sibiri. *Vestnik Moskovskogo Universiteta* 3: 96–129.

Larin, S. I., & N. P. Matveyeva. 1997. Rekonstruktsiya sredy obitaniya cheloveka v rannem zheleznom veke severnoi chasti Tobolo-Ishimskoi lesostepi. *Vestnik arkheologiyi, anthropologiyi i etnographiyi* 1: 133–40.

Lattimore, O. 1951. *Inner Asian Frontiers of China*. New York: American Geographical Society.

Latyshev, V. V. 1947a. Izvestiya drevnikh pisatelei o Skifiyi i Kavkaze. *Vestnik drevnei istoriyi* 1: 253–316.

———. 1947b. Izvestiya drevnikh pisatelei o Skifiyi i Kavkaze. *Vestnik drevnei istoriyi* 2: 249–99.

———. 1947c. Izvestiya drevnikh pisatelei o Skifiyi i Kavkaze. *Vestnik drevnei istoriyi* 3: 149–60.

———. 1947d. Izvestiya drevnikh pisatelei o Skifiyi i Kavkaze. *Vestnik drevnei istoriyi* 4: 230–300.

———. 1992. *Izvestiya drevnikh pisatelei o Skifiyi i Kavkaze*. St. Petersburg: Institute for Oriental Studies.

Lavrushin, Y. A., & E. A. Spiridonova. 1999. Osnovnyje geologo-paleoekologicheskiye sobytiya kontsa pozdnego pleistitsena i golotsena

na vostochnom sklone Yuznogo Urala. In *Prirodnyje sistemy Yuzhnogo Urala*, ed. L. L. Gaiduchenko. Chelyabinsk: Chelyabinsk State University: 66–103.

Leshchinskaya, N. A. 1995. Vyatski bassein v I-nachale II tys. do n.e.. Ph.D. dissertation: Izhevsk, Udmurt State University.

Levin, M. G., & N. N. Cheboksarov. 1955. Khozyaistevenno-kulturnye tipy i istoriko-kulturnyje oblasti: k postanovke voprosa. *Sovetskaya etnografiya* 4: 3–17.

Levina, L. M., & L. V. Chizhova. 1995. O nekotorykh anthropomorfnykh i zoomorfnykh izobrazheniyakh v dzhetyasarskikh pamyatnikakh. In *Dzetyasrskaya kultura*, ed. L. M. Levina. Nizovy'a Syrdary'i v drevnosti. Moscow: Institute of Ethnology and Anthropology: 185–201.

Levshin, A. I. 1832. *Opisaniye kirgiz-kazachyikh ili kirgiz-kaisakskikh ord i stepei*. Izvestiya etnograficheskiye III. St. Petersburg.

Litvinski, B. A. 1972. *Kochevniki 'Kryshi mira'*. Moscow: Nauka.

Livshits, V. A. 2002. Three silver bowles from he first burial ground of Isakovka. *Vestnik drevnei istoriyi* 2: 43–56.

Logvin, V. N. 2002. The Cemetery of Bestamak and the Structure of the Community. In *Complex Societies of Central Eurasia from the 3rd to the 1st Millennium BC: Regional Specifics in Light of Global Models*, ed. K. Jones-Bley, & D. Zdanovich. Journal of Indo-European Studies. Monograph Series 45. Washington, D.C.: Institute for Study of Man: 189–201.

Lubchansky, I. E., & N. O. Ivanova. 1996. Mogilnik Ily'assky I – novyi pogrebalnyi kompleks srubno-alakulskogo vremeni. In *Materialy po arkheologiyi i etnografiyi Urala*, ed. S. Y. Zdanovich. Chelyabinsk: Center "Arkaim": 89–107.

Lubo-Lesnichenko, E. I. 1985. Velikii shelkovyi put'. *Voprosy istoriyi* 9: 13–20.

———. 1987. Pazyryk i Zapadnyi Meredianalnyi put'. *Strany i narody Vostoka* XXV: 237–44.

———. *Kitai na Shelkovom Puti*. Moscow: Vostochnaya Literatura.

Lukashev, A. V., & V. A. Demkin. 1989. Topografiya arkheologicheskikh pamyatnikov VI-I vv. do n.e. Severo-Zapadnoi chasti Volgo-Uralskogo mezdurechy'a. In *Arkheologiya Vostochno-Evropeiskoi stepi*, ed. I. V. Sergatskov. Saratov: Saratov State University: 157–61.

Machinsky, D. A. 1971. O vremeni pervogo aktivnogo vystupleniya sarmarov v Podneprovy'e po dannym pismennykh svidetelstv. *Arkheologicheski sbornik Gosudarstvennogo Ermitazha* 13: 30–54.

———. 1972. Nekotorye problemy etnogeografiyi vostochnoevropeiskikh stepei vo II v. do n.e.-I v.n.e. *Arkheologicheski sbornik Gosudarstvennogo Ermitazha* 14: 122–32.

Makarova, L. A. 1976. Kharakteristika kostnogo materiala iz poseleniya Sargary. In *Proshloye Kazakhstana po arkheologicheskim istochnikam.* Alma-Ata: Nauka: 211–26.

Malashev, V. Y., & L. T. Yablonsky. 2004. Ranniye kochevniki Yuzhnogo Priuraly'a. *Materialy i issledovaniya po arkheologiyi Rossiyi* 6: 117–46.

Mallory, J. P. 1989. *In Search of the Indo-Europeans. Language, Archaeology and Myth.* London and New York: Thames and Hudson.

———. 1998. A European Perspective on Indo-Europeans in Asia. In *The Bronze and Iron Age peoples of Eastern Central Asia,* ed. V. Mair. Philadelphia: Institute for Study of Man: 175–201.

Malov, N. M. 1995. Indoevropeiskaya neurbanisticheskaya tsivilizatsiya epokhi paleometalla evrasiiskoi skotovodcheskoi istoriko-kulturnoi provintsiyi – zveno mozaichnoi tselostnosti. In *Konverguentsyja i diverguentsiya v razvitiyi kultur epokhi eneolita-bronzy Srednei i Vostochnoi Evropy,* ed. V. Bochkarev. Saratov: Saratov State University: 7–10.

———. 2002. Spears – Signs of Archaic leaders of the Pokrovsk Archaeological Culture. In *Complex Societies of Central Eurasia from the 3rd to the 1st Millennium BC: Regional Specifics in Light of Global Models,* ed. K. Jones-Bley, & D. Zdanovich. Journal of Indo-European Studies Monograph Series 45. Washington, D.C.: Institute for Study of Man: 314–36.

Malov, N. M., & V. V. Filipchenko. 1995. Pamyatniki katakombnoi kultury Nizhnego Povolzhy'a. *Arkheologicheskiye vesti* 4. St. Petersburg: Institute for History of Material Culture: 52–62.

Malutina, T. S. 1990. Poseleniya i zhilishcha fedorovskoi kultury volgo-uralskikh stepei. In *Arkeologiya volgo-uralskikh stepei,* ed. G. Zdanovich. Chelyabinsk: Chelyabinsk State University: 28–39.

———. 1991. Stratigraficheskaya pozitsiya materialov fedorovskoi kul'tury na mnogo-sloinykh poseleniyakh kazahstanskikh stepei. In *Drevnosti vostochno-evropeiskoi lesostepi,* ed. N. Y. Merpert. Samara: Samara State University: 141–62.

Mandelshtam, A. M. 1978. K vostochnym aspektam istorii rannikh kochevnikov Srednei Aziyi i Kazakhstana. *Kratkiye soobshcheniya Intituta arkheologiyi AN SSSR* 154: 19–24.

Marazov, I. 1998. *Ancient Gold: The Wealth of the Tracians. Tresures from the Republic of Bulgaria.* New York: Harry N. Abrams, INC Publishers.

Margulan, A. K. 1979. *Begazy-Dandybayevskaya kultura Tsentralnogo Kazakhstana.* Alma-Ata: Nauka.

Markov, S. V. 1973. Nektoryje problemy vozniknoveniya i rannikh etapov kochevnichestva v Aziyi. *Sovetskaya etnografiya* 1: 101–13.

———. 1976. *Kochevniki Aziyi. Struktura khozyaistva i obshchestvennoi organizatsiyi.* Moscow: Moscow State University.

Martynov, A. I. 1989a. O stepnoi skotovodcheskoi tsivilizatsiyi I tys. do n.e. In *Vzaimodeistviye kochevykh kultur i drevnikh tsivilizatsyi,* ed. V. M. Masson. Alma-Ata: Nauka: 284–92.

———. 1989b. *Skifo-Sibirski mir – stepnaya skotovodcheskaya tsivilizatsiya V-II vv. do n.e.* Paper presented to the Problemy arkheologiyi skifo-sibirskogo mira, Kemerovo, 1989b: 5–12.

Masanov, N. E. 1995. *Kochevaya tsivilizatsiya kazakhov: osnovy zhiznedeyatelnosti nomadnogo obshchestva.* Almaty-Moscow: Sotsinvest-Gorizont.

Masson, V. M. 1989. *Pervyje tsivilizatsiyi.* Moscow: Nauka.

———. 1998. Epokha drevnikh velikikh stepnykh obshchestv. *Arkheologicheskiye vesti* 5: 255–67.

———. 1999. Drevniye tsivilizatsiyi Vostoka i stepnye plemena v svete dannykh arkheologiyi. *STRATUM plus* 5: 265–84.

Matushchenko, V. I. 1974. *Drevnyaya istoriya naseleniya lesnogo i lesostepnogo Prioby'a (neolit i bronzovyi vek). Elovsko-Irmenskaya kultura.* Tomsk: Tomsk State University.

———. 1989. Pogrebenniye voina sargatskoi kultury. *Izvestia Sibirskogo otdeleniya AN SSSR. Seria: Istoriya, phililogiya i philosifiya* I: 51–9.

———. 1994. Epokha bronzy. Lesnaya i lesostepnaya polosa. Doandronovskoye vremya In *Mir realnyi i potustoronnij,* ed. V. I. Matushchenko. Ocherki kulturogeneza narodov

Zapadnoi Sibiri. Tomsk: Tomsk State University Press: 73–111.

———. 1999a. *Drevnaya istoriya Sibiri.* Omsk: Omsk State University.

———. 1999b. *Eshche raz o seiminsko-turbinskom fenomene.* Paper presented to the XIV Uralskoye Arkheologicheskoye soveshchaniye, Chelybinsk: 1999b, 90–2.

Matushchenko, V. I., & G. V. Sinitsina. 1988. *Mogilnik u d. Rostovka vblizi Omska.* Tomsk: Tomsk State University.

———. 1997. *Mogilnik Sidorovka v Omskom Priirtyshye.* Novosibirsk: Nauka.

Matveyev, A. V. 1986. Nekotorye itogi i problemy izucheniya irmenskoi kultury. *Sovetskaya arkheologiya* 2: 56–69.

———. 1993. *Irmenskaya kultura v lesostepnom Prioby'e.* Novosibirsk: Novosibirsk State University Press.

———. 1998. *Pervyje andronovtsy v lesakh Zauraly'a.* Novosibirsk: Nauka.

Matveyev, A. V., & N. P. Matveyeva. 1987. Yuvelirnyje izdeliya Tutrinskogo mogilnika (k probleme Sibirskoi kollektsityi Petra 1). In *Anthropomorfnye izobrazheniya:pervobytnoye iskusstvo,* ed. R. S. Vasilyevski. Novosibirsk: Nauka: 191–201.

———. 1992. *Tutrinski mogilnik.* Tumen: Tyumen State University.

Matveyeva, G. I. 1962. Raskopki kurganov u g. Troitsk. *Voprosy arkheologiji Urala* 2: 33–7.

Matveyeva, N. P. 1993. *Sargatskaya kultura na Srednem Tobole.* Novosibirsk: Nauka.

———. 1994. *Rannii zheleznyi vek Priishimy'a.* Novosibirsk: Nauka.

———. 1995. *O svyazyakh lesostepnogo naseleniya Zapadnoi Sibiri s Tcentralnoi Aziyei v rannem zheleznom veke.* Paper presented to the Russia and the East, Chelyabinsk: 1995, 53–8.

———. 1997. O torgovykh svyzyakh Zapadnoi Sibiri i Tsentralnoi Aziyi v rannem zheleznom veke. *Rossijskaya arkheologiya* 2: 63–77.

———. 2000. *Sotsialno-ekonomicheskiye struktury naseleniya Zapadnoi Sibiri v rannem zheleznom veke (lesostepnaya i podtayezhnaya zony).* Novosibirsk: Nauka.

Matveyeva, N. P., & N. E. Ryabogina. 2003. Rekonstruktsiya priorodnykh uslovij Zauraly'a v rannem zheleznom veke (po palonologicheskim dannym). *Archaelogy, Ethnography and Anthropology of Eurasia* 16: 30–5.

McGovern, W. M. 1939. *The Early Empires of Central Asia.* New York: Van Rees Press.

Medvedev, A. P. 1999a. Lesostepnoye Podony'e na rubezhe epokhi bronzy i rannego zheleznogo veka. In *Evrasiiskaya lesostep v epokhu metalla,* ed. A. D. Pryakhin. (Arkheologiya vostochno-evropeiskoi lesostepi). Voronezh: Voronezh University Press: 92–107.

———. 1999b. *Ranni zheleznyi vek lesostepnogo Podonya.* Moscow: Nauka.

———. 2002a. Avestan "Yima's Town" in Historical and Archaeological Perspective. In *Complex Societies of Central Eurasia from the 3rd to the 1st Millennium BC: Regional Specifics in Light of Global Models,* ed. K. Jones-Bley, & D. Zdanovich. Journal of Indo-European Studies. Monograph Series 45. Washington, D.C.: Institute for Study of Man: 42–67.

———. 2002b. Antichnaya traditsiya i arkheologicheskiye realiyi skifskogo vremeni na Srednem i verkhnem Donu. *Vestnik drevnei istoriyi* 3: 153–9.

Medvedskaya, I. N. 1980. Metallicheskiye nakonechniki strel Perednego Vostoka i evraziiskikh stepei II – pervoi poloviny I tys. do n.e. *Sovetskaya arkheologiya* 4: 23–37.

Mei, J. 2000. *Copper and Bronze Metallurgy in Late Prehistoric Xinjiang: its Cultural Context and Relationship with Neighboring Regions* (BAR Inetrantional Series 865). Oxford: Archaeopress.

Mei, J., & C. Shell. 1999. The Existence of Andronovo Cultural Influence in Xinjiang during the 2nd Millennium BC. *Antiquity* 73: 570–78.

Milukova, A. I. 1964. *Vooruzheniye skifov* (Svod archaeologicheskikh istochnikov D1–4). Moscow: Nauka.

———. 1989. (ed.) *Stepi evropeiskoi chasti SSSR v skofo-sarmatskoye vremya* (Arkheologiya SSSR). Mosow: Nauka.

Merpert, N. Y. 1954. *Materialy po arkheologiyi Sredenego Zavolzhy'a* (Materialy i issledovaniya po arkheologiyi SSSR 42). Moscow: Academy of Sciense Press.

———. 1974. *Drevneishiye skotovody Volgo-Uralskogo mezhdurechya.* Moscow: Nauka.

———. 1977. Iz istoriyi drevneyamnykh plemen. In *Problemy arkeologiyi Evraziyi i Severnoi Ameriki.* Moscow: Nauka.

———. (ed.) 1985. *Srubnaya kulturno-istoricheskaya obshchnost'.* Moscow: Nauka.

———. 1995a. K voprosu o drevneishikh krugloplanovykh ukreplenykh poseleniyakh

Evraziyi. In *Rossiya i Vostok: Problemy vzaimod-eistviya*, ed. G. B. Zdanovich, N. O. Ivanova, & A. D. Tairov. Chelyabinsk: Chelyabinsk State University: 116–9.

———. 1995b. O planirovke poselkov rannego bronzovogo veka v Verkhneyefratskoi doline. *Rossijskaya arkheologiya* 3: 28–46.

Mochalov, O. D. 1997. Ornament keramiki aba-shevskikh pogrebenii Priuraly'a. In *Istoriko-kulturnye izyskaniya*, ed. S. G. Gushchin. Samara: Samara State University: 54–73.

Mogi'nikov, V. A. 1992. Lesostep' Zauraly'a i Zapadnoi Sibiri. In *Stepnaya polosa aziatskoi chasti SSSR v skifo-sarmatskoye vremya*, ed. M. G. Moshkova (Arkheologiya SSSR). Moscow: Nauka: 247–311.

Molodin, V. I. 1983. Pogrebeniye liteishchika iz mogilnika Sopka-2. In *Drevniye gornyaki i metallurgu Sibiri*, ed. Yu.F. Kirushin. Barnaul: Altai State University: 96–109.

———. 1985. *Baraba v epokhu bronzy*. Novosi-birsk: Nauka.

———. 2001. Westsibirien, der Altai und Nordkazachstan in der entwickelten und spaten Bronzezeit. In *Migration und Kultur-transfer. Der Wandel vorder- und zentalasiatischer Kulturen im Umbruch vom 2.zum1. vorchistlichen Jarhrtausend*, ed. H. Parzinger. Bonn: Dr. Rudolf Habelt GmbH: 85–100.

Molodin, V. I., & I. G. Glushkov. 1989. *Samus'skaya kultura v verkhnem Prioby'e*. Novosibirsk: Nauka.

Molodin, V. I., & H. Partzinger. (eds.) 2001. *Chicha – gorodishche perekhodnogo ot bronzy k zhelezu vremeni v Barabinskoi lesostepi*. Novosibirsk: Institute of Archaeology and Ethnography SD RAS.

Morgunova, N. L. 1992. K voprosu ob obs-chestvennom ustroistve drevneyamnoi kul-tury. In *Drevnaya istoriya naseleniya Volgo-Uralskikh stepei*, ed. N. L. Morgunova. Orenburg:. Pedagogical Institute: 25–36.

———. 2000. Bolshoi Boldyrevskii kurgan. *Arkheologicheskiye pamyatniki Orenburzhy'a* IV, 55–61.

———. 2002. Yamnaya (Pit-Grave) Culture in the Southern Urals Area. In *Complex Societies of Central Eurasia from the 3rd to the 1st Millennium BC: Regional Specifics in Light of Global Models*, ed. K. Jones-Bley & D. Zdanovich. Journal of Indo-European Studies Monograph Series 45. Washington, D.C.: Institute for Study of Man: 249–50.

Morgunova, N. L., O. S. Khokhlova, G. I. Zaitseva, O. A. Chichagova, & A. A. Goly'eva. 2003. Rezultaty radiouglerodnogo datirovaniya arkheologicheskikh pamyatnikov Yuzhnogo Priuralya. In *Shumaevkiye kurgany*, ed. N. L. Morgunova. Orenburg: Orenburg Pedagogical Institute: 60–4.

Morgunova, N. L., & A. Y. Kravtsov. 1994. *Pamyatniki drevneyamnoi kultury na Ileke*. Ekaterinburg: Nauka.

Morgunova, N. L., & M. A. Turetski. 2002. Nekotoryje rezultaty kompleksnykh issle-dovanij pamyatnikov Yamnoi kultury v Yuzhnom Priuraly'e. In *Severnaya Evrasia v epokhu bronzy: prostranstvo, vremya, kultura*, ed. Y. P. Kirushin & A. A. Tishkin. Barnaul: Altai State University: 180–1.

———. 2003. *Novye nakhodki povozok yamnoi kultury v Yuzno-Uralskom regione*. Paper presented to the Chteniya, posvyashchennye 100-letiyu deyatelnosti V. A. Gorodtsova v Gosudarstevennom Istoricheskom Muzeye, Moscow, 2003: 84–7.

Morozov, Y. A. 1981. Proyavleniye spetsal-izatsii proizvodstva v khozyaistve srubnogo naseleniya Yuznogo Urala. In *Materialy po khozyaistvu i obshchestvennomu stroju plemen Yuzhnogo Urala*, ed. N. A. Mazhitov & A. K. Pshenichnuk. Ufa: BF AN SSSR: 57–67.

———. 1982. Srubnyje pamyatniki Priuraly'a (voprosy periodizatsy i khronologiyi). In *Priuraly'e v epokhu bronzy i rannego zheleza*, ed. V. A. Ivanov & A. K. Pshenichnuk. Ufa: Baskirski filial RAS. Institut istoriyi, yazyka i literatury, 3–19.

———. 1995. Istoriografiya voprosa perekho-dnogo perioda ot epokhi bronzy k kulturam rannikh kochevnikov Yuzhnouralskikh stepei. In *Kurgany kochevnikov Yuzhnogo Urala*, ed. B. B. Ageyev. Ufa: Gilem: 5–17.

Moshkova, M. G. 1974. *Proiskhozhdenie ran-nesarmatskoi (prokhorovskoi) kuetury*. Moskva: Nauka.

———. 1982. Pozdnesarmatskiye pogrebeniya Lebeoevskogo mogilnika v Zapadnom Kaza-khstane. *Kratkie soobshcheniya Instituta Arkhe-ologii SSSR* 170: 80–6.

———. 1988. Ponyatiye "arkheologicheskaya kultura" i savromato-sarmatskaya kulturno-istoricheskaya obshchnost'. In *Problemy sar-matskoi arkheologiyi i iistoriyi*, ed. V. E. Mak-simenko. Azov: Azov Museum: 89–108.

———. (ed.) 1992. *Stepnaya polosa Asiatskoi chasti SSSR v skofo-sarmatskoye vremya* (Arkheologiya SSSR). Moscow: Nauka.

———. (ed.) 1994. Le cimetier sarmate de Lebedevka dans le Sud de l'Oural. In *Archeologie. Dossiers d'Archeologie* 194: 84–7.

———. (ed.) 2002. *Statisticheskaya obrabotka porebalnykh pamyatnikov Aziatskoi Sarmatiyi. Srednesarmatskaya kultura.* Moscow: Institute of Archaeology RAS.

Mosin, V. S. 1996. Stoyanka Burli II i nekotorye voprosy eneolita Yuzhnogo Zauraly'a. In *Novoye v arkheologiyi Yuzhnogo Urala*, ed. S. A. Grigory'ev. Chelyabinsk: Rifei: 48–61.

Murzabulatov, M. V. 1979. Skotovodcheskoye khozyaistvo zauralskihk bashkir v XIX-nachale XX v. In *Khozaystvo i kultura bashkir v XIX – nachale XX v.*, ed. R. G. Kuzeev, & N. B. Bikbulatov. Moscow: Nauka: 62–77.

Murzin, V. Y. 1990. *Proiskhodgdeniye skifov: osnovnyje etapy formirovaniya skofskogo etnosa.* Kiev: Naukova Dumka.

Napolskikh, V. V. 1997. *Vvedeniye v istoricheskuyu uralistiku.* Izhevsk: Udmurt State University.

Nelin, D. V. 2000. Novaya nakhodka psaliya so spiralnym ornamentom v Yuzhnom Zuraly'e. *STRATUM plus* 2: 569–70.

Nemkova, V. K. 1978. Stratigraphiya pozdnei poslelednikovykh otlozhenyi Preduraly'a. In *K istoryi pozdnego pleistotsena i golotsena Yuzhnogo Urala i Preduralyja*, ed. V. L. Yakhimovich. Ufa: BF AN SSSR: 4–45.

Nikitenko, N. I. 1998. Nachalo osvoyeniya zheleza v belozerskoi kulture. *Rossijskaya arkheologiya* 3: 36–47.

Novokreshchennykh, I. N. 1914. *Glyadenovskoye kostishche* (Trudy permskoi uchenoi arheologicheskoi komissiyi XI). Perm.

Obydennov, M. F. 1996. Svedeniya o nakhodkakh metallicheskikh izdelij. In *Aktualnye problemy drevnei istoriji i arkheologiji Yuzhnogo Urala*, ed. N. A. Mazhitov & M. F. Obydennov. Ufa: Eatern University: 105–25.

———. 1998. *Mezhevskaya kultura.* Ufa: VEK.

Obydennov, V. F., & G. T. Obydennova. 1992. *Severo-vostocnaya periferiya srubnoi kulturno-istoricheskoi obshchnosti.* Saratov: Saratov State University.

Ochir-Goryaeva, M. 2000. A Comparative Study of the Early Iron Age Cultures in the Low Volga and the Southern Urals Regions. In *Kurgans, Ritual Sites, and Settlements: Eurasian Bronze and Iron Age*, ed. J. Davis-Kimball, E. Murphy, L. Koryakova, & L. T. Yablonsky. BAR International Series, 890. Oxford: Archaeopress: 194–206.

Okladnikov, A. P. (ed.). 1968. *Istoriya Sibiri.* Leningrad: Nauka.

Olkhovsky, V. S. 1997. Obychai i obryad kak forma traditsiyi. *Rossijskaya arkheologiya* 2: 159–67.

Orlova, L. A. 1995. Radiouglerodnoye datirovaniye arkheologicheskikh pamyatnikov Sibiri i Dalnego Vostoka. In *Metody estestvennykh nauk v arkheologicheskikh rekonstruktsiyakh*, ed. Y. P. Kholushkin. Novosibirsk: Institute of Archaeology and Ethnology SB of RAS: 207–32.

Ostanina, T. I. 1997. *Naseleniye Srednego Prikamy'a v III-V vv. n.e.* Izhevsk: Udmurt Institute of History, Language and Literature.

Otroshchenko, V. V. 2000. K voprosu o pamyatnikaklh novokumakskogo tipa. In *Problemy izucheniya eneolita i bronzovogo veka Urala.*, ed. S. Zasedateleva. Orsk: Institute for studies of Eurasian steppe UD RAS: 66–71.

———. 2003. The Economic Peculiarities of the Srubnaya Cultural-historical Entity. In *Prehistoric Steppe Adaptation and the Horse*, ed. M. G. Levin, C. Renfrew, & K. Boyle. Oxford: McDonald Institute for Archaeological Research: 319–51.

Ozcen, I., & Osturk, J. 1996. *The Lydian Treasure.* Istanbul: Ministry of Culture. Republic of Turkey.

Parzinger, H. 2000. Seima-Turbino phenomenon and formation of the Siberian Animal style. *Archeology, Ethnography and Anthropology* 1: 66–75.

Pashkevich, G. A. 2000. Zemledeliye v stepi i lesostepi Vostochnoi Evropy v neolite. *Stratum plus* 2: 404–17.

Patrushev, V. S. 1984. *Mariisky krai v VIII-VI vv. do n.e. (Starshii Akhmylovsky mogilnik).* Yoshkar-Ola: Mariskoye Izdatelstvo.

———. 1990. Novye issledovaniya Pustomorkvashanskogo mogilnika. In *Novye istochniki po etnicheskoi i sotsialnoi istorii finno-ugrov Povolzhy'a I tys. do n.e. – I tys. n.e.*, ed. Y. A. Zeleneyev. Yoshkar-Ola: Mari State University: 25–74.

Pershits, A. I. 1994. Voina i Mir na poroge tsivilizatsiyi. Kochevye skotovody. In *Voina i Mir v pervobytnosti.*, ed. A.I. Pershits, Yu. I. Semenov, & A. I. Shnirelman. Moscow: Nauka: 131–300.

Petrenko, A. G. 1984. *Drevneye i srednevekovoye zhivotnovodstvo Srednego Povolzhy'a i Priuraly'a.* Moscow: Nauka.

Petrin, V. T., T. I. Nokhrina, & A. F. Shorin. 1993. *Arkheologicheskie pamyatniki Argazinskogo vodokhranilischa (epokhi kamnya i bronzy).* Novosibirsk: Nauka.

Pfrommer, M. 1993. *Metal Work from the Hellenized East. Catalog of the Collections.* Malibu, California: The J. Paul Getty Museum.

Pleiner, R. 2000. *Iron Age Archaeology: the European Bloomery Smelters.* Prage: Archeologicky Ustav AV CR.

Pletneva, L. M. (ed.) 1994. *Poseleniya i zhilishcha* (Ocherki kulturogeneza narodov Zapadnoi Sibiri, Vol. 1). Tomsk: Tomsk State University.

Pletneva, S. A. 1982. *Kochevniki srednevekovy'a. Poiski istoricheskikh zakonomernostei.* Moscow: Nauka.

Podgayevski, G. V. 1935. Gorodishche Voronezh. In *Arkheologicheskiye issledovaniya v RSFSR (1934–1936). Kratkiye otchety i svedeniya,* ed. V. V. Golmsten. Moscow-Leningrad: Academy of Sciences Press: 156–60.

Pogodin, L. I. 1989. *Otchet ob arkheologicheskikh issledovaniyakh v Nizhneomskom I Gorkovskom raionakh Omskoi oblasti v 1989.* Institute of Archaeology RAS. Manuscript P-1, 13932.

Pogodin, L. I. 1996. Zolotoye shity'e Zapadnoi Sibiri. In *Istoricheski ezhegodnik,* ed. V. I. Matushchenko. Omsk: Omsk State University: 123–34.

———. I. 1998a. Lakovye izdeliya iz pamyatnikov Zapadnoi Sibiri rannego zheleznogo veka. In *Vzaimodeistviye sargatskikh plemen s vneshnim mirom,* ed. L. I. Pogodin. Omsk: Omsk State University: 26–38.

———. 1998b. *Vooruzheniye naseleniya Zapadnoi Sibiri rannego zheleznogo veka.* Omsk: Omsk State University.

Pogodin, L. I., & A. Y. Trufanov. 1991. Mogilnik sargatskoi kultury Isakovka-3. In *Drevniye pogrebeniya Ob'-Irtyshy'a,* ed. V. M. Kulemzin. Omsk: Omsk State University: 98–126.

Polevodov, A. V. 2003. Suzgunskaya kultura v lesostepi Zapadnoi Sibiri. Ph.D. dissertation: Moscow, Institute of Archaeology, RAS.

Polevodov, A. V., & A. Y. Trufanov. 1997. *O pogrebalnom obryade suzgunskoi kultury.* Paper presented to the "Russia and East. Archaeology and Ethnic History," Omsk, 1997: 19–23.

Polos'mak, N. V. 1987. *Baraba v epokhu rannego zheleza.* Novosibirsk: Nauka.

———. 1994. *Steregushchiye zoloto griphy.* Novosibirsk: Nauka.

———. 2000. *Vsadniki Ukoka.* Novosibirsk: Nauka.

Polyakov, Y. A. 2001. Glyadenovskaya kultura. In *Arkheologiya i etnografiya Srednego Priuraly'a,* ed. A. F. Melnichuk. Berezniki: Perm State University: 10–9.

Polyakova, E. L. 2002. Megality Yuzhnogo Zauraly'a. In *Vestnik obshchestva otkrytykh issledovani drevnosti,* ed. F. N. Petrov. Chelyabinsk: Obshchestvo otkrytykh issledovanii drevnosti: 49–56.

Popov, N. S. 1813. *Khozyaistvennoye opisaniye Permskoi guberniyi.* St. Petersburg.

Popov, V. A. (ed.) 1993. *Ranniye formy sotsialnoi stratifikatsiyi.* Moscow: Nauka

———. (ed.) 1995. *Ranniye formy politicheskoi organizatsiyi: ot pervobytnosti k gosudarstvennosti.* Moscow: Nauka.

Porokh, A. N. 1999. Istoriya kuznechnogo proizvodstva u kochevnokov Niznego Povolzhy'a skifskoi epokhi. In *Nauchnye shkoly Volgogradskogo Universiteta. Arkheologiya Volgo-Uralskogo regiona v epokhu rannego zheleznogo veka i srednevekovy'a,* ed. A. S. Skripkin. Vogograd: Volgograd State University: 300–18.

Posrednikov, V. A. 1992. O yamnykh migratsiyakh na vostok i afanasyevsko-prototokharskaya problema. In *Donetskii arkheologicheskii sbornik* I, ed. V. A. Posrednikov. Donetsk: AVERS: 9–20.

Potyemkina, T. M. 1979. O sootnosheniyi alekseyevskikh i zamaraevskikh kompleksov v lesostepnom Zauraly'e. *Sovetskaya arkheologiya* 2, 35–70.

Potyemkina, T. M. 1985. *Bronzovyj vek lesostepnogo Pritoboly'a.* Moscow: Nauka.

———. 1995. Problemy svyazei i smena kultur Zauraly'a v epokhu bronzy (rannij i srednij etapy). *Rossijskaya arkheologiya* 1: 14–27.

Potyemkina, T. M., O. N. Korochkova, & V. I. Stefanov. 1995. *Lesnoye Tobolo-Irtyshy'e v kontse epokhi bronzy.* Moscow: PAIMS.

Privat, K. 2002. Preliminary report of paleodietary analysis of human and founal remains from Bolshekaraganski kurgan 25. In *Arkaim: Nekropol,* ed. D. Zdanovich. Chelyabinsk: South Ural Press: 167–71.

Pryakhin, A. D. 1971. *Abashevskaya kultura v Podony'e.* Voronezh: Voronezh State University.

————. 1973. *Drevneye poseleniye Peschanki.* Voronezh: Voronezh State University.

————. 1976. *Poseleniya abashevskoi obshchnosti.* Voronezh: Voronezh State University.

————. 1977. *Pogrebalnyje abashevskiye pamyatniki.* Voronezh: Voronezh State University.

————. 1996. *Mosolovskoye poseleniye metallurgov-liteishchikov epokhi pozdnei bronzy.* Voronezh: Voronezh State University.

Pryakhin, A. D., & A. K. Khalikov. 1987. Abashevskaya kultura Yuzhnogo Priuraly'a. In *Arkeologiya SSSR. Epokha bronzy lesnoi polosy SSSR*, ed. O. N. Bader, D. A. Krainov, & M. F. Kosarev. Moscow: Nauka: 124–31.

Pshenichnuk, A. K. 1983. *Kultura rannikh kochevnikov Yuzhnovo Urala.* Moscow: Nauka.

————. 1989. *Raskopki tsarskogo kurgana na Yuzhnom Urale.* Ufa: Bashkir Center of RAS.

————. 2000. Drevnaya posuda rannikh kochevnikov Yuzhnogo Urala. In *Ufimskij arkheologicheski sbornik*, ed. A. H. Pshenichnuk. Ufa: National Museum of Bashkortostan: 76–93.

Pustovalov, S. Zh. *Vozrastnaya, polovaya i sotsialnaya kharakterisika katakombnogo naseleniya Severnogo Prichernomory'a.* Kiev: Naukova Dumka.

————. 1994. Economy and social organization of northern Pontic steppe – forest-steppe pastoral population: 2750–2000 BC (Catacomb culture). In *Nomadism and Pastoralism in the Circle of Baltic-Pontic Early agrarian Cultures: 5000–1650 BC*, ed. A. Kosko. Poznan: Adam Mickiewicz University: 86–134.

Pyankov, I. V. 2002. Arkaim and Indo-Iranian Var. In *Complex Societies of Central Eurasia from the 3rd to the 1st Millennium BC: Regional Specifics in Light of Global Models*, ed. K. Jones-Bley, & D. Zdanovich. Journal of Indo-European Studies Monograph Series 45. Washington, D.C.: Institute for Study of Man: 42–52.

Pyankova, L. T. 1989. *Drevniye skotovody Yuzhnogo Tadzhikistana.* Dushanbe: Nauka.

Pyatkin, B. N. 1987. Predstavleniya drevnikh ludei o prostranstve i vremeni po kurgannym sooruzheniyam. In *Skofo-Sibirski mir. Iskusstvo i ideologiya*, ed. A. I. Martynov. Novosobirsk: Nauka: 30–7.

Radloff, V. V. 1989. *Iz Sibiri: Stranitsy dnevnika (From Siberia: Pages of dairy).* Moscow: Nauka.

Rassamakin, Y. 1999. The Eneolithic of the Black See Steppe: Dynamics of Cultural and Economic Development 4500–2300 BC (trans.) C. Scarre. In *Late prehistoric exploitation of the Eurasian steppe*, ed. Y. R. M. Levine, A. Kislenko, N. Tatarintseva. McDonald Institute Monographs. Cambridge: McDonald Institute for Archaeological Research: 59–182.

Razhev, D. I. 2001. Naseleniye lesosotepi Zapadnoi Sibiri rannego zheleznogo veka: rekonstruktsiya antropologicheskikh osobennostei. Ph.D. dissertation: Ekaterinburg, Institute of History and Archaeology UD RAS.

Rostovtseff, M. 1922. *Iranians and Greeks in Southern Russia.* Oxford: Clarendon Press.

————. 1925. *Scythia i Bospor. Kriticheskoye obozreniye pamyatnikov literaturnykh i arkheologicheskikh.* Leningrad.

Rostovtseff, M. 1929. *The Animal Style in South Russia and China* (Princeton Monographs in Art and Archaeology 29). Princeton: Princeton University Press.

Rudenko, S. I. 1952. *Gornoaltaiskiye nakhodki i skify.* Moscow-Leningrad: Academy of Sciences Press.

————. 1961. K voprosu o formakh skotovodcheskogo khozyaistva i o kochevnikakh. *Materialy po otdeleniyu etnografiyi* 1. Moscow: Nauka: 3–8.

————. 1962. *Sibirskaya kollektsiya Petra 1.* (Arkheologiya SSSR. Svod arkheologicheskikh istochnikov D3–9). Moscow: Academy of Sciences Press.

————. 1970. *The Frozen Tombs of Siberia: The Pazyryk Burials of Iron Age Horsmen.* Berlkeley and Los Angeles: University of California Press.

Ryabogina, N. E., N. P. Matveyeva, & L. A. Orlova. 2001a. Novyje dannyje po prirodnoi srede Zauraly'a v drevnosti (palinilogicheskiye issledovaniya otlozhenii Nizhne-Ingalskogo-3 poseleniya). *Vestnik arkheologiyi, anthropologiyi i etnographiyi* 3: 205–12.

Ryabogina, N. E., & L. A. Orlova. 2002. Pozdnegolotsenovyi torfyanik Gladilovskyi Ryam kak indicator izmeneniya paleoekologicheskikh uslovii Ishimskoi ravniny. *Vestnik arkheologiyi, anthropologiyi i etnographiyi* 4: 203–13.

Ryabogina, N. E., T. G. Semochkina, & S. N. Ivanov. 2001b. Rekonstruktsiya uslovii obitaniya naseleniya nizhnego Priisety'a v pozdnem bronzovom i rannem zhelznom vekakh. In *Problemy vzaimodeistviya cheloveka i prirodnoi sredy*, ed. V. P. Tsibulsky. Tumen: Institut problem osvoyeniya Severa: 33–8.

Ryndina, N. V. 1998. *Drevneisheye metalloobrabatyvayushcheye proizodstvo Yugo-Vostochnoi Evropy*. Moscow: Moscow State University.

Ryndina, N. V., & A. D. Degtyareva. 2002. *Eneolit i bronzovyi vek*. Moscow: Moscow State University.

Saenz, C. 1991. Lords of Wast: perdition, pastoral production, and the process of stratification among the eastern Twargs. In *Chiefdom: Power, Economy and Ideology*, ed. T. Earle. Cambridge: Cambridge University Press: 100–20.

Salnikov, K. V. 1940. *Andronovskyi kurgannyi mogilnik u s. Fyodorovki* (Materialy i issledovaniya po arkheologiyi SSSR 1). Moscow: Academy of Sciences Press: 58–68.

———. 1951. *Bronzovyj vek Yuzhnogo Zauraly'a* (Materialy i issledovaniya po arkheolohiyi SSSR 21). Moscow: Academy of Sciences Press.

———. 1952. *Kurgany na ozere Alakul* (Materialy i issledovaniya po arkheologiyi SSSR 24). Moscow: Nauka: 51–71.

———. 1954. Abashevskaya kultura na Yuzhnom Urale. *Sovetskaya arkheologiya* XXI: 52–94.

———. 1962. K istoriyi drevnei metallurgiyi na Yuzhnom Urale. In *Arkeologiya i etnografiya Bas'kiriyi*. Vol. I. Ufa: Baskirski Nauchyi Tsentr: 62–74.

———. 1967. *Ocherki drevnei istoriyi Yuzhnogo Urala*. Moscow: Nauka.

Sarianidi, V. I. 1987. Baktriyski tsentr zlatodeliya. *Sovetskaya arkheologiya* 1: 72–83.

Savelyeva, E. A. 1984. *Arkheologiya Komi ASSR*. Syktyvkar: Syktyvkar University.

Schmidt, A. V. 1928. Otchet o komandirovke v 1925 g. v Uralskuyu oblast'. *Sbornik muzeya antropologii i etnografiyi ANSSSR*.

Sementsov, A. A., G. I. Zaitseva, I. Gursdorf, N. A. Bokovenko, H. Parzinger, A. Nagler, K. V. Chugunov, & L. M. Lebedeva. 1997. Voprosy khronologiyi pamyatnikov kochevnikov skifskoi epokhi Yuzhnoi Sibiri i Tsentralnoi Aziyi. In *Radiouglerod i Arkheologiya*, ed. G. I. Zatseva. Arkheologicheskiye Vesti 37. St. Petresburg: Institut for History of Material Culture: 86–93.

Semochkina, N. G., & N. T. Ryabogina. 2001. Palinologicheskaya kharakteristika razreza kurgana 15 Chistolebyazhskogo mogilnika.

Vestnik arkheologiyi, antropologiyi i etnografiyi 3: 115–20.

Sergatskov, I. V. 2002. Analiz sarmatskikh pogrebalnykh pamyatnikov I-II vv. do n.e. In *Statisticheskaya obrabotka porebalnykh pamyatnikov Aziatskoi Sarmatiyi. Srednesarmatskaya kultura*, ed. M. G. Moshkova. Moscow: Institute of Archaeology RAS: 22–129.

Shakhmatov, V. F. 1962. O pastbishchno-kochevoi (zemelnoi) obshchine u kazakhov. In *Trudy Instituata istoriyi, arkheologiyi i etnografiyi AN Kaz. SSR*, ed. V. F. Shakhmatov, T. Z. Shoinbayev, & V. S. Kuznetsov. Alma-Ata: Nauka: 3–37.

Shakhmatov, V. F. 1964. *Kazakhskaya pastbishno-kochevaya obsgchina*. Alma-Ata: Nauka.

Shamiladze, V. M. 1982. O nekotorykh voprosakh klassifikatsiyi i terminologiyi skotovodstva Kavkaza. *Sovetskaya etnografiya* 3: 70–6.

Sharapova, S. V. 2004. Trans-Urals Iron Age ceramics – A new outlook. In *European Journal of Archaeology* 7 (2): 177–97.

Shchukin, M. B. 1994. *Na rubezhe er* (Russian Archaeological Bibliothek. 2). St. Petersburg: Farn Ltd.

Shilov, V. P. 1975. *Ocherki po istorii drevnikh plemen Nizhnego Povolzhy'a*. Leningrad: Nauka.

Shnirelman, V. A. 1980. *Proiskhozhdenoye skotovodstava: kulturno-istoricheskaya problema*. Moscow: Nauka.

———. 1988. Proizvodstevennye predposylki razlozheniya pervobytno-obshchinnogo obshchestva. In *Istoria pervobytnogo obshchestva. Epokha klassoobrazovaniya*, ed. Y. V. Bromlei. Moscow: Nauka: 5–139.

Shorin, A. F. 1999. *Eneolit Urala i sopredelnykh territorii: problemy kulturogeneza*. Ekaterinburg: Institute of History and Archaeology RAS.

Shramko, B. A. 1962. Novyie dannye o dobyche zheleza v Skifiyi. *Kratkiye soobshcheniya Instituta Arkheologii Academii Nauk* 62: 72–7.

———. 1969. Orudiya skifskoi epokhi dlya obrabotki zheleza. *Sovetskaya arkheologiya* 3: 52–69.

———. 1987. *Belskoye gorodishche skifskoi epokhi*. Kiev: Naukova Dumka.

Shramko, B. A., & Y. G. Mashkarov. 1993. Issledovaniye bimetallicheskogo nozha iz pogrebeniya katakombnoi kultury. *Rossijskaya arkheologiya* 2: 163–70.

Shramko, B. A., L. A. Solntsev, & L. D. Fomin. 1963. Tekhnika obrabotki zheleza v lesostepnoi Skifiyi. *Sovetskaya arkheologiya* 4: 36–57.

————. 1977. Nachalnayi etap obrabotki zhe-leza v Vostochnoi Evrope (doskifski period). *Sovetskaya arkheologiya* 1: 52–80.

Sinuk, A. T. 1981. Repinskaya kultura epokhi eneolita-bronzy v basseine Dona. In *Sovetskaya arkheologiya* 4, 8–19.

————. 1996. *Bronzovyi vek basseina Dona*. Voronezh: Voronezh State Pedagogical University.

Sinuk, A. T., & I. A. Kozmirchuk. 1995. Neko-torye aspekty izuchenija abashevskoi kultury v basseine Dona. In *Drevniye indoiranski kultury Volgo-Urala*, ed. I. B. Vasily'ev. Samara: Samara Pedagogical Institute: 37–70.

Skripkin, A. S. 1990. *Asiatskaya Sarmatiya. Prob-lemy khronologii i ee istoricheskii aspect*. Saratov: Saratov State University.

————. 1996. K voprosu ob etnicheskoi istoriyi sarmatov pervykh vekov nashei ery. *Vestnik drevnei istoriyi* 1: 160–9.

————. 2000. *O kitaiskikh traditsiaykh v sarm atskoi kulture*. Paper presented to the Antich-naya tsivilizatsiya i varvarskij mir, Krasnodar, 2000: 96–9.

Smirnov, A. P. 1952. *Ocherki drevnei i sredn-evekovoi istoriyi narodov Srednevo Povolzhya i Prikamy'a* (Materialy i issledovaniya po arkheologiyi SSSR 30). Moscow: Moscow: Academy of Sciences Press.

Smirnov, K. F. 1961. *Vooruzheniye savromatov* (Materialy i issledovania po arkhrologii SSSR 101). Moskow: Nauka.

————. 1964. *Savromaty: rannaya istoria i kultura Sarmatov*. Moscow: Nauka.

————. 1975. *Sarmaty na Ileke*. Moskow: Nauka.

Smirnov, K. F., & E. E. Kuzmina. 1977. *Proiskhozhdeniye indoirantsev v svete noveishikh arkheologicheskikh otkrytij*. Moscow: Nauka.

Smoline, V. 1927. La nécropole d'Abashevo. *Eurasia Septentrinalis Antiqua* 1.

Snodgrass, A. 1980. Iron and Early metallurgy in the Mediterranean. In *The Coming of the Iron Age*, ed. J. D. Muhly. New Haven and London: Yele University Press: 335–74.

Solovyev, A. I. 2003.*Oruzhiye i dospekhi: Sibir-skoye vooruzheniye ot kamennogo veka do srednevekovya*. Novosibirsk: INFOLIO-press.

Solovyev, B. S. 1994. *Chirkovskaya kultura Srednego Povolzhy'a*. Izhevsk: Udmurt State University.

Sorokin, V. S. 1962. *Mogilnik bronzovoi epokhi Tasty-Butak I v Zapadnom Kazakhstane* (Materialy i issledovaniya po arkheologiyi SSSR 120). Moscow: Nauka.

Spitsin, A. A. 1893. Kostenosnye gorodishcha. *Materialy po arkheologii vostochnykh gubernii Rossii*. St. Petersburg.

————. 1901. *Drevnosti basseinov Oki i Kamy* (Materialy po ackheologiyi Rossiyi). St. Petersburg.

————. 1914. *Glyadenovskoye kostishche* (Trudy Permskoi arkheologicheskoi komissii XI). Perm.

Stavisky, B. Y. 1997. Velikij shelkovyi put. In *Cultural Values*, ed. P. G. Muradov. Biblioteka Turkmenica. St. Peterburg: Eropean House: 19–29.

Steblin-Kamenskij, I. M. 1995. Ariisko-uralskiye svyazi: Mif ob Jime. In *Rossiya i Vostok: prob-lemy vzaimodeistviya.*, ed. G. B. Zdanovich. Chelyabinsk: Chelyabinsk State University: 166–7.

Stefanov, V. I. 1996. Poseleniya alakulskoi kultury Uzhnogo Urala. In *Materialy po arkhe-ologiji i etnografiji Uzhnogo Urala*, ed. A. D. Tairov. Chelyabinsk: Kamennyi Poyas: 43–63.

Stefanov, V. I., & O. N. Korochkova. 2000. *Andronovskiye drevnosti Tumenskogo Pritoboly'a*. Ekaterinburg: Poligrafist.

————. 2006. *Urefty I – Zauralski pamyatnik v andronovskom kontexte*. Ekaterinburg: Ural State University.

Stefanov, V. I., Koryakov, I. O., Chemyakin, Yu. P. & S. V. Kuzminykh. 2001. Igralnye kosti iz srubno-andronovskikh pamyatnikov Urala I Zapadnoi Sibiri. In *Bronzovyi vek Vostochnoi Evropy: kharakteristika kultur, khronologiya i periodizatsiya*, ed. Yu. I. Kolev, P. F. Kuznetsov and O. V. Kuzmina. Samara: Samara State Pedagogical University: 290–8.

Stepanova, N. F. 1997. Inventar iz pogrebeni afanasyevskoi kultury Gornogo Altaya. In *Sotsialno-ekonomicheskiye struktury drevnikh obshchestv Zapadnoi Sibiri*, ed. Y. F. Kirushin & A. B. Shamshin. Barnaul: Altai University: 32–36.

Stokolos, V. S. 1962. Kurgany epokhi bronzy u s. Stepnoye. *Krayevedcheskiye zapiski* I: 3–19.

————. 1972. *Kultura naselenija bronzovogo veka Uzhnogo Zauraly'a*. Moscow: Nauka.

Strabo. 1994. *Geography*. Moscow: Nauka.

Sulimirski, T. 1970. *The Sarmatians*. London: Thames and Hudson.

Sunchugashev, Y. I. 1969. *Gornoye delo i vyplavka metallov v drevnei Tuve*. Moscow: Nauka.

————. 1979. *Drevnaya metallurgiya Khakassiyi.* Moscow: Nauka.

Tainter, J. A. 1988. *The Collapse of Complex Societies.* Cambridge: Cambridge University Press.

Tairov, A. D. 1991. *Ranniye kochevniki yuzhnovo Zauralya v VII-II vekakh do novoi ery.* Ph.D. dissertation: Moscow: Institute of Archaeology RAS.

————. 1993. Pastbishchno-kochevaya sistema i istoricheskiye sudby kochevnokov Ural-Kazakhstanskikh stepei v I tys. do n.e. In *Kochevniki Uralo-Kazakhstanskikh Stepei*, ed. A. D. Tairov. Ekaterinburg: Nauka: 3–23.

————. 1995. *Torgovyje kommunikatsiyi v Zapadnoi chasti Uralo-Irtyshskogo mezhdurechy'a.* Chelyabinsk: Chelyabinsk State University.

————. (ed.) 1999. *Kurgan s usami "Solochanka".* Chelyabinsk: Chelaybinsk State University.

————. 2000. Rannii zheleznyi vek. In *Drevnyaya istoriya Yuzhnogo Zauraly'a*, ed. N. O. Ivanova Chelyabinsk: South Ural State University: 4–205.

————. 2003. *Izmemeniya klimata stepei i lesostepei Tsentralnoi Evraziyi vo II-I tys. do n.e.: meterialy k istoricheskim rekonstruktsiyam.* Chelyabinsk: Rifei.

Tairov, A. D., & S. G. Botalov. 1988. Kurgan u sela Varna. In *Problemy arkheologiyi Uralo-Kazakhstanskikh stepei*, ed. G. Zdanovich. Chelyabinsk: 100–25.

Talgren, A. M. 1919. *L'epoque dite d Ananino dans la Russie orientale* (Souomen Muinaismuistoyhdistyksen Aikakanshirja XXXI). Helsinki: K. F. Puromienen Kirjapaino O.-Y.

————. 1937. The Arctic Bronze Age in Europe. *Eurasia Septentrinalis Antiqua* XI: 1–46.

Taskin, V. S. 1989. *Materialy po istoriyi kochevykh narodov v Kitaye III-V v. Sunnu.* Moscow: Nauka.

Telegin, D. Y. (ed.) 1985. *Archeologiya Ukrainskoi SSR. Pervobytnaya arkheologiya* (1). Kiev: Naukova Dumka.

Teploukhov, S. A. 1927. *Drevniye pogrebeniya v Minusinskom kraye* (Materialy po etnographiyi III). Leningrad: Academy of Sciences Press.

Terekhova, N. N., & V. R. Erlikh. 2000. Drevneishii chernyi metall na Severo-Zapadnom Kavkaze. In *Skify i Sarmaty v VII-III vv. do n.e. Paleoekologiya, antropologiya i arckheologiya*, ed. V. I. Gulayev & V. S. Olkhovsky. Moscow: Institute of archaeology RAS: 281–6.

Terekhova, N. N., L. S. Rozanova, V. I. Zavy'alov, & V. V. Tolmacheva. 1997. *Ocherki po istoriyi drevnei zhelezoobrabotki v Vostochnoi Evrope.* Moscow: Metallurgiya.

Tkachev, A. A. 2002. *Tsentralnyi Kazakhstan v epokhu bronzy.* Tyumen: Izdatelstvo TGNGU.

Tkachev, V. V. 1995. O sootnosheniyi sintashtinskikh i petrovskikh pogrebalnykh kompleksov v stepnom Priuralye. In *Rossiya i Vostok: problemy vzaimodeistviya.*, ed. G. B. Zdanovich. Chelyabinsk: Chelyabinsk State University: 168–70.

————. 1998. K probleme proiskhozhdeniya petrovskoi kultury. In *Arkheologicheskije pamyatniki Orenburzhy'a* II, ed. N. L. Morgunova. Orenburg: DIMUR: 38–56.

————. 2000. O yugo-zapadnykh svyazyakh naseleniya Yuzhnogo Urala v epokhu rannei i srednei bronzy. In *Problemy izucheniya eneolita i bronzovogo veka Urala*, ed. S. Zasedateleva. Orsk: Institute evrazijskikh issledovanij: 37–54.

Tkachev, V. V., & Y. Gutsalov. 2000. Novyje pogrebeniya eneolita-srednej bronzy vostochnogo Orenburzhya i Severnogo Kazakhstana. In *Arkheologicheskye pamyatniki Orenburzhy'a* IV, ed. N. L. Morgunova. Orenburg: Orenburgskaya guberniya: 27–47.

Tolmachev, V. 1912. *Drevnosti Vostochnogo Urala* (Zapiski Uralskogo Obshchestva lubitelei estestvoznaniya). Ekaterinburg: UOLE.

Tolstov, S. P. 1948. *Drevnij Khorezm. Opyt istoricheskikh issledovanij.* Moscow: Moscow State University.

Tolybekov, S. E. 1971. *Kochevoye obchshestvo kazakhov v XVII-nachale XX veka: politiko-ekonomicheskiy analiz.* Alma-Ata: Nauka.

Tomilov, N. A. 1986. *Turkoyazchnoye naseleniye Zapadnosibirskoi ravniny v kontse XVII – pervoi chetverti XIX v.* Tomsk: Tomsk State University.

Treister, M. Y., & S. A. Yatsenko. 1997/98. About the Centers of Manufacture of Certain Series of Horse-Harness Roundels in 'Gold-Turquoise Animal Style' of the 1st-2nd Centuries AD. *Silk Road Art and Archaeology* V: 51–106.

Trever, K. V. 1940. *Pamyatniki Greko-Baktriiskogo iskusstva.* Moscow-Leningrad: Izdatelstvo Akademii Nauk.

Trifonov, V. A. 1996a. K absolutnomu datirovaniju "mikenskogo" ornamenta epokhi razvitoi bronzy Evraziji. In *Radiouglerod i arkheologija*, ed. G. Zaitseva, V. Dergachev,

& V. Masson. St-Petereburg: Institute for History of Material Culture RAS: 60–4.

———. 1996b. Popravki k absolutnoi khronologiji kultur eneolita-bronzy Severnogo Kavkaza. In *Mezhdu Evropoi i Aziyei. Kavkaz IV-I tys. do n.e.*, ed. V. Bochkarev. St. Petersburg: Institute for History of Material Culture: 43–9.

———. 2001. Popravki k absolutnoi khronologiji kultur epokhi eneolota – srednei bronzy Kavkaza, stepnoi I lesostepnoi zon Vostochnoi Evropy (po dannym radiouglerodnogo datirovaniya). In *Bronzobyi vek Vostochnoi Evropy: kharakteristika kultur, khronologiya i periodizatsiya*, ed. Yu.I. Kolev, P. F. Kuznetsov and O. V. Kuzmina. Samara: Samara State Pedagogical University: 71–84.

Tsalkin, V. I. 1964. Nekotorye itogi izucheniya kostnykh ostatkov zhivotnykh iz raskopok pozdnego bronzovogo veka. *Kratkie soobshcheniya Instituta Arkheologii SSSR* 101: 20–9.

———. 1966. *Drevneye zhivotnovodstvo Vostochnoi Evropy i Sredeni Azii* (Materialy i issledovaniya po arkheologii SSSR 135). Moscow: Moscow: Academy of Sciences Press.

Tsimidanov, V. V. 1990. *Predposylki usileniya voyennoi verkhushki v stepnykh obshchestvakh epokhi bronzy*. Paper presented to Problemy isucheniya katakombnoi kul'turno-istoricheskoi obshchnosti. Zaporozhy'e: 103–7.

———. 1997. Triada srubnykh isigniy vlasti: mesto slozheniya. In *Epokha bronzy i ranniy zheleznyi vek v istorii drevnikh plemyon yuzhnorusskikh stepei*, ed. A. I. Yudin. Saratov: Saratov State Pedagogical University.

Turetski, M. A. 2004. Razvitiye kolesnogo transporta u plemen yamnoi kultury. In *Arkheologicheskiye pamyatniki Orenburzhya*, ed. N. L. Morgunova. Orenburg: Orenburg State University: 31–6.

Usachuk, A. N. 2002. Regional peculiarities of technology of the shield cheekpieces production (based on materials of the Middle Don, Volga, and Southern Urals). In *Complex Societies of Central Eurasia from the 3rd to the 1st Millennium BC. Reginal Spesifics in Light of Global Models*, ed. K. Jones-Bley, & D. Zdanovich. Journal of Indo-European Studies Monograph Series 45. Washington, D.C.: Institute for the Study of Man: 237–43.

Usmanova, E. R., & V. N. Logvin. 1998. *Zhenskie nakosnye ukrashenia Kazakhstana: (epokha bronzy)*. Lisakovsk: Lisakovsk Museum.

Vainberg, B. I. 1999. *Etnogeografiya Turana v drevnosti. VII v. do n.e.-VIII v. n.e.* Moscow: Vostochnaya Literatura.

Vainshtein, S. I. 1972. *Istoricheskaya etnographiya tuvintsev. Problemy kochevogo khozyaistva*. Moscow: Nauka.

———. 1973. *Problema proiskhozhdeniya i formirovaniya khozyaistvenno-kulturnogo tipa kochevykh skotovodov umerennogo poyasa Evraziyi* (IX Mezhdnarodnyi Kongress Antropologicheskikh i Etnograficheskikh Nauk). Moscow: Nauka.

———. 1980. *Nomads of Southern Siberia*. Cambridge: Cambridge University Press.

Van der Plicht, J. 2004. Radiocarbon, the calibration curve and Scythisn chronology. In *Impact of the Environment on Human Migration in Eurasia*, ed. Marian Scott, E., Alexeyev, A. Yu. & G. Zaitseva. London: Kluwer Academic Publishers: 45–62.

Varfolomeyev, V. V. 1991. Sary-Arka v kontse bronzovoi epokhi. Ph.D. dissertation: Alma-Ata, Institute of Archaeology KAZ AS.

———. 2003. Kent i ego okruga (nekotoryje itogi paleoekonomicheskogo i sotsiokulturnogo analiza pamyatnikov vostochnoi Sary-Arki). In *Stepnaya tsivilizatsiya vostochnoi Evraziyi*, ed. K. A. Akishev. Astana: Kultegin: 88–108.

Vasily'ev, I. B. 1980. Mogilnik yamnopoltavkinskogo vremeni u s. Utevka v Srednem Povolzhy'e. In *Arkheologiya vostochno-evropeiskoi lesostepi*, ed. A. D. Pryakhin. Voronezh: Voronezh University: 32–58.

Vasily'ev, I. B., P. F. Kuznetsov, & A. P. Semenova. 1992. Pogrebeniya znati epokhi bronzy v Srednem Povolzhy'e. In *Arkheologicheskiye vesti* I, ed. V. M. Masson. S-Petresburg: Institute for Hstory of Material Culture: 52–63.

———. 1994. *Potapovski kurgannyi mogilnik indoiranskikh plemen na Volge*. Samara: Samara State University.

Vasily'ev, S. S., V. A. Dergachev, & V. F. Chistyakov. 1997. Vyjavlenie 2400-letnego tsikla v kontsentratsiyi C-14 i vospriyimchivost povedeniya cheloveka k krupnomasshtabnym izmeneyam klimata. In *Radiocarbon and Archaeology*, ed. G. I. Zaitseva, V. A. Dergachev, & V. M. Masson. St.

Petersburg: Institute for History of Material Culture: 13–35.

Vichtomov, A. D. 1967. Periodizatsiya i local'nye grouppy pamyatnikov ananyinskoi kul'tury Srednevo Prikamya. *Uchenye zapiski Permskovo universiteta* 148: 78–110.

Viktorora, V. D. 2002. Pochemu na ptitsevidnykh izobrazheniyekh poyavilis' lichiny. *Uralskij istoricheskij vestnik* 8: 74–92.

Vildanov, P. F., & A. F. Melnichuk. 1999. *Dalniye yugo-vostochnye svyazi naseleniya Permskogo Priuralya v rannem zheleznom veke.* Paper presented to the XIV Uralskoye arkheologicheskoye soveshchsniye, Chelyabinsk, 1999: 119–20.

Vinogradov, N. B. 1982. Kulevchi III – pamyatnik petrovskogo tipa na Yuzhnom Urale. *Kratkiye soobshcheniya Instituta Arkheologiyi SSSR* 169: 94–100.

———. 1983. Yuzhnoye Zauraly'e i Severnyi Kazakhstan v rannealakulski period. Ph.D. dissertation: Moscow, Institute of Archaeology.

———. 1984. Kulevchy VI – novyi alakulskij mogilnik v lesostepyakh Yuzhnogo Zauraly'a. *Sovetskaya arkheologiya* 3: 136–53.

———. 1991. Poseleniye Kinzhitai – pamyatnik perekhodnogo vremeni ot epokhi bronzy k rannemu zheleznomu veku v Uzhnom Zauraly'e. In *Konvergentsiya i divergentsiya v razvitiji kul'tur epokhi eneolita-bronzy Srednei i Vostochnoi Evropy*, ed. V. S. Bochkarev. Arkheologicheskiye izyskaniya. St. Petersburg: Institute for History of Material Culture: 71–4.

———. 1995a. Khronologiya, soderzhaniye i kulturnaya prinadlezhnost' pamyatnikov sintashtinskogo tipa bronzovogo veka v Yuzhnom Zauraly'e. *Vestnik Chelyabinskogo pedagogicheskogo instituta. Istoricheskije nauki* 1: 16–26.

———. 1995b. Yuzhnye motivy v keramicheskikh kompleksakh epokhi bronzy v Yuzhnom Zaural'ye. In *Konvergentziya i divergentziya v razvitii kul'tur epokhi eheolita-bronzy Srednei i Vostochnoi Evropy*, ed. V. S. Bochkarev. (Arkheologicheskie izyskaniya 25). St. Peterburg: Institute for History of Material Culture: 71–4.

———. 2000. Mogilnik epokhi bronzy Kulevchy VI v Yuzhnom Zauraly'e (po raskopkam 1983 g.). *Problemy istoriyi, filologiyi, kultury* VIII: 24–53.

Vinogradov, N. B., & A. V. Epimakhov. 2000. From a Settled Way of Life to Nomadism: Variants in Models of Transition. In *Kurgans, Ritual Sites, and Settlements: Eurasian Bronze and Iron Age*, ed. J. Davis-Kimball, E. M. Murphy, L. Koryakova, & L. T. Yablonsky. BAR International Series 890. Oxford: Archaeopress: 240–6.

Vinogradov, N. B., V. P. Kostukov, & S. V. Markov. 1996. Mogil'nik Solntse-Talika i problema genezisa fedorovskoi kultury bronzovogo veka v Yuznom Zauraly'e. In *Novoye v arkheologiyi Yuznogo Urala*, ed. S. A. Grigory'ev. Chelyabinsk: Rifei: 131–50.

Vostrov, V. V. 1962. Rodoplemennoi sostav i rasseleniye kazakhov na territoriyi Turgaiskoi oblasti (konets XIX – nachalo XX veka). *Trudy Instituta Istoriyi, Arkheologiyi i Etnografiyi AN Kazakhskoi SSR* 16: 72–94.

Voznesenskaya, G. A. 1967. Metallograficheskiye issledovanoiya kuznechnykh izdeli iz ranneslavyanskikh pamyatnikov. *Kratkie soobshcheniya Instituta Arkheologii SSSR* 110: 125–28.

———. 1978. Kuznechnoye proizvodstvo u vostochnykh slavyan v tretyei chetverti I tys. do n.e. In *Drevnaya Rus' i slavyane*, ed. V. V. Sedov. Moscow: Nauka: 61–65.

Wason, P., & M. Baldia. 2000. Religiya, kommunikatsiya i genesis slozhnoi sotsialnoi organizatsiyi v neoliticheskoi Evrope. In *Alternativnye puti k tsivilizatsiyi*, ed. N. N. Kradin, A. V. Korotayev, D. M. Bondarenko, & V. A. Lynsha. Moscow: Logos: 219–34.

Yablonsky, L. T. (ed.) 1996a. *Kurgany levoberezhnogo Ileka.* Moscow: Institute of Archaeology RAS.

———. 1996b. *Saki Yuzhnovo Priaralya.* Moscow: Timp.

———. 2000. "Scythian Triad" and "Scythian World". In *Kurgans, Ritual Sites, and Settlements. Eurasian BronZe and Iron Age*, ed. J. Davis-Kimball, E. M. Murphy, L. N. Koryakova, & L. T. Yablonsky. BAR International Series 890. Oxford: Archaeopress: 3–8.

———. 2001. The Scyths, Sarmatians and Other in Context of Achievements of Russian Archaeology in the 20th Century. *Rossijskaya arkheologiya* 1: 56–65.

Yablonsky, L. T., & V. A. Bashilov. 2000. Some Current Problems Concerning the History of Early Iron Age Eurasian Steppe Nomadic Societies. In *Kurgans, Ritual Sites, and Settlements. Eurasian Bronze and Iron Age*, ed. L. T. Yablonsky. BAR International Series 890. Oxford: Archaeopress: 9–12.

Yablonsky, L. T., J. Davis-Kimball, Y. V. Demidenko, & V. Y. Malyshev. 1996. Raskopki mogilnikov Pokrovka 1,2,7,10 v 1995 g. In *Kurgany levoberezhnogo Ileka*, ed. L. T. Yablonsky. Moscow: Institute of Archaeology RAN: 7–48.

Yablonsky, L. T., & A. A. Khokhlov. 1994. Kraniologiya naseleniya yamnoi kultury Orenburgskoi oblasti. In *Pamyatniki drevneyamnoi kultury na Ileke*, ed. N. L. Morgunova & A. Y. Kravtsov. Ekaterinburg: Nauka: 116–52.

Yakar, J. 1985. *The Later Prehistory of Anatolia. The Late Chalcolithic and Early Bronze Age* (BAR International Series 268). Oxford: Oxford University Press.

Yaminov, A. F., & N. S. Savely'ev. 1999. *Baishevskij arkheologicheskij mikrorayon*. Paper presented to the XIV Uralskoye Arkheologicheskoye soveshchaniye, Chelyabinsk, 1999: 110–1.

Yatsenko, S. A. 1993. Alanskaya problema i tsentral'no-aziatskije elementy v kul'ture kochevnikov Sarmatii rubezha 1–2 vv. n.e. *Peterburgski arkheologicheski vestnik*, 3: 60–72.

———. 2003. Peculiarities of Social Development of the Sarmato-Alans and their Images in Evidence of Other Cultures. In *Nomadic Pathways in Social Evolution*, ed. N. N. Kradin. Moscow: Russian State University of Humanities.

Yessen, A. A., & B. E. Degenom-Kovalevski. 1935. K voprosu o drevneishei metallurgiji medi na Kavkaze. *Izvestija gosudarstvennoi akademiji istoriji materialnoi kultury* 120: 7–237.

Yessen, A. A. 1946. O drevnei dobyche zolota na Urale. In *200 let zolotodobychi na Urale*. Sverdlovsk.

———. 1948. Chusovskaya expeditsiya 1942 g. *Sbornik Gosudarstevennogo Ermitazha* 5: 38–40.

Zaibert, V. F. 1993. *Eneolit Uralo-Irtyshskogo mezhdurechy'a*. Petropavlovsk: Petropavlovsk Pedagogical Institute.

Zaikov, V. V. 1995. Mineralno-syry'evaya basa pamyatnikov epokhi bronzy na Yuzhnom Urale (Strana gorodov). In *Rossia i Vostok: Problemy vzaimodeistviya*, ed. G. B. Zdanovich. Chelyabin.sk: Chelyabinsk State University: 147–51.

Zaikov, V. V., A. V. Yuminov, A. P. Bushmakin, E. V. Zaikova, A. D. Tairov, & G. B. Zdanovich. 2002. Ancient Copper Mines and Products from Base and Noble metals in the Southern Urals. In *Complex Societies of Central Eurasia from the 3rd to the 1st Millennium BC (Regional Specifics in Light of Global Models)*, ed. K. Jones-Bley, & D. Zdanovich. Journal of Indo-European Studies Monograph Series 45. Washington, D.C.: Institute for Study of Man: 417–42.

Zaitseva, G. I., J. Possnert, A. Y. Alekseyev, V. A. Dergachev, & A. A. Sementsov. 1997a. Radiouglerodnye daty kluchevykh pamyatnikov Evropeiskoi Skifiyi. In *Radiocarbon and Archaeology*, ed. G. I. Zatseva, V. A. Dergachev, & V. M. Masson. St. Petersburg: Institute for HIstory of Material Culture: 76–83.

Zaitseva, G. I., S. S. Vasily'ev, L. S. Marsadolov, v.d. Pliht, I., A. A. Sementsov, V. A. Dergachev, & L. M. Lebedeva. 1997b. Radiouglerod i dendrokhronologiya kluchevykh pamyatnikov Sayano-Altaya:statisticheski analiz. In *Radiouglerod i arkheologiya*, ed. G. I. Zatseva. Arkheologicheskiye vesti. 37. St. Petresburg: Institute for History of Material Culture: 36–44.

Zakh, V. A. 1995. *Poselok drevnikh skotovodov na Tobole*. Novosibirsk: Nauka.

Zbruyeva, A. V. 1952. *Istoriya naseleniya Prikamiya v ananyinskuyu epokhu* (Materyaly i issledovaniya po arkheologiyi SSSR 30). Moscow: Nauka.

———. 1960. *Pamyatniki epokhi bronzy v Prikazanskom Povolzhy'e i Niznem Prikamy'e* (Materialy i issledovaniya po arkheologiyi SSSR 80). Moscow: Nauka.

Zdanovich, D. G. 1997a. *Sinatshtinskoye obshchestvo: sotsialnyje osnovy "kvazigorodskoi" kultury Yuzhnogo Zauraly'a epokhi srednei bronzy*. Chelyabinsk: Chelyabinsk State University.

———. 2002a. Arkheologiya kurgana 25 Bolshekaraganskogo mogilnika. In *Arkaim-nekropol*, ed. D. G. Zdanovich. Chelyabinsk: South Ural Press: 17–110.

———. 2002b. Introduction. In *Complex Societies of Central Eurasia from the 3rd to the 1st Millennium BC: Regional Specifics in Light of Global Models*, ed. K. Jones-Bley & D. Zdanovich. Journal of Indo-European Studies Monograph Series 45. Washington, D.C.: Institute for Study of Man: ix–xxxviii.

———. 2005. *Zhertvopronosheniya zhivotnykh v pogrebalnom obryade naseleniya stepnogo Zauraly'a epokhi srednei bronzy*. Ph.D. dissertation: Ekaterinburg, Institute of History and Archaeology of the Ural Branch of RAS.

Zdanovich, D. G., & L. L. Gaiduchenko. 2002. Sintashta Burial Sacrifice: The Bolshekaraganski Cemetery in Focus. In *Complex Societies of Central Eurasia from the 3rd to the 1st Millennium BC: Regional Specifics in Light of Global Models*, ed. K. Jones-Bley, & D. Zdanovich. Journal of Indo-European Studies Monograph Series 45. Washington, D.C.: Institute for Study of Man: 202–31.

Zdanovich, G. B. 1970. Novoye naseleniye epokhi bronzy v Severnom Kazakhstane. In *Po sledam drevnikh kultur*, ed. M. Kadyrbayev. Alma-Ata: Nauka: 147–53.

———. 1973. Keramika epokhi bronzy Severo-Kazakhstanskoi oblasti. *Voprosy arkheologiyi Urala* 12: 21–43.

———. 1988. *Bronzovyi vek Uralo-Kazakhstanskikh stepei (osnovy periodizatsii)*. Sverdlovsk: Ural State University Press.

———. 1989. Phenomen prototsivilizatsiyi bronzobogo veka Uralo-Kazakhstanskikh stepei. Kulturnaya i sotsialno-ekonomicheskaya obuslovlennost. In *Vzaimodeistviye kochevykh kultur i drevnikh tsivilizatsii*, ed. V. Masson. Alma-Ata:. 58–76.

———. 1995. Arkaim: Ariyi na Urale ili nesostaoyavsheyesya tsivilizatsiyia. In *Arlaim: Issledovaniya. Poiski. Otkrytiya*, ed. G. Zdanovich. Chelyabinsk: Kamennyi Poyas: 21–42.

———. 1997b. Arkaim – kulturnyi kompleks epokhi srednei bronzy Uzhnogo Zaural'ya. *Rossijskaya arkheologiya* 2: 47–62.

———. 1999. *Garmonizatsiya prostranstva "Strany gorodov."* Paper presented at the XIV Uralskoye arkheologicheskoye soveshchaniye, Chelyabinsk, 1999: 76–7.

Zdanovich, G. B., & I. M. Batanina. 1995. "Strana gorodov" – ukreplennyje poseleniya epokhi bronzy XVII–XV v. do n.e. na Yuznom Urale. In *Arkaim. Issledovaniya. Poiski. Otkrytiya.*, ed. G. Zdanovich. Chelyabinsk: Kamennyi poyas: 54–62.

———. 2002. Planography of the Fortified Centers of the Middle Bronze Age in the southern Trans-Urals according to Aereal Photography Data. In *Complex Societies of central Eurasia from the 3rd to the 1st Millennium BC: Regional Specifics in Light of Global Models*, ed. K. Jones-Bley, & D. Zdanovich. Journal of Indo-European Studies Monograph Series 45. Washington, D.C.: Institute for Study of Man: 120–38.

Zdanovich, G. B., I. V. Ivanov, & M. K. Khabdulina. 1984. Opyt ispolzovaniya v arkheologii paleopochvennykh metodov issledovaniya (kurgany Kara-Oba i Obaly v Severnom Kazakhstane). *Sovetskaya arkheologiya* 4: 35–48.

Zdanovich, G. B., & D. G. Zdanovich. 1995. Protogorodsakaya tsivilizatsija "Strana Gorodov" Yuzhnogo Zauraly'a (opyt modeliruyushchego otnosheniya k drevnosti). In *Rossiya i Vostok: Problemy vzaimodeistviya*, ed. G. B. Zdanovich. Chelyabinsk: Chelyabinsk State University: 48–62.

———. 2002. The 'Country of Towns' of Southern Trans-Urals. In *Ancient Interactions: east and west of Eurasia*, ed. M. G. Levin. Cambridge: McDonald Institute for Archaeological Research: 249–64.

Zdanovich, S. Y. 1981. Novyje materialy k istoriyi skotovodstava v Zauraly'e i Severnom Kazakhstane v epokhu finalni bronzy. In *Materialy po khozyaistvu i obshchestvennomu stroyu plemen Yuzhnogo Urala*, ed. N. A. Mazhitov & A. H. Pshenichnuk. Ufa: Baskirski filial AN SSSR: 44–56.

———. 1983. Proiskhozhdeniye sargarinskoi kultury. In *Bronzovyi vek stepnoi polosy Uralo-Irtyshskogo mezhdurechy'a*, ed. Z. G. B. Chelyabinsk: Chelaybinsk State University: 69–80.

———. 1984. Keramika sargarinskoi kultury. In *Bronzovyi vek Uralo-Irtyshskogo mezhdurechy'a*, ed. S. Y. Zdanovich. Chelyabinsk: Chelyabinsk State University: 79–96.

———. 2003. The Steppe of the Urals and Kazakhstan during the Late Bronze Age. In *Prehistoric Steppe Adaptation and the Horse*, ed. K. Boyle. Oxford: McDonald Institute for Archaeological Research: 329–404.

Zdanovich, S. Y., & T. S. Malutina. 1976. Kulturnyi kompleks Sargary. In *Problemy arkheologiyi Povolzhy'a i Priuraly'a*, ed. I. B. Vasily'ev. Kuibyshev: Kuibyshev Pedagogical Institute: 90–101.

Zhelezchikov, B. F. 1980. Ranniye kochevniki Yuzhnovo Priuraly'a. Ph.D. dissertation: Moscow, Institute of Archaeology of AN SSSR.

Zhelezchikov, B. F. 1983. Ecologiya i nekotorye voprosy khozyastvennoi deyatelnosti sarmatov Yuzhnogo Priuralya i Zavolzhy'a v VI v. do n.e. – I v. n.e. In *Istoriya i kultura sarmatov*, ed. A. S. Skripkin. Saratov: Saratov State University: 48–60.

———. 1984. Veroyatnaya chislennost' savromato-sarmatov Yuzhnogo Priuraly'a i Zavolzhy'a v VI v. do n.e. – I v. n.e. po demographicheskim i ecologicheskim dannym. In *Drevnosti Evraziyi v skifo-sarmatskoye vremya*, ed. A. I. Milukova, M. G. Moshkova, & V. G. Petrenko. Moscow: Nauka: 65–8.

———. 1988. Stepi Vostochnoi Evraziyi v VII-II vv. do n.e. In *Problemy sarmatskoi arkheologiyi i istoriyi*, ed. V. E. Maksimenko. Azov: Azov Museum: 57–64.

Zhuravleva, G. N. 1995. Narodonaseleniye Srednego Prikamy'a v pianoborskuyu epokhu: (opyt paleodemograficheskikh rekonstruktsii).

Ph.D. dissertation: Izhevsk, Udmurt State University.

Zinyakov, N. M. 1997. *Chernaya metallurgiya i kuznechnoye remeslo Zapadnoi Sibiri*. Kemerovo: Kuzbassvuzizdat.

Zinyakov, N. V. 1988. *Istoriya chernoi metallurgiyi i kuznechnogo remesla Drevnego Altaya*. Tomsk: Tomsk State University.

Zuyev, Y. A. 1995. Sarmato-Alany Priaraly'a (Yattsy-Abzoya). In *Kultura kochevnokov na rubezhe vekov: problemy genezisa i transformatsiyi*, ed. K. V. Kekibayev. Almaty: Nauka: 38–45.

Zykov, A. P. 1993. Zheleznye kinzhaly Severo-Zapadnoi Sibiri. In *Znaniya i navyki uralskogo naseleniya v drevnosty*, ed. L. N. Koryakova. Ekaterinburg: Ural Division of RAS: 144–69.

INDEX

Italics indicate figures

Abashevo context, 180
Abashevo cultural area, 33, 57
Abashevo cultural intercommunity, 180, 340n3
Abashevo culture, 57, *58*, 79, 83, 97, 111, 136, 178
  animals, 64
  burial grounds, 61
  elite kurgans, 65
  funeral tradition, *63*
  groups, 122
  influence, 66
  metal, 34, 35, 60, *62*
  ornaments, 60
  pottery, 60, 74, 86
  settlement material, 60
  settlements, *59*, 60
    living architecture, 60
  territory, 109
Abashevo groups, 45, 66, 99
Abashevo metallurgical center, 37
Abashevo sites, 34, 36, 57, 62, 112
Abashevo tradition, 59, 319
Achaemenid, 225, 236, 238, 304, 305
adzes, 34, 37, 41, 42, 50, 93, 189, 196
Aegean, 91, 96
Afanasyevo culture, 53, 123, 188, 343n2
agriculture, 54, 65, 121, 146, 149, 167, 204, 206, 265, 324, 326
Alakul culture, 65, 97, 98, 126, 127, 136, 182
  burial grounds, 130
  female hair decoration, 134, *137*
  funeral ritual, 134
  northern complex in, 150
  origin, 137, 138
  periodization, 136
  pottery, 130, *132*, 136
  settlements, 128
    houses, *131*
Alans, 220, 225, 228, 229, 249, 250, 310

Alanya, 228. *See* Yagn-Tsai
Alexander the Great, 223, 225, 229
Altai, 27, 42, 53, 104, 108, 139, 161, 169, 170, 175, 187, 188, 230, 231, 241, 292, 311, 340n4
  cassiterite deposits, 42
  frozen tombs, 216
  tin, 323
Altai, mountains, 6, 27, 43, 108, 285, 310, 331
  area, 40, 41
Amu-Darya, river, 112, 228
Ananyino burial ground, 252
Ananyino cosmological model, 260
Ananyino cultural groups, 194
Ananyino culture, 195, *195*, 196, 251, *253*, 258, 259, 312, 330
  animals, 257
  burials, 254
  pottery, 257
  settlements, 254, 276
Ananyino intercommunity, 251, 276
Ananyino metallurgical center, 194, 200
Ananyino metallurgy, 195, 196, 200
  influence, 194
Ananyino sites, 194, 252, 258
Ananyino society, 258
  symbolic system of, 260
Anatolia, 26, 91, 181
Andronovo area
  row materials, 43
  site distribution, *124*
Andronovo cultural and historical community, 342n3
Andronovo cultural and historical intercommunity, 126
Andronovo cultures
  characteristics, 127
  history of study, 123–126
Andronovo family of cultures
  composition, 126
Andronovo groups, 158